THEORY AND PRACTICE OF EXCISE TAXATION

Theory and Practice of Excise Taxation

Smoking, Drinking, Gambling, Polluting, and Driving

Edited by
SIJBREN CNOSSEN

UNIVERSITY PRESS

OXFORD
UNIVERSITY PRESS

Great Clarendon Street, Oxford OX2 6DP

Oxford University Press is a department of the University of Oxford.
It furthers the University's objective of excellence in research, scholarship,
and education by publishing worldwide in

Oxford New York

Auckland Cape Town Dar es Salaam Hong Kong Karachi Kuala Lumpur
Madrid Melbourne Mexico City Nairobi New Delhi Shanghai Taipei Toronto

With offices in

Argentina Austria Brazil Chile Czech Republic France Greece
Guatemala Hungary Italy Japan South Korea Poland Portugal
Singapore Switzerland Thailand Turkey Ukraine Vietnam

Published in the United States
by Oxford University Press Inc., New York

© Oxford University Press, 2005

British Library Cataloguing in Publication Data

Data available

Library of Congress Cataloging in Publication Data

Data available

ISBN 0-19-927859-8

3 5 7 9 10 8 6 4 2

Typeset by Kolam Information Services Pvt. Ltd, Pondicherry, India
Printed in Great Britain
on acid-free paper by
Biddles Ltd., King's Lynn, Norfolk.

Preface

Excise taxes on smoking, drinking, gambling, polluting, and driving are very much in the news these days. Not only are these taxes convenient sources of government revenue, they can also be designed to reflect the external costs that consumers or producers of excisable products impose on other people. Global warming, acid rain, traffic congestion, and the economic costs of cigarette and alcohol consumption are problems that can be corrected through selective excise taxes and other regulatory instruments. Excise taxes, moreover, are increasingly looked upon as revenue substitutes for distortionary taxes on capital and labour.

These and other issues are addressed in this volume, which contains seven essays by a group of internationally recognized experts who analyse the current state of the art in excise taxation. The essays were initially presented at a conference on Excise Tax Policy and Administration held at the Dutch Ministry of Finance in The Hague, and attended by academics, government officials, and representatives of industry from numerous countries.

The essays provide a systematic, insightful, and often provocative treatment of a major fiscal instrument that policy-makers tend to ignore and that gets little attention in the professional literature. The authors show a sound knowledge, not only of relevant economic theory, but also of the myriad institutional details that are crucial for the practical application of that theory. No doubt, for many years to come, the volume can serve as a comprehensive guide to the debate on a wide range of excise tax policy and administration issues.

This volume and the conference that preceded it would not have been possible without the sponsorship of the International Tax and Investment Center in Washington DC. The hospitality of the Dutch Ministry of Finance and the Netherlands Institute for Advanced Study, where this volume was completed, were much appreciated. I especially would like to thank the authors, discussants, and referees of the essays, who have all been very generous with their time. Profound thanks are due to Judith Payne, Production Editor of *Fiscal Studies*, who cheerfully yet meticulously prepared the essays for publication.

Sijbren Cnossen

Contents

List of Figures

List of Tables

Participants: Conference on Excise Tax Policy and Administration

(Affiliation at time of Conference)

Richard Arnott, Boston College
Jean-Philippe Barde, OECD
Carl Bartone, World Bank
Richard Bird, University of Toronto
Nils Axel Braathen, OECD
Charles Clotfelter, Duke University, North Carolina
Sijbren Cnossen, University of Maastricht
Bruce Davie, US Department of the Treasury
Reiner Eichenberger, University of Fribourg
Bruno Frey, University of Zurich
Don Fullerton, University of Texas at Austin
Peter Heller, International Monetary Fund
John Kay, Economist
Molly Macauley, Resources for the Future, Washington DC
Charles McLure, Jr., Hoover Institution
Muthukumara Mani, International Monetary Fund
David Newbery, University of Cambridge
Agnar Sandmo, Norwegian School of Economics
Michael Smart, University of Toronto
Stephen Smith, University College London
Emil Sunley, International Monetary Fund
Joy Townsend, London School of Hygiene and Tropical Medicine
François Vaillancourt, University of Montreal
Leighton Vaughan Williams, Nottingham Trent University
Herman Vollebergh, Erasmus University Rotterdam
Dan Witt, International Tax and Investment Center, Washington DC

Chapter 1

Economics and Politics of Excise Taxation[*]

SIJBREN CNOSSEN
University of Maastricht

1.1 WHY ARE EXCISE TAXES IMPORTANT?

Selective taxes on goods and services, often referred to as excise taxes, are among the oldest forms of taxation in the world.[1] The salt excise, for instance, was considered a gold mine for the European sovereign during the Middle Ages, because sources of supply were few and could be easily controlled. Interestingly, the prominence of excise taxation in the sixteenth and seventeenth centuries owed much to the Dutch, whose duties on beer, sugar, salt, spirits, and other goods were called *excijsen*.[2] In fact, excise taxation was so widely applied that an English observer noted that 'a fish dish eaten in Holland pays 30 excises'.[3] From *la terre classique de la fiscalité*, as Holland was called at that time, excise taxation spread to other European countries. Many German states, for instance, followed the Dutch example, and the apparent success of the 'new imposts' also led to their introduction in England[4] and its colonies, including the USA.

In Europe, during the nineteenth century, many of the 'small' excises (so-called because they yielded comparatively little revenue) were abolished or absorbed into general taxes on goods and services, often referred to as sales taxes, which were widely introduced in the first quarter of the twentieth century and transformed into general consumption or value added taxes (VATs) during the 1970s and 1980s. The 'big' excises – on tobacco products, alcoholic beverages, and petroleum products – remained, but little attention was given to them in the professional literature.

This has changed greatly in recent years, primarily due to the rise and awareness of environmental problems. Greenhouse gases, for instance, lead to global warming; they are generated by the burning of fossil fuels, such as coal, petroleum, and natural gas. This has led to a burgeoning literature on the use of 'economic instruments', such as excises, to restrain harmful emissions. As another example, the perceived health costs of smoking have induced the

* The author is grateful for the stimulating comments of Stephen Smith, Judith Payne, and Lans Bovenberg on a draft of this chapter.

World Health Organization to initiate a campaign to reduce tobacco consumption, among others through an increase in the tobacco excises. More generally, the difficulties in extracting revenue from the capital income tax base due to greater capital mobility and the distortionary effects of high taxes on labour supply and demand have induced various governments to re-examine the revenue-substituting potential of excise taxation.

The seven essays in this volume examine in considerable detail the relative merits of the 'new' excise taxes on smoking, drinking, gambling, polluting, and driving, as well as the politics and psychology of excise taxation. In most cases, the authors provide surveys of the existing excise structures, mainly in Europe and the USA, and review the literature. They attempt to show what we have learned, focusing on such issues as external costs, regulation, incidence, revenue, trade deflection, harmonization, and various administrative aspects of excise taxation. In addition, they explore avenues for new research. Clearly, excise taxes have come a long way from the simple efficient revenue-raising measures they once were to the complex policy tools that they have become today. This chapter summarizes the main findings of the essays, following a brief exploration of the definition, objectives, and design of excise taxes.

1.2 DEFINITION OF EXCISES

Broadly speaking, the distinguishing features of excise taxation are selectivity in coverage, discrimination in intent, and often some form of quantitative measurement in determining the tax liability. This contrasts with general consumption taxes, such as VATs and retail sales taxes (RSTs), which are typically defined to include all goods and services for sale in the tax base other than those specifically exempted. VATs and RSTs, moreover, are levied only to raise revenue, whereas excises are often also justified on other grounds, or viewed as serving a special purpose. Beyond that, excise tax collection is usually linked to physical controls, whereas the VAT or RST liability is generally verified through checks on books of account and other documentary evidence.

As indicated above, history supports a broad interpretation of the concept 'excise'. In fact, following usage in the professional literature (Cnossen, 1977), all selective taxes on goods, services, and motor vehicles can be considered part of excise systems. Arguably, profits of government-owned tobacco, alcohol, and gambling monopolies should also be considered part of excise systems, in addition to the taxes on these products and activities. A further subcategory is taxes on the ownership or use of goods, as distinct from taxes on the goods themselves, and taxes on permission to perform certain activities. Examples are the important recurrent or user taxes on motor vehicles and taxes on licences to sell alcoholic beverages; these taxes are also selective in nature.[5] In sum, excise systems comprise all selective taxes and related levies and charges on tobacco, alcohol, gambling, pollution, driving, and other specific goods, services, and activities.

1.3 OBJECTIVES OF EXCISE TAXATION

The objectives that can be identified in relation to the use of excise taxes are the following.

1.3.1 *To Raise Revenue for General Purposes*

In practice, most excises have probably been enacted for revenue purposes, the main consideration being that they could be administered more easily than other taxes. Excises on tobacco, alcohol, petrol, and motor vehicles are good potential sources of revenue, because the products are easy to identify, the volume of sales is high, and the fact that there are few producers simplifies collection. Also, there are few substitutes that consumers would find equally satisfactory, so that consumption remains high despite excise-induced price rises. Not surprisingly, in Denmark for example, excise tax receipts account for 11 per cent of total tax revenue (including social security contributions) or 5.6 per cent of gross domestic product (GDP).

The differentially higher taxation of excisable products for revenue purposes also has an economic rationale. The absence of close substitutes for addictive or indispensable products, such as tobacco, alcohol, and energy, implies that the demand for them is inelastic. This means that the potential for distortion of economic decisions by the imposition of excise taxes is relatively small. More generally, economic theory prescribes that as long as goods are unrelated in consumption, tax rates should be higher on the good with the lowest elasticity. This finding is known as the Ramsey rule (1927), which holds that, subject to certain conditions about the range of other tax instruments available to the authorities, the rate of tax on the sale of each good should be set inversely proportional to its elasticity of demand (holding the elasticity of supply constant).[6]

As an extension of the Ramsey rule, Corlett and Hague (1953) have proved that, since leisure cannot be taxed, efficient taxation requires taxing products that are consumed jointly with leisure at a relatively high rate. As a result, the second-best situation in which leisure cannot be taxed is moved closer to the first-best situation in which leisure would be taxed and a general, equal-rate, consumption tax would be equivalent to a lump-sum tax without excess burden, i.e. there would be no loss of welfare above and beyond the tax revenue collected. Therefore, if cigarettes and beer, or, perhaps more likely, pleasure boats, are complements to leisure, then taxing them improves resource allocation.

1.3.2 *To Reflect External Costs*

Furthermore, excises are often rationalized as charges for the external cost that consumers or producers of excisable products impose on others. Although the principle of consumer sovereignty implies that rational, fully informed persons who weigh up all the costs and benefits of their actions should be free to smoke, drink, gamble, pollute, and drive, physical, financial, and psychological costs imposed on others should be accounted for in price if they cannot be charged directly or indirectly (for example, through higher insurance premiums) to the perpetrators. Thus, the existence of external costs could establish a case for government intervention, among others through excise taxation.

Charging consumers or producers for external costs is known as the Pigouvian prescription (Pigou, 1918), which holds that efficient consumption or production can be achieved through the tax system by imposing an excise on the activity equal to the marginal cost of the damage caused to other people.[7] The identification and measurement of marginal costs are often difficult, however, because they depend on who does what, where, and under what circumstances. In practice, therefore, average external costs are estimated and a 'pooling' approach (akin to insurance) is adopted in charging for these costs. Perpetrators as a group meet the costs by paying a uniform excise calculated as the total external costs divided by, say, the number of packs of cigarettes or drinks consumed. This average-cost approach seems acceptable if damage – for example, through smoking – is approximately proportional to cost.[8]

Global warming through fossil-fuel burning perhaps represents the classic case for internalizing external costs through appropriately designed excise taxes imposed on carbon emissions or, less directly, energy. The impact of burning fossil fuels on global climate change is a pure public 'bad' and the damage caused to the global climate is a function simply of the total amount of carbon dioxide and other greenhouse gases emitted, which in turn can be directly related to the quantities of different fossil fuels used and their characteristics. This observation has induced various countries to redesign their energy taxes in line with environmental objectives by differentiating the related excises by type of fossil fuel. The effects of lead pollution, acid rain, and other environmental 'bads', furthermore, have been countered by favouring less-polluting products (for example, unleaded versus leaded petrol) and by introducing new taxes to raise the price of polluting products or processes (for example, on fertilizers, pesticides, sulphur, disposable containers, basic chemicals, and batteries).

An important question regarding the taxation of pollution (as well as of smoking, drinking, and gambling) is whether duty rates should exceed Pigouvian levels when governments need revenue, and non-distortionary lump-sum taxes are unavailable. Surprisingly, perhaps, Bovenberg and de Mooij (1994) argue that revenue considerations generally lead to taxes on 'dirty' goods that are below Pigouvian levels. The reason is that in their model, government revenue is best collected with a uniform tax on all consumption; and, as the overall level of taxation increases, the marginal excess burden of a Pigouvian tax rises relative to its external benefits. Hence, differential taxation of polluting goods should fall as the overall level of taxation rises.

1.3.3 *To Discourage Consumption*

Information failures are other instances that justify government intervention, even in the absence of explicit external costs. Thus, research has indicated that the price elasticity of demand for cigarettes and alcoholic beverages among the young is, on average, twice the price elasticity among adults. In the event, excise-induced price rises would have a powerful effect in deterring the young from smoking and drinking. More generally, public health objectives – paternalistic or not – can be furthered through the imposition of excises which restrain the consumption of products regarded as unhealthy. Although economists have little to say on the objectives as such, they can analyse the efficacy of one instrument over another in achieving the objectives. In the example, this would be the choice between an increase in the tobacco and alcohol excises, or, perhaps more appropriately, better dissemination of information on the health hazards of smoking and drinking, coupled perhaps with legislation restricting supply or (place of) consumption.

1.3.4 *To Charge Road Users for Government-Provided Services*

Excise taxation can also play an important role in regulating various external (including environmental) and other costs associated with road transport. Road (and similar transport) services resemble goods produced in the private sector that are used optimally when their price, commonly referred to as the economic user charge, equals the total social costs of operating the road network. Accordingly, road user charges should contain charges for efficient road use and for damage, as well as charges for externalities, such as congestion, pollution, noise, and accidents. Road user charges can be set to cover the total costs of operating the road network or the difference between the marginal social cost and the average private cost of road use.

Motor fuel taxes (in contrast to motor vehicle taxes) can be set at a level that is a reasonable proxy for road maintenance charges as they reflect varying consumption per vehicle-kilometre. If most motorized traffic uses the surfaced portion of the highway system, setting the economic user charge according to the variable maintenance cost of surfaced roads may be a fair approximation of marginal cost. This applies to consumers as well as producers. In the event, the taxation of motor fuels used as production inputs does not violate the Diamond–Mirrlees (1971) theorem, which prescribes that, subject to certain general conditions, intermediate goods should not be subject to revenue-raising taxes (if they were, producers would incur excess burdens in trying to pass the tax on to consumers in addition to the tax itself).[9] After all, the fuel excise, although levied on an intermediate good, is a quid pro quo for the cost of government-provided road services. A charge, even if indirect, is therefore fully appropriate. In addition to this user charge, externality taxes for congestion, pollution, noise, and accidents, imposed on business users at equivalent levels to those on private users, may, of course, be warranted.

1.3.5 *Other Objectives*

In addition to these four main objectives, there are other goals of excise taxation. Thus, excises (including higher-than-standard VAT or RST rates) on (luxury) goods and services, whose income-elasticity of demand exceeds unity, can be used in an attempt to improve the progressivity of tax systems. Such taxes are difficult to justify, however, in industrial economies with sufficient administrative capacity to levy comprehensive, graduated income taxes. Accordingly, they are not dealt with in this volume. Similarly, no attention is paid to differentially higher duties on imports to protect domestic industry, because 'it would be just as sensible to drop rocks into our harbours because other nations have rocky coasts' (Robinson, 1947). Differentially higher taxes on the export of natural resource products, such as oil and gas, are not dealt with either. They are not permitted in the European Union (EU).

1.4 ISSUES IN EXCISE TAX DESIGN

Obviously, the objectives specified above require appropriately designed instruments to achieve or approximate them. In the field of taxes on tobacco, alcohol, and petroleum, for instance, there is the question of whether specific rates (fixed amounts per quantity) or *ad valorem* rates (fixed percentages of trade price), or some combination of these rates, should be used. Uniform specific rates reduce relative price differences between low-priced and high-priced brands, whereas uniform *ad valorem* rates increase absolute price differences. As discussed in the next chapter, in imperfect markets, the choice between these two rates depends on whether the primary aim of tax policy is to discourage consumption or to raise revenue, and on whether improvements in product quality are deemed desirable or not.

Since the damage caused by smoking, drinking, or polluting is independent of price, correction of externalities favours specific over *ad valorem* taxation. Where it is clear that the tax instrument should be specific, further choices may have to be made about the precise form of the instrument. Thus, specific tobacco excises can be designed by reference to the weight of tobacco, the number of cigarettes, or their nicotine or tar content, while the specific alcohol excise can be based on volume, alcohol content, or some combination of these attributes. Similarly, in the environmental field, harmful emissions can be restrained through taxes, tradable pollution permits, or command-and-control regulations. In theory, pollution permits and Pigouvian taxes are identical, but from a practical point of view, they are not. Pollution permits reduce uncertainty about the ultimate level of pollution but tend to deter new firms from entering a market dominated by large firms that are able to buy up pollution licences in excess of the firms' cost-minimizing requirements. Nevertheless, taxes and permits tend to be more efficient in controlling pollution than command-and-control regulations. By imposing across-the-board standards, regulations do not take account of differences in firm-specific costs.

Another issue concerns the proper coordination of excises and general consumption taxes, such as VATs and RSTs. To ensure fiscal neutrality, excisable products, regardless of whether they are domestically produced or imported, should be included in the consumption tax base. Levying the general consumption tax on the excise-duty-inclusive value of manufactured or imported items would then effect coordination. Accordingly, and properly so, the resource allocation function of the excises would be given priority over the revenue-raising role of the consumption tax. But this assumes that corrective excises reflect external costs and as such should be subject to the standard rate of VAT. If the amount of the excises exceeds external costs, however, there will be additional VAT on the excess of these excises over the corrective component, and that part of the total VAT should be considered to be part of the residual tax system rather than the VAT as such.

Yet another policy issue concerns the desirable degree of harmonization in a single market such as the EU or the USA. Harmonization would improve the efficiency of exchange and reduce incentives for tax-base snatching, i.e. setting low excise duty rates to attract consumers from other states. Furthermore, if fuel and motor vehicles are used in the production process, harmonization of the related excises reduces intercountry distortions from excise-induced differences in cost structures.

1.5 SUMMARY OF CONTRIBUTIONS AND CONFERENCE DISCUSSION

These preliminaries set the stage for summarizing the individual contributions on the taxation of smoking, drinking, gambling, polluting, and driving in succeeding chapters, as well as some thoughts on the politics and psychology of excise taxation in the concluding chapter. In addition, some major points of the conference discussion are highlighted.

1.5.1 *Taxation of Tobacco*

In Chapter 2, *Sijbren Cnossen* and *Michael Smart* survey and analyse the effects of tobacco taxation. They start their contribution with an overview of tobacco taxes in Europe (the EU member states plus the accession countries in central and eastern Europe as well as the Mediterranean) and the US states. In the EU, tobacco taxes (specific and *ad valorem* excises plus VAT), at more than 300 per cent of the pre-tax retail price, are the highest on any single product in the world (by comparison, the VAT is, on average, 19 per cent in the EU). The level of tobacco taxation differs widely. In the UK, for instance, total taxes on a pack of twenty cigarettes are nearly €6 and four times the level found in Spain. A wide range of tobacco tax levels is also found among the US states, although the overall average level (as a share of the tax-inclusive retail price) is only half the EU level. Interestingly, the *ad valorem* excise is mainly an EU phenomenon. It tends to protect the cheap tobaccos grown in southern member states.

Cnossen and Smart conclude that concern about revenue (Ramsey rule) is the main reason for levying differentially higher taxes on tobacco products. A further argument in favour of high tobacco taxes is the restraining effect they appear to have on the young, who may have a poor appreciation of the risk of smoking and a tendency to undervalue future health damage. But apart from this special case of information failure (which should perhaps be remedied through better dissemination of data on the health hazards of smoking), the case for high tobacco taxes appears weak. The net external costs (Pigou term) of smoking, which allow for the cost savings of premature deaths, may be low or even negligible. The high tobacco taxes, therefore, seem to violate consumer sovereignty. Moreover, their burden distribution is highly regressive and there are difficulties in ensuring compliance. Illegal bootlegging and smuggling, which undermine public revenue and health objectives, have reached alarming proportions, particularly in Europe. Accordingly, the authors conclude that there are conceptual and empirical limits to excessively high levels of tobacco taxation.

In his cogent comments on tobacco taxation, *Peter Heller* pointed out that the World Bank and the International Monetary Fund have both emphasized the 'win–win' aspects of reliance on tobacco taxation, at least in developing countries and transition economies, from the point of view of revenue mobilization as well as containment of smoking levels. In this context, the discussion had made him aware of the practical tax administration issues of high tobacco tax levels, including the significant financial incentives associated with smuggling. Importantly, he noted that the approach taken to tobacco taxation was relevant for its implications toward any tax policy regime that might be adopted in the context of the legalization of narcotics. Sooner or later, governments may need to accept that the social costs of maintaining the illegality of narcotics – in terms of the financial profitability to international crime syndicates and the cost of narcotics-associated crimes – far exceed the benefits. If legalization occurs, governments were likely to look to tobacco tax regimes as an element of an overall policy regime toward narcotics.

Joy Townsend focused in particular on smoking as a public health issue. Referring to her own work (Townsend, Roderick, and Cooper, 1994), she pointed out that increasingly those most affected by smoking diseases are the poorer members of society who are at the greatest risk of dying from lung cancer, heart ailment, and chronic obstructive airways disease, largely due to their higher smoking prevalence. The lower the socio-economic group or income, the higher the price elasticity of demand and the higher the externality costs of smoking tend to be, and so tobacco tax increases have the effect of reducing health and mortality inequalities. Tax increases would also deter young people from smoking. Furthermore, lower socio-economic groups tend to be less responsive to health publicity, so tax is seen to work where information does not reduce health inequalities.

1.5.2 *Economic Issues in Alcohol Taxation*

In similar vein to the previous contribution, *Stephen Smith*, in Chapter 3, surveys the taxation of alcoholic drinks in the EU. Alcohol tax revenue, measured on a per capita basis, varies widely from over €100 in Scandinavian countries to less than €30 in Mediterranean countries. In the main, this reflects widely differing levels of taxation; in Mediterranean countries, Austria, and Germany, for instance, there is no excise on still wine. Smith proceeds to discuss the revenue-raising efficiency, externality-correcting properties, and distributional incidence of alcohol taxation. He notes that it is unlikely that the price elasticity of alcohol demand is sufficiently low to warrant significantly higher-than-average taxation of alcohol on 'inverse-elasticity' grounds. It is unclear, moreover, whether alcohol would be a complement with or a substitute for leisure. As regards the Pigou term, he concludes that the taxation of alcohol sales helps to reduce the external costs generated by abusive consumers, but at the cost of reducing the consumer satisfaction of non-abusive consumers. On incidence, he notes that the concerns that are sometimes raised about the regressivity of tobacco taxes do not apply with anything like the same force to alcohol taxes.

Subsequently, Smith reviews the external costs associated with abusive alcohol consumption, including its effects on wages and productivity, healthcare, and accidents. In US studies, a very large proportion of the net external cost is accounted for by the valuation of alcohol-related traffic fatalities, whereas in UK studies, the largest items appear under the heading 'social cost to industry'. Smith cites evidence that the average external cost of alcohol consumption in the UK might be of the order of 17 per cent of the pre-tax price of alcohol. Since external cost is closely related to excessive consumption, the marginal external cost would be higher than the average cost. Although this would be an argument in favour of excises differentiated on the basis of drinks consumed per occasion, on practical grounds Smith prefers uniform taxation of alcohol content across beer, wine, and spirits. In concluding his contribution, the author addresses the cross-border shopping issues that arise from differences in levels of alcohol taxation in EU member states. Narrowing these differences, he believes, would reduce the economic and fiscal costs associated with legal cross-border shopping.

In discussing the economics of alcohol taxation, *Bruce Davie* noted that the variation in excises across US states has created a veritable cottage industry of research devoted to relating differences in taxes on alcoholic beverages to a wide variety of changes in social conditions. Although an increasing number of medical studies conclude that moderate alcohol consumption improves the consumer's health, his sampling dealt only with negative externalities. Davie's survey listed the following results: (a) a 1 per cent increase in the price of alcohol decreases the rate of wife abuse by 3.1–3.5 per cent but has no effect on abuse of husbands (Markowitz, 1999); (b) a 10 per cent increase in the excise tax on beer would reduce severe domestic violence against children by 2.3 per cent (Markowitz and Grossman, 1999); (c) a 78 per cent increase in the beer tax (restoring the real rate to its 1975 level) would reduce highway fatalities by 7–8 per cent (Ruhm, 1996); (d) raising the beer tax to the alcohol equivalent tax on distilled spirits would reduce the drinking of under-age drinkers who drink frequently by 32 per cent (Grossman et al., 1994); (e) a 10 per cent increase in the price of alcohol would decrease drunk driving by 7.4 per cent for men and 8.1 per cent for women (Kenkel, 1993); (f) a 10 per cent increase in the beer tax would reduce rapes by 1.32 per cent, robbery by 0.9 per cent, murder by 0.3 per cent, and assaults by 0.3 per cent (Cook and Moore, 1993); and (f) a US$0.20 per six-pack increase in the beer tax could reduce the overall gonorrhoea rate by 8.9 per cent (Harrison and Kassler, 2000).

Agnar Sandmo made the more general point that acceptance or non-acceptance of the principle of consumer sovereignty lies at the heart of controversies in the area of the efficiency aspects of alcohol taxation. Although it can hardly be denied that there is an externalities case for the taxation of alcohol, many people – perhaps primarily non-economists – would also argue that there is an 'internalities' case. Alcohol consumption causes damage not only to others but also to the drinkers themselves, and high taxation of alcohol is a means to protect consumers against unforeseen effects on their future selves. This is paternalism, which is a moral attitude with a low standing among economists. However, we also know from analytical models that people's actions are not necessarily time consistent, and my future self might in fact be grateful to the government for its efforts to induce my past self to consume less than I would have done in the absence of taxes and regulations on the consumption of alcohol. With the habit formation associated with alcohol use, this could be developed into an independent argument for alcohol taxation.

1.5.3 *Gambling Taxes*

In addition to smoking and drinking, gambling is often singled out for differentially higher or 'sumptuary' excise taxation in the apparent belief that there is something immoral about it. In Chapter 4, *Charles Clotfelter* observes that gambling has experienced rapid growth in recent decades,[10] marked by the legalization of heretofore forbidden games and increasing rates of participation among households. This legalization is invariably accompanied by both regulation and taxation, or implicit taxation through profits of government-operated gambling establishments. Because the forms of gambling are so diverse, the institutional structures for taxation are both complex and variegated. Governments collect revenue in the form of excises, such as taxes on admissions and on profits of government-operated gambling enterprises. The tax base, which should approximate net consumer expenditure, is either gross revenue (for example, for slot machines and casino table games) or gross wager (for example, for lotteries). In addition, winnings may be subject to income tax. Overall, gambling products tend to be subject to quite high explicit or implicit tax rates approximating those on tobacco and alcohol, but because collection costs are high, net revenues are small.

Clotfelter points out that the taxation of gambling cannot be wholly separated from its legalization and regulation. While the joint legalization and taxation probably conveys net welfare gains (occasional gamblers are better off), the legalization nevertheless imposes some external costs (compulsive gamblers, particularly of gaming machines, are worse off). Presumably, these costs can be corrected through Pigouvian taxation, in parallel with similar taxes on tobacco and alcohol. Owing to prevailing expenditure patterns, the incidence of gambling taxes is usually regressive. Clotfelter concludes that the taxation of gambling is bound up with other policy issues relating to a society's attitude towards gambling. A middle ground is to accommodate the existing, unstimulated demand for gambling, without doing anything to stimulate that demand. Besides limiting the availability of gambling opportunities, this approach would be consistent with differentially higher tax rates.

François Vaillancourt illustrated the discussion on gambling taxes with references to the Canadian experience. In Canada, gambling gains are considered akin to life insurance payments: spending is paid out of after-tax income and payouts are random. On these grounds, life insurance payments and gambling gains are not seen as income and hence not taxed as such.

Leighton Vaughan Williams pointed out that since 2000, the aim of the UK government has been to base betting taxation policy explicitly on economic criteria, such as maintaining competitiveness and reducing allocative inefficiency. Thus, the decision to reduce the overall level of betting taxation demonstrated an awareness of changing market conditions in the betting industry which has become especially vulnerable to the growth in e-commerce. Furthermore, the proposed switch from a general betting duty to a gross profits tax is likely to lead to lower prices and enhanced consumer welfare. The intuition behind this result is that by levying the tax on margins instead of turnover, producers with at least some market power have an incentive to reduce their price. A potential disadvantage of the move to a gross profits tax, however, is that the revenue stream from betting taxes is likely to become less stable. In effect, the risk burden will be shifted from the private to the public sector.

1.5.4 *Environmentally Related Levies*

Whereas the Ramsey rationale is important for sumptuary excises, the Pigou rationale is paramount in analysing environmentally related taxes, charges, and tradable permits. Although the need for greater use of these economic instruments is widely recognized, in practice, as *Jean-Philippe Barde* and *Nils Axel Braathen* emphasize in Chapter 5, command-and-control types of regulations still dominate the environmental landscape. On the basis of a comprehensive survey of their use in OECD countries, Barde and Braathen conclude, moreover, that green taxes and other environmentally related levies on motor fuel, electricity, packaging, and landfill waste still exhibit a large number of shortcomings. In most cases, the externality–tax linkage is weak, the rates are low, the bases are riddled with exemptions (for example, for coal, which is often subsidized, and electricity), taxes overlap with regulations, and international coordination, required to contain border-crossing externalities, is not forthcoming.

Nevertheless, the case for appropriately designed 'green taxes' is strong, particularly as part of a wider tax reform that enables governments to introduce appropriate supporting measures. Although green tax reforms have been pioneered in Scandinavian countries, elsewhere two main fears seem to stall further progress – the perceived regressivity of environmental levies and their negative impact on sectoral competitiveness. The authors believe that the negative effect on low-income households can be dealt with by *ex-post* compensation measures that might take the form of tax credits, income-tested benefits, and tax shifts that do not defeat the environmental purpose of the tax. The perceived loss of competitiveness is often countered by *ex-ante* measures, such as exemptions and reduced rates, which, however, undermine the effectiveness of the environmentally related levies. Accordingly, green tax reform is unlikely to make much progress unless some minimum level playing field is agreed upon between OECD countries. It would be unfortunate if international coordination were not forthcoming, because environmentally related levies are a potentially effective way of protecting the environment and thus enhancing economic efficiency.

In his comments, *Muthukumara Mani* observed that environmentally related levies are making some headway in developing countries but are still a long way from becoming widely accepted. Moreover, there is considerable scope for restructuring existing taxes in line with environmental objectives. As part of its adjustment programmes, the International Monetary Fund often recommended raising energy taxes mainly on revenue grounds, although the environmental impact was also a real consideration. Fortunately, the distributional impact of gasoline taxes tends to be very progressive in developing countries.

Herman Vollebergh pleaded for a contingency approach in designing environmental taxes. He posited that the choice of particular tax bases and rates should be viewed in relation to their environmental benefits or goals, given the specific characteristics of the economy or the sector on which the levy is imposed. The multi-dimensionality of green taxes in terms of goals and instruments should be heeded. Furthermore, policy-makers should be cognizant of the fact that the implementation of environmental taxes is not costless. Importantly, the costs and benefits of the introduction of expensive new emission taxes should be balanced against the costs and benefits of using less-well-targeted but cheaper existing output or input taxes.

1.5.5 *An Excise Tax on Municipal Solid Waste?*

Don Fullerton's contribution, in Chapter 6, presents an interesting application of Pigouvian environmental tax reform, i.e. the role of excise taxes on waste in achieving efficient levels of waste disposal and recycling, as well as a means of raising revenue for state governments in the USA. Because taxing waste can lead to illegal dumping, the author discusses the use of a tax–subsidy scheme as an alternative to a tax on disposal. The tax–subsidy or deposit–refund system, as the author calls it, would involve taxing product sales at retail stores and subsidizing recycling and legal garbage collection. As a result, the scheme can match all of the effects of having both the tax on garbage and the unavailable 'tax on dumping'.

Fullerton places his innovative scheme against the background of some basic information about household garbage and recycling in the USA. Under current policies, the marginal cost to an individual household for disposal of another bag of garbage is essentially zero, even though collection and disposal costs increase with the amount of garbage. Instead, the full social cost per bag of garbage should be the product's price plus the optimal tax rate. The author develops a theoretical model to characterize optimal waste taxes and tax–subsidy policies. Furthermore, he reviews the empirical literature on how unit pricing of solid waste affects disposal and recycling, and analyses the welfare costs of illicit disposal. Later sections of his contribution include an analysis of optimal waste fees and estimates of the size and importance of the potential revenue that state governments might raise from taxing waste. Fullerton's chapter provides an impetus for taking a closer look at waste taxes, including a theoretical framework for thinking about the optimal price per bag, the welfare gain from charging such a price, and the administrative costs of alternative means by which to collect that price.

Carl Bartone and *Molly Macauley* commented on the US experience with municipal solid waste deposit management schemes. Drawing on his extensive experience with environmental issues at the World Bank, Bartone noted the difference between the US landfill-based approach and the approach by the EU which has mandated a waste management policy based on principles of integrated waste management and a 'hierarchy' of options that go from waste minimization, to resource recovery, recycling, and reuse, to waste treatment and disposal. In contrast to the USA, the trend in the EU is to limit landfilling to inert waste and to rely more heavily on incineration and instruments such as packaging regulations in combination with environmental taxes. The findings of various studies, however, call into question the blind adherence to the concept of the waste hierarchy as followed in the EU, at least in the case of the Netherlands (Dijkgraaf and Vollebergh, 1998), and could be used to argue that the US waste management industry is properly structured from an economic point of view.

1.5.6 *Road User and Congestion Charges*

Various economic theorems – Pigou, Ramsey, Diamond–Mirrlees, Corlett – Hague – come together in the analysis of the taxation of road use. Appropriately, therefore, *David Newbery*'s contribution is the last analysis of particular product-specific forms of excise taxation. As he sets out in Chapter 7, designing an efficient set of road user taxes and charges involves charging for scarce road space, setting corrective taxes for environmental externalities, and possibly employing additional taxes to improve the overall efficiency and equity of the tax system. Analogously with other network utilities, revenue from road charges can be set to cover total road costs, including interest on the capital, while their structure (fuel excises, licence fees, and road prices such as cordon tolls) can improve the efficiency of road use and reduce congestion. With constant returns and efficient road provision, moreover, there is no conflict between efficient and cost-recovering charges. This clarification simplifies moves to more efficient road pricing.

Newbery then proceeds to show how to set road user charges, illustrating the method with data from Britain. Congestion costs comprise the largest part of the efficient road user charge, with road damage costs and externalities a relatively small part. The best approach to internalizing congestion costs is a cordon toll, although its efficient design turns out to be very complex. Road fuel taxes should probably be set at a level that accounts for the average long-run marginal cost of inter-urban roads for typical cars, with the vehicle excise duty set to adjust total payments by type of vehicle. The author opines that although accident externalities might be appreciable, the appropriate level of charges might be considerably reduced if punishment and insurance charges already induced sufficient care. Furthermore, the external cost of emissions of greenhouse gases, nitrogen oxides, and particulates can be reduced through tailpipe emission standards as well as met by differentially higher excises on, say, leaded than on unleaded petrol. An *ad valorem* tax on the component of car insurance that covers accident costs would internalize accident externalities.

In summing up his contribution, Newbery calculates the pure road charge and green tax elements in Britain at 36p/litre (€0.60/litre) for petrol and 40p/litre (€0.67/litre) for diesel. If this applied generally across the EU, the Netherlands and Germany would be taxing petrol at about the right rate and only the UK would be overcharging it. All countries except the UK are probably undercharging diesel. In conclusion, Newbery argues for revenue-neutral adjustments in total revenue from road use to improve efficiency by shifting over to better-targeted congestion taxes, such as cordon tolls and road pricing.

In the discussion, *Richard Arnott* noted that the literature has considered the interaction between congestion-related externalities and the labour–leisure distortion, but appears to have overlooked another interaction which might be substantially more important – that between congestion-related externalities and interaction externalities. To illustrate, he hypothesized an annular economy of constant width. Individuals reside around the annulus on equal-size plots. At each location, a proportion w of the land is allocated to a congestible road. The economy is knowledge-based and knowledge is exchanged through non-market interaction. Opportunities for interaction between pairs of individuals are generated by a stochastic process. For an interaction, individual i invites individual j to visit him. Both gain from the interaction, but in deciding whether to accept the invitation, individual j weighs his *private* benefit from the interaction against his *private* travel cost. It should be evident that if interaction is not subsidized (which in fact it is not, presumably because of measurement problems), the optimal (second-best) congestion toll is below the Pigouvian level and may even be negative. Arnott had no idea how quantitatively important interaction externalities are, but he observed that the majority of urban economists believe that the benefits from interaction are the principal force leading to the spatial agglomeration of economic activity. If this belief is correct, then the standard analysis of congestion pricing may be seriously misguided.

If road pricing is so efficient, *Reiner Eichenberger* asked, why is there in fact so little effective political support to implement it? Eichenberger believed that the answer must be found in voters' fear that the government may use road pricing to increase overall taxation. In addition, road pricing gives the government an incentive to reduce road capacity in order to set monopolistic prices (resulting in more, instead of less, congestion). Similarly, local governments have an incentive to export road taxes by unduly increasing the taxes on roads that are used heavily by commuters. According to Eichenberger, these issues can only be resolved in the context of direct democracy in which citizens are able to control taxes. Democratic road districts could be drawn up based on the concept of functional, overlapping, and competing jurisdictions (Frey and Eichenberger, 1999) – in analogy to the school districts in several US states. These districts would have their own institutions with a specific power to tax. A pricing scheme adopted in Saas Fee in the Canton of Valais provides proof that this idea was the way forward.

1.5.7 *Economics, Politics, and Psychology*

Excise taxation, as *Bruno Frey* argues in the last chapter, is only one instrument in the fiscal toolbox to combat externality and immorality. Excise taxes, along with tradable permits and command-and-control measures, provide external incentives for desirable conduct, i.e. they induce extrinsic motivation. In addition, as the author emphasizes, the importance of socially desirable behaviour for its own sake (i.e. intrinsic motivation) should be recognized. In fact, intrinsic motivation should be seen as a regulatory resource or tool that must be explicitly considered as an alternative to the usual conventional instruments. Specifically, a key consideration in the analysis and evaluation of external regulatory instruments and strategies is whether they undermine intrinsic behaviour (crowding-out effect) or reinforce it (crowding-in effect). Crowding-out is a 'hidden cost' that should be accounted for.

Frey argues that tax-price instruments bolster intrinsic motivation in so far as they provide regulated agents freedom of choice and thus enhance moral agency. In addition, these instruments may help consumers to overcome their weakness of will; they may restrain consumers from taking short-run decisions that they themselves consider to be suboptimal over the long run. At the same time, the author notes that tax-price instruments may impair intrinsic motivation by signalling that once the price has been paid for an activity, such as pollution, there is no reason, moral or otherwise, not to engage in it. Frey also believes that tradable permits, by contrast, have a damaging effect on intrinsic motivation; he likens their sale to the selling of indulgences. Clearly, the concept of 'intrinsic motivation' and its relation to external regulatory incentives deserve a place in regulatory theory and practice, particularly since the costs of external incentives, such as excise taxes, weigh most heavily on the poor. Excise taxes should be combined with other policy instruments to achieve desired policy objectives, and due attention should be paid to psychological and politico-economic considerations.

In the discussion, *Richard Bird* expressed sympathy with this conclusion. He observed that there is, it seems, a lot we do not know about excise taxes despite their antiquity and ubiquity. Thus, little is uncontested and uncontestable about how substantial most of the negative externalities associated with excise products are, let alone how effective the tax 'solution' to the problems might be. Furthermore, the real 'externality' with which many who talk and write about special taxation are concerned is perhaps less one of mortality than of morality. Higher excises are often justified because the consumption of the taxed products is in some sense bad for people. Similarly, industry protection may be a reason for not increasing excise taxes or not providing inflation adjustments to specific rates. Indeed, although externality and morality may be the language of the debate, revenue and interest – reflecting the ordinary political process – are still often the real currencies. In short, welfare economics does not rule; politics does. This does not mean, of course, that fiscal economists do not provide valuable and valid contributions to public policy, but rather that excise taxes should be viewed as simply one instrument in a complex social and economic policy process.

John Kay expanded on this point by noting that differences in social values among EU member states, for example, are translated, among others, into large differences in excise taxes. No doubt, the differences impose economic distortions, yet there is not one economic argument that can demonstrate that the cost of these distortions is greater than the loss from imposing homogeneity (or the converse). These costs are sunk costs that should be evaluated in the context of embedded markets. To illustrate, for reasons that are little more than historical accidents, northern EU member states mainly imposed specific excises on tobacco, while southern ones preferred *ad valorem* taxes. The structures of the domestic industry and the preferences of consumers were framed by these choices. In markets with predominantly *ad valorem* structures, consumers became used to low-cost and low-quality European tobaccos, while smokers whose habits had been formed under specific taxation preferred longer cigarettes manufactured from American tobacco. Local industries developed to meet these preferences. That is why, once trade liberalization and tax harmonization became an issue in the EU, some countries lobbied for *ad-valorem*-based structures and others for specific systems. And yet, it is not apparent that there are substantial benefits from harmonization (and, in particular, from harmonization of structure rather than broad level). In this context, the danger is that harmonization is used, not as a means of achieving a single optimal European tax system, or even as a means of finding a set of common European values, but as a mechanism by which the producers of one state can seek to advance their competitive positions at the expense of others.

1.6 INVITATION

As this summary of the contributions to this volume and the discussions indicates, excise taxes on smoking, drinking, gambling, polluting, and driving nearly always involve lively, insightful, and provocative exchanges of views at academic, government, and industry levels. Inevitably, the summary is selective and to some extent subjective, but hopefully it has stimulated the reader sufficiently to study the contributions on the various excise taxes more closely. No doubt, he or she will benefit from their analysis and learn from the perspectives they offer.

Notes

1 Cnossen (1977), on which this paragraph draws, notes that in China, during the time of the Han dynasty, excises were levied on tea, liquor, fish, and reeds for fuel and thatching. Furthermore, salt and iron were considered convenient sources of government revenue and their production was organized as a government enterprise so that all net proceeds would accrue solely to the State. Elsewhere, in India, during the Mauryan period, excises were imposed on liquor and salt, and, later, coverage was expanded to perfumery, indigo, cotton, carding, soap making, edible oil, and printed cloth.

2 According to Webster's *Third New International Dictionary*, the word 'excise' derives from the Middle Dutch *excijs*, which is probably a modification of the old French *assise*: session, settlement, assessment.

3 From a reference made by van der Poel (1963 and 1964), who surveys the development of excise taxation in the Netherlands; the quotation is from p. 1012.

4 In seventeenth-century England, the term excise or new impost was not only applied to eatables, drinks, tobacco, and other goods, but also to houses, trades (hackney coaches, hawkers), bachelors, and services performed in connection with burials, births, and marriages.

5 In the terminology of the Organisation for Economic Co-operation and Development (OECD), excise systems therefore comprise all selective taxes on the production, sale, transfer, leasing, and delivery of goods and the rendering of services (item 5120 in the OECD (2003) classification), as well as all selective taxes on the use of goods, or on the permission to use goods or perform activities (item 5200), other than general taxes on goods and services (item 5110).

6 A disturbing feature of Ramsey's analysis is that it assumes that all individuals are identical, in which case a uniform lump-sum tax would be indicated. However, Atkinson and Stiglitz (1976) have extended the analysis to include multiple persons and redistributional goals.

7 Coase (1960) has pointed out that government intervention to deal with externalities would not be required if property rights to, say, air and water were established. But the application of this important finding is limited if resource owners cannot identify the source of damages to their property (and legally prevent the damages) or if the cost of bargaining deters the parties involved from finding their way to an efficient solution. (Even if these conditions were met, the assignment of property rights would still, of course, affect income distribution.)

8 Of course, measurement problems come back in full force if there are threshold levels of consumption below which adverse effects are absent or attenuated – one or two glasses of wine per day are good for you. In this situation, Pigouvian taxes should exceed average external cost.

9 More generally, the Diamond–Mirrlees theorem holds that the pursuit of production efficiency (all firms face the same input and output prices) as a policy objective takes precedence over the pursuit of exchange efficiency (all consumers face the same product prices).

10 In 2000, per capita lottery sales in the USA, for instance, were $127, based on the entire US population, or $144, based on the population of the lottery states. Clotfelter's figures show that there is considerable variation in gambling tax revenue across OECD countries. Italy, Australia, and Finland are the only countries, however, where gambling taxes contribute as much as 1–2 per cent of total tax revenue.

References

Atkinson, A. B., and Stiglitz, J. E. (1976), 'The design of tax structure: direct versus indirect taxation', *Journal of Public Economics*, 6: 55–75.

Bovenberg, A. L., and de Mooij, R. (1994), 'Environmental levies and distortionary taxation', *American Economic Review*, 84: 1085–9.

Cnossen, S. (1977), *Excise Systems: A Global Study of the Selective Taxation of Goods and Services*, Baltimore, MD: Johns Hopkins University Press.

Coase, R. H. (1960), 'The problem of social cost', *Journal of Law and Economics*, 3: 1–44.

Cook, P. J., and Moore, M. J. (1993), 'Economic perspectives on reducing alcohol-related violence', in National Institute on Alcohol Abuse and Alcoholism, *Alcohol and Interpersonal Violence: Fostering Multidisciplinary Perspectives*, Research Monograph 24, Bethesda, MD.

Corlett, W. J., and Hague, D. C. (1953), 'Complementarity and the excess burden of taxation', *Review of Economic Studies*, 21: 21–30.

Diamond, P. A., and Mirrlees, J. A. (1971), 'Optimal taxation and public production, I: production efficiency', *American Economic Review*, 61: 8–27.

Dijkgraaf, E., and Vollebergh, H. R. J. (1998), *Incineration or Dumping? A Social Cost Comparison of Waste Disposal Options*, Research Memorandum 9808, Rotterdam: Research Centre for Economic Policy, Erasmus University Rotterdam.

Frey, B. S., and Eichenberger, R. (1999), *The New Democratic Federalism for Europe: Functional, Overlapping and Competing Jurisdictions*, Cheltenham: Edward Elgar Publishing.

Grossman, M., Chaloupka, F. J., Saffer, H., and Laixuthai, A. (1994), 'Effects of alcohol price policy on youth: a summary of economic research', *Journal of Research on Adolescence*, 4: 347–64.

Harrison, P., and Kassler, W. J. (2000), 'Alcohol policy and sexually transmitted disease rates – United States, 1982–1995', US Department of Health and Human Services, Center for Disease Control, Epidemiology Program Office, *MMWR Weekly*, 49: 364–9.

Kenkel, D. S. (1993), 'Drinking, driving and deterrence: the effectiveness and social cost of alternative policies', *Journal of Law and Economics*, 26: 877–913.

Markowitz, S. (1999), 'The price of alcohol, wife abuse, and husband abuse', National Bureau of Economic Research, Working Paper 6916.

—— and Grossman, M. (1999), 'Alcohol regulation and domestic violence towards children', *Contemporary Economic Policy*, 16: 309–21.

OECD (2003), *Revenue Statistics of OECD Member Countries 1965–2002*, Paris: Organisation for Economic Co-operation and Development.

Pigou, A. C. (1918), *The Economics of Welfare*, London: Macmillan.

Ramsey, F. (1927), 'A contribution to the theory of taxation', *Economic Journal*, 37: 47–61.

Robinson, J. (1947), *Essays in the Theory of Employment*, London: Macmillan.

Ruhm, C. J. (1996), 'Alcohol policies and highway vehicle fatalities', *Journal of Health Economics*, 15: 435–54.

Townsend, J., Roderick, P., and Cooper, J. (1994), 'Cigarette smoking by socio-economic group, sex, and age: effects of price, income and health publicity', *British Medical Journal*, 309, 923–7.

Van der Poel, J. (1963 and 1964), 'De evolutie der accijnzen', *Weekblad voor Fiscaal Recht*, nos. 4682–6; 1963: 1009–14, 1032–40; 1964: 14–18, 37–42, 61.

Chapter 2

Taxation of Tobacco*

SIJBREN CNOSSEN
University of Maastricht

MICHAEL SMART
University of Toronto

2.1 PRELIMINARIES

2.1.1 *Introduction*

The level and structure of tobacco taxation are very much in the news these days. The level of tobacco taxation is believed to be an important instrument by which government can curtail tobacco consumption. An increase in the tax level, it is argued, will reduce the demand for cigarettes and thus improve health. Recently, the health issue has been forcefully brought to the fore by the publication of a joint study (Jha and Chaloupka, 2000) by the World Bank (WB) and the World Health Organization (WHO). Focusing in particular on developing countries, the WB/WHO study advocates higher taxes and tight controls on smuggling, among a host of other measures.[1] In the study's wake, the WHO is promoting the adoption of a worldwide Framework Convention on Tobacco Control.

Next to the level, the structure of tobacco taxation is considered important. As is well known, the tobacco excise can be levied at a fixed amount per quantity (specific rate), a fixed percentage of the product's retail price (*ad valorem* rate), or some combination of these rates. It is the appropriate balance between specific and *ad valorem* taxation that governs the debate on the harmonization of tobacco excises in the fifteen member states of the European Union (EU) and, by extension, the twelve accession countries in central and eastern Europe and the Mediterranean. Harmonization is prescribed by the Treaty of Rome, which established the European Economic Community (the EU's predecessor) in 1958.

This chapter reviews the issues involved in choosing the most appropriate level and structure of tobacco taxation. As background to the review,

* We would like to thank Jonathan Gruber, Peter Heller, Charles McLure, Emil Sunley, Joy Townsend, and, especially, Judith Payne for their perceptive comments on an earlier version of this chapter. Of course, we alone are responsible for any remaining errors.

Section 2.2 surveys the tobacco tax regimes in Europe and in the USA, two regions where the economic aspects of tobacco consumption and taxation have been studied most extensively. Interestingly, total tax levels and excise rate structures differ widely between as well as within these regions. Section 2.3 examines the interrelated issues involved in taxing tobacco: external costs, specific versus *ad valorem* taxation, equity considerations, revenue aspects, bootlegging, and smuggling. Section 2.4 draws some conclusions.

Throughout the chapter, the emphasis is mainly on taxes on cigarettes, which account for more than 90 per cent of tobacco consumption in the EU and the USA. Other tobacco products – cigars, pipe tobacco, snuff, and chewing tobacco – generally subject to *ad valorem* rates and consumed much less widely, are not discussed.

2.1.2 *Tobacco Tax Design*

The workings of the tobacco tax regimes in the EU and elsewhere can be illustrated by reviewing the design of the Dutch regime. In accordance with EU codification directive 95/59/EC (Council, 1995),[2] the tax on cigarettes in the Netherlands comprises three elements:

- a specific excise, expressed as a fixed amount of €53.27 per 1,000 cigarettes, or €1.07 per pack of twenty;
- an *ad valorem* excise, levied at a fixed percentage, i.e. 20.51 per cent, of the tax-inclusive retail price of the most popular price category of cigarettes (MPPC), also called the reference price;
- the value added tax (VAT) of 19 per cent, or 15.97 per cent if expressed as a percentage of the retail price inclusive of tax.

On this basis, Table 2.1 specifies the current cigarette tax structure in the Netherlands for two packs of cigarettes, brand A and brand B, that are sold at retail for €2.83 and €2.33, respectively. The retail price, inclusive of taxes, can be broken down into the price exclusive of taxes (ex-factory cost plus profit and trade margins) and the taxes, i.e. excises and VAT.

Obviously, the *ad valorem* excise and the VAT are fully identical in effect. Therefore, only the sum of *ad valorem* excise and VAT, hereafter called *ad valorem* levy, is relevant for the analysis. It is often argued that the VAT should be left out of consideration, because its imposition would not affect the price of cigarettes relative to other consumer goods. This would be correct if the excises, specific and *ad valorem*, reflected the social cost of tobacco use. To the extent that this is not the case, the VAT on the excess of the amount of the excises over the social cost represents an additional tax. The amount involved can be large. In the case of brand A in Table 2.1, a VAT on the retail price excluding taxes would amount to €0.14. However, the absolute amount of VAT, €0.45, is more than three times that amount. Thus the effective VAT rate is 62 per cent instead of 19 per cent. Because of this substantial tax-on-tax effect, we include the VAT in the analysis.

Table 2.1. *Netherlands: Specification of the Retail Price of Cigarettes (euro)*

	Brand A	Brand B	Difference
1. Retail price (p) including taxes	2.83	2.33	0.50
2. Taxes			
a. Specific excise (t_s)	1.07	1.07	0.00
b. *Ad valorem* excise ($t_{a1}p$)	0.58	0.48	0.10
c. VAT ($t_{a2}p$)	0.45	0.37	0.08
d. Total tax ($t_s + t_a p$)	2.10	1.92	0.18
3. Retail price ($p0$) excluding taxes	0.73	0.41	0.32

From the breakdown in Table 2.1, a number of important ratios can be derived:

- The total tax burden T on the MPPC – say, brand A – is equal to the ratio of the sum of all taxes, i.e. €2.10, to the retail price, i.e. €2.83, or 74 per cent – approximately 285 per cent of the retail price exclusive of taxes.
- The share S of the specific excise, i.e. €1.07, in total tax, i.e. €2.10, is 51 per cent – a percentage that plays an important role in the harmonization debate in the EU.[3]
- The share E of the sum of the specific excise and the *ad valorem* excise, i.e. €1.65, in the retail price, i.e. €2.83, is approximately 58 per cent – just above the minimum of 57 per cent required under the codification directive.
- The ratio M of the difference in retail price including taxes, i.e. €0.50, to the difference in retail price excluding taxes, i.e. €0.32, is 1.6 (rounded). More generally, this figure, called the multiplier, means that for every euro increase in factory cost, the retail price has to be increased by €1.60. The multiplier increases with the sum of *ad valorem* excise and VAT; it is independent of the specific excise.[4]

The various ratios can also be expressed algebraically. Let the retail price be denoted by p, the specific excise by t_s, the sum of *ad valorem* excise $t_{a1}p$ and VAT $t_{a2}p$ by $t_a p$, and the pre-tax price by $p0$. Then the relationship between post-tax and pre-tax prices is

$$(1) \qquad p = p0 + (t_s + t_a p) = \frac{p0 + t_s}{1 - t_a}.$$

Furthermore, if we denote the total tax burden by T, the share of the specific excise in total tax by S, the share of the sum of t_s and $t_{a1}p$ in the retail price by E, and the multiplier by M, then the various ratios can be expressed as follows:

$$(2) \qquad T = \frac{t_s + t_a p}{p};$$

(3)
$$S = \frac{t_s}{t_s + t_a p};$$

(4)
$$E = \frac{t_s + t_{a1} p}{p};$$

(5)
$$M = \frac{1}{1 - t_a} = \frac{1}{1 - T(1 - S)}.$$

2.2 TOBACCO TAX REGIMES IN EUROPE AND THE USA

The previous analysis sets the stage for a discussion of the tobacco tax regimes in the EU and the USA. As described below, tobacco taxes – levels and structures – differ markedly between as well as within the EU and the USA. In contrast to the EU, tobacco excises in the USA are wholly specific.

2.2.1 *European Union*

The founding fathers of the EU believed that differential excises could be used as protectionist trade barriers even if levied on a destination basis (imports taxed, exports free of tax). Excise tax rate structures could be so designed that they would effectively, if not legally, discriminate against products that were predominantly imported. Hence, the Treaty of Rome mandated the harmonization of excise taxes. Although little progress has so far been made in aligning the various tobacco excise tax structures, some discussion of the evolving debate is of interest before the actual tax structures are analysed. In turn, the binding framework on tobacco taxation (called *acquis communautaire*) agreed to by the EU is a benchmark for the accession countries in central and eastern Europe and the Mediterranean.[5]

Developments

Early on, the southern member states, under France's leadership, tried to reduce the specific element of the tobacco excise in favour of the *ad valorem* element. The reason is protection.[6] The tobaccos of the southern member states are cheaper than the higher-quality American blends that the northern member states import for their consumers. Since a specific tax regime tends to shrink relative price differences between low-cost and high-cost brands, whereas an *ad valorem* regime does not, the latter is more propitious to southern European producers.[7]

Throughout the years, the *ad valorem* lobby has been hard at work to promote its interests. Thus, in 1972, just before the accession of Denmark,

Ireland, and the UK (all specific excise rate countries!), agreement was reached on the gradual reduction of the role of the specific excise, which would be 'harmonized' in three stages. The share of the specific excise S would have to lie in the range 5–75 per cent in the first stage, 5–55 per cent in the second stage, and 5–35 per cent in the third stage. The second stage started 1 July 1978, but, in the face of growing opposition, the third stage has never been implemented. Instead, the second stage has been extended repeatedly, and, in 1986, the implementation of the third stage (which was originally planned for 1 January 1980!) was removed from the directive. Currently, the 5–55 per cent band is still in effect.

The stalemate in the early 1980s manifested itself in a controversy between the European Commission and the Economic and Social Committee (ECO-SOC) of the European Parliament. The European Commission (1982) wanted harmonization to proceed on the basis of the ratio of the specific excise to total tax; in the end, the ratio should become some 20 per cent. ECOSOC (1981), however, favoured harmonization on the basis of the *ad valorem* excise. At a given tax burden, this appears to be a case of six of one and half a dozen of the other, because the sum of the proportional elements equals the tax burden multiplied by one minus the ratio of specific excise to total tax.

But as Kay and Keen (1982) point out in an early but still relevant publication, the respective positions represented more subtle points of view. The proposal of the Commission implied a multiplier of 3 (corresponding to an *ad valorem* rate of about 56 per cent), while ECOSOC had a multiplier of 2 in mind, which implied an *ad valorem* rate of 40 per cent (inclusive of VAT) and a ratio of specific excise to total tax of 43 per cent. In other words, an increase in the tax burden on cigarettes under the Commission's proposal would involve an increase in the *ad valorem* rate, whereas an increase in total tax under ECOSOC's recommendation would involve an increase in the specific excise. The controversy was not resolved.

The matter was tabled again following the publication, in 1985, of the European Commission's White Paper, *Completing the Internal Market*. The elimination of border controls between the member states, it was argued, might lead to trade diversion, among others of tobacco products. Hence, further tax rate harmonization seemed called for. On the basis of the arithmetic averages of the member states, the Commission proposed, in 1987, to harmonize the specific rate at €19.5 per 1,000 cigarettes[8] and the *ad valorem* rate at 52–54 per cent. Again, ECOSOC (1988) rejected the Commission's proposal, arguing that it violated competition policy, would force some member states to raise tobacco taxes, and would be detrimental to poor member states.

Subsequently, the Commission tabled a proposal, which was discussed by the Economic and Finance Ministers (ECOFIN) in Luxembourg on 24 June 1991. Agreement was reached on the following points:

- the maintenance of the earlier agreed rate band of 5–55 per cent as regards the share S of the specific excise in total tax;

- a total excise burden *E*, specific and *ad valorem*, of at least 57 per cent of the retail price;
- the application of the standard rate of VAT, which would have to be at least 15 per cent, or 13.04 per cent of the price inclusive of VAT.

The new 57-per-cent criterion on the minimum total excise burden favoured harmonization on the basis of the *ad valorem* excise, similar to the earlier proposal to harmonize on the basis of the ratio of the specific excise to total tax. This time, the Economic and Monetary Affairs Committee (EMAC) of the European Parliament considered the proposal flawed. In its view, the 57 per cent criterion, which is a function of each member state's MPPC, would create different minimum excise amounts per member state. Therefore, EMAC proposed an alternative minimum, which became known as the 'adjunct', of €35 per 1,000 cigarettes. This proposal was approved in plenary session on 10 March 1992. However, ECOFIN did not adopt the adjunct when it passed directive 92/79/EEC (Council, 1992), based on the deliberations in Luxembourg, a few weeks later.[9]

It soon transpired that various perverse consequences flowed from the new criterion. In a volatile market, the MPPC could change from the top of the price range to the bottom. Hence, member states could be conforming to the 57 per cent rule one day and be in breach of it the next, without having made any changes to their rate structures. To avoid a situation in which the dog would be chasing its own tail, the European Commission (1995) therefore recommended the Council and the Parliament to amend the codification directive, so that member states whose absolute level of total excise on cigarettes was higher than a prescribed amount would be deemed to meet the minimum excise rule.[10] The most recent directive (Council, 2002) maintains the 57 per cent rule, but also stipulates that the resulting amount shall not be less than €60 per 1,000 cigarettes. Furthermore, member states that levy an overall minimum excise duty of €95 per 1,000 cigarettes shall be deemed to meet the 57 per cent rule.[11]

Tobacco Tax Regimes

Clearly, the *acquis communautaire* permits widely different tobacco excise regimes. Thus, most northern member states, as well as Portugal, have opted for a predominantly specific excise regime. On the other hand, southern member states favour a predominantly *ad valorem* regime. Also, in Finland and, more recently, Sweden, the share of the *ad valorem* excise in total excise is greater than the share of the specific excise.[12]

Table 2.2 presents an overview of taxes on cigarettes in all fifteen member states of the EU. It provides interesting information on the similarities and differences between 'northern' and 'southern' member states:[13]

- In all member states, the total tax burden *T* on cigarettes clusters around 76 per cent of the retail price, or 317 per cent of the retail price exclusive of tax. No single product is taxed so highly as tobacco.

Table 2.2. *European Union: Taxes on Cigarettes as of April 2003*

Member state[a]	Specific excise (euro per pack of 20)	Proportional elements (% of retail price)			Absolute amounts (euro per pack of 20)			Tax burden (%)	Important ratios			Multiplier
		Ad valorem excise	VAT	Total ad valorem levy	Total excise	Total tax	Retail price[b]		Share of specific excise in total tax (%)	Share of total excise in retail price (%)		
	t_s	t_{a1}	t_{a2}	$t_a = t_{a1} + t_{a2}$	$t_s + t_{a1}P$	$t_s + t_a P$	p	$T = \dfrac{t_s + t_a P}{p}$	$S = \dfrac{t_s}{t_s + t_a P}$	$E = \dfrac{t_s + t_{a1}P}{p}$		$M = \dfrac{1}{1 - t_a}$
Specific rates												
UK	3.09	22.00	14.89	36.89	4.67	5.74	7.18	80	54	65		1.6
Ireland	2.50	18.46	17.36	35.82	3.42	4.29	5.00	86	58	68		1.6
Denmark	1.63	21.22	20.00	41.22	2.49	3.30	4.04	82	49	62		1.7
Germany	1.23	24.23	13.79	38.02	2.05	2.51	3.37	75	49	61		1.6
Netherlands	1.07	20.51	15.97	36.48	1.65	2.10	2.83	74	51	58		1.6
Portugal	0.81	23.00	15.97	38.97	1.30	1.63	2.10	78	50	62		1.6
Ad valorem rates												
Finland	0.30	50.00	18.03	68.03	2.30	3.03	4.00	76	10	58		3.1
France	0.15	55.19	16.39	71.58	2.30	2.94	3.90	75	5	59		3.5
Sweden	0.44	39.20	20.00	59.20	2.05	2.88	4.12	70	15	50		2.5
Belgium	0.37	45.84	17.36	63.20	1.67	2.15	2.82	77	17	59		2.7
Austria	0.43	42.00	16.67	58.67	1.56	2.01	2.69	75	21	58		2.4
Greece	0.09	53.86	15.25	69.11	1.35	1.71	2.35	73	5	57		3.2
Italy	0.08	54.26	16.67	70.93	1.20	1.54	2.07	75	5	58		3.4
Luxembourg	0.24	46.84	10.71	57.55	1.21	1.44	2.08	69	17	58		2.4
Spain	0.08	54.00	13.79	67.79	1.13	1.40	1.95	72	6	58		3.1

[a] Specific excise regime if specific excise as a percentage of total tax is approximately the same as or higher than percentage of *ad valorem* excise; otherwise, *ad valorem* regime. Ranked within each group by total tax per pack of twenty cigarettes. Figures may have been rounded.

[b] Value of the most popular price category (MPPC) in April 2003.

Source: Computed from Mogensen (2003*a*). Figures may have been rounded. Exchange rates used for non-euro member states are: Denmark – 1DKK=€0.13; Sweden – 1SEK=€0.10; UK – £1=€1.62.

- In the northern member states, the share S of the specific excise in total tax lies close to the upper limit of the agreed band of 5–55 per cent. In the southern member states, by contrast, the share of the specific excise is closer to the lower limit of 5 per cent. The situation with respect to the *ad valorem* excise and the VAT is the other way around: on average, 37.9 per cent of the retail price in the northern member states as opposed to, on average, 65.1 per cent in the southern member states.
- In all member states except Sweden, the share E of the sum of specific and *ad valorem* excise in retail price is 57 per cent or higher. Sweden meets the alternative minimum requirement of €95 per 1,000 cigarettes (€1.90 per pack). For this reason, the UK, Ireland, Denmark, Germany, Finland, and France would not have to comply with the 57 per cent criterion either.
- One member state – Spain – does not comply with the supplementary criterion of €60 per 1,000 cigarettes or €1.20 per pack. It has until the end of 2004 to fall in.
- Approximately equal relative total tax burdens, but large differences in the share of the sum of *ad valorem* excise and VAT in total tax, imply large differences in multipliers M. In the northern member states, M clusters around the value 1.6; in the southern member states, M fluctuates around 2.9.
- Although relative total tax burdens are close to each other, substantial differences show up in the absolute amounts of total tax burdens and retail prices. The northern member states levy, on average, €3.26 tax per pack of twenty cigarettes (of which, €1.72 from the specific rate) against €2.12 by the southern member states (of which, €0.24 from the specific rate). Not surprisingly, retail prices average €4.09 and €2.89 per pack, respectively – a difference of €1.20 per pack.

As these figures indicate, the EU is deeply divided on the appropriate balance between specific and *ad valorem* taxation. On the north side, Denmark, Germany, Ireland, the Netherlands, and the UK have dug in to defend their specific excises. Austria, Belgium, France, Greece, Italy, Luxembourg, and Spain are entrenched on the south side, staunchly clinging onto their *ad valorem* rates. Finland, Portugal, and Sweden are the only member states whose tobacco excise regime is at variance with their geographical location.

EU Accession Countries

Analogous to Table 2.2, Table 2.3 shows the various tobacco taxes in the accession countries. The information in the table can be summarized as follows:

- The total tax on cigarettes T for eleven accession countries for which information is available is around 65 per cent, 11 percentage points lower than in the EU. The variation of T among the accession countries is greater than that among EU member states.

Table 2.3. *EU Accession Countries: Taxes on Cigarettes as of April 2003*

Country[a]	Specific excise (euro per pack of 20)	Proportional elements (% of retail price)			Absolute amounts (euro per pack of 20)			Important ratios			
		Ad valorem excise	VAT	Total ad valorem levy	Total excise	Total tax	Retail price[b]	Tax burden (%)	Share of specific excise in total tax (%)	Share of total excise in retail price (%)	Multiplier
	t_s	t_{a1}	t_{a2}	$t_a = t_{a1} + t_{a2}$	$t_s + t_{a1}P$	$t_s + t_aP$	P	$T = \dfrac{t_s + t_aP}{P}$	$S = \dfrac{t_s}{t_s + t_aP}$	$E = \dfrac{t_s + t_{a1}P}{P}$	$M = \dfrac{1}{1 - t_a}$
Specific rates											
Cyprus	1.35[c]	—	13.04	13.04	1.35	1.64	2.22	74	82	61	1.1
Hungary	0.41	20.00	20.00	40.00	..	..	..	..	..	..	1.7
Slovak Republic	0.46	—	16.70	16.70	0.46	0.64	1.08	59	72	42	1.2
Lithuania	0.25	10.00	15.25	25.25	0.32	0.44	0.77	57	56	42	1.3
Latvia	0.20[d]	—	15.25	15.25	0.20	0.27	0.52	53	71	37	1.2
Ad valorem rates											
Malta	0.19	53.10	13.04	66.14	1.79	2.19	3.03	72	9	59	3.0
Slovenia	0.21	39.07	16.67	55.74	0.79	1.04	1.49	70	20	53	2.3
Czech Republic	0.24	22.00	18.03	40.03	0.53	0.76	1.32	58	31	40	1.7
Estonia	0.27	24.00	15.25	39.25	0.52	0.68	1.05	65	39	49	1.6
Poland	0.28	25.00	18.03	43.03	0.50	0.66	0.88	75	42	57	1.8
Romania	0.10	32.00	19.00	51.00	0.31	0.43	0.64	67	24	48	2.0
Bulgaria	0.02[d]	40.00	16.67	56.67	0.27	0.37	0.62	60	5	43	2.3

[a] Specific excise regime if specific excise as a percentage of total tax is approximately the same as or higher than percentage of *ad valorem* excise; otherwise, *ad valorem* regime. Ranked within each group by total tax per pack of twenty cigarettes. Figures may have been rounded.

[b] Value of the most popular price category (MPPC) in April 2003.

[c] The specific excise depends on the origin of the tobacco (Cyprus/EU or third country) and the selling price band. The source provides data on total tax, retail price, and VAT. Accordingly, the authors have calculated the specific excise by subtracting the VAT from the total tax.

[d] Specific rates apply to filter cigarettes.

Source: Computed from Mogensen (2003*b*). Figures may not add because of rounding.

- The accession countries are about evenly divided between specific-rate and *ad-valorem*-rate countries. In Malta, like most other Mediterranean countries, the share of specific excise in total tax is very low. By contrast, the excise regime in Cyprus (as well as the Slovak Republic and Latvia) is exclusively specific.
- Cyprus, Malta, and Poland are the only accession countries that meet the overall minimum requirement for E, i.e. that the share of the total excise in the retail price should be 57 per cent or higher. At least nine countries do not even come close to meeting the adjunct of €1.20 per pack of cigarettes, let alone the alternative minimum of €1.90 at which the 57 per cent criterion is waived.
- The multiplier M averages 1.8; generally, variations are smaller than among EU member states.
- As in the EU, retail prices differ widely between countries, from €0.52 in Latvia to €3.03 in Malta, an island that should have fewer difficulties in controlling smuggling.

Obviously, most accession countries will have to make substantial (upward) adjustments to their tobacco excises to bring them into line with the EU *acquis communautaire*. Latvia would have to increase its tobacco taxes more than fivefold to match the total tax burden of €1.40 in Spain, which is the lowest in the EU. It is likely that further increases in the tobacco taxes of eastern European countries will exacerbate the smuggling problem (see below). The accession countries would be hard put to raise their total tobacco excises to €95 per 1,000 cigarettes – the level at which the 57 per cent rule is waived. Hence, the discussion focuses mainly on the 57 per cent rule and its adjunct, the minimum total excise of €60 per 1,000. The 57 per cent rule can be met more easily by increasing the *ad valorem* excise, the €60 minimum by raising the specific excise. The accession countries will have to make their own choices, since the European Commission cannot promote a specific excise regime over an *ad valorem* regime or vice versa. In negotiations, gradual phase-in schedules have been agreed to, under which most adjustments will be completed by 2010.

2.2.2 USA

In contrast to the EU, tobacco tax harmonization is not an issue in the USA. The federal government imposes a uniform specific excise of $0.39 per pack of twenty cigarettes, but, as shown in Table 2.4, state and local tobacco excises, all specific, vary widely, from $1.51 per pack in Massachusetts to $0.03 in Kentucky and Virginia (the unweighted average is $0.60). Furthermore, retail sales taxes (RSTs), ranging from 4 per cent to 7 per cent (exclusive of local sales taxes, unless they are uniform across the state), are imposed in forty-four states and the District of Columbia.[14] In 2001, state cigarette excise revenues totalled $8.4 billion, while the federal government collected $7.4 billion from the same source.[15]

Table 2.4. *USA: Taxes on Cigarettes as of October 2002 (US dollars per pack of twenty cigarettes)*

State (ranked by total tax)	Specific state / federal excise[a] t_s	RST (tax-exclusive) (%)[b] t_r	Total tax $t_s + t_r p(1 - t_r)$	Total 'tax' including Master Settlement (MS)[c]	Average retail price p	Tax burden including MS (%) $T = \dfrac{t_s + t_r p + MS}{p}$	Share of excise + MS in total tax (%) $S = \dfrac{t_s + MS}{t_s + t_r p + MS}$
New Jersey	1.89	6	2.17	2.48	4.90	51	89
Washington	1.82	6.5	2.12	2.43	4.98	49	88
Massachusetts	1.90	5	2.11	2.42	4.32	56	91
New York	1.89	4	2.11	2.42	5.80	42	91
Rhode Island	1.71	7	2.01	2.32	4.61	50	87
Michigan	1.64	6	1.90	2.21	4.68	47	88
Hawaii	1.59	4	1.77	2.08	4.65	45	91
Connecticut	1.50	6	1.76	2.07	4.53	46	87
Oregon	1.67	—	1.67	1.98	4.34	46	100
Pennsylvania	1.39	6	1.63	1.94	4.25	46	88
Illinois	1.37	6.25	1.62	1.93	4.26	45	87
Maryland	1.39	5	1.60	1.91	4.36	44	89
Maine	1.39	5	1.59	1.90	4.25	45	89
California	1.26	7	1.55	1.86	4.38	42	84
Vermont	1.32	5	1.53	1.84	4.37	42	89
Alaska	1.39	—	1.39	1.70	4.55	37	100
Wisconsin	1.16	5	1.36	1.67	4.16	40	88
Kansas	1.09	4.9	1.27	1.58	3.76	42	89
Utah	1.09	4.75	1.26	1.57	3.83	41	89
Washington DC	1.04	5.75	1.26	1.57	4.05	39	86
Nebraska	1.03	5	1.21	1.52	3.88	39	88
Arizona	0.97	5	1.16	1.47	3.91	38	87
Ohio	0.94	5	1.13	1.44	3.96	36	87
Indiana	0.95	5	1.13	1.43	3.72	38	88
Minnesota	0.87	6.5	1.10	1.41	3.83	37	84
North Dakota	0.83	5	1.01	1.32	3.68	36	86

State						
Texas	0.80	6.25	1.01	1.32	3.60	37	84
Nevada	0.74	6.5	0.96	1.27	3.56	36	83
Florida	0.73	6	0.94	1.25	3.65	34	83
New Hampshire	0.91	—	0.91	1.22	3.65	33	100
Arkansas	0.73	5.13	0.91	1.22	3.60	33	85
Iowa	0.73	5	0.90	1.21	3.48	35	85
Louisiana	0.75	4	0.88	1.19	3.50	34	89
South Dakota	0.72	4	0.86	1.17	3.53	33	88
Idaho	0.67	5	0.83	1.14	3.33	34	86
Mississippi	0.57	7	0.79	1.10	3.43	32	80
Tennessee	0.59	6	0.78	1.09	3.38	32	83
Oklahoma	0.62	4.5	0.77	1.08	3.40	32	86
New Mexico	0.60	5	0.77	1.08	3.49	31	84
West Virginia	0.56	6	0.74	1.05	3.25	32	83
Missouri	0.56	4.23	0.69	1.00	3.29	30	87
Alabama	0.56	4	0.69	0.99	3.48	28	88
Wyoming	0.51	4	0.64	0.95	3.35	28	86
Georgia	0.51	4	0.64	0.94	3.31	28	87
Delaware	0.63	—	0.63	0.94	3.29	29	100
South Carolina	0.46	5	0.62	0.93	3.30	28	83
Kentucky	0.42	6	0.60	0.91	3.23	28	80
Colorado	0.59	0	0.59	0.90	3.18	28	100
Montana	0.57	—	0.57	0.88	3.21	27	100
North Carolina	0.44	4	0.56	0.87	3.15	28	86
Virginia	0.42	4.5	0.56	0.86	3.20	27	85
Unweighted average	0.99	4.6	1.16	1.47	3.86	37	88

[a] The federal excise is $0.39 per pack of twenty cigarettes.

[b] RST rates, t_r, are in tax-exclusive form, i.e. specified as a proportion of the net-of-tax price (in contrast to the VAT rates in Tables 2.1, 2.2, and 2.3). RST amounts are calculated by applying the state RST rate (including local sales tax rates if uniform across state) to the estimated average retail price, not including RST, of a pack of cigarettes in each state. New York State's retail price also reflects New York City's $1.50 cigarette tax. Colorado's RST does not apply to cigarettes, and Alabama, Georgia, and Missouri do not apply their RST to that portion of retail cigarette prices that represents the state's cigarette excise tax. Alaska, Delaware, Montana, New Hampshire, and Oregon have no RST at all.

[c] The Master Tobacco Settlement Agreement provides for the payment of $246 billion by tobacco companies to the states (and various trust funds) over twenty-five years ending in 2025. The payment in 2002 of $8.9 billion is equivalent to a specific excise of $0.31 per pack.

Source: www.tobaccofreekids.org/reports/prices, downloaded 10 October 2002.

Beyond this, mention should be made of the Master Tobacco Settlement Agreement (MTSA), concluded in 1998, under which tobacco companies are expected to pay $206 billion to the states over a period of twenty-five years ending in 2025. The payments are in settlement of actual and potential product liability suits.[16] In 2002, the states received $8.9 billion – $0.5 billion more than state tobacco excise tax collections. Since annual consumption was approximately 28.6 billion packs in 2001, the payment was equivalent to $0.31 per pack.[17] This amount can be viewed as an additional specific excise.[18] In Table 2.4, therefore, the settlement payment has been added to the total specific state/federal excises and the RST levied per pack of cigarettes in each state. The MTSA, sizeable increases in tobacco excises, and other factors have raised the price of a pack of cigarettes by, on average, $1.25 over a period of four years since 1998.

Table 2.4 shows the following information:

- The unweighted average total tax burden *T*, inclusive of the MTSA payments, is 37 per cent of the retail price, compared with 76 per cent in the EU. In absolute amounts, the unweighted average total tax is $1.47 per pack of cigarettes, half of the average total tax in the EU of €2.57.[19]

- As in the EU, the average masks wide differences in absolute amounts. The ratio of the highest total tax ($2.48 in New Jersey) to the lowest total tax ($0.86 in Virginia) is 2.9, compared with 4.1 in the EU. In high-tax US states, the total tax on cigarettes approaches or slightly exceeds the Belgian level in the EU.

- In contrast to EU member states, the total tax in US states is predominantly specific. The unweighted average state and federal excise is $0.99 plus the MTSA payment of $0.31, i.e. $1.30 – nearly two-thirds of the total excise in the EU of €2.02. The share of the specific tax in total tax ranges from 80 per cent in Kentucky and Mississippi to 100 per cent in states without RST; the unweighted average is 88 per cent.

- The *ad valorem* element consists solely of the RST, which adds, on average, $0.18 to the price. The tax-on-tax effect of, on average, $0.07 is small, because RST rates in US states are, on average, less than one-third of average VAT rates in the EU. This implies that there is not much of a multiplier effect. Cost increases roughly result in correspondingly higher retail prices.

- As in the EU, northern states tend to levy higher excises than tobacco-growing southern states (Kentucky, Virginia, North Carolina, South Carolina, Georgia, and Tennessee), although there are some exceptions to this rule. In addition, the excises in most states that have borders with Canada tend to be lower than those in adjacent states, allegedly because cigarettes that are exported free of tax from Canada are often not reported in the USA.[20]

- As in the EU, retail prices differ markedly, ranging from $5.80 per pack of cigarettes in New York to $3.15 in North Carolina, a tobacco state. The price in New York is higher than the price in all but one EU member state (the UK). The price in North Carolina is still higher than the price in eight EU member states on account of the higher pre-tax price of cigarettes. Cigarette retail prices across the USA differ less than prices across the EU. This should be attributed to the use of qualitatively similar tobaccos and the greater share of the specific excises in total tax.

2.2.3 *Summary*

Tobacco taxes in the EU are the highest in the world. The total tax (excises and VAT) on cigarettes is, on average, 76 per cent of the retail price, which equals 317 per cent of the retail price exclusive of tax. In comparison, the VAT rate of, on average, 19.3 per cent, which is also calculated on the price exclusive of tax, is very modest indeed. At, on average, 65 per cent of the retail price, the total tax on cigarettes in the accession countries is a third of the average total tax in the EU. In the USA, taxes (federal and state excises, RST, plus the MTSA charge) on cigarettes are, on average, 38 per cent of the retail price inclusive of tax, or 61 per cent of the price exclusive of tax, compared with RSTs of 4–7 per cent.

Within these regions, tax burdens differ widely among EU member states, various accession countries, and US states. In fact, the wide variability of tobacco taxes observed in the USA raises the question of the extent to which harmonized taxes, prescribed by treaty, are necessary or even desirable within the EU. This issue is important, since the new accession countries will have considerable difficulties in conforming to the EU minimum taxes on tobacco. A notable difference between the EU and the USA is that the EU attaches importance to the *ad valorem* excise which is absent in the USA.

The high taxes on tobacco raise a number of questions which are addressed in the next section. What and how high are the costs that smokers impose on other people? Accordingly, how high should the level of tobacco taxes be? What considerations enter into the choice of the appropriate balance between specific and *ad valorem* excises? What are the implications of the burden distribution of tobacco taxes across various income groups? Are tobacco taxes an efficient source of government revenue? How serious are the problems of cross-border shopping and smuggling in view of the high tax rates? As argued below, the answers to these questions depend on the goal that is being pursued, i.e. charging for external costs, maximizing revenue, excise tax harmonization, or some combination of these and other goals.

2.3 ISSUES IN TOBACCO TAXATION

2.3.1 *External Costs*

Smoking, like bad eating habits and lack of exercise, has detrimental effects on a person's health. In the case of smoking, the causal link to future health problems is by now extremely well documented. Smoking is a primary cause of lung cancer, emphysema, and chronic bronchitis, and a major cause of heart disease and stroke; it is also associated with other diseases and other forms of cancer. Smoking by pregnant women in particular is known to lead to low-birth-weight babies, neonatal death, and sudden infant death syndrome (Chaloupka and Warner, 2000). Smoking therefore gives rise to a number of economic costs, related primarily to the expense of treating smoking-related illnesses, as well as the well-being and market earnings that are lost as a consequence of smoking-related illness and death.

While the health consequences of smoking are important, in principle they are irrelevant to public policy unless the costs imposed are external, i.e. imposed on others, rather than borne privately by the smoker. The principle of consumer sovereignty implies that a rational person who weighs up all the costs and benefits of his actions should be free to smoke as long as he is fully informed about the consequences of his choice and does not impose costs on others. External costs (physical, financial, psychological) and information failures (lack of knowledge about addiction and health risks) establish a case for government intervention through regulation, education, and taxation (Jha et al., 2000).

Measuring Costs

Once external costs have been identified and measured, the Pigouvian prescription for taxation is clear. Efficient consumption of tobacco can be achieved through the tax system by imposing a tax on cigarettes equal to the cost of the damage caused to other people. That is, the Pigouvian tax should be equivalent to the marginal external cost per cigarette consumed.[21]

How high should Pigouvian tobacco taxes be? Whether the costs of smoking are external or internalized by the smoker is, to some extent, in the eye of the beholder. At one extreme, environmental or 'second-hand' tobacco smoke is now known to cause health problems in 'passive' smokers. Such costs are certainly external to the smoker. However, much second-hand smoke is experienced within the family home, so that it might be argued that such costs are internalized by the smoker, either through altruism or through explicit negotiation among family members (Manning et al., 1989).

Further, marginal health expenditures associated with smoking will not be borne by the patient who has health insurance, unless the health insurer has taken steps to observe the smoking behaviour of customers and sets premiums and policies to control moral hazard. In fact, some private health insurance schemes do quote separate prices for smokers and non-smokers; however, there appears to be no real effort to verify customers' reports, and significant moral hazard remains even in private healthcare systems. In the presence of such insurance market failures, then, incremental costs are analogous to physical externalities, and government intervention to internalize costs is appropriate (Greenwald and Stiglitz, 1986).

In short, identification and measurement of marginal costs are difficult. The true external cost depends on who smokes what, where, and under what circumstances. Obviously, this kind of information is not available and, even if it were, it would not be feasible to impose a separate tax on each cigarette that goes up in smoke. In practice, therefore, a 'pooling' approach is adopted in charging for the external costs of smoking. Similar to motor fuel taxes paid by road users (Newbery, this volume), smokers as a group meet these costs by paying a uniform tax on tobacco products.

Some improvements in targeting over current practice can be envisaged, however. Since health damage is greater when the tar content of cigarettes is greater, taxes on high-tar cigarettes should be higher too. However, some research (for example, Evans and Farrelly (1998)) shows that addicts smoke low-tar and low-nicotine cigarettes differently, inhaling more to increase the amount of nicotine they ingest. So Pigouvian taxes might not be proportional to tar content, but some differentiation is likely to be appropriate still. Moreover, a 'tar tax' would give manufacturers an incentive to develop palatable low-tar cigarettes, which would have long-term health benefits (Bulow and Klemperer, 1998).

For most economists, this much is gospel. But, as Lightwood et al. (2000) point out, public health and medical researchers have often taken a different approach, estimating the total of external and private costs of smoking, including the costs of lost earnings and suffering experienced by smokers themselves. Related to this, advocates sometimes argue that cigarette taxes should rise to offset the costs of government-financed health services used by smokers. By this logic, therefore, cigarette taxes should presumably be higher in European countries that have extensive government-financed healthcare systems than in the USA, where the share of private healthcare spending is much higher.[22]

Of course, the distinction between total and external costs is extremely important in practice. Virtually all empirical research (described in more detail below) suggests that the net external costs of smoking are quite small. To the extent that this is so, the high levels of tobacco taxation we observe seem to reflect paternalistic attitudes to smoking, rather than externality considerations appropriate to a government that respects consumer sovereignty.

Addiction and Information Failures

Consumer sovereignty proceeds from the premise that smokers are fully aware of the consequences of their habits. However, if smokers, especially teenagers, are poorly informed about the costs of smoking, then, to that extent, costs of smoking are external. Further, as Peck et al. (2000) point out, the fact that nicotine is addictive undermines the consumer-sovereignty argument against government intervention. If smokers behave myopically in choosing to consume an addictive drug, the rationality condition ceases to apply, because the addicted smoker is to some extent a different person from the one who decided to start smoking. In this perspective, the injured party is the smoker's future self, and high taxes may in principle be justified on welfare grounds.

Similar conclusions follow even in a model of 'rational' addiction (Becker and Murphy, 1988), if smokers' preferences are such that they behave in a dynamically inconsistent fashion. Thus, in Gruber and Koszegi (2001), consumers are rational and forward-looking, but they discount costs and benefits in the near-term future to a greater extent than those in the long term. With such preferences, smokers have a 'self-control' problem: they continually plan to smoke less in the future than they actually can.[23] It follows that taxes may raise smokers' own welfare, by reinforcing a commitment to quit in the future.[24]

This view justifies the formulation of public health objectives aimed at reducing the level and number of smokers, among other methods through the tax system. Prima facie, information failures and myopia establish a case for government intervention, even in the absence of explicit external costs. Again, however, taxation is a poor instrument if lack of information is central to smoking. This problem is best addressed through prominent warning labels and the dissemination of information about health hazards through the media.[25] Based on evidence from the USA, it may be assumed that over 90 per cent of consumers in developed countries are aware of the long-term health effects of smoking (Kenkel and Chen, 2000).[26]

Higher taxes are particularly effective in reducing the incidence of smoking among teenagers, even though taxes are second-best to better education about the addictive nature of smoking and its long-term costs. Research (Chaloupka et al., 2000) indicates that the price elasticity of demand for cigarettes in high-income countries is, on average, −0.8 among the young, compared with, on average, −0.4 among adults. Generally, teenagers are better able to kick the habit (the addiction has not taken hold) and more susceptible to peer pressure (Guindon, Tobin, and Yach, 2002). Estimates for the USA suggest that a tax increase of $2 per pack would reduce overall youth smoking by about two-thirds (National Cancer Policy Board, 1998).[27] This could have beneficial long-term effects, because future abstention depends to a large extent on current abstention (Chaloupka et al., 2000). It is difficult to rationalize, however, why tax increases should penalize habitual smokers. As Shoup (1983) notes, 'If ... we put aside the problem of negative externalities, there seems to be no acceptable principle that justifies higher taxation of addicts.'

Empirical Research

A number of researchers have attempted to provide empirical estimates of the external costs of smoking. The essence of the most common approach is to use healthcare utilization rates to forecast the incremental health expenditures for the current generation of smokers, make some additions for healthcare costs associated with environmental tobacco smoke, and then divide the total amount by the number of packs of cigarettes currently consumed, to arrive at an estimate of the Pigouvian tax rate. Necessarily, then, these studies estimate the average external damage of smoking, rather than the marginal external damage discussed in the theory.[28] Further, these studies have been criticized for omitting many of the diseases associated with environmental tobacco smoke and omitting the pain and suffering experienced by passive smokers from the calculations entirely. In this approach, pain and suffering of smokers themselves are omitted from the analysis, on the grounds that such costs should be internalized if smokers are rational.

In one influential study of this type, Manning et al. (1989) estimated the gross external costs of smoking in the USA to lie in a range centred around 43 cents per pack of cigarettes consumed (66 cents in April 2003 if adjusted for changes in the consumer price index). Once reductions in healthcare expenditures resulting from smokers' premature deaths were netted out, the estimate declined to just 16 cents per pack (25 cents in April 2003). This figure is supported by other studies, though at the low end of the range of all estimates.

On the basis of a careful review of a large number of studies, Lightwood et al. (2000) conclude that estimates of gross costs range from 0.1 to 1.1 per cent of gross domestic product (GDP) in high-income countries.[29] Smokers, however, tend to live shorter lives than non-smokers, which saves on pension payments and healthcare costs of age-related diseases (Shoven et al., 1989).[30] From an economic point of view, therefore, it is *net* costs, which assess all government social security expenditures over a lifetime, that should be the focus of analysis. While there is greater controversy about estimates of net costs, Lightwood et al. (2000) conclude that the majority of the cross-section studies indicate that the net costs of smoking are small but positive.

There are notable exceptions in the literature. Atkinson and Townsend (1977) found that the actual cost savings to the UK exchequer from a hypothetical 40 per cent reduction in cigarette smoking were relatively small. A study for Finland (Pekurinen, 1992) concluded that smoking could involve net healthcare cost savings. In an updated version of the Manning et al. study, Viscusi (1995) found that net external costs were negligible for the USA. Barendregt et al. (1997) calculated the length of time it takes for the cost savings from smoking cessation to be balanced by the increased costs from the longer life expectancies of non-smokers. Their results imply that smoking reduces net healthcare costs. The results of these studies, however, are sensitive to the choice of the discount rate at which the net present value of future costs is estimated. Many of these studies, moreover, have been criticized for underestimating the costs of environmental tobacco smoke (Chaloupka and Warner, 2000).

Nevertheless, this evidence is striking. If the external costs of smoking are negligible, government measures to reduce smoking through higher taxes would seem to be a form of paternalism on which economics has little to say.

Finally, it should be noted that a small literature has recently taken a different approach, directly estimating the health benefits of increasing tobacco taxes rather than estimating the health costs of smoking. Notice that from the Pigouvian perspective, such information is irrelevant: the tax rate should be set to the marginal external damage, at which price smokers may choose to smoke or not at no cost to efficiency. The estimates are valuable, however, if there is uncertainty about the cost to smokers of 'abating' the externality, or if taxation is to be compared with alternative public health strategies, such as education programmes.

As an example, Evans and Ringel (1999) examined the impact of changes in state-level cigarette taxes on the health of new-born children, using data from a census of all births in the USA during the 1989–92 period. Smoking increases the likelihood that children are of low birth weight, which is an important indicator of post-natal health problems. Through its effects on smoking behaviour (the authors calculated a price elasticity of smoking participation for pregnant women of −0.5), the cigarette tax variable, however, is estimated to have a significant positive impact on the probability that children are of normal birth weight. This study is a useful corroboration of clinical studies of the impact of maternal smoking, where it is difficult to control for the effect of other characteristics and behaviours of the mother that may be correlated with the decision to smoke. In the same vein, Moore (1996) examines the impact of state cigarette taxes on smoking-related mortality during the 1954–88 period. On the basis of the evidence, he argues that a 10 per cent increase in cigarette taxes would prevent 5,200 deaths annually.

2.3.2 *Specific versus* Ad Valorem *Taxation*

While most work on tobacco taxation has focused on the appropriate level of total taxation, considerable importance may be attached to whether taxes take a specific or *ad valorem* form. As indicated above, in the EU in particular, this issue has been controversial. In a perfectly competitive market for a homogeneous good, the choice between *ad valorem* and specific taxation is irrelevant: any specific tax could be replaced by its percentage equivalent with no effect on consumer and producer prices or on government revenue. For a number of reasons, actual markets for tobacco products differ from this idealized framework. Here, we focus chiefly on the implications of quality differences among brands and on the market power of tobacco producers.

Certainly, tobacco is not a homogeneous product. Someone who smokes knows that there are large differences in quality among brands: a Virginia tastes better than two sticks of sawdust. Since the revenue authorities would surely be hard-pressed to choose appropriate tax rates for each quality level independently, they are faced with a choice between a common specific tax rate, which reduces relative price differences between low-price and high-price brands, and a common *ad valorem* rate, which does not. In a competitive market with quality differences, standard optimal tax considerations would therefore seem to argue for *ad valorem* taxation. The relative price of high- and low-quality cigarettes would be unchanged, and consumers would continue to choose brand on the basis of cost rather than tax differences.[31]

The Pigouvian perspective leads to a very different conclusion, however: the damage caused by a cigarette is independent of the price at which it is sold, so that correction of externalities favours specific over *ad valorem* taxation. All else equal, the share of specific in total taxation should be smaller when the marginal cost of public funds is higher and the importance of tobacco taxes for generating revenue correspondingly greater. To some extent, this reasoning is consistent with the *ad valorem* excise element in EU tobacco tax structures and its absence in US structures.

These arguments apply to competitive markets in which the set of quality levels on offer is given exogenously. With imperfect competition, firms' incentives to raise price and to distort quality may be quite different under specific and *ad valorem* taxation. Consider first the case of a monopolist who faces an inverse demand curve $P(q)$ and must pay a specific tax at rate t_s on each unit of output sold. Profit maximization requires

$$(6) \qquad\qquad MR = MC + t_s,$$

where $MR = P + qP'$ is marginal revenue and MC is marginal cost. In contrast, *ad valorem* taxation at rate t_a causes the producer price to fall from p to $(1 - t_a)p$, so that the profit maximization condition becomes

$$(7) \qquad\qquad MR = \frac{MC}{1 - t_a}.$$

In words, specific taxation increases marginal costs by a fixed amount, whereas *ad valorem* taxation acts as a proportional tax on costs, together with a proportional (lump-sum) tax on monopoly profits. This is the 'multiplier' effect of *ad valorem* taxation discussed above.

By taxing marginal revenue, *ad valorem* taxation increases the firm's perceived demand elasticity by the multiplier $1/(1 - t_a)$ and so diminishes incentives for the firm to raise price above marginal cost. Thus one might expect consumer prices to be lower under *ad valorem* than under specific taxation. Indeed, it is possible to show, in the monopoly case, that replacing a specific tax t_s by its *ad valorem* equivalent $t_a = t_s/p$ causes consumer prices to fall and tax revenue and monopoly profits to rise (Skeath and Trandel, 1994).[32] So everyone gains from *ad valorem* taxation – except the public health advocate. In the Cournot model of an oligopoly industry, the story is largely the same: a shift to *ad valorem* taxation will reduce prices and increase government revenues. In this case, however, industry profits may fall, as competition among firms intensifies.

A further, testable implication of the theory is that the pass-through of tax increases to consumer prices should be greater under specific than under *ad valorem* taxation (Delipalla and Keen, 1992). There is some evidence that specific taxes in the EU are more likely to be 'over-shifted' (consumer prices rise by more than the tax) than *ad valorem* taxes (Delipalla and O'Donnell, 2001).

Just as *ad valorem* taxation seems to induce firms to cut prices, it also creates a clear incentive to downgrade product quality (Barzel, 1976). Examining again the first-order conditions for profit maximization under the two tax systems, notice that the specific tax causes a fixed increase in costs, whereas *ad valorem* taxation acts like a proportional increase. This multiplier effect of *ad valorem* taxation makes improvements in product quality more expensive for the firm. Likewise, it reduces incentives to invest in advertising, promotion, and other demand-enhancing fixed costs of production. In contrast, specific taxation does not directly distort manufacturers' decisions to invest in product quality.[33]

In this respect, then, *ad valorem* taxation may be a useful tool in 'deglamorizing' cigarettes and reducing consumption in the long run, especially among young people (Bulow and Klemperer, 1998). But not all investments in product quality are detrimental to health, and *ad valorem* taxation based on the retail price of cigarettes discourages 'good' and 'bad' quality improvements alike. The cost of coal filters, for instance, which purify the tobacco of tar and other harmful substances, is subject to the multiplier effect. As argued previously, such desirable investments by manufacturers could be encouraged by differentiated taxation of cigarettes. But, in the absence of such differentiation, *ad valorem* taxation could have perverse effects.[34]

Other, more immediate, considerations might also govern the choice of tax structure. Thus, a specific tax can be imposed at the manufacturer's or importer's stage where it is easiest to collect, whereas, under a system of free trade prices, an *ad valorem* levy must be collected at the retail stage if trade distortions and tax avoidance are to be avoided. In the EU, of course, these issues are circumvented by determining the *ad valorem* levy by reference to the (fixed) retail price of the most popular price category of cigarettes. In effect, the *ad valorem* levy becomes a specific tax as long as the designated cigarettes remain 'most popular' and cigarette producers do not negotiate a new retail price with the excise tax authorities. Generally, a disadvantage of a specific tax is that its value erodes with inflation, unless the excise administration has the authority to adjust the tax on the basis of the consumer price index. Again, in the EU, this is less of an issue, because inflation would compel producers to approach the excise authorities with a proposal for a new retail price.

We summarize these arguments as follows:

- In imperfectly competitive markets, a shift from specific to *ad valorem* taxation has a clear tendency to reduce mark-ups, and so to increase government revenue and cigarette consumption.
- With quality differences, specific taxation induces consumers to 'upgrade' their choice of brand (at fixed producer prices), whereas *ad valorem* taxation discourages firms with market power from making costly investments to increase quality.[35]
- The choice between specific and *ad valorem* taxation therefore depends on whether the primary aim of the policy is to discourage smoking or to raise revenue and on whether improvements in cigarette quality are deemed desirable or not.
- If the goal of policy is to reduce smoking, there is some tension between the tendency of specific taxes to lead to higher consumer prices and the tendency of *ad valorem* taxes to discourage investments in quality that keep smokers 'hooked'. The solution is likely to be *ad valorem* taxation at

a higher equivalent rate to achieve the desired level of consumer prices, and with concomitant gains for government treasuries.

2.3.3 *Equity Considerations*

Tobacco taxes are highly discriminatory and regressive, more so than any other tax. In high-income countries, only 38 per cent of men and 21 per cent of women pay tobacco taxes (Gajalakshimi et al., 2000). Tobacco taxes are regressive because, proportionately, the poor spend a higher share of their income on cigarettes than the rich, assuming that the prevalence of smoking is the same. As a group, however, the poor smoke more than the rich, which tends to exacerbate the regressivity problem across income classes. In fact, smoking is becoming increasingly concentrated in lower classes – variously defined by income, education, occupation, or social class. While the poor were the last to pick up smoking, they are also the last to quit.

Townsend, Roderick, and Cooper (1994) collected evidence on the standardized mortality ratios from smoking diseases by social class in England and Wales. They found that the incidence of lung cancer was three times (women) to four times (men) as high among unskilled manual labourers as among professional workers. Similar ratios were found for other smoking-related illnesses, such as coronary heart disease and chronic obstructive airways disease. The differences in smoking-related illnesses could largely be attributed to differences in smoking prevalence. The authors also found that the lower the socio-economic group or income, the higher the price elasticity of demand tended to be (and the lower the response to health publicity).[36] They concluded that tobacco tax increases would both reduce smoking in lower socio-economic groups and help reduce the differences in health and mortality inequalities between poor and rich.[37]

On the basis of these findings, Warner et al. (1995) suggest that an increase in tobacco taxes would redistribute the relative burden of tobacco taxes in a progressive manner. While this might be true for the tobacco tax burden distribution measured by income class ('might', because average tax burdens could still go up), it would not be true, of course, for the more appropriate comparisons of the burden distribution between the smoking poor and the non-smoking poor or between the smoking poor and the smoking rich. The smoking poor would be faced with an unjustifiable increase (in terms of tax burden distribution) in the tobacco taxes they pay.

In addition, Warner et al. (1995) suggest that the regressivity of tobacco taxes should be viewed in the context of the net effects of the overall tax system combined with the redistributional effects of the expenditure side of government. Unfortunately, however, it is difficult to compensate the effect of the discriminatory regressivity of tobacco taxes by progressive income taxes or social benefit systems. In fact, it might be argued that if the poor were subject to lower tobacco taxes, families at the lower end of the income distribution might have more to spend on food. As Shoup (1969) has pointed out, regressive excises may reduce gainful consumption, defined as 'consumption of a type such that, in the event that it decreases, the output of the economy will decrease, either now or later, by more than the decrement in consumption'.

Finally, similar to regressivity, there is the issue of affordability between smokers in countries with different income levels – between, say, the member states of the EU and the accession countries. Per capita income in the accession countries of, on average, €3,900 is only a quarter of per capita income in Greece (and less than one-fifth of per capita income in the EU). Nevertheless, tobacco tax levels and retail prices are, on average, half of those in Greece. Consequently, relative to per capita income, the accession countries tax cigarettes twice as highly as Greece. In the same vein, Guidon, Tobin, and Yach (2002) found that an employee in Greece has to work, on average, 24 minutes (see Table 2.5) to be able to buy a pack of Marlboro cigarettes (17 minutes for a local brand), compared with 56 minutes in Poland (40 minutes for a local brand) and 71 minutes in Hungary (54 minutes for a local brand). Even in the UK, which has the highest tobacco taxes in the world, cigarettes are more affordable (in terms of minutes of paid labour required to buy a pack) than in most accession countries.

2.3.4 *Revenue Aspects*

The discussion on external costs indicated that the Pigouvian tax on tobacco should probably be lower than current tax levels found in most countries. But the externality arguments ignore the revenue considerations that evidently also influence governments when tobacco tax rates are chosen.[38] When governments need revenue, and non-distortionary lump-sum taxes are unavailable, should cigarette tax rates exceed the Pigouvian level? Bovenberg and de Mooij (1994) posed an analogous question about excise taxes on energy intended to reduce external effects from greenhouse gases. Surprisingly, perhaps, they argued that revenue considerations generally lead to optimal taxes on 'dirty' goods that are *below* Pigouvian levels. The reason is that, in their model, government revenue is best collected with a uniform tax on all consumption; and, as the overall level of taxation increases, the marginal deadweight loss of a Pigouvian tax rises relative to its external benefits. Hence, differential taxation of polluting goods (in this case, tobacco) should fall as the overall level of taxation rises.

The argument of Bovenberg and de Mooij relies on the notion that uniform taxation is the least costly way to raise revenue. Because the demand for cigarettes is highly inelastic, however, tobacco taxes may remain an efficient source of revenue.[39] The fact that consumers' demand is little affected by price changes (deadweight losses are minimal) will minimize consumers' loss of utility associated with a tax causing them to forgo consumption they would prefer in order to avoid paying the tax. This efficiency property is associated with the Ramsey rule, which prescribes that tax rates should vary inversely with the elasticity of demand for products (holding the elasticity of supply constant).[40] Thus, optimal tobacco tax rates may indeed be higher than the marginal external damage attributable to smoking.

Table 2.5 shows the revenue contribution of tobacco taxes in the EU and the USA (data for the accession countries are not available). In 2000, specific-rate member states in the EU collected, on average, 2.4 per cent of total tax revenue (defined to include social security contributions) or 0.9 per cent of GDP from excises and VAT on tobacco products. Revenues from excises and VAT in the *ad-valorem* member states were, on average, 2.0 per cent of total tax revenue or 0.9 per cent of GDP.[41] The differences in revenue should mainly be attributed to differences in absolute tax burdens. Per pack of cigarettes, revenue in Italy is only a half of revenue in Denmark. Differences in consumption (and income) appear to be less important. The percentage of smokers among the population in the various member states centres around 30 per cent of adults aged 15 or over. Portugal and Sweden are notable exceptions.

As pointed out by Kay and Keen (1982), governments interested solely in revenue would probably wish to keep the retail price as low as possible under a specific regime, so as not to depress sales volume. Under an *ad valorem* regime, on the other hand, governments have an interest in keeping the retail price as high as possible. This suggests that there is a combined rate at which revenue is independent of retail price. This situation occurs if the share of the *ad valorem* levy in total tax is equal to the price elasticity of demand. If, at a given price p, tax revenue from cigarettes is denoted by R_p and the demand by D_p, then

$$(8) \qquad R_p = (t_s + t_a p) D_p$$

Tax revenue will then be independent of price if

$$(9) \qquad \frac{t_a p}{t_s + t_a p} = E_p,$$

where E_p denotes the price elasticity of demand.

To illustrate, if the price elasticity equals -0.4, then 40 per cent of revenue should come from the *ad valorem* levy and 60 per cent from the specific excise. This implies a multiplier of nearly 1.7.

2.3.5 *Bootlegging and Smuggling*

Naturally, large inter-country differences in tobacco taxes are a fertile breeding ground for bootlegging (the legal or illegal purchase, depending on quantity, of cigarettes in one country for consumption or resale in another country) and smuggling (the illegal purchase of untaxed cigarettes in the country of consumption or another country). Greater trade liberalization and increases in tobacco taxes have made bootlegging and smuggling important issues in recent years. The reward for illegal trade and production of cigarettes is closely related to the difference in tax between legally and illegally sold cigarettes, the probability of detection, and the magnitude of punishment.

Table 2.5. *European Union and USA: Tobacco Tax Revenues (2000)[a] and Other Statistics*

Country	Percentage of total tax revenue	Percentage of GDP	Price per pack (euro)	Total tax per pack (euro)	Percentage of smokers	Affordability (minutes of labour per pack of Marlboro)	Smuggling as a percentage of domestic sales	Corruption index[b]
Specific rates								
UK	2.71	1.01	7.18	5.74	29	40	2	8.7
Ireland	3.84	1.19	5.00	4.29	32	31	4	6.9
Denmark	1.60	0.78	4.04	3.30	31	23	n.a.	9.5
Germany	1.85	0.70	3.37	2.51	37	18	10	7.3
Netherlands	1.24	0.51	2.83	2.10	33	19	8	9.0
Portugal	3.40	1.17	2.10	1.63	19	26	n.a.	6.3
Ad valorem rates								
Finland	1.24	0.58	4.00	3.03	24	29	n.a.	9.7
France	1.65	0.75	3.90	2.94	33	20	2	6.3
Sweden	0.96	0.52	4.12	2.88	19	28	2	9.3
Belgium	1.56	0.70	2.82	2.15	29	22	7	7.1
Austria	1.74	0.76	2.69	2.01	24	22	15	7.8
Greece	4.85	1.83	2.35	1.71	37	24	8	4.2
Italy	1.99	0.83	2.07	1.54	25	26	12	5.2
Luxembourg	6.03	2.50	2.08	1.44	33	12	7	9.0
Spain	n.a.	n.a.	1.95	1.40	33	21	15	7.1
USA	0.55	0.16	3.85	1.47[c]	31	18	n.a.	7.7

[a] Excises and VAT. Tobacco tax revenue has been computed by multiplying actual excise revenues shown in OECD (2002) by R_t/R_e, where R_t and R_e are the total tax and total excise yield, respectively, as calculated in Table 2.2.

[b] Perception index ranging from 0 (highly corrupt) to 10 (highly clean), based on surveys of business people, risk analysts, and the general public.

[c] Including Master Settlement – see Table 2.4.

Sources: Revenue – individual country tables in OECD (2002); price per pack – Tables 2.2 and 2.4 in this chapter; affordability – Guindon, Tobin, and Yach (2002); percentage of smokers – downloaded from www.ash.org.uk; smuggling – table 15.3 in Merriman, Yurekli, and Chaloupka (2000); corruption perceptions index – downloaded from www.transparency.org (August 2002).

In the EU, more than 12 per cent of the population lives near internal frontiers, i.e. within 30 kilometres of a neighbouring member state. Smokers within this 30-kilometre band will have an incentive to buy cigarettes across the border if the price differential is substantial. Merriman, Yurekli, and Chaloupka (2000) estimate that in a European country with the mean level of incentive, bootlegged imports account for about 3 per cent of domestic consumption. Luxembourg is an important provider of cigarettes to Germany, France, and Belgium. Joossens and Raw (1995) estimated that only 15 per cent of tobacco products bought in Luxembourg are consumed there. In Finland, 12 per cent of domestic sales come from bootlegged imports. Legal bootlegging may have decreased in the EU following the elimination of duty-free shopping in 1999.[42]

Illegal bootlegging, however, should still be a considerable problem. To illustrate, Table 2.5 indicates that the reference price of cigarettes is €4.04 in Denmark, but only €2.08 in Luxembourg – a spread of €1.96 per pack. The temptation to exploit this price differential illegally is enormous.[43] A trip from Luxembourg to Copenhagen with a 7.5-tonne lorry loaded with 60,000 packs of cigarettes yields gross profits of €117,600. The net proceeds of a day trip with the same lorry from Luxembourg to Amsterdam are approximately €45,000. Obviously, legal and illegal bootlegging within the EU could be minimized if price differentials between member states were narrowed through the harmonization of the specific excises (which narrow price differences between low- and high-price brands).

In addition, smuggling is a growing menace. According to anecdotal evidence, one in every five cigarettes smoked in the UK is bought on the black market (*NRC/Handelsblad*, 21 August 2002).[44] Also, Germany, with its borders with eastern European countries, is a focal market for smuggled cigarettes. Many illegal shipments originate in China, which is the world's largest producer of contraband cigarettes. These cigarettes present a special health problem because they have not been controlled regarding toxic and hazardous remnants of pesticides or excessive tar and nicotine. Furthermore, large quantities of cigarettes that are ostensibly legally shipped to eastern European countries, mainly from the UK, Germany, and the Netherlands,[45] do not arrive at the final destination.[46] In the EU, in 2000, approximately 5.1 billion cigarettes were seized by customs (down from nearly 7 billion in 1999).[47] This represents the annual consumption of 1 million smokers (approximately the smoking population of Ireland) on the assumption that each smoker consumes 13–14 cigarettes per day.

The overall size of the smuggling phenomenon can be estimated by comparing export and import data on cigarettes. According to Joossens and Raw (1998), recorded worldwide exports of cigarettes are consistently about 1.3 times as great as imports. In 1996, the difference between exports and imports amounted to 6 per cent of world cigarette consumption or some 400 billion cigarettes (approximating the annual consumption in the USA). This means that a third of global exports find their way to the contraband market. The EU portion of this is about 60 billion cigarettes per year, with an annual loss of revenue to EU governments of €7.7 billion. In the EU, as shown in Table 2.5, the unweighted average of smuggled cigarettes as a percentage of in-state consumption is about 7.7 per cent. The population-weighted average is 8.9 per cent.

The amount of smuggled imports should be positively associated with the relative price of cigarettes in a country and negatively correlated with enforcement activities in local markets.[48] The corruption indices shown in Table 2.5 are an indication of the quality of these activities. The European Commission (1998, 2001) is concerned about the illegal trade in cigarettes. In 1998, it reported that over fifty criminal networks had been identified by investigations of large-scale smuggling of various products, including tobacco. In 2001, the Commission concluded that the illegal trade between eastern European countries and the EU 'has reached alarming proportions and is disrupting the domestic market'.[49] As a percentage of domestic consumption, smuggling has moved into the double-digit category in Latvia (39 per cent), Lithuania (30 per cent), Estonia (16 per cent), Romania (20 per cent), Poland (15 per cent), and Bulgaria (15 per cent) (Merriman, Yurekli, and Chaloupka, 2000). It is doubtful whether tobacco taxes can be sustained if smuggling exceeds 15–20 per cent of domestic sales. The problem could become worse if the accession countries have to comply with the *acquis communautaire* on the tobacco excises.

Studies for the USA focus mainly on bootlegging. Price Waterhouse (1991), for instance, concluded that the various state treasuries lost some $US179 million in revenue in 1989 as a result of the tax-induced diversion of cigarette purchases (mainly by the Mafia). It was estimated that some 2.4 per cent of all sales were traded illegally in that year. At that time, taxes on cigarettes (federal excise, state excise, and retail sales tax) ranged from $0.03 per pack in North Carolina to $0.48 in Minnesota and average retail prices from $2.25 in Atlanta to $1.35 in Kentucky.

Since 1989, tax differentials between US states have risen along with the average level. Recent studies infer the level of bootlegging between US states by calculating the difference between the demand for cigarettes predicted by econometric models and the observed level of tax-paid sales. Saba et al. (1995) found that in most states, border crossing accounted for less than 2 per cent of sales, but that the phenomenon was much more important in low-tax states (New Hampshire, the District of Columbia) with a border with a high-tax state. Thursby and Thursby (2000) found that, in most years, 3–5 per cent of US consumption results from bootlegging and smuggling. This represents 2.5–4.5 million smokers.

2.4 CONCLUDING COMMENTS

The reasons for levying high taxes on tobacco products are the predictability of the revenue (as indicated by the low price elasticity of demand), the desire to protect children (who may have a poor appreciation of the risk and a tendency to undervalue the future), the belief that smokers should pay for the burden they impose on others (external costs), and the objective to improve public health. Perhaps the strongest argument for high tobacco taxes is the effect they have of discouraging young people from taking up smoking (Warner et al., 1995).

The reasons for moderating the level of tobacco taxes are the principle of consumer sovereignty (high taxes imposed on fully informed individuals are a form of paternalism), the finding that the net external costs of smoking (which allow for the cost savings of premature deaths from smoking) may be low, equity considerations (tobacco taxes are highly discriminatory and regressive), and difficulties in ensuring compliance control (illegal bootlegging and smuggling, which undermine public health objectives, have reached alarming proportions, particularly in Europe).

The choice between specific and *ad valorem* taxation depends on whether the primary aim of government policy is to discourage smoking or to raise revenue and on whether improvements in cigarette quality are deemed desirable or not. Specific excises, which tend to narrow price differentials, would also tend to minimize cross-border shopping if rates were harmonized.

This chapter has illustrated the difficulties in tailoring a tobacco tax regime in the context of multiple objectives and constraints. The question of what the right level and structure of tax should be is a complex one. For the economist, there are conceptual and empirical limits to excessively high levels of tobacco taxation, at least if based on Pigouvian argumentation. As a single policy instrument, even with ideal excise tax administration, tobacco taxation cannot alone meet the multiple objectives of 'social-welfare-maximizing' governments (even if one ignores the political economy factors that may be involved). In addition, of course, the 'value weights' in the social welfare functions are by no means universally agreed, whether across countries or even within countries in terms of different groups within the electorate. Excise tax administration, moreover, is not ideal, as the quantitative and growing significance of smuggling indicates.

Notes

1 These other measures include comprehensive bans on the promotion and advertising of tobacco products, better and more widely publicized research into the consequences of smoking, prominent warning labels, and deregulated access to nicotine-replacement therapies.

2 This directive codified the provisions of the harmonization directive of 1972, which aimed at approximating the rate structures, and the definition directive of 1978, which provided uniform concepts for tobacco products. These directives were repealed.

3 Over the years, the Netherlands has seen one of the most spectacular shifts between specific and *ad valorem* taxation, particularly during the 1980s. In the 1970s, the share of the specific excise in total tax on cigarettes was only 5 per cent and roll-your-own bore no specific excise at all. The share was raised to 10 per cent in 1980, to 25 per cent in 1984, and to 50 per cent in 1987, applying to cigarettes as well as roll-

your-own. The Dutch government opted for a much heavier dose of the specific rate to bolster revenues from tobacco taxation and to increase their predictability (Keen, 1998).

4 The trade margin also functions as an *ad valorem* rate for the producer if it is set at a fixed percentage of the retail price. Such percentages are or used to be legislated in Belgium, France, Portugal, Italy, Luxembourg, and Spain.

5 The accession countries, to be admitted in 2004, comprise the Baltic countries (Estonia, Latvia, and Lithuania), Cyprus, the Czech Republic, Hungary, Malta, Poland, the Slovak Republic, and Slovenia. Bulgaria and Romania will probably be admitted in 2007.

6 This situation resembles the early approach to alcohol taxation in France, which used to levy low excises on spirits made from grapes, e.g. cognac, but high excises on spirits made from grains, e.g. gin. Although the alcohol excise structure did not discriminate on the basis of product origin, nevertheless it protected home-made spirits, because grain-based spirits were mainly imported. The European Court of Justice ruled, however, that the excise should be based on alcohol content rather than the raw material. For a reference, see Cnossen (1987).

7 Tobacco, moreover, is the most heavily subsidized product under the Common Agricultural Policy (CAP). If it were desirable, however, to provide income support to growers of tobacco, then it would be far better to do so directly than through the excise structure and price support measures. Recently, the European Commission has tabled proposals under which the current price support measures will be replaced by income support measures.

8 Value figures originally denoted in ecu are shown in euro on a one-to-one basis.

9 In implementing the Luxembourg agreement, member states tried to keep the number of changes to a minimum. Changes in specific and *ad valorem* excise rates could be offsetting as long as the 57-per-cent criterion was satisfied. Also, increases in VAT rates could be compensated by reductions of *ad valorem* excises, and vice versa.

10 The proposal and recent developments are reviewed in a report on tobacco taxation from the European Commission (2001) to the Council and the European Parliament.

11 The supplementary minimum amount of the total excise shall be €64 from 1 July 2006 and the minimum excise duty under which the 57 per cent rule is waived shall be €101 from 1 July 2006. In addition, the directive prescribes various minimum overall excise duties on other types of tobacco: (a) roll-your-own – 32 per cent of the retail price or €27 per kilogram; (b) cigars and cigarillos – 5 per cent of the retail price or €10 per 1,000 items or per kilogram; (c) fine-cut smoking tobacco – 32 per cent of the retail price or €27 per kilogram; and (d) other smoking tobaccos – 20 per cent of the retail price or €19 per kilogram.

12 For an account of the confusing developments in Sweden, which in a few years switched from a specific regime to an *ad valorem* regime, see Joossens et al. (2000). Reportedly, an earlier significant increase in tobacco excises was rescinded following popular opposition and anecdotal evidence that the tax hike had increased smuggling.

13 In the following, 'northern member states' is used to refer to Denmark, Germany, Ireland, the Netherlands, and the UK, plus Portugal, and 'southern member states' is used to refer to Austria, Belgium, France, Greece, Italy, Luxembourg, and Spain, plus Finland and Sweden.

14 Alaska, Delaware, Montana, New Hampshire, and Oregon have no RST at all. Colorado has a RST but it does not apply to cigarettes. Interestingly, and in contrast to EU practice, Alabama, Georgia, and Missouri do not apply their state sales tax to that portion of retail cigarette prices that represents the state's cigarette excise tax.

15 Source: www.tobaccofreekids.org/reports/prices, downloaded 10 October 2002.

16 The MTSA was concluded with the five largest tobacco manufacturers by all but four states, and these four had previously settled with tobacco manufacturers. The amounts received by the states will be adjusted for inflation and various other developments. In addition, the MTSA provides for various upfront payments and mandatory trust fund contributions, prescribes restrictions on marketing and advertising, youth access, and lobbying, makes provision for changes in corporate culture, compliance, and disclosure practices, and sets up agricultural and rural assistance programmes. In all, payments are expected to total $246 billion.

17 The information in this paragraph was computed from data downloaded from www.tobaccofreekids.org/reports/prices (10 October 2002).

18 However, because of the way that payments are apportioned among manufacturers, the MTSA may have economic effects substantially different from those of the equivalent excise tax. The payments stipulated in the MTSA and individual state agreements are lump sums apportioned to individual manufacturers on the basis of their market shares. But then policies that affect market shares (including price changes and advertising) also affect the producer's tax bill. The result is that marginal cost changes by a different amount from (probably less than) the average tax rate used in the table. A further issue is that the MTSA also settled various legal claims, which reduced manufacturers' expected future legal costs. So perhaps for this reason too, the payment per cigarette overestimates the true tax rate. See Bulow and Klemperer (1998).

19 At current exchange rates (April 2003), one dollar is approximately equivalent to 90 euro cents.

20 Conversely, in 1994, this argument persuaded the Canadian government to lower its tobacco taxes. For an account, see Joossens and Raw (1995), who report that a threefold difference in price in 1991 increased smuggling from 1.3 billion cigarettes in 1990 to 14.2 billion in 1993. Cigarettes manufactured in Canada were exported duty-free to the USA and subsequently smuggled back into Canada. As discussed below, smuggling also occurs in Europe.

21 However, see below for a discussion of how revenue considerations should lead taxes away from Pigouvian levels.

22 As noted above, the distinction between public and private healthcare expenditures seems irrelevant if private health insurers do not successfully control moral hazard by smoking clients. In this case, virtually all smoking-related healthcare expenditures are properly classified as external costs that should be internalized through Pigouvian taxation.

23 In support of this view, Gruber and Mullainathan (2002) provide evidence that higher cigarette taxes increase smokers' self-reported happiness.

24 However, Bernheim and Rangel (2002) provide an alternative model of partially rational addictive behaviour, which they call 'characterization' failure, in which taxation of addictive substances can never generate efficiency gains.

25 Some have expressed doubt about the effectiveness of information dissemination. See Warner et al. (1995) and the literature cited therein.

26 Although this may generally be true, there is still some doubt about the extent to which smokers internalize the risks of smoking, as suggested by Weinstein (1998).

27 Interestingly, since 1998, cigarette prices in the USA have increased by, on average, $1.25 per pack (see www.tobaccofreekids.org/reports/prices (10 October 2002)). However, we do not know of any studies that have measured the impact on youth smoking.

28 The difference may be important, if damage is not approximately proportional to consumption. In particular, if there are threshold levels of consumption below which adverse health effects are attenuated, as some research has suggested, then Pigouvian tax rates should exceed average external cost.

29 The higher estimates are found in countries where healthcare costs account for a relatively large share of GDP. As regards EU member states, research in the UK for 1986–7 estimated gross costs at between 0.08 and 0.13 per cent of GDP. Furthermore, gross costs in Finland for 1987 were estimated at 0.07–0.08 per cent of GDP. For the references, see Lightwood et al. (2000).

30 Obviously, this does not mean that death is an economically desirable event. As Warner et al. (1995) point out, it simply means that as long as early death reduces the extra social costs in the form of social security benefits and pensions, smokers should receive a 'credit' for the associated savings. This calculation is independent of the value of life per se, which is impossible to judge. Clearly, the value of the loss in years of life as a result of premature death to the individual concerned, his family members, and society at large far outweighs the narrow fiscal gains that may accrue because governments save on medical, social security, and pension payments.

31 Of course, the tax would still have income effects that might induce consumers to choose lower-quality brands, but so would a non-distortionary lump-sum tax. The theory of optimal taxation implies that a uniform percentage tax on a subset of commodities is desirable only under restrictive conditions on preferences (Atkinson and Stiglitz, 1980); but in this context, those restrictions seem plausible.

32 Since the monopolist could guarantee the same profit by producing the same output as before, profits can only rise with the change. Government revenue must rise because the monopolist operates on the elastic portion of the demand curve, so that a price cut must increase total revenue.

33 However, specific taxation may induce consumers to opt for higher-quality brands, if the degree of tax shifting is independent of product quality. In support of this view, Sobel and Garrett (1997) find that specific tax increases in US states are associated with significant declines in the market share of generic brands.

34 Evans and Farrelly (1998), cited in Warner et al. (1995), suggest that higher taxes encourage smokers to switch from higher-priced brands to lower-priced (and other higher-tar and higher-nicotine) generic and discounted brands, thereby possibly increasing smokers' exposure to the toxic substances in cigarette smoke.

35 Keen (1998) constructs examples in which product quality may be least distorted either by specific or by *ad valorem* taxation.

36 Townsend et al. (1994) reported that price elasticities of demand for cigarettes were highest in (low) socio-economic group V (-1.0 for men and -0.9 for women) and lowest (not significantly different from zero) in (high) socio-economic groups I and II. The gradient in price elasticities was significant for men and for women. Price significantly affected smoking prevalence in socio-economic group V and for all women.

37 Bobak et al. (2000) provide five hypotheses for the continuous upward gradient in smoking from high to low socio-economic groups: the poor are less educated and hence less aware of the health risks of smoking; smoking may be a self-medication to ameliorate stress; smoking may be a replacement reward; the poor have less to lose from future health problems; and nicotine dependence may be greater among the poor.

38 It is interesting to note that Pigouvian and revenue considerations in tobacco taxation have long gone hand in hand. It was James I of England, a vocal early antagonist of tobacco and author of the philippic *A Counterblaste to Tobacco* (1604), who introduced the first significant taxation of tobacco there: import duties were raised by 4,000 per cent in 1604. In the process, however, he may have discovered the Laffer curve: the duties were later decreased substantially (Gately, 2001).

39 To illustrate, assume that the price elasticity of demand for cigarettes is constant at -0.4 and that cigarettes are taxed at 75 per cent of the retail price. In this situation, a tax increase of 10 per cent that is fully passed on to consumers would reduce demand by 3 per cent but raise cigarette tax revenue by 6.7 per cent.

40 Recently, however, the revenue efficiency of high tobacco taxes has been questioned. Becker, Grossman, and Murphy (1994) have found that the long-run price elasticity of demand may be twice as high as the short-run elasticity. If, in the above example, the long-run price elasticity of demand for cigarettes were -0.8 (instead of -0.4), a 10 per cent tax increase would reduce demand by 6 per cent and increase revenue by 3.4 per cent.

41 Luxembourg has been left out in calculations for the *ad-valorem* states. This country's tobacco tax revenue is very high because it engages in considerable tax-base snatching from neighbouring countries by following a low-tax/high-turnover sales strategy.

42 Previously, duty-free shopping within the EU accounted for nearly half of global duty-free sales, which in turn represented 1 per cent of global cigarette consumption (Market Tracking International, 1998).

43 Although individuals can buy cigarettes in other member states for their own consumption needs, wholesale bootlegging is prohibited in the EU.

44 The abrupt decline in tobacco tax revenues in the UK would seem to support this allegation. In 1999, tobacco excise revenues were halved (OECD, 2002).

45 In 2000, these three countries produced 476 billion cigarettes, 63 per cent of production in the EU. In turn, the EU accounted for 13.6 per cent of world production of 5,557 billion cigarettes. Other important cigarette-producing countries are China (30.1 per cent), the USA (11.6 per cent), the Russian Federation (4.9 per cent), and Japan (4.8 per cent). Furthermore, the EU is the most important exporting region of the world, accounting for 40 per cent of world exports.

46 For recommendations to control cigarette transit trade, see Joossens and Raw (2000).

47 For the information in this paragraph, see www.ash.org.uk/?smuggling.

48 Merriman, Yurekli, and Chaloupka (2000) find that corruption in a country is a stronger indicator of cigarette smuggling than price. To some extent, however, this seems to beg the question, because to some extent corruption and smuggling go hand in hand.

49 Recent administrative measures, implemented 1 January 2001, have considerably
tightened the rules on transit trade in cigarettes. This should reduce the levels of
bootlegging and smuggling.

References

Atkinson, A. B., and Stiglitz, J. E. (1980), *Lectures on Public Economics*, Maidenhead:
McGraw-Hill.

—— and Townsend, J. (1977), 'Economic aspects of reduced smoking', *Lancet*, 2: 492–5.

Barendregt, J. J., Bonneux, L., and van der Maas, P. J. (1997), 'The health care costs of
smoking', *New England Journal of Medicine*, 337: 1052–7.

Barzel, Y. (1976), 'An alternative approach to the analysis of taxation', *Journal of
Political Economy*, 84: 1177–97.

Becker, G. S., Grossman, M., and Murphy, K. M. (1994), 'An empirical analysis of
cigarette addiction', *American Economic Review*, 84: 396–418.

—— and Murphy, K. M. (1988), 'A theory of rational addiction', *Journal of Political
Economy*, 96: 675–700.

Bernheim, D., and Rangel, A. (2002), 'Addiction, cognition, and the visceral brain',
Stanford University, mimeo.

Bobak, M., Jha, P., Nguyen, S., and Jarvis, M. (2000), 'Poverty and smoking', in P. Jha
and F. J. Chaloupka (eds), *Tobacco Control in Developing Countries*, Oxford: Oxford
University Press on behalf of the World Bank and the World Health Organization.

Bovenberg, A. L., and de Mooij, R. (1994), 'Environmental levies and distortionary
taxation', *American Economic Review*, 84: 1085–9.

Bulow, J., and Klemperer, P. (1998), 'The tobacco deal', *Brookings Papers on Economic
Activity: Microeconomics*, 323–94.

Chaloupka, F. J., Hu, T., Warner, K. E., Jacobs, R., and Yurekli, A. (2000), 'The taxation
of tobacco products', in P. Jha and F. J. Chaloupka (eds), *Tobacco Control in Developing Countries*, Oxford: Oxford University Press on behalf of the World Bank and
the World Health Organization.

—— and Warner, K. E. (2000), 'The economics of smoking', in A. J. Cuyler and
J. P. Newhouse (eds), *Handbook of Health Economics*, Amsterdam: Elsevier.

Cnossen, S. (1987), 'Tax structure developments', in S. Cnossen (ed.), *Tax Coordination
in the European Community*, Deventer: Kluwer.

Council (1992), 'Directive of 19 October amending directives 72/464/EEC and 79/32/
EEC on taxes other than turnover taxes which are levied on the consumption of
manufactured tobacco', *Official Journal* L316 (31 October).

—— (1995), 'Directive of 27 November on taxes other than turnover taxes which affect
the consumption of manufactured tobacco', *Official Journal* L291 (6 December).

—— (2002), 'Directive of 12 February amending directives 92/79/EEC, 92/60/EEC and
95/59/EEC as regards the structure and rates of excise duty applied on manufactured
tobacco', *Official Journal* L046 (16 February).

Delipalla, S., and Keen, M. J. (1992), 'The comparison between *ad valorem* and specific
taxation under imperfect competition', *Journal of Public Economics*, 49: 351–67.

—— and O'Donnell, O. (2001), 'Estimating tax incidence, market power and market
conduct: the European cigarette industry', *International Journal of Industrial Organization*, 19: 885–908.

ECOSOC (1981), *Report on the Commission's Proposal for a Council Directive Amending Directive 72/464/EEC on Taxes Other than Turnover Taxes which Affect the Consumption of Manufactured Tobacco*, CES 242/81, Brussels.

—— (1988), 'ECOSOC opinion', *Official Journal of the European Communities*, C/237 (12 September).

European Commission (1982), *Implications of Further Harmonisation of the Excises on Manufactured Tobacco*, COM (82)61, Brussels.

—— (1985), *Completing the Internal Market*, White Paper from the Commission to the European Council, Brussels.

—— (1995), *Commission Report to the Council and European Parliament*, COM/95/285 final (13 September), Brussels.

—— (1998), *Fight against Fraud*, COM(98)276 Final, Brussels.

—— (2001), *Report from the Commission to the Council and the European Parliament on the Structure and Rates of Excise Duty Applied on Cigarettes and Other Manufactured Tobacco Products*, COM (2001) 133 final (14 March), Brussels.

Evans, W. N., and Farrelly, M. C. (1998), 'The compensating behavior of smokers: taxes, tar and nicotine', *RAND Journal of Economics*, 29: 578–95.

—— and Ringel, J. S. (1999), 'Can higher cigarette taxes improve birth outcomes?', *Journal of Public Economics*, 72: 135–54.

Gajalakshimi, G. K., Prabhat, J., Ranson, K., and Nguyen, S. (2000), 'Global patterns of smoking and smoking-attributable mortality', in P. Jha and F. J. Chaloupka (eds), *Tobacco Control in Developing Countries*, Oxford: Oxford University Press on behalf of the World Bank and the World Health Organization.

Gately, I. (2001), *La Diva Nicotina*, Boston, MA: Simon & Schuster.

Greenwald, B. C., and Stiglitz, J. E. (1986), 'Externalities in economies with imperfect information and incomplete markets', *Quarterly Journal of Economics*, 101: 229–64.

Gruber, J., and Koszegi, B. (2001), 'Is addiction "rational"? Theory and evidence', *Quarterly Journal of Economics*, 116: 1261–303.

—— and Mullainathan, S. (2002), 'Do cigarette taxes make smokers happier?', National Bureau of Economic Research, Working Paper 8872.

Guindon, G. E., Tobin, S., and Yach, D. (2002), 'Trends and affordability of cigarette prices: ample room for tax increases and related health gains', *Tobacco Control*, 11: 0–8.

James I of England (1604), *A Counterblaste to Tobacco*.

Jha, P., and Chaloupka, F. J. (eds) (2000), *Tobacco Control in Developing Countries*, Oxford: Oxford University Press on behalf of the World Bank and the World Health Organization.

——, Musgrove, P., Chaloupka, F. J., and Yurekli, A. (2000), 'The economic rationale for intervention in the tobacco market', in P. Jha and F. J. Chaloupka (eds), *Tobacco Control in Developing Countries*, Oxford: Oxford University Press on behalf of the World Bank and the World Health Organization.

Joossens, L., Chaloupka, F. J., Merriman, D., and Yurekli, A. (2000), 'Issues in the smuggling of tobacco products', in P. Jha and F. J. Chaloupka (eds), *Tobacco Control in Developing Countries*, Oxford: Oxford University Press on behalf of the World Bank and the World Health Organization.

—— and Raw, M. (1995), 'Smuggling and cross border shopping of tobacco in Europe', *British Medical Journal*, 310: 1393–7.

—— and—— (1998), 'Cigarette smuggling in Europe: who really benefits?', *Tobacco Control*, 7: 66–71.

Joossens, L., and Raw, M. (2000), 'How can cigarette smuggling be reduced?', *British Medical Journal*, 321: 947–50.

Kay, J. A., and Keen, M. J. (1982), *The Structure of Tobacco Taxes in the European Community*, Report Series 1, London: Institute for Fiscal Studies.

Keen, M. J. (1998), 'The balance between specific and *ad valorem* taxation', *Fiscal Studies*, 19: 1–37.

Kenkel, D., and Chen, L. (2000), 'Consumer information and tobacco use', in P. Jha and F. J. Chaloupka (eds), *Tobacco Control in Developing Countries*, Oxford: Oxford University Press on behalf of the World Bank and the World Health Organization.

Lightwood, J., Collins, D., Lapsley, H., and Novotny, T. E. (2000), 'Estimating the costs of tobacco use', in P. Jha and F. J. Chaloupka (eds), *Tobacco Control in Developing Countries*, Oxford: Oxford University Press on behalf of the World Bank and the World Health Organization.

Manning, W. G., Keeler, E. B., Newhouse, J. P., Sloss, E. M., and Wasserman, J. (1989), 'The taxes of sin: do smokers and drinkers pay their way?', *Journal of the American Medical Association*, 261: 1604–9.

Market Tracking International (1998), *World Tobacco File 1998*, London: DMG Business Media.

Merriman, D., Yurekli, A., and Chaloupka, F. J. (2000), 'How big is the worldwide cigarette-smuggling problem?', in P. Jha and F. J. Chaloupka (eds), *Tobacco Control in Developing Countries*, Oxford: Oxford University Press on behalf of the World Bank and the World Health Organization.

Mogensen, T. (2003*a*), *Excise Duty Tables* (April), Brussels: Directorate General of Taxation and Customs Union, European Commission.

——— (2003*b*), *Excise Duty Tables* (July) (special version I with information from the candidate countries to the European Union), Brussels: Directorate General of Taxation and Customs Union, European Commission.

Moore, M. J. (1996), 'Death and tobacco taxes', *RAND Journal of Economics*, 27: 415–28.

National Cancer Policy Board (1998), *Taking Action to Reduce Tobacco Use*, Washington, DC: National Academy Press.

Newbery, D. M. (this volume), 'Road user and congestion charges'.

OECD (2002), *Revenue Statistics of OECD Member Countries, 1965–2000*, Paris: Organisation for Economic Co-operation and Development.

Peck, R., Chaloupka, F. J., Jha, P., and Lightwood, J. (2000), 'A welfare analysis of tobacco use', in P. Jha and F. J. Chaloupka (eds), *Tobacco Control in Developing Countries*, Oxford: Oxford University Press on behalf of the World Bank and the World Health Organization.

Pekurinen, M. (1992), *Economic Aspects of Smoking: Is There a Case for Government Intervention in Finland?*, Helsinki: VAPK Publishing.

Price Waterhouse (1991), *Study of the Demand for Cigarettes and the Implications for Cross-Border Activity*.

Saba, R. P., Beard, R. T., Ekelund, R. B., Jr., and Ressler, R. W. (1995), 'The demand for cigarette smuggling', *Economic Inquiry*, 33: 189–202.

Shoup, C. S. (1969), *Public Finance*, London: Weidenfeld & Nicolson.

——— (1983), 'Current trends in excise taxation', in S. Cnossen (ed.), *Comparative Tax Studies*, Amsterdam: North-Holland.

Shoven, J. B., Sundberg, J. O., and Bunker, J. P. (1989), 'The social security cost of smoking', in D. A. Wise (ed.), *The Economics of Aging*, Chicago, IL: University of Chicago Press.

Skeath, S. E., and Trandel, G. E. (1994), 'A Pareto comparison of *ad valorem* and specific taxation in noncompetitive environments', *Journal of Public Economics*, 53: 53–71.

Sobel, R. S., and Garrett, T. A. (1997), 'Taxation and product quality: new evidence from generic cigarettes', *Journal of Political Economy*, 105: 880–7.

Thursby, J. G., and Thursby, M. C. (2000), 'Interstate cigarette bootlegging: extent, revenue losses and effects of federal intervention', *National Tax Journal* (March): 59–77.

Townsend, J., Roderick, P., and Cooper, J. (1994), 'Cigarette smoking by socio-economic group, sex, and age: effects of price, income and health publicity', *British Medical Journal*, 302: 922–7.

Viscusi, W. K. (1995), 'Cigarette taxation and the social consequences of smoking', in J. M. Poterba (ed.), *Tax Policy and the Economy*, Cambridge, MA: MIT Press.

Warner, K. E., Chaloupka, F. J., Cook, P. J., Manning, W. C., Newhouse, J. P., Novotny, T. E., Schelling, T. C., and Townsend, J. (1995), 'Criteria for determining an optimal cigarette tax: the economist's perspective', *Tobacco Control*, 4: 380–6.

Weinstein, N. D. (1998), 'Accuracy of smokers' risk perceptions', *Annals of Behavioral Medicine*, 20: 135–40.

Chapter 3

Economic Issues in Alcohol Taxation

STEPHEN SMITH
University College London

3.1 INTRODUCTION

There is considerable diversity across European Union (EU) member states in the taxation of alcoholic drinks. All apply excise taxes, in addition to value added tax (VAT), to at least some categories of alcoholic drink, but the scale of these taxes varies widely. In the Scandinavian member states, Ireland, and the UK, alcoholic drinks are particularly heavily taxed, and alcohol[1] taxes are a significant source of public revenues, contributing over €100 in tax revenue per head of population. Elsewhere in the EU, alcohol taxes are lower, and in the Mediterranean EU countries, alcohol taxes are, in the main, of trivial economic and revenue significance.

This diversity of tax treatment creates problems of fiscally induced cross-border shopping and various forms of illegal tax evasion and fiscal fraud. These problems are mainly experienced in the high-tax countries, and have been amplified by the greater freedom of movement and reduction in fiscal control on cross-border transactions after the abolition of intra-EU frontiers as part of the '1992' programme. The severity of these problems would be reduced by tax changes to reduce the alcohol tax differentials between member states. The key question for EU policy is the process by which greater convergence in alcohol tax rates should arise. It could be achieved without any need for EU coordination as a result of national policy decisions taken by the countries most severely affected. Since the economic costs of the existing differentials are largely borne by high-tax countries, the process of market-driven convergence would then involve tax reductions in high-tax member states, and therefore lower average alcohol taxes across the EU. Alternatively, convergence could be achieved through a less asymmetric process, in the form of negotiated EU coordinated tax rates, with the average level and range of EU alcohol taxes chosen as the outcome of policy choice rather than unregulated tax competition.

The EU has already recognized the potentially unsatisfactory consequences of relying on unregulated fiscal competition to determine excise tax policies. Minimum excise rates, to set a floor to excise levels in all member states, were agreed as part of the 1992 fiscal negotiations. The significance of this floor in the case of alcohol taxes is, however, limited. For all types of alcoholic drinks, it left scope for significant tax differentials between existing tax rates in high-tax member states and lower taxes elsewhere, and in the case of still wine, the 'floor' was actually set at zero. The Commission's May 2001 strategy statement on future EU tax policy (European Commission, 2001) indicated that the Commission was giving consideration to a number of alcohol tax issues, including effects of alcohol taxes on the functioning of the Internal Market, competition between categories of drinks, and health and agricultural policy aspects.

In deciding how far the EU needs to go in underpinning the high alcohol taxes in some member states by enforcing a higher EU-wide floor to rates, a central question is the economic justification for special taxation of alcoholic drinks, above the general VAT. On what economic grounds could high-tax member states justify their existing high levels of excise taxes on alcohol, and are these grounds applicable EU-wide, or, alternatively, sufficiently compelling to justify constraints on the tax policies of other member states?

This chapter reviews the economic case for taxing alcohol more heavily than the generality of consumer spending.[2] Following this Introduction, Section 3.2 presents data on existing alcohol taxes and tax revenues in EU member states. Section 3.3 sets alcohol taxation in the context of the economic reasons for differential taxation of commodities more generally. Section 3.4 considers distributional aspects of the taxation of alcoholic drinks, and Section 3.5 discusses one of the main lines of argument to support additional taxes on alcohol – the use of taxes to regulate social costs of alcohol consumption. Section 3.6 looks at issues relating to the choice of tax base, and Section 3.7 considers alcohol tax policy issues raised by cross-border shopping. Section 3.8 draws some conclusions.

3.2 TAXATION OF ALCOHOLIC DRINKS IN THE EU

Taxation of alcoholic drinks generates widely varying amounts of tax revenue in different member states, largely (although not entirely) attributable to differences in the level of taxation on alcoholic drinks. Table 3.1 shows per capita alcohol excise tax revenues in each of the member states in 2001. (VAT revenues from alcohol are excluded in these figures.) Revenues exceeded €200 per capita in Finland and Ireland, and exceeded €100 per capita in the UK, Sweden, and Denmark. The lowest per capita revenues from alcohol excises were in Italy (€13 per head of population), Portugal, Greece, and Spain (all under €30 per head).

All EU member states levy VAT on all categories of alcoholic drink, and, in addition, all levy additional excises over and above VAT on at least some categories of alcoholic drink. Since the VAT on alcoholic drinks is generally levied at the member state's standard rate, the issues relating to the special tax treatment of alcohol concern the existence and structure of these excise taxes.

Excise taxes are levied on spirits in all member states on the basis of the alcohol content of the product (in other words, in terms of a duty rate per

Table 3.1. *Revenues from Excise Taxes on Alcoholic Drinks in EU Member States, 2001 (euros per capita)*

	Spirits	Wines etc.	Beer	Total
Austria	9.17	2.80	24.68	36.66
Belgium	20.31	15.53	20.28	56.13
Denmark	43.17	30.73	38.03	111.94
Finland	103.42	44.41	104.83	252.66
France	33.38	5.37	5.15	43.90
Germany	26.11	5.95	9.99	42.05
Greece	20.81	0.00	5.83	26.64
Ireland	58.71	42.54	117.88	219.13
Italy	8.15	0.28	4.54	12.96
Luxembourg	61.84	2.41	7.62	71.86
Netherlands	25.45	10.79	17.80	54.04
Portugal	13.47	1.45	9.88	24.80
Spain	21.85	0.43	5.44	27.72
Sweden	65.29	50.53	31.98	147.80
UK	52.36	57.79	78.90	189.06

Source: Calculated from data in European Commission, Directorate General for Taxation and Customs Union, *Excise Duty Tables April 2003* (REF 1.016). Downloaded from http://europa.eu.int/comm/taxation_customs/publications/info_doc/taxation/c4_excise_tables.pdf.

hectolitre of pure alcohol). There are some minor tax concessions for the products of small distilleries in four member states, and also some reduced rates for low-strength spirits, but with these exceptions, the structure of the spirits excise is defined on a consistent basis throughout the EU. Excise tax rates per hectolitre of pure alcohol in April 2003 ranged from €5,505 in Sweden to €645 in Italy, leading to the levels of duty per bottle (70cl) of 40 per cent spirits shown in Table 3.2. Excise taxation on this 'typical' bottle of spirits thus ranges from over €15 in Sweden to less than €2 in Italy.

Beer is taxed on the basis of alcoholic strength in all member states. In most member states, the duty on standard beers is simply proportional to alcohol content (for example, in the UK, it is the equivalent of about €0.20 per litre per degree of alcohol in the final product). In three member states, the duty on standard beers is graduated, with higher rates of duty per unit of alcohol being levied on stronger beers. A number of member states apply lower rates of duty on 'low-alcohol' beers and on the output of independent small breweries. The level of duty charged on a typical litre of beer (at 5 per cent alcohol strength, equivalent to 12.5 degrees Plato) ranges from €1.43 in Finland to €0.10 in Germany, Luxembourg, and Spain (Table 3.2).

There is considerable diversity in the excise taxes applied to wine. Still wine, where it is taxed, is generally taxed at a flat rate per litre, but seven member states apply no duty at all to still wine. The highest taxation of wine, above €2 per typical bottle (75cl at an alcohol content of 12.5 per cent abv), occurs in

Table 3.2. *Excise Duty Rates on Alcoholic Drinks in EU Member States, April 2003 (euros)*

	Beer per litre	Still wine per 75 cl bottle	Spirits per 70cl, 40%
Austria	0.26	0.00	2.80
Belgium	0.21	0.35	4.65
Denmark	0.47	0.71	10.37
Finland	1.43	1.77	14.13
France	0.13	0.03	4.06
Germany	0.10	0.00	3.65
Greece	0.14	0.00	2.54
Ireland	0.99	2.05	10.99
Italy	0.17	0.00	1.81
Luxembourg	0.10	0.00	2.92
Netherlands	0.25	0.44	4.21
Portugal	0.15	0.00	2.47
Spain	0.10	0.00	2.07
Sweden	0.81	1.82	15.41
UK	0.97	1.90	8.73
Minimum adopted by Council, 19 October 1992	0.09	0	1.54 /2.80

Note: In some member states, the rate of tax on beer and still wine varies with strength. The figures here assume beer at 5 per cent abv (or 12.5 degrees Plato) and still wine at 12.5 per cent abv.

Source: Calculated from data in European Commission, Directorate General for Taxation and Customs Union, *Excise Duty Tables April 2003* (REF 1.016). Downloaded from http://europa.eu.int/comm/taxation_customs/publications/info_doc/taxation/c4_excise_tables.pdf.

Ireland, and six other member states also apply non-trivial excises (Table 3.2). Sparkling wine is generally taxed at higher rates, although, again, some member states levy no duty. There are also various lower duty rates applicable to low-strength wines.

Since 1992, the EU has stipulated minimum levels of excise for alcoholic drinks. For beer, the minimum was set at €1.87 per degree of alcohol. For spirits, the minimum was €550 per hectolitre of alcohol, with an additional stipulation that member states with an existing duty rate above €1,000 per hectolitre of alcohol could not reduce their rate below €1,000. For still and sparkling wine, the minimum excise was set at zero (Directive 92/84/EEC of 19 October 1992). These minima were intended to set a floor to duty rates in the EU, and were introduced as part of the fiscal measures that accompanied the elimination of intra-EU frontiers from the start of 1993. The equivalents of these minimum rates, converted to the rate applicable to the typical purchase, are also shown in Table 3.2.

Although the taxation of some alcoholic drinks is related to alcohol strength, excise duty on alcoholic drinks is not systematically related to alcohol content, and the implicit taxation of alcohol varies across different categories of drink.

In general, spirits are taxed more heavily, per unit of alcohol, than wine and beer. On average across the fifteen member states, beer is taxed at about €8.4 per litre of pure alcohol, wine at about €6.4, and spirits at €21.6, but there is considerable variation, both in average duty levels and in relative taxation of the different drink categories, across different member states.

3.3 THE THEORETICAL FRAMEWORK: ECONOMIC THEORY AND COMMODITY TAXATION

Other things being equal, uniform taxation of commodities, through a value added tax or sales tax applied at a single rate to all goods and services, has substantial practical appeal. It minimizes the amount of detailed information needed for the administration of the commodity tax. Only the total value of sales needs to be recorded, and the revenue authorities have no need to be concerned with the nature of the goods and services traded. In addition, by making no fiscal distinction between commodities, the tax authorities have no need to police the blurred boundaries between different goods, and (public and private) resources are not dissipated in litigation over the tax treatment of particular borderline items.

In most European countries, alcoholic drinks, like motor fuels and tobacco products, have been taxed more heavily than other goods for many years. The special excise duties levied on these products date from a period when general commodity taxation was less well developed than it is now, and less capable of supporting substantial revenues. Taxation of alcohol, tobacco, and petrol contributed significant revenues at low administration and enforcement cost. The retention of these taxes in current circumstances, when VAT has the capacity to raise large revenues from a more widely spread general commodity tax, may simply reflect a hangover from the past and the operation of various political-economy impediments to reform. However, the retention of these taxes may also be justified on the grounds that there are particular reasons to want to tax these commodities more heavily than others. Such arguments are increasingly acting to maintain these taxes at high levels and, in some cases, are being used to argue for increases in the relative taxation of these commodities.

Arguments for differential taxation of commodities fall into three broad groups: revenue-raising efficiency arguments, efficiency arguments relating to the use of taxes in correcting externality problems, and distributional arguments. The remainder of this section considers the two efficiency arguments, while Section 3.4 discusses distributional issues.

3.3.1 *Revenue-Raising Efficiency*

The principal efficiency arguments for differential taxation of commodities stem from Ramsey's (1927) analysis. Where commodity taxes have to be used for raising public revenues, and where distributional considerations can be ignored, Ramsey demonstrates that the efficiency cost of raising revenues will be minimized by non-uniform commodity taxes having the effect that the taxes should lead to equal proportionate reductions in consumption of each taxed commodity. The implications of this condition for the pattern of optimal tax rates are not straightforward, except in the special case where demand for each good is independent of the prices of other goods. In this case, the optimal tax rates will be inversely proportional to the elasticity of demand for each good. Goods with inelastic demand should therefore be taxed more heavily than average, and goods with price-elastic demand less heavily.

It will be noted that since goods that have a low price elasticity will tend also to have a low income elasticity, the 'inverse-elasticity' policy rule would imply heavier taxation of necessities than of luxuries, a policy prescription which may run counter to concerns about equity (which would typically suggest that necessities should be taxed less heavily than other goods).

A different perspective on essentially the same problem is provided by Corlett and Hague (1953), who show that if goods differ in their degree of substitutability for or complementarity with leisure, non-uniform taxation will reduce the welfare cost of raising given revenues. The efficient pattern of commodity tax rates would levy higher taxes on goods that are more complementary with leisure and lower taxes on goods that are substitutes for leisure. The intuition behind this result is that leisure is a commodity that enters into individual utility but is untaxed in a system of commodity taxation. Taxing goods that are complements with leisure more heavily than other goods in effect acts as a proxy for the 'missing' tax on leisure.

Subsequent literature has shown that the circumstances in which differential commodity taxation may be warranted on efficiency grounds are likely to be somewhat restricted. Atkinson and Stiglitz (1980) and Deaton and Stern (1986) show that relaxing one of the key assumptions of the Ramsey analysis – that ruling out lump-sum transfers – can lead to a prescription for uniform commodity taxation in a reasonably broad set of circumstances (primarily those where labour supply and commodity demands are weakly separable, a condition which rules out the Corlett-and-Hague cases). The policy conclusion is frequently drawn that the case for differential commodity taxation is then rather weak, except in countries with poorly developed systems of income taxation and social assistance (which may not be capable of making the required lump-sum transfers). However, it should be noted that weak separability of leisure and commodity demands is not an innocuous and trivial restriction, and differential commodity taxation may still be justified in these terms, even in developed countries with sophisticated mechanisms capable of targeting lump-sum transfers to individual households on the basis of complex criteria.

What evidence is there that alcohol might be a commodity for which above-average taxation might be appropriate under either the inverse-elasticity or Corlett-and-Hague leisure-complement policy rules?

The available evidence on elasticities is mostly based on work using US data, including a number of studies estimating price elasticities from the cross-section variation in alcohol prices between US states, resulting from different state-level tax policies. The widely cited study by Leung and Phelps (1993) reviewed the results of studies estimating the price elasticity of alcohol demand. Although the studies show considerable variation, the broad pattern of results would be consistent with elasticities of -0.3 for beer, -1.0 for wine, and -1.5 for spirits. The price elasticity of demand for an addictive commodity would be expected to be higher over the long run than in the short run (Becker and Murphy, 1988), and Grossman, Chaloupka, and Sirtalan (1998) find that the long-run elasticity in a model with addiction is some 50 per cent higher than the short-run elasticity. Differences of some significance for policy are found in the price elasticity of different subgroups in the population. Young people are substantially more price-responsive than older drinkers. Also, estimated price elasticities appear to vary with consumption levels. Manning, Blumberg, and Moulton (1995) find a greater price elasticity among moderate drinkers than among light drinkers and heavy drinkers; the consumption of heavy drinkers was found to have little sensitivity to price. On the other hand, Kenkel (1993) found a high price elasticity for the number of 'heavy-drinking days' reported by individuals, of around -0.9 over all age groups and -2.24 for youths aged 18–21. While the overall picture is clearly complex, it is unlikely that the price elasticity of alcohol demand is sufficiently low to warrant significantly higher-than-average taxation of alcohol than other goods on 'inverse-elasticity' grounds.

It is unclear, a priori, whether alcohol would be a complement with or a substitute for leisure. More leisure means more time to consume alcohol and also reduces the risk that the consequences of overconsumption (hangovers and so on) will negatively affect work performance. On the other hand, some level of alcohol consumption may be complementary with time spent working (and hence a leisure substitute), either because drinking helps workers unwind after a stressful day or because of social drinking with colleagues. The balance between these two effects may vary with individual alcohol consumption. At low consumption levels, alcohol may be complementary with work, but at higher levels of individual consumption, alcohol may be complementary with leisure. No clear implications can be drawn for taxation policy.

3.3.2 *Externality-Correcting Taxes*

Each of the three major excises, on alcohol, tobacco, and motor fuels, might also be justified in terms of their role in discouraging consumption activities that give rise to external costs. The external costs in the case of alcohol are discussed in more detail in Section 3.5. They include direct externalities experienced by other individuals, such as the harm that drunken drivers cause to others, and collectively borne costs such as the cost of publicly funded medical treatment for alcohol-related conditions. In both these examples, individual consumption decisions will not reflect the full social costs of consumption, because the individual consumer does not bear the marginal costs of medical treatment or of direct externalities that follow from their alcohol consumption decisions.

The case for using taxes to discourage socially harmful activities was set out by Pigou (1920) and has been developed subsequently in the context, primarily, of environmental policy. In the first-best context in which the Pigouvian tax can be set to achieve cost-effective correction of the externality, and in which prices are not distorted by taxation, monopoly, or other factors, a tax equal to the marginal external damage of each unit consumed would achieve efficient 'abatement' of the externality.

Recognition of the revenue-raising role that Pigouvian taxes can also perform has led to an extensive literature on the 'double dividend' of such taxes. The main policy implication relevant to the present discussion that can be drawn from this literature is that in an economy that is significantly distorted by a high level of initial taxation, it may be efficient to tax externality-generating activities at a lower level than would have been efficient in an undistorted economy (Bovenberg and de Mooij, 1994). The intuition is that the welfare costs of discouraging consumption of the externality-creating good through taxation are magnified where the externality tax is imposed on top of existing distortionary taxes (because, roughly speaking, the welfare costs of tax-induced changes in behaviour rise more than proportionately with the level of taxation).

Alcohol taxes, like many other practical instances of Pigouvian taxation, take the form of taxes levied on the production and sale of a commodity, and not specifically on the externality generated by its use. Sale of the commodity is effectively acting as a proxy for the level of the externality associated with its use, and its value as a proxy will depend on the stability of the relationship between the commodity and the externality (Sandmo, 1976). Literature looking at these types of proxy Pigouvian taxes suggests that if an imperfect proxy tax base is used, rather than direct taxation of measured externalities, there may be circumstances in which it might be efficient to subsidize or tax other goods that are substitutes for or complements with the externality-generating activity, rather than simply to rely on the proxy tax base alone (Green and Sheshinski, 1976). The policy rules in these second-best cases can be complex, and may be counter-intuitive in some cases (Balcer, 1980).

In the case of alcohol taxes, it is clear that the relationship between commodity sale and consumption is far from precise. The bulk of the external costs arise as a result of excessive or abusive consumption. Only some ('abusive') consumers may cause externalities, and the relationship between their alcohol consumption and the externalities may not be linear. As Pogue and Sgontz (1989) discuss, the taxation of alcohol sales helps to reduce the external costs generated by abusive consumers, but at the cost of reducing the consumer satisfaction of non-abusive consumers.

3.4 DISTRIBUTIONAL INCIDENCE OF ALCOHOL TAXES

As a general rule, the distributional incidence of individual components of the tax system is of less concern than the overall distributional incidence of all taxes (or, indeed, all government fiscal interventions) taken together. The fact that a particular regressively distributed component of the tax system may bear disproportionately heavily on poorer households may be unimportant if other taxes exhibit corresponding progressivity.

Nevertheless, where, as with alcohol taxes, taxes are distributed unevenly across households at similar income levels, there may be reason to look at the separate distributional incidence of the alcohol tax, since any adjustment to other taxes can only offset on average the distributional impact of taxes on alcohol. The distributional incidence of taxation on high consumers of alcohol will be more heavily influenced by the distributional characteristics of the alcohol tax; and for non-consumers of alcohol, the incidence of the alcohol tax will be an irrelevance.

Figure 3.1 shows the distributional incidence of UK excise duties on alcohol across households at different levels of gross income. Alcohol taxes overall are broadly proportional to income in the UK. Within the total, the tax on beer is broadly proportional to income, the tax on wine has a progressive incidence, and the tax on spirits is marginally regressive. The concerns that are sometimes raised about the regressivity of tobacco taxes[3] do not apply with anything like the same force to alcohol taxes.

Pechman (1985) showed that the assessment of the distributional incidence of taxation may be affected by the length of the accounting period used for the analysis. A tax that appears regressive when analysed on the basis of household income in a single year might – and, he suggests, would – appear less regressive when analysed over a longer period. Subsequent research, including Poterba (1989) and Lyon and Schwab (1995), has investigated this conjecture in more detail, comparing tax incidence analysed with respect to both current income and longer-period income estimates or proxies.

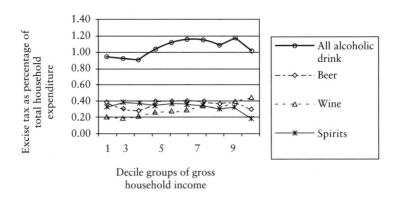

Figure 3.1. *Excise Tax on Alcohol as a Percentage of Total Household Expenditure, 1999–2000*

Source: Author's calculations, based on expenditure data from the UK Family Expenditure Survey, 1999–2000, table 1.3, and using excise duty rates, expressed as a percentage of selling price, for beer, wine, and spirits of 15.1 per cent, 36.1 per cent, and 47.1 per cent, respectively

There are three principal reasons for the distributional incidence of indirect taxes to vary depending on the time frame of the analysis – consumption-smoothing across transitory income fluctuations and across predictable life-cycle variations in income, and systematic life-cycle changes in consumption propensities. For example, temporary income shocks (such as the effect of unemployment) might have little effect on the level of current consumption, or on the pattern of goods consumed, because households might run down savings or borrow to maintain their consumption, despite the temporary drop in income. The average-income household experiencing what it perceives as a temporary income shock that places it in the lowest 10 per cent of the income distribution in a particular year does not immediately reduce its consumption to that of the permanently poor, nor does it change the pattern of goods consumed to reflect the lifestyles of the permanently poor. Instead, if it maintains the alcohol consumption of the average-income household (and if alcohol spending is a normal good), then it will have higher alcohol consumption than the permanently poor households in the bottom decile.

Further reasons for distributional analyses of taxation to vary according to whether they are based on lifetime or current income are the existence of predictable life-cycle variations in income, which may be smoothed through borrowing and saving, and the possibility that consumption patterns may vary over the life cycle. Suggestive evidence of systematic variation in alcohol consumption propensities over the life cycle in the UK is given in Figure 3.2, which shows alcohol budget shares for household income quintiles within each age group (where age groups are defined by the age of the head of the household). While budget shares among the top two quintiles are more convergent, there is a clear tendency among the lowest three deciles for alcohol budget shares among the under-30 age group to be some 2 percentage points higher than those among the over-65s.

Studies for the USA have found that alcohol taxes appear substantially less regressive when a longer time frame is used for analysis than when analysed on the basis of current income. A study by the Congressional Budget Office (1990) compares distributional analyses, in which the tax burden is expressed first as a percentage of current (annual) income and second as a percentage of total household consumption (though households remain classified to deciles throughout on the basis of current income). It finds that for all three of the major excises (on alcohol, tobacco, and motor fuels), the current-income analysis makes the tax burden appear more regressive than the alternative. Taxes on alcohol are found to be regressive when analysed with respect to current income and slightly progressive on the basis of aggregate household consumption.

In a study that uses income and consumption both as the basis of classification to deciles and to calculate shares, Poterba (1989) shows that alcohol excises look substantially more regressive when analysed on the basis of current income than when using measures more consistent with life-cycle analysis. Analysed on the basis of current income, alcohol taxes would look sharply regressive, because household alcohol spending as a percentage of income for

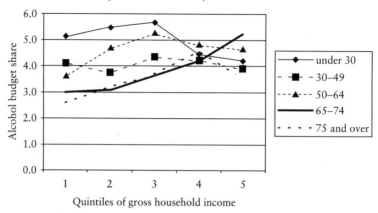

Figure 3.2. *Alcohol Budget Shares of Alcoholic Drinks across Quintiles of Gross Household Income, for Households Analysed by Age of Head of Household*

Source: Calculated from data in the UK Family Expenditure Survey, 1999–2000.

the poorest income quintile is some five times that for the richest quintile. On the other hand, analysed on the basis of household spending quintiles, alcohol taxes would look considerably less regressive, because the average alcohol budget share for the lowest-spending quintile is only some 30 per cent higher than that for the highest-spending quintile.

Lyon and Schwab (1995) use data from the US Panel Survey of Income Dynamics (PSID) to measure directly the effect of using different time periods to analyse distributional incidence. They find that alcohol taxes look somewhat less regressive when analysed using data on income and consumption for a five-year period than when using a single year's data, suggesting that transitory fluctuations in income account for some of the regressivity of alcohol and other excise taxes when analysed using current income. The Suits[4] index, used by Lyon and Schwab to summarize the distributional incidence of taxes under each income measure, falls in absolute value by about 22 per cent, from −0.135 to −0.105, when the perspective is changed from annual to five-year data. A further reduction in regressivity is found if the analysis is based on lifetime, rather than five-year, income. Nevertheless, alcohol tax in the USA remains regressive after this correction, and lifetime shares of income devoted to alcohol consumption are about 40 per cent greater in the poorest lifetime-income quintile than in the richest.

Whether a longer time frame makes any quantitatively significant difference to distributional analysis will in practice depend on three main factors:

- the extent of income volatility;
- the extent of consumption-smoothing behaviour – which will be affected by the prevalence and pattern of credit constraints;
- the extent to which predictable life-cycle differences in consumption propensities reinforce or offset effects arising from life-cycle changes in income.

All the above are likely to have important institutional and cultural determinants, which make it hazardous to generalize, either from country to country or from commodity to commodity. It is unlikely that the quantitative conclusions from analyses of US excises can be carried over to the European context, where different institutional arrangements in the labour market give rise to less income volatility at the individual level, so that adjusting distributional analyses to recognize the stochastic component of current income may be less important than it is in the USA. Equally, within Europe, the significance of the life-cycle perspective may vary. Differences in the way that alcohol is consumed are large between European member states, and it is quite probable that these cultural differences lead to different age-related consumption profiles.

3.5 SOCIAL COSTS OF ALCOHOL CONSUMPTION

Section 3.3 introduced the theoretical argument that the external costs associated with the consumption of goods such as alcohol and tobacco might warrant supplementary taxes, in addition to standard VAT, on these commodities. While individual consumers would be generally regarded as best placed to identify the pattern of consumption that best satisfies their needs, and to decide whether or not to purchase a particular good on the basis of whether the benefits of consuming it are sufficient to justify the price, we cannot assume that individual decision-making will result in the socially optimal pattern of consumption of goods that impose costs on people other than the individual decision-maker. Thus, while we may generally be happy to assume that individual choice properly reflects the costs and benefits of consumption to the individual concerned, externality-correcting taxes may be needed if we are to ensure that costs imposed on others are properly considered. This section addresses the question of the nature and size of the external costs of alcohol consumption.

The costs that this section considers are those borne by society collectively, or by individuals *other than the individual alcohol consumer*. The consumption of alcohol – like the consumption of tobacco – involves various consequences that extend beyond the immediate pleasure of consumption to the individual consumer. Frequently, the discussion of whether alcohol consumption is socially harmful includes discussion of the consequences for the individual consumer's own health, employment prospects, accident risks, and so on. Such costs to the individual consumer are not, however, externalities. Arguments that they might warrant higher taxation to discourage consumption involve an element of paternalism or 'society knows best', perhaps reflecting a concern that individuals may be poorly informed about some of the consequences for themselves of consumption.[5] Unless there are grounds to believe that consumers are poorly informed about some of the consequences of consumption, there are no reasons to overrule their consumption choices in their own interests; and where people are poorly informed, a better first response might be to provide better information rather than to dictate consumption decisions. For these reasons, pater-

nalist arguments for taxation generally meet with scepticism among economists.

Nevertheless, in the case of alcohol consumption, as with tobacco, the case
for discouraging consumption, *in the individual's own interest*, should not be
dismissed too lightly. Some of the individual costs of alcohol consumption arise
as a result of the addictive nature of consumption, and this adds a further
dimension to the problem. Current consumption may increase the risk of future
addiction. A well-informed and rational consumer would presumably be less
willing to consume alcohol, particularly in the manner or circumstances most
likely to give rise to future addiction, than if there were no risk of future
addiction. However, it is unrealistic to assume that all individual users of
alcohol are fully informed about the addictive risks associated with each unit
of consumption. In addition (except in an empty and tautological sense), it is
unrealistic to assume that all alcohol consumption decisions are based on a
rational calculus of the costs and benefits of each unit consumed.[6]

Aside from this issue, the 'social-costs' argument for higher alcohol taxes
requires us to identify, and appropriately charge for, the external costs of
alcohol consumption. The consequences of alcohol consumption that are felt
by individuals other than the consumer, and are unlikely to have been taken
into account by the consumer when choosing how much alcohol to consume,
fall into three broad categories. The first consists of direct externalities experienced by other individuals, including the victims of accidents, property
damage, and violence caused by other people's drinking. The second comprises
collectively borne costs, such as the cost of publicly funded medical treatment
for alcohol-related conditions, and other public expenditure costs. The third
category of externalities arise through the tax system. Alcohol consumption
may have consequences for the individual consumer's income and expenditure.
While these effects would be wholly internal in a 'first-best' world without
distortionary taxes, the presence of income taxes and spending taxes means
that the government partly shares in the benefits of additional income or
spending. This gives rise to what is, in effect, a tax revenue externality, and,
given the efficiency cost of raising public revenues through distortionary taxation, induced changes in revenues have a clear social value.

A considerable proportion of the literature on the social costs of alcohol
consumption is not directly relevant to the estimation of externality taxes,
because an insufficiently clear distinction is drawn between costs experienced
and internalized by the individual consumer and external costs experienced by
others. This is true, in particular, of studies using the 'cost-of-illness' (COI)
approach, which is directed at a social cost–benefit analysis of measures to
prevent illness. Such studies typically draw a clear distinction between resource
costs and transfer payments, but include resource costs experienced by the
individual consumer as well as those experienced by others.

The most widely quoted US estimates of alcohol consumption externalities,
appropriately defined, are those of Manning et al. (1989), who estimate that net
external costs are equivalent in value to about 35 per cent of the producer price

of alcohol. A very large proportion of the net external cost is accounted for by the valuation of alcohol-related traffic fatalities. Since the number of alcohol-related traffic fatalities seems to vary quite widely across countries, this would suggest that these US estimates may not be a good indication of alcohol externalities in other countries. Parry (2001) notes that there are fewer serious alcohol-related road traffic accidents in the UK than in the USA, and that marginal external costs are consequently also likely to be lower in the UK.

Estimates of external costs of alcohol consumption for the UK by Maynard, Godfrey, and Hardman (1994) are shown in Table 3.3. The estimates include various categories of direct externality (such as the damage caused in road traffic accidents) and also the cost of defensive measures (such as policing costs and the costs of research on alcohol problems). The costs of collectively funded medical treatment in the UK National Health Service of

Table 3.3. *Social Costs of Alcohol: England and Wales (1992 prices)*

	£ million (1992 prices)	Percentage of pre-tax alcohol expenditure
1. The social cost to industry		14.2
Sickness absence	1,059	
Housework services	71	
Unemployment	244	
Premature deaths	956	
2. The social cost to the NHS		1.0
In-patient costs—direct alcohol diagnosis	41	
In-patient costs—other alcohol-related diagnosis	120	
General Practice costs	3	
3. Society's response to alcohol-related problems		0.01
Expenditure by national bodies	0.5	
Research	0.9	
4. Social cost of material damage		0.9
Road traffic accidents (damage)	152	
5. Social cost of criminal activities		0.3
Police involvement in traffic offences (excluding road accidents)	7	
Police involvement in traffic accidents (including judiciary and insurance administration)	21	
Drink-related court cases	27	
Total (excluding unemployment and premature death)	1,503	9.2
Total (including unemployment and premature death)	2,703	16.5

Source: Maynard, Godfrey, and Hardman, 1994, table 1. (Author's calculations in final column, based on rough estimate of 1992 England and Wales consumer spending on alcoholic drinks of approximately £20.9 billion, minus £4.5 billion of duty, giving £16.4 billion of sales net of sales taxes.)

alcohol-related illnesses are also included. However, the largest items appear under the heading 'social cost to industry', including the substantial costs of sickness absence and unemployment. Quite how far these should count as external costs depends on what is assumed about alcohol-induced productivity effects on individual wages, an issue discussed in more detail below. Overall, Maynard et al. calculate the total externalities associated with alcohol consumption in the UK to be around £2.7 billion, equivalent to some 17 per cent of pre-tax alcohol expenditure.

The externality case for taxing alcohol at higher rates than other goods requires clear identification and measurement of the external costs of alcohol consumption. Nevertheless, attempts to draw a clear boundary between internalized and external costs are not straightforward, and a number of areas of conceptual and practical difficulty can be identified.

3.5.1 *Effects on Family Members*

One controversial area is the treatment of costs borne by family members. Family members of an abusive alcohol user may experience considerable costs, including costs of violence, costs of injury, and pain and distress as a result of the alcohol-related illness and premature death of the alcohol abuser. Many of the consequences of alcohol abuse during pregnancy, including damage to the lifetime health and happiness of the child, also come under this heading (although there are, in addition, further important costs for the healthcare system). Whether, and to what extent, costs experienced by other family members should count as externalities has been controversial. As Viscusi (1995) notes, it turns, in principle, on whether the welfare of other members enters into the utility function of the alcohol consumer, and, in other areas of policy, it is often assumed that family members are assumed to care for each other's welfare to the extent that the welfare of the household can be considered as a single entity. In the case of alcohol abuse, however, this seems implausible, and the costs of domestic violence and the injuries inflicted on unborn children would seem best treated as externalities.

3.5.2 *Effects on Wages and Productivity*

A large part of the total social cost of alcohol estimated by Maynard, Godfrey, and Hardman (1994) consists of effects on industrial output. Whether the income or output loss from sickness absence and other alcohol-related productivity effects should be counted as an externality depends primarily on how far the effects of alcohol on worker productivity are reflected in wages. There are a number of cases of interest:

1. If workers are paid their actual marginal product, and if there is no income taxation, then there is no externality. Alcohol abusers who are less productive receive correspondingly lower wages.

2. When there are taxes on wages, or on consumption out of wages, then the loss in wages experienced by an alcohol abuser is partly shared by the rest of society, through the reduction in tax revenues, and is no longer a matter of social indifference.

3. However, employers may not always be able to differentiate the wages paid to alcohol abusers and non-abusers, to reflect their different individual marginal products. In this case, the lower productivity of alcohol abusers generates externalities of two forms. First, the employer paying an alcohol abuser wages that exceed the worker's marginal product will experience a real income externality. Secondly, since the overall marginal product has fallen and the employer is unable to differentiate the wages paid to different workers, both abusers and non-abusers will receive lower wages as a result of the lower productivity of abusers.[7]

Quite how far the productivity effect of individual alcohol abuse is reflected in individual wages, and how far it is collectively borne, is unclear. Even where there is no immediate impact on the abusers' wage (because of contractual provisions or collective bargaining), it is likely that abusers with poor sickness records will be less frequently promoted, and thereby suffer longer-term income losses.

There is, however, an empirical literature on the effect of alcohol consumption on wages and occupational attainment at the individual level. MacDonald and Shields (2001) analyse the relationship between drinking patterns and occupational attainment (measured by hourly wages) in the UK, taking account of the possibility that there may be a reciprocal relationship between drinking and wages: higher wages may permit greater alcohol consumption, but at the same time, alcohol consumption may have an effect on wages. The authors find an inverse U-shaped drinking–wage profile, with moderate consumers of alcohol having higher wages than either heavy drinkers or non-drinkers. The maximum wage appears to be at around 210 ml[8] of alcohol per week for men and 140 ml for women, somewhat above the mean levels of weekly consumption in the study's data (180 ml for men and 70 ml for women). A male worker consuming 210 ml per week would have a wage premium of some 14 per cent over a non-drinker and some 25 per cent over a male consuming three times as much alcohol.

3.5.3 *Healthcare Finance and External Costs*

How far are the costs of medical treatment and healthcare internalized when alcohol consumption decisions are made, and how far should they be counted as an externality? In the case of publicly funded, tax-financed systems such as the UK National Health Service, the answer is straightforward: the treatment costs of illnesses resulting from individual consumption decisions are collectively financed. The same may largely be true of other collectively financed systems, such as employer-financed healthcare. By contrast, a system of private insurance capable of appropriate differentiation of insurance premiums (for example, through experience rating at the individual level) might be able to internalize a large part of the healthcare costs associated with alcohol abuse.

This suggests that the classification of healthcare costs into internal and external is institution-dependent and will vary between countries depending on the institutional arrangements. In European welfare states, where healthcare costs are substantially funded out of direct taxation or quasi-tax social contributions, healthcare costs are an important part of the externality calculation, and, other things being equal, alcohol externalities (and hence the optimal rate of alcohol taxation) may be higher in such countries than in countries where healthcare costs are largely individually borne. Nevertheless, it is clear that defining the precise boundary between collectively financed and individually borne healthcare costs will often be difficult, especially in systems that are neither wholly tax-financed nor wholly individually financed.

3.5.4 *Implications of Externality Estimates for Tax Rates*

Translating the externality estimates into appropriate rates of Pigouvian taxation on alcoholic drinks is complicated by the fact that most of the available estimates of social costs of alcohol consumption concern total social costs. While the average external cost can be straightforwardly derived, the marginal external cost of consumption may well differ sharply from the average. Unlike the case of the externalities from tobacco consumption, which may well be almost constant across each unit consumed, the externalities from alcohol consumption largely relate to abusive consumption. Excessive consumption, leading to serious drunkenness in individual episodes, or alcoholism over time, is the source of the externalities, and the external costs associated with moderate consumption may be close to zero. While Table 3.3 suggests that the average external cost from alcohol consumption in the UK might be of the order of 17 per cent of the pre-tax price of alcohol, the marginal external cost may be different.

Diamond (1973) discusses externality taxation in a context where all individuals causing externalities must be taxed at the same rate, but where the externalities from some are more damaging than those from others. He shows that in the case where there is separability between the externality and consumption, the tax should simply be the weighted average of the marginal contributions to the externality, across different individuals, where the weights are given by the sensitivities of demand for the good that generates the externality. If differences in the external costs of alcohol arise from differences between individuals, rather than between units of drink consumed by a particular individual, then this result may provide some support for regarding the average external costs as a rough-and-ready indicator of the optimal externality tax. However, if the external damage caused by alcohol consumption varies across units consumed by each individual (for example, if it is 'the one drink that makes you drunk' that causes all the problems), then the appropriate externality tax would be considerably higher.

Pogue and Sgontz (1989) investigate further the implications for optimal alcohol taxation of the requirement that the alcohol sold to abusive and non-abusive drinkers must be taxed at the same rate. Their analysis is directed at quantifying the trade-off between the reduction in welfare of non-abusive drinkers and the social benefits from the reduction in consumption by abusive drinkers. The balance will depend on the size of marginal social costs from abusive consumption, the size of the welfare loss from distorted non-abusive consumption, the relative numbers of abusive and non-abusive consumers, and the price elasticities of the two groups. (There is also the difficult issue of principle of whether alcohol-dependent consumers of alcohol should be treated as deriving utility from their abusive consumption, or not.) Overall, Pogue and Sgontz estimate that US alcohol taxes in 1983 were at about half the socially optimal level.

A broadly similar difference between actual and optimal taxes in the USA is estimated by Manning et al. (1989). Kenkel (1996) estimates a higher optimal tax – about equal to the pre-tax alcohol price. Saffer and Chaloupka (1994) reckon that the weighted average optimal US tax on alcohol (allowing separately for taxes on beer, wine, and spirits) is 2.3 times the 1991 level.

3.6 TAX BASE

In addition to the question of the level of taxes on alcohol, there is a question about the precise specification of the tax base. One issue is whether alcohol excises should continue to be wholly specific (as at present in the EU) or should contain an *ad valorem* component. Keen (1998) surveys the issues in the choice between specific and *ad valorem* taxes. He observes that *ad valorem* taxation will tend to have a multiplier effect, in the sense that actions that increase, or reduce, the producer price by a given amount will have a larger effect on the price charged to the consumer. As a result, *ad valorem* taxes will tend to discourage costly improvements in product quality and will tend to promote more vigorous price competition between producers. Specific taxes, on the other hand, will tend to have an upgrading effect on product quality. The overall implications for consumer welfare and tax revenue of the choice between specific and *ad valorem* taxation will vary, depending on the market structure. *Ad valorem* taxation of goods will tend to be more attractive where producers exert a degree of monopoly power and where there is little product differentiation. Specific taxes would be preferred where there are reasons to want to maintain product quality or where taxation is partly intended to affect an externality that is broadly related to the quantity of the product rather than to its value.

A further issue is the form of the specific base, and in particular the role of both volume and alcohol content in the determination of the taxation of different products. There are issues here about the role of alcohol content in defining the tax payable, both within a single category of drink (beer, wine, or spirits) and across the three principal categories of drink.

In all EU member states, the taxation of spirits is defined in terms of alcohol content, so that dilution or concentration makes no difference to the excise tax burden per unit of alcohol content. The taxation of beer is also related to alcohol content, although in some countries not linearly. By contrast, the excise taxation of wine is based on an excise per unit volume, although in some member states this excise is banded according to the alcohol strength of the product. To some extent, there are good practical reasons for this difference in treatment. The large-scale industrial processes involved in the production of most beer and spirits can regulate alcohol content precisely and permit reasonably straightforward administration and enforcement of an excise based on alcohol content. The smaller-scale and less-predictable processes involved in the production of wine give both the producer and the revenue authorities less control over alcohol content, and make volume-based excises a more practical solution. In addition, perhaps rather less scope exists for producers to make a significant change to the alcohol content of wine than with beer or spirits, and therefore volume-based taxation of wine may be a closer approximation to alcohol content taxation than would be volume-based beer or spirits taxation.

Arguments for uniform taxation of alcohol content across the three principal categories of drink (beer, wine, and spirits) appear quite persuasive, and this has been advocated by Crooks (1989) among others. Uniform taxation of alcohol would avoid distortion of sales between competing drinks and would relate the taxation of each drink to the ingredient responsible for externalities.

Currently, spirits are taxed much more heavily per unit of alcohol than beer and wine in all EU member states. Table 3.4 shows that the typical tax rate per unit of alcohol levied on beer is less than 65 per cent of the tax on spirits per unit of alcohol in all member states, and less than 50 per cent in all but five member states. The excise tax on still wine per unit of alcohol is about 60 per cent of the spirits tax per unit of alcohol in the UK and Ireland, but less than 40 per cent in all other member states (and zero in seven member states).

How significant is this differential treatment, both for consumer welfare and for producers? A key issue here is the extent to which different drinks are close substitutes for one another. Evidence in Smith (1999) and in Customs Associates Ltd (2001) on cross-price elasticities suggests that beer, wine, and spirits are not particularly close substitutes, and that wine and spirits may in fact be mild complements.

A move towards uniformity in taxation per unit of alcohol across the three main categories of alcoholic drink would seem a natural way to structure the Pigouvian taxation of alcohol, in that it would appear to target the externality tax precisely to the underlying source of the externalities. Nevertheless, the issue is not straightforward, especially where there is relatively limited substitution between the three categories of drink.

First, different drinks may differ in their propensity to generate external costs per unit of alcohol content. This is, however, to some extent a function of the pricing of different drinks, and evidence on the current pattern of abuse across different drinks is not necessarily particularly informative in designing optimal alcohol taxes, since it is partly a result of existing tax and price decisions. For example, spirits might not currently generate major externalities, if the high price restricts consumption to more-affluent consumers interested in non-alcohol attributes, but this does not tell us what level of externalities would be associated with spirits consumption if spirits were taxed at the same rate per unit of alcohol as beer and wine. Indeed, there is at least anecdotal evidence that some abusive consumers select drinks with the lowest price per unit of alcohol content, so that the abuse related to different drinks is then endogenous to tax policy decisions. Recognition of this does not, however, automatically lead to uniform taxation of alcohol content, since, in the hands of abusers, different drinks may still generate different levels of externalities. Arguably, spirits offer the greatest potential to get very drunk very quickly, which may exacerbate some of the externality problems. If uniform taxation of alcohol content would make low-cost industrially produced spirits the cheapest form of alcohol, the shift of abusers to spirits consumption might then not be a matter of social indifference.

Secondly, Pigouvian taxation of alcohol content involves balancing the welfare losses to non-abusive consumers against the social gains from deterring abusive consumption, and this balance may differ across drinks. Nevertheless, since the welfare losses to non-abusive consumers will tend to rise more than in

Table 3.4. *EU Duty Rates per Litre of Alcohol Content, relative to Taxation of Spirits, April 2003*

	Beer (5% abv)	Still wine (12.5% abv)	Spirits
Minimum adopted by Council, 19 October 1992	19	0	100
Austria	52	0	100
Belgium	26	23	100
Denmark	25	21	100
Finland	57	37	100
France	18	2	100
Germany	15	0	100
Greece	31	0	100
Ireland	51	56	100
Italy	54	0	100
Luxembourg	19	0	100
Netherlands	33	31	100
Portugal	35	0	100
Spain	27	0	100
Sweden	29	35	100
UK	62	65	100

Source: Calculated from data in European Commission, Directorate General for Taxation and Customs Union, *Excise Duty Tables April 2003* (REF 1.016). Downloaded from http://europa.eu.int/comm/taxation_customs/publications/info_doc/taxation/c4_excise_tables.pdf.

proportion to the tax rate (in the linear case, in proportion to the square of the tax rate), it would be expected that significant departures from uniformity of taxation will tend to increase the aggregate level of these costs. Saffer and Chaloupka (1994) present a calculation for the USA, based on the methodology of Pogue and Sgontz (1989), which suggests that there would be gains from greater uniformity in the taxation of alcohol across beer, wine, and spirits. A significant factor behind this result is that the costs to non-abusive consumers are non-linear in the tax rate.

Thirdly, optimal externality taxation needs to take account of the presence of other forms of regulation.[9] Non-fiscal control measures designed to regulate alcohol consumption, and the various costs associated with abusive alcohol consumption, have a regulatory effect which may be regarded as having a 'tax-equivalent' value, which should, broadly speaking, be deducted from the level of the Pigouvian tax that would be set in the absence of these regulatory policies. In principle, it would be possible for these non-fiscal regulatory measures to vary in importance across categories of drink. Drinks subject to more-stringent non-fiscal regulation could then be taxed accordingly less, while maintaining broadly similar levels of regulation per unit of alcohol across all categories of drink.

3.7 CROSS-BORDER SHOPPING AND TAXATION

A growing tax policy issue in the UK and some other high-tax EU member states is the revenue loss from legal cross-border shopping and from various forms of illegal tax evasion and smuggling. Both problems arise as a result of large tax-induced price differentials between member states, especially between adjacent member states.

The problem of revenue losses from legal cross-border shopping by individuals has come into particular prominence as a result of the abolition of border controls between EU member states from 1 January 1993. Prior to 1993, most member states applied restrictive travellers' allowances on personal imports of alcoholic drinks from other EU countries, as well as from the rest of the world, and this kept legal cross-border shopping within tightly constrained bounds. As a result of the abolition of border controls, individuals can purchase goods in another member state and bring them home without restriction or fiscal adjustment, so long as the goods are for their personal use and not for resale.

The requirement that individual imports should be for personal use is underpinned by agreed 'indicative levels' of duty-paid imports, below which imports would normally be accepted as being for the individual's personal use, and above which the claim of personal use might be challenged. These are comparatively unrestrictive. The indicative levels were set at 110 litres for beer, 90 litres for wine, and 10 litres for spirits. Transitional arrangements were agreed for the high-tax Scandinavian countries – Sweden and Finland – as part of the arrangements for their accession to the EU. These, for example, limited personal duty-paid imports initially to 15 litres of beer, to be gradually adjusted to the standard EU indicative level of 110 litres by the start of 2004.

The scale of revenue losses from both legal and illegal cross-border movements of alcohol is controversial. Estimates by HM Customs and Excise, the UK tax administration concerned, assessed the UK revenue loss from legitimate cross-Channel shopping for alcohol in 1998 at £285 million (€420 million), about 5 per cent of total UK alcohol duty revenues.[10] Some part of this revenue loss would have arisen as a result of duty-free purchases, rather than tax-paid purchases in other member states, though it is a reasonable guess that a significant part of the alcohol purchased duty-free would have been purchased outside the UK in the absence of the opportunity to make duty-free purchases.[11] HM Customs and Excise estimated that illegal cross-Channel smuggling of alcohol in 1998 involved a revenue loss to the UK of some £230 million (€340 million), around 4 per cent of total alcohol excise revenue.[12]

For individual member states with high duty rates on alcohol, alcohol tax policy needs to take account of the potential revenue losses through legal and illegal cross-border activities. Crawford and Tanner (1995) and Crawford, Smith, and Tanner (1999) consider whether the revenue losses through cross-border shopping induced by duty differentials are sufficiently large that UK revenues could be increased by cutting the rates of UK excise duties. They observe that the post-1992 abolition of border controls acts so as to increase the price elasticity of demand for UK-bought alcohol. As the price is increased, some consumers reduce their consumption of alcohol altogether (the normal effect, in the absence of cross-border shopping opportunities), while others may switch to buying abroad. The higher elasticity for UK-bought alcohol might suggest that UK tax rates on alcohol should be reduced (on grounds basically similar to the Ramsey optimal commodity tax argument). Also, if the increase in elasticity is sufficiently large, it is possible that the existing rates of duty might exceed the revenue-maximizing duty rates.

Using data from the UK Family Expenditure Survey for the years spanning completion of the Single Market, Crawford, Smith, and Tanner (1999) find, however, no evidence of a significant change in elasticities. Whether a reduction in duty rates would increase or reduce UK tax revenues depends on the own-price and cross-price elasticities of demand for the various categories of alcoholic drinks. Crawford et al. find that the UK tax rates on beer and wine are still lower than revenue-maximizing tax rates, meaning that a cut in duty on these drinks would reduce total revenues (even though it would repatriate a certain amount of cross-border shopping). On the other hand, the study is unable to reject the hypothesis that the current UK tax rate on spirits is the revenue-maximizing rate. This suggests that the duty on spirits may be closer to the level at which a cut in duty might reduce cross-border shopping by enough to compensate for the revenue lost on each unit.

For the EU, the policy issue is whether there is a collective gain to be made from policies to reduce the duty differentials between member states that give rise to cross-border shopping and smuggling. Lee, Pearson, and Smith (1988) argue that fiscal externalities between member states warrant some level of EU tax coordination to control cross-border shopping. These externalities include revenue losses, the time and travel costs of cross-border shoppers, and a loss of business (perhaps entailing adjustment costs) to retailers on the high-tax side of the border. The authors note that there is an asymmetry between the effects of increasing and lowering tax rates. A member state that raises its tax rate relative to taxes in neighbouring member states increases cross-border shopping, but the costs are largely internal to the member state concerned. On the other hand, a member state that reduces its tax rate attracts cross-border shopping and revenues, imposing external costs on other member states. Observing that the greatest priority for the EU is to regulate those member state policies that have negative effects on other member states, Lee et al. argue that this implies that the EU should set an EU-wide floor to excise duty (and VAT) levels in member states, to restrict the negative externalities that duty reductions would impose on other member states, but that there are no compelling grounds to place any upper limit on member states' duty rates.

The subsequent formal literature on tax policy in the presence of cross-border shopping has explored in more detail the robustness of these policy rules. Using a simple two-country model with revenue-maximizing governments, Kanbur and Keen (1993) show that imposition of a minimum tax rate (a tax floor) in both countries may improve welfare in both, while a policy imposing uniform rates in both countries is undesirable. Other results in this literature vary in the scope they find for collective policies to improve on non-cooperative tax competition. Some papers (for example, Brennan and Buchanan (1980) and Edwards and Keen (1996)) suggest that unregulated tax competition may be a useful mechanism to control the tendency to excessive growth in government. The case for the EU imposing some form of duty coordination thus, to a certain extent, turns on fundamental differences of philosophy about the nature and value of governments. Those who view governments as choosing tax and spending policies to maximize social welfare may regard tax coordination as a way to ease what would otherwise be an undesirable constraint on the choice of a socially optimal pattern of taxation, while those who believe that there is a natural tendency towards excessive growth in government spending may view tax coordination in a less-positive light.

3.8 CONCLUSIONS

This chapter has reviewed the range of arguments that could justify taxing alcohol at higher rates than other commodities. Alcohol demand is insufficiently price-inelastic to warrant higher-than-average taxation on the basis of the Ramsey inverse-elasticity rule. While short-run price elasticities for alcohol may be quite low, demand is more price-elastic in the long run (this pattern reflecting the addictive nature of alcohol overconsumption). Likewise, there do not seem to be strong grounds for taxing alcohol heavily as a leisure complement (the Corlett-and-Hague argument). The relationship between demands for alcohol and leisure is likely to be complex, and it is unclear that alcohol is a good that is uniformly complementary with leisure.

The main justification for levying additional excise taxes on alcohol, over and above standard VAT, lies in the role that alcohol tax can play in reducing the externalities associated with alcohol consumption (and, especially, abusive overconsumption). Using alcohol taxes for this purpose involves targeting the incentive somewhat imprecisely to the underlying externality, since alcohol externalities are not proportional to alcohol consumption but are largely confined to abusive overconsumption by a subset of all consumers. Externality taxation of alcohol thus involves a compromise between the potential gains from reducing external costs of abusive consumption and the welfare costs of discouraging non-abusive consumption.

The external costs of alcohol consumption are likely to be heavily affected both by the institutional arrangements for financing healthcare, pensions, and so on, and by the cultural context in which alcohol is consumed. It is therefore unlikely that US estimates can be carried over without modification to the European context, or that externalities will be uniform throughout Europe. Because healthcare in many European countries is financed through taxation, or through contributions that have much of the character of taxes, and because European countries have more-significant tax-funded pensions and higher levels of income taxation, some of the major items in US calculations of alcohol externalities would be different in Europe. A study for the UK by Maynard, Godfrey, and Hardman (1994) estimates the annual external costs of alcohol consumption to be around £2.7 billion, or some 17 per cent of the value of pre-tax consumer expenditure on alcohol. It is unlikely that this result can be straightforwardly extrapolated to other European countries because of significant social differences in how alcohol is used in different parts of the EU. There is clearly a need for further systematic and comparative research on alcohol externalities in European countries.

Some of the US literature has observed that alcohol taxes are regressively distributed with respect to current household income and significantly less regressive from a lifetime perspective. Further evidence is also needed on this for European countries. At least, however, alcohol taxation does not appear to be so regressively distributed as tobacco taxes, and therefore distributional concerns may not be a major constraint on European alcohol tax policies.

Because of the differences across European countries in alcohol consumption patterns and – probably – external costs of alcohol consumption, it is unlikely that the optimal tax treatment of alcoholic drinks will be identical in all members of the EU. Imposing greater uniformity on the very diverse pattern of EU alcohol taxation may thus involve some economic inefficiency (as well as some limitations on national fiscal sovereignty). Nevertheless, narrowing differences in alcohol taxes between EU member states would reduce the economic and fiscal costs associated with legal cross-border shopping and with the various forms of illegal smuggling and tax evasion that are encouraged by significant tax differences. The most appropriate form for such EU fiscal coordination to take would be significant increases in the agreed EU-wide floors to alcohol taxes. There is no obvious EU-wide reason to prevent member states setting higher duty levels than those elsewhere.

Notes

1 Throughout this chapter, the term 'alcohol' is used as a shorthand general term covering all forms of alcoholic drinks, including beers, wines, and spirits, except where this is liable to lead to ambiguity.

2 Existing literature on this issue includes Crooks (1989), Grossman et al. (1993), O'Hagan and Reilly (1995), and Buck, Godfrey, and Richardson (1996).

3 See, for example, the discussion in O'Hagan (1998).

4 The index developed by Suits (1977) compares the cumulative distribution of tax burden and of income. It is bounded by -1 and $+1$, with -1 meaning a tax borne entirely by the poorest income group, 0 denoting a proportional tax, and $+1$ meaning a tax borne entirely by the richest income group.

5 Viscusi (1995), for example, discusses whether individuals accurately perceive the health risks of cigarette smoking.

6 This is not to deny the argument that certain categories of action which may appear irrational when viewed alone – such as crimes committed while drunk – may be regarded as the outcome of a rational decision whether or not to put oneself in the state of drunkenness.

7 It is possible that wages might fall by more than the average reduction in productivity of the two groups. The situation is one of asymmetric information, and an employer paying alcohol abusers wages reflecting average productivity could end up with a workforce comprising an above-average proportion of abusers (for conventional adverse-selection reasons). All wages may thus be driven down towards the marginal product of abusers.

8 MacDonald and Shields express their results in terms of consumption of the alcohol 'units' used in UK health education. One 'unit' is defined as 8 grams, or approximately 10 ml, of pure alcohol.

9 In his discussion of the tax treatment of gambling in this volume, Clotfelter observes that differences across countries in the level of regulation have implications for the optimal pattern of gambling taxation.

10 Written parliamentary answer by Dawn Primarolo, 26 November 1999, *Hansard*, column 253W.

11 Since July 1999, the EU countries have abolished duty-free sales on intra-EU travel. Christiansen and Smith (2001) discuss the tax policy implications.

12 Written parliamentary answer by Dawn Primarolo, 26 November 1999, *Hansard*, column 253W.

References

Atkinson, A. B., and Stiglitz, J. E. (1980), *Lectures on Public Economics*, Maidenhead: McGraw-Hill.

Balcer, Y. (1980), 'Taxation of externalities: direct versus indirect', *Journal of Public Economics*, 13: 121–9.

Becker, G. S., and Murphy, K. M. (1988), 'A theory of rational addiction', *Journal of Political Economy*, 96: 675–700.

Bovenberg, A. L., and de Mooij, R. (1994), 'Environmental levies and distortionary taxation', *American Economic Review*, 84: 1085–9.

Brennan, G., and Buchanan, J. M. (1980), *The Power to Tax: Analytical Foundations of a Fiscal Constitution*, Cambridge and New York, NY: Cambridge University Press.

Buck, D., Godfrey, C., and Richardson, G. (1996), 'Should alcohol be taxed for the public good?', in N. Lunt and D. Coyle (eds), *Welfare & Policy: Research Agenda and Issues*, London: Taylor and Francis.

Christiansen, V., and Smith, S. (2001), 'The economics of duty-free shopping', CESifo, Working Paper 595.

Clotfelter, C. T. (this volume), 'Gambling taxes'.

Congressional Budget Office (1990), *Federal Taxation of Tobacco, Alcoholic Beverages and Motor Fuels*, Washington, DC: US Government Printing Office.

Corlett, W. J., and Hague, D. C. (1953), 'Complementarity and the excess burden of taxation', *Review of Economic Studies*, 21: 21–30.

Crawford, I., Smith, Z., and Tanner, S. (1999), 'Alcohol taxes, tax revenues and the Single European Market', *Fiscal Studies*, 20: 287–304.

——and Tanner, S. (1995), 'Bringing it all back home: alcohol taxation and cross-border shopping', *Fiscal Studies*, 16(2): 94–114.

Crooks, E. (1989), *Alcohol Consumption and Taxation*, Report Series 34, London: Institute for Fiscal Studies.

Customs Associates Ltd (2001), *Study on the Competition between Alcoholic Drinks*, summary of the final report for the European Commission, February 2001. Available at http://europa.eu.int/comm/taxation_customs/publications/reports_studies/taxation /study_al_drinks/al_drinks.htm.

Deaton, A., and Stern, N. (1986), 'Optimally uniform commodity taxes, taste differences and lump-sum grants', *Economics Letters*, 20: 263–6.

Diamond, P. (1973), 'Consumption externalities and imperfect corrective pricing', *Bell Journal of Economics*, 4: 526–38.

Edwards, J., and Keen, M. (1996), 'Tax competition and Leviathan', *European Economic Review*, 40: 113–34.

European Commission (2001), *Tax Policy in the European Union: Priorities for the Years Ahead*, Communication from the Commission to the Council, the European Parliament, and the Economic and Social Committee, COM(2001) 260 final. Available at http://europa.eu.int/comm/taxation_customs/publications/official_doc/com/ taxation/com2001260/com2001260_en.pdf.

Green, J., and Sheshinski, E. (1976), 'Direct versus indirect remedies for externalities', *Journal of Political Economy*, 83: 797–808.

Grossman, M., Chaloupka, F., and Sirtalan, I. (1998), 'An empirical analysis of alcohol addiction: results from the Monitoring the Future panels', *Economic Inquiry*, 36: 39–48.

Grossman, M., Sindelar, J. L., Mullahy, J., and Anderson, R. (1993), 'Policy watch: alcohol and cigarette taxes', *Journal of Economic Perspectives*, 7(1): 211–21.

Kanbur, R., and Keen, M. J. (1993), 'Jeux sans frontières: tax competition and tax coordination when countries differ in size', *American Economic Review*, 83: 877–92.

Keen, M. J. (1998), 'The balance between specific and *ad valorem* taxation', *Fiscal Studies*, 19: 1–37.

Kenkel, D. S. (1993), 'Drinking, driving and deterrence: the effectiveness and social costs of alternative policies', *Journal of Law and Economics*, 36: 877–913.

——(1996), 'New estimates of the optimal tax on alcohol', *Economic Inquiry*, 34: 296–319.

Lee, C., Pearson, M., and Smith, S. (1988), *Fiscal Harmonisation: An Analysis of the Commission's Proposals*, Report Series 28, London: Institute for Fiscal Studies.

Leung, S., and Phelps, C. (1993), 'My kingdom for a drink ... ? A review of estimates of the price sensitivity of alcoholic beverages', in M. E. Hilton and G. Bloss (eds), *Economics and the Prevention of Alcohol-Related Problems*, NIH Publication 93-3513, Rockville, MD: National Institutes of Health.

Lyon, A. B., and Schwab, R. M. (1995), 'Consumption taxes in a life-cycle framework: are sin taxes regressive?', *Review of Economics and Statistics*, 77: 389–406.

MacDonald, Z., and Shields, M. (2001), 'The impact of alcohol consumption on occupational attainment in England', *Economica*, 68: 427–53.

Manning, W. G., Blumberg, L., and Moulton, L. H. (1995), 'The demand for alcohol: the differential response to price', *Journal of Health Economics*, 14: 123–48.

——, Keeler, E. B., Newhouse, J. P., Sloss, E. M., and Wasserman, J. (1989), 'The taxes of sin: do smokers and drinkers pay their way?', *Journal of the American Medical Association*, 261: 1604–9.

Maynard, A., Godfrey, C., and Hardman, G. (1994), 'Conceptual issues in estimating the social costs of alcohol', prepared for an international symposium on the Economic Costs of Substance Abuse, Banff, Canada, 11–13 May. Available at www.ccsa.ca/Costs/maynard.htm.

O'Hagan, J. (1998), 'The taxation of tobacco', in C. Sandford (ed.), *Further Key Issues in Tax Reform*, Bath: Fiscal Publications.

—— and Reilly, A. (1995), 'The taxation of alcoholic beverages', in C. Sandford (ed.), *More Key Issues in Tax Reform*, Bath: Fiscal Publications.

Parry, I. W. H. (2001), 'On the costs of excise taxes and income taxes in the UK', Resources for the Future, mimeo, October.

Pechman, J. A. (1985), *Who Paid the Taxes: 1966–1985*, Washington, DC: Brookings Institution.

Pigou, A. C. (1920), *The Economics of Welfare*, London: Macmillan.

Pogue, T. F., and Sgontz, L. G. (1989), 'Taxing to control social costs: the case of alcohol', *American Economic Review*, 79: 235–43.

Poterba, J. M. (1989), 'Lifetime incidence and the distributional burden of excise taxes', *American Economic Review*, 79: 325–30.

Ramsey, F. (1927), 'A contribution to the theory of taxation', *Economic Journal*, 37: 47–61.

Saffer, H., and Chaloupka, F. (1994), 'Alcohol tax equalization and social costs', *Eastern Economic Journal*, 20: 33–43.

Sandmo, A. (1976), 'Direct versus indirect Pigovian taxation', *European Economic Review*, 7: 337–49.

Smith, Z. (1999), *The Revenue Effect of Changing Alcohol Duties*, Briefing Note 4, Institute for Fiscal Studies, www.ifs.org.uk/consume/alcohol.pdf.

Suits, D. B. (1977), 'Measurement of tax progressivity', *American Economic Review*, 67: 747–52.

Viscusi, W. K. (1995), 'Cigarette taxation and the social consequences of smoking', *Tax Policy and the Economy*, 9: 51–101.

Chapter 4

Gambling Taxes

CHARLES T. CLOTFELTER[*]
Duke University

4.1 INTRODUCTION

With deep roots in history and dozens of modern manifestations, gambling is an activity that governments have typically either forbidden or taxed. Governments in most parts of the world use it to raise revenue, though the amounts raised are paltry in comparison with the mainstays of modern tax systems. As a form of personal expenditure, gambling has grown rapidly in many countries over the past four decades. This growth has been fuelled by new forms of commercial gambling and by increasing social acceptance of the activity itself. Because gambling has historically existed under a cloud of unrespectability, if not outright condemnation, and because governments have correspondingly outlawed it, or legalized it only with reluctance, the point must be made from the start that its taxation cannot be separated wholly from its legalization and regulation. The history of governments' policies towards gambling suggests that most societies cannot tolerate legalization of gambling without its regulation. So, while it is not the purpose of the present chapter to discuss aspects of the regulation of gambling, it will be important in applying norms of welfare economics to gambling taxation to recall that taxation is inextricably bound up with legalization and regulation.

As one chapter in a volume examining various aspects of excise taxation, the present chapter addresses the taxation of gambling. But not all the revenue-raising devices associated with gambling are strictly excise taxes, although most serve the same function. For that reason, this chapter considers not only conventionally defined excise taxes (levied on expenditures by betters or on receipts by operators) but also the profits made by government-operated gambling. By conventional public accounting standards, such profits are not strictly taxes. But since they serve essentially the same function, they are referred to in the present chapter as implicit taxes.[1] These distinctions are discussed at greater length in this chapter.

[*] The author is grateful to Eugene Martin Christiansen, Philip Cook, François Vaillancourt, Leighton Vaughan Williams, and two anonymous referees for helpful comments on an earlier draft, and to Abiskar Mitra and Jason DeRousie for research assistance.

By way of introduction, it is worth distinguishing four classes of gambling. The first, arguably the most important, and, in any case, the only one that is taxable is commercial gambling. As commonly used, this term includes all legal forms of gambling undertaken by organized firms or governments. It includes, for example, privately operated casinos, government-operated lotteries, and the organized gambling offered on Indian reservations in North America. In all cases of which I am aware, these forms of commercial gambling are subject to taxation or implicit taxation. A second form of gambling is that conducted by charitable or other public-service organizations. Often regulated but typically not taxed, the proceeds of such charitable gaming may be difficult to separate from taxation, as is noted below. A third form of gambling is informal, consisting of bets between individuals. Not only can such wagering not be easily regulated, but also few governments believe it to be anything that ought to be regulated or otherwise attended to. In contrast, governments do worry about the fourth category of gambling – the organized gambling operations that are conducted in violation of government restrictions. While it raises no more revenue than informal gambling, illegal gambling is very much a consideration to policy-makers when deciding questions related to the regulation and taxation of legal commercial gambling.

Gambling is practised all over the world, and in most of the world at least some form of it is legal. The ancient Egyptians, Chinese, Persians, Greeks, and Romans gambled, and this popularity has continued into modern times. Francis I of France authorized a lottery in 1638, the Republic of Venice legalized casinos beginning in 1638, and Napoleon legalized gambling clubs in 1806, which raised millions of francs in the early nineteenth century. As an instrument of public finance, gambling has been used to finance many projects in modern times, among them a bridge over the Seine in the sixteenth century and the Continental Army of the American Revolution in the eighteenth (France, 1901, pp. 2–4; Barnhart, 1997, p. 451; Barnhart, 1991, p. 541; Ezell, 1960, pp. 2–3). In its contemporary forms, gambling has grown in recent decades, with new forms being legalized in many countries and rates of participation rising where gambling has been established.

Gambling taxes bear several similarities to two other common excise taxes – those on tobacco and alcohol. All three of these forms of excise taxation have been used through much of modern history to raise revenue for governments at all levels. Besides their pragmatic value as sources of public revenue, all of these taxes at some time have been justified as 'sumptuary' taxes, designed in part for the same reason as the sumptuary laws of ancient Greece, to discourage forms of consumption that are not favoured by public opinion. To some extent, the structures of the excise taxes applying to gambling are comparable to those used for tobacco and alcohol taxation. Each commodity comes in different forms, and taxing authorities have chosen to tax the various forms differently, employing a mix of unit and *ad valorem* taxes. Yet gambling beats the other two by far in terms of variety of form and institutional detail. As a result, gambling taxes are unusually complex, making it important to devote attention to matters of tax structure in an assessment such as the present one. Accordingly, the chapter unapologetically takes as one of its principal aims to offer a description of current structures for the taxation of gambling. As the subsequent pages will illustrate, however, the present chapter can claim only limited success in explaining these complexities.

The purpose of this chapter is to consider the taxation of gambling as a whole, describing the ways that gambling is taxed and offering an economic assessment of such taxation. Section 4.2 provides an overview of commercial gambling as it is practised today, with some description of the variety of games, or products, that are available for taxation. Section 4.3 examines some of the institutional detail involved in the taxation of gambling, noting differences among countries in the structure of taxes employed. Because the rules, operation, and institutional structures differ widely across the various forms of gambling and across countries, it will become evident that the structure of gambling taxes cannot be summarized simply. The next three sections of the chapter employ traditional normative constructs of public finance to evaluate gambling taxes. Section 4.4 focuses on efficiency aspects; Section 4.5 applies the conventional criteria of tax equity, citing evidence on the incidence of gambling taxation and the distributional consequences of earmarking gambling revenues; and Section 4.6 notes two other related normative criteria, concerning the adequacy of gambling taxation to raise revenue and the stability of such revenues. Section 4.7 reflects on the political economy of gambling taxation. The chapter ends with a brief concluding section.

4.2 THE DIVERSITY OF COMMERCIAL GAMBLING

Illustrating both the reach and diversity of commercial gambling around the world, Table 4.1 shows the geographical coverage of various forms of gambling by continent in 1996. Measuring prevalence simply by the number of countries in which each game is legally operated at least somewhere in the country, it shows that gambling is virtually a worldwide phenomenon. The most widespread product is lotteries, which were legally available in 102 of the 128 countries that had any form of legal gambling (though, to be sure, gambling was not necessarily legal in every part of those 102 countries). Virtually every country in Europe and the Americas had some form of lottery. (Separate figures are given for several specific lottery products, including instant scratch-off games, lotto and numbers, and football pools.) Casinos were legal in almost as many countries (ninety-four), although they would be found in far fewer locations than lottery outlets. Next most common were slot machines, horse racing, at the track and in off-track locations, and bingo. The remaining forms of gambling shown were all relatively uncommon. There were, in addition, other forms of commercial gambling not recorded in the table, among them betting on boat and bicycle races. As a whole, the table demonstrates two relevant facts about gambling as a potential tax base. First, it is a source available to most governments. Secondly, because the products themselves

Table 4.1. *Types of Legal Gambling, Worldwide, 1996*

	Africa	Asia / Oceania	Europe	North America	South and Central America, Caribbean	World
Number of countries						
Total	48	62	43	3	32	188
With any legal gambling	34	31	29	3	31	128
Number of countries with:						
Lotteries						
General	22	21	28	3	28	102
Instant	18	15	25	3	19	80
Lotto/Numbers	13	11	26	3	15	68
Toto/Football pools	13	8	23	3	12	59
Casinos	27	15	25	2	25	94
Slot machines	19	11	25	2	22	79
Racing						
Horse	14	16	23	3	19	75
Greyhound	0	4	7	2	2	15
Off-track betting	7	10	20	3	12	52
Bingo	4	6	11	2	23	46
Cock fighting	0	2	1	1	12	16
Jai alai	0	1	1	2	0	4

Sources: McQueen, 1996; www.worldatlas.com/cntycont.htm, visited on 6 May 2002.

differ so much, as do the institutions that deliver them, no single formula for taxation can be applied to all of them. In order to assess gambling taxes, it is necessary first to have some understanding of the similarities and differences among the principal commercial games.

4.2.1 *The Leading Games*

Lotteries

As shown in Table 4.1, lotteries are the most widespread form of commercial gambling in the world. Lotteries offer several main products, which differ in probability of winning, prize structure, frequency of drawings, and the sense of 'player participation'. Instant or scratch-off games are tickets with thin coverings that, once scratched off, reveal what prize, if any, the purchaser has won. Lotto requires players to predict a set of winning numbers out of a larger set of possibilities; to win the French 6/49 lotto, for example, a player would have to predict which six numbers out of forty-nine will be drawn. Owing to its long odds, large number of players, and the accumulation of grand prize 'jackpots' when there is no winner, lotto has produced a few prizes in the hundreds of millions of dollars.[2] In some countries, winners are determined by the outcomes of sporting events, but such pools are effectively random drawings.

The traditional British football pool, for example, was based on a better's success in predicting which eight soccer matches, out of a total of fifty, would end in ties (not including scoreless ties) (Forrest, 1999). Owing to the nature of the sport and the high number of independent matches, this game is akin to a random draw.[3] In Germany, another variant of football pools is operated by government lottery agencies as pari-mutuel pools (Albers and Hubl, 1997, p. 127). Lotteries also offer games based on the illegal daily numbers game, on the casino game keno, and on traditional raffles (the so-called passive lottery). Lotteries generate net profits because they award in prizes only a portion of the gross amount wagered on tickets.[4]

Essentials of Lottery Finance

To illustrate the essentials of lottery finance, Table 4.2 displays for the thirty-eight state lotteries in the USA their sales, revenues, distribution of revenues, and importance of the implicit tax in state revenue. On average, the US state lotteries in the fiscal year ending in 2000 (FY2000) paid out 56 cents in prizes for each dollar of gross sales. Lottery agencies have gradually increased this 'payout rate' in recent years in an effort to increase sales. After subtracting commissions and other operating expenses, the lottery agencies ended up making a profit of about 32 cents per dollar. Depending on the level of lottery sales, this very healthy profit rate has the potential to raise sizeable funds for state governments. In FY2000, the revenue raised amounted to some 1.4 per cent of total own-source revenue for the states.

A key factor in the potential importance of lotteries as a public finance instrument is obviously the level of lottery purchases. In FY2000, per capita lottery sales in the USA were $144, based on the population of lottery states, or $127, based on the entire US population.[5] To be sure, since tickets may be purchased by residents of non-lottery states or by foreign nationals, any calculation of per capita sales can only be approximate. To see how this level of demand compares internationally, Table 4.3 presents worldwide data on lottery sales. Based on sales data collected on eighty-six countries with lotteries, it shows a wide variation by continent, ranging from $106 per capita in North America to just $2 in Africa. Per capita sales are sizeable in many developed countries, as illustrated by the selected countries listed. While lotteries are widespread, therefore, the intensity of lottery play is quite uneven. In an analysis of international lottery sales data for 1999, Garrett (2001, table 1) shows that, as a share of GDP, lottery sales were much lower in Africa (0.10 per cent) and Asia (0.21 per cent) than in the Americas (0.50 per cent), Europe (0.55 per cent), and Australia and New Zealand (0.57 per cent).

Casinos

If lotteries are the gambling game of the masses, the casino – at least in popular imagination – is the venue for the tuxedo and evening dress elite. While this

Table 4.2. *Lottery Sales, Expenses, and Government Revenue: US States, FY2000*[a]

State	Sales ($m)[b]	Sales per capita ($)	Revenue ($m)[c]	As percentage of sales			Lottery revenues as percentage of state own-source revenue
				Prizes	Operating expenses	Revenue	
Arizona	255.6	50	75.6	53.8	16.6	29.6	0.7
California	2,598.4	77	885.8	52.7	13.2	34.1	0.7
Colorado	371.0	86	87.5	60.3	16.1	23.6	0.8
Connecticut	837.5	246	255.9	60.0	9.4	30.6	1.9
Delaware	102.5	131	32.8	49.9	18.2	31.9	0.9
DC	215.8	377	67.8	52.3	16.3	31.4	1.9
Florida	2,248.5	141	889.5	49.2	11.2	39.6	2.2
Georgia	2,313.6	283	672.1	58.8	12.1	29.1	3.1
Idaho	86.5	67	17.6	58.9	20.7	20.4	0.5
Illinois	1,466.5	118	507.6	54.5	10.9	34.6	1.5
Indiana	582.5	96	161.8	57.8	14.4	27.8	1.1
Iowa	178.2	61	43.7	55.2	20.3	24.5	0.5
Kansas	192.6	72	55.8	54.2	16.8	29.0	0.8
Kentucky	583.7	144	160.2	58.6	14.0	27.4	1.2
Louisiana	276.4	62	96.6	50.2	14.9	34.9	0.7
Maine	147.9	116	38.2	58.9	15.3	25.8	0.9
Maryland	1,172.9	221	406.7	56.0	9.3	34.7	2.6
Massachusetts	3,691.6	581	829.2	70.0	7.6	22.5	3.7
Michigan	1,694.8	171	572.1	54.3	11.9	33.8	1.5
Minnesota	397.3	81	83.4	60.8	18.2	21.0	0.4
Missouri	507.8	91	152.3	55.2	14.8	30.0	1.0
Montana	29.9	33	5.7	52.1	28.7	19.2	0.2
Nebraska	68.2	40	15.1	54.1	23.8	22.1	0.4
New Hampshire	190.9	155	58.2	56.9	12.6	30.5	2.0
New Jersey	1,838.8	219	695.9	53.8	8.3	37.8	2.2
New Mexico	110.8	61	24.1	56.3	21.9	21.8	0.4
New York	3,629.3	191	1,445.6	48.7	11.4	39.8	2.0
Ohio	2,150.4	189	636.6	59.3	11.1	29.6	1.5
Oregon	323.7	95	55.9	65.0	17.7	17.3	0.5
Pennsylvania	1,686.8	137	650.9	51.5	9.9	38.6	1.7
Rhode Island	193.3	184	51.6	59.3	14.0	26.7	1.2
South Dakota	23.6	31	4.6	55.5	24.9	19.5	0.2
Texas	2,657.3	127	838.9	56.8	11.6	31.6	1.5
Vermont	75.0	123	19.2	62.4	12.1	25.5	0.9
Virginia	973.0	137	313.3	55.2	12.6	32.2	1.4
Washington	452.8	77	100.1	64.0	13.9	22.1	0.4
West Virginia	164.8	91	41.2	57.6	17.4	25.0	0.7
Wisconsin	406.7	76	114.9	57.1	14.6	28.2	0.5
Total	34,896.7	144	11,163.9	56.4	11.6	32.0	1.4

[a] Data are for the fiscal year ending in 2000, except for own-source revenue which is for 1999 (1998 for DC).

[b] Excludes video lottery terminals.

[c] Revenue calculated as Sales – Prizes – Operating expenses. Due to accounting practices, this may differ from reported revenue. For all states, total reported revenue was $11,186 million.

Sources: McQueen, 2001*a*, table 1; state own-source revenues – US Census Bureau, *Statistical Abstract of the United States: 2001*, tables 428 and 437.

Table 4.3. *Per Capita Lottery Sales, by Continent and Selected Countries, 2000*

	Per capita sales (US$)	Number of countries
Continents and world		
Africa	2	16
Asia /Middle East	10	11
Oceania	95	2
Europe	71	39
Central /South America	10	13
North America	106	5
World	35	86
Selected countries		
Japan	68	
Malaysia	78	
Australia	100	
New Zealand	74	
Belgium	93	
France	101	
Germany	110	
Italy	168	
Netherlands	63	
Sweden	207	
UK	135	
Argentina	24	
Mexico	7	
Canada	177	

Sources: McQueen, 2001*b*; *population* – *CIA World Factbook*, www.cia.gov/cia/publications/factbook/index.html; author's calculations.

elitist image has been democratized through the spread of the traditional casino table games and slot machines to new locations, including river boats and Indian reservations, it remains the fact that casinos are not as widely accessible to the general population as lotteries. Although many are private, casinos may be owned, and in some cases operated, by governments. Governments raise revenues from casinos in much the same way regardless of ownership and operation, however. Most commonly, casinos are taxed on their gross revenue (money taken in by the casino after prizes are paid out), sometimes under a progressive rate structure. A separate set of taxes may be levied on slot machines and other electronic gaming machines; these taxes are often levied simply as a per-machine licence fee, with the rate sometimes a function of the top possible prize.

To illustrate the variety of operating levels among countries, Table 4.4 shows the number of casinos operating in European countries as of 1998 and the gross gaming revenue they generated per capita. These per capita figures suggest that the reach and importance of casinos are less than those of lotteries, but nonetheless sufficient to generate large gross revenues in the aggregate. In

Table 4.4. *European Casinos: Numbers and Gross Revenue per Capita, 1998*

Country	Number of casinos[a]			Gross gaming revenue per capita (US$)[a, b]
	State-run	Privately owned	Total casinos	
Austria	0	12	12	28
Belgium	0	8	8	4
Czech Republic	0	51	51	25
Denmark	0	6	6	4
France	0	163	163	31
Germany	34	14	48	11
Great Britain	0	116	116	13
Greece	2	7	9	28
Netherlands	12	0	12	23
Hungary	11	9	20	3
Italy	4	0	4	7
Poland	0	34	34	1
Portugal	0	8	8	20
Spain	3	26	29	6
Switzerland	0	24	24	33

[a] *International Gaming and Wagering Business*, 2000.

[b] Author's calculations; exchange rates – OECD, www.oecd.org/xls/M00023000/M00023777.xls; population—*CIA World Factbook*, www.cia.gov/cia/publications/factbook/index.html.

1998, the gross revenues from casinos in the fifteen European countries listed amounted to $5.9 billion (*International Gaming and Wagering Business*, 2000). Significantly, casinos have experienced substantial growth in recent years. In the USA, where casinos could be found in only one state as late as 1976, they operate in twenty-eight states today, counting casinos operated by Native American tribes (Volberg, 2001, p. 24). In France, the number of casinos grew by 20 per cent between 1990 and 1999 and casino gross revenues increased from FF 1.25 billion to FF 9.4 billion[6] over the same period, an increase largely due to slot machines (*The Economist*, 1999).

Other Forms of Gambling

Of the remaining forms of commercial gambling, three are worth special mention, particularly for readers who are not themselves regular participants. First, betting on horse racing is a time-honoured form of gambling. Similar forms of betting apply to greyhound racing, boat racing, and jai alai and may occur at the track or event or at remote betting sites. Most typically, wagering takes the form of pari-mutuel betting, whereby the pay-off to a bet is determined by the distribution of wagers. Less often, fixed odds are offered, guaranteeing certain pay-offs to winning bets. Under either of these payout approaches, the operator makes money by arranging that the amounts paid out to winners will usually be less than the gross amount wagered.

A second form to be distinguished is gaming machines, which include traditional slot machines as well as newer generations of electronic machines, known variously as electronic gaming machines (EGMs), video poker machines, video lottery terminals (VLTs), and AWPs (amusement machines with limited money prizes) (Albers and Hubl, 1997, p. 127). These machines typically offer electronic versions of poker, bingo, blackjack, keno, or traditional 'reel' games from slot machines (Volberg, 2001, p. 58). Found in pubs, clubs, hotels, and amusement arcades as well as in casinos, these machines feature a small cost per bet, instantaneous winning or losing, the chance to win a prize many times the size of the cost of a single play, a high ratio of winnings to cost per play (payout rate), and the opportunity to recycle or 'reinvest' winnings into subsequent play. Largely because of the immediacy of pay-offs, these games are thought to have high potential for aggravating problem gambling.[7] Probably because of the administrative difficulty of keeping track of amounts taken in and paid out by such machines, most taxing authorities choose to tax such machines by means of per-machine licence taxes.

The third form that deserves particular note is sports betting. The form of sports betting that actually merits the term is that conducted through bookmakers. Seeking to profit by balancing betters on both sides of a contest, bookmakers set odds or point spreads to allow themselves to walk away with a small portion of the total amount bet as profit. Bookmaking on sporting events is legal in a few places, such as the UK and Nevada in the USA, but sports organizations generally oppose legalizing bookmaking because of the dangers of corrupting players. As noted above, sports pools are really lotteries dressed up with an inconsequential sports connection.

4.2.2 *Gross Wager or Gross Revenue?*

For a study of taxation of gambling, it would be highly desirable to have a comparable measure of gambling activity that could be used to compare magnitudes across types of gambling. Two candidates for measuring gambling activity are gross wager and gross revenue. *Gross wager* (also referred to as *turnover*, *sales*, or *handle*) is the total amount of bets placed. Since much of this amount is returned to betters as winnings, sometimes right away, this amount is thought to overstate what would be thought of as consumer expenditure. Johnson (1985) argues that a better measure of expenditure is *gross revenue*, which is gross wager minus prizes, in some games referred to as *net takings* or *player loss*. For many forms of gambling, gross revenue does come closest to approximating consumer expenditure and thus parallels the base for other excise taxes.

However, a case can be made that gross revenue does not do equal justice to all forms of gambling, as I argue below. In the case of US lotteries, portrayed in Table 4.2, gross wager was $34.9 billion in FY2000. Subtracting prizes of $19.7 billion yielded $15.2 billion as gross revenue. These figures imply that the average payout rate (prizes as a percentage of gross wager) for US lotteries was 56 per cent. Subtracting operating expenses of $4.1 billion yielded net revenue collected by state governments of $11.2 billion (after rounding). To show how gross revenues can be used to compare gambling magnitudes, Table 4.5 gives estimates for all forms of commercial gambling in the USA for 1982 and 2000. Looking only at 2000, the table indicates that casinos and lotteries were by far the most important forms of gambling, exceeding gambling on Indian reservations and vastly overshadowing horse racing, bingo, and bookmaking. The table also shows the average percentage of gross wager in each form of gambling that was retained by the provider in 1996. For example, casinos kept an average of 4.4 per cent of the total amount wagered, whereas traditional lotteries kept 45.2 per cent. The table also reflects impressive growth in commercial gambling in the USA, with gross revenues in constant dollars increasing at an impressive annual rate of 6.8 per cent over the eighteen-year period.

Despite the attraction of using a single concept – gross revenue – to compare all gambling activity, I believe it is not as good a measure of consumer spending for lotteries as it is for other games, such as slot machines and casino table games. Inherent in table games and slot machines is a pattern of play wherein winnings are often 'reinvested' in the form of new wagers on succeeding rounds of betting.[8] The total amount a better leaves in the casino after a session – gross revenue for the casino – is indeed a fair expression of that better's expenditure. For most lottery games, including lotto, daily numbers games, and the older raffle-type passive draw lotteries, $10 spent on tickets is really just that, and represents $10 not saved or spent on other goods or services. Should a prize be won, it will happen at another time and place and be more akin to income than to winnings subject to 'reinvestment'. The prize, in effect, is just one attribute of lotteries as a consumer expenditure. Consumer expenditure on the game is the amount typically left at the counter when the tickets are purchased, not the expected loss. For this reason, gross wager seems a better measure of lottery play than gross revenue.

4.3 HOW GAMBLING IS TAXED

One manifestation of the diversity in gambling forms is that there is a plenitude of portals through which government may enter in order to extract revenue. In an effort to achieve as much precision as possible, this section specifies what is reasonable to study under the heading of gambling taxation. As a companion question, it considers how to define the rate of taxation. Next, the institutional variety in gambling taxation is illustrated by looking in detail at the taxes used in several countries.

4.3.1 *What Is a Gambling Tax?*

It is possible to distinguish at least three generic means of collecting revenues from gambling. First are excise taxes, whose form may be quite similar to those

Table 4.5 *Gross Revenues and Taxes, by Type of Gambling: USA*

	Gross revenue, 1982 ($m)[a]	Gross revenue, 2000 ($m)[b]	Percentage retained, 1996[c]	Gross revenue, 1982, in 2000 dollars ($m)[d]	Growth rate of gross revenue, 1982–2000 (%)[e]
Pari-mutuels					
Horse total	2,250.0	3,338.9	21.0	4,015.0	−1.0
Greyhound total	430.0	457.1	21.8	767.3	−2.9
Jai alai total	112.0	46.6	22.7	199.9	−8.1
Total pari-mutuels	2,792.0	3,842.5	21.1	4,982.2	−1.4
Lotteries					
Video lotteries	0.0	1,657.0	9.8	0.0	
Traditional games	2,170.0	15,558.7	45.2	3,872.3	7.7
Total lotteries	2,170.0	17,215.6	37.8	3,872.3	8.3
Casinos					
Nevada /NJ slot machines	2,000.0	9,146.9	5.7	3,568.9	5.2
Nevada /NJ table games	2,200.0	4,407.6	2.1	3,925.8	0.6
River boats and cruise ships	0.0	9,634.3	19.5	0.0	
Other land-based casinos	0.0	1,428.0	5.9	0.0	
Other commercial gambling	0.0	171.0	36.4	0.0	
Non-casino devices	0.0	1,558.2	10.3	0.0	
Total casinos	4,200.0	26,346.0	4.4	7,494.7	7.0
Legal bookmaking					
Sports books	7.7	123.8	3.1	13.7	12.2
Horse books	18.0	6.8	7.7	32.1	−8.6
Total bookmaking	25.8	130.6	3.3	46.0	5.8
Card rooms	50.0	949.3	6.9	89.2	13.1
Charitable bingo	780.0	994.2	23.6	1,391.9	−1.9
Charitable games	396.0	1,483.8	26.0	706.6	4.1
Indian reservations					
Class II	0.0	1,198.1	30.0	0.0	
Class III	0.0	9,238.5	7.5	0.0	
Total Indian reservations	0.0	10,436.6	8.2	0.0	
Internet gambling	0.0	2,207.5	0.0	0.0	
Grand total	10,413.8	63,606.1	7.7	18,583.0	6.8

[a] Christiansen, 1998, table 2.

[b] Christiansen and Sinclair, 2001.

[c] Christiansen, 1998, table 1.

[d] Consumer price index (CPI-U) in 1982 and 2000, respectively, was 96.5 and 172.2.

[e] Exponential growth rate: $100 \times \ln[(\text{gross revenue } 2000)/(\text{gross revenue } 1982 \text{ in } 2000 \text{ dollars})]/18$.

imposed on alcohol, tobacco, road fuel, and other items of consumption. Taxes on admissions into gambling establishments or on gross revenue received by casinos would fall into this category. So, too, would special taxes on the net revenue of gambling establishments, though they would have the form of business income taxes. It would also be reasonable to count as excises the licence fees that are levied on establishments or individual gaming machines, although these may have the form of a property tax. Excises should also cover other negotiated payments from operators of commercial gambling to governments, such as the agreed-upon payments of Indian tribes to US state governments.

A second important category counted in the present chapter as gambling taxation is the profit from government-run or government-sanctioned gambling enterprises. The most prominent example here is lotteries, operated in the USA and Canada exclusively by government or quasi-government units but also by private companies elsewhere. The government derives revenue by using its monopoly position to sell lottery products at a profit. After paying the costs of running the lottery (prizes, commissions paid to retail outlets, and other operating costs), the government keeps the rest. Though not a tax by the usual definition (and not counted, for example, in OECD statistics on gambling taxes), this source of revenue looks and acts in every other way just like a tax. I refer to this form of revenue as an implicit tax.[9] Counted here also are the moneys devoted to 'good causes' in the UK national lottery. Because the allocation of these funds is done through public but non-governmental entities, the funds themselves are tantamount to a tax expenditure, if not a direct government expenditure because it is authorized by government. It therefore seems logical to count these allocated profits as implicit taxes, just as with funds earmarked for categories of government expenditure.

A third category of revenue that one might want to count as a gambling tax is the income tax that in some countries is placed on winnings. From the perspective of a well-conceived income tax, it is perfectly justifiable to tax gambling winnings (net of gambling losses and other expenses). But, since the opposite policy – to exempt gambling winnings – also seems defensible, the decision to tax them can be viewed as a part of the overall tax on gambling. On balance, I believe the argument for so counting this tax is the stronger. In practice, however, I can do no more than to guess at how large this amount may be.

4.3.2 *Tax Rate, Base, and Revenue*

As stated in the various laws covering gambling taxes, the rates of taxation present no particular conceptual problem. They can be stated with precision, along with their associated tax bases. It is only in the attempt to compare rates of taxation – between types of gambling or between gambling and other types of excise taxation – that ambiguity creeps in. The source of the ambiguity is the question noted above as to whether gross wager (the total amount bet) or gross revenue (the amount betters lose) is the better measure of gambling activity. For forms of gambling that involve repeated bets during a single betting session, such as gaming machines, gross revenue seems a much better measure than gross wager. But for the important case of lotteries, the total amount spent – gross wager – seems to approximate consumer expenditure better.

To illustrate the importance of the choice of base, consider the estimated tax rates calculated by Australia's Productivity Commission (1999, p. 19.17). Expressed as *ad valorem* rates as a percentage of tax-exclusive expenditures, the Commission calculated an average tax rate for casino games of 26 per cent. (Taxes were 21 per cent of gross revenues, thus 26 per cent of gross revenues exclusive of taxes.) By comparison, the commission's calculated rates were 42 per cent for gaming machines and 52 per cent for wagers on races, compared with 89 per cent for beer and 211 per cent for tobacco, rates that imply that taxes constituted 47 per cent of the tax-inclusive price of beer and 68 per cent of the gross price of tobacco. Using this same approach for lotteries, however, the commission calculated a tax rate of 455 per cent. Although the details of that calculation are not available, it would be consistent with a breakdown per dollar of sales of something like 45 per cent for prizes, 10 per cent for operating expenses, and 45 per cent for government revenue (45/10 ≈ 455%). A more reasonable calculation of the *ad valorem* tax rate for this case is 82 per cent (45/ 55), since 55 cents per dollar would be the cost of providing the product that was bought for a dollar. This is still a high rate of tax, but it is more comparable to *ad valorem* rates as usually stated.

A comparison based on twenty-one developed countries is presented in Table 4.7. Using revenue statistics from the OECD, the table summarizes tax revenue derived from gambling. In judging the revenue importance of those gambling revenues in federal countries, it is obviously necessary to note what level of government receives the revenues. Unfortunately, these data do not cover all of the major sources of revenue from gambling. In particular, they omit profits generated by government-operated gambling enterprises, including state and provincial lotteries and state-run casinos. As a result, the implied per capita government revenue figures are clearly too low for some countries. For the USA, per capita revenue from state lotteries alone was about $46 in FY2000 (since per capita lottery sales were $144 and about 32 per cent of lottery sales went to state governments, as given in Table 4.2). Thus the actual per capita figure would be at least $60. Similarly, Canada's lotteries were not counted in the OECD numbers. By contrast, the per capita figure given for the UK is higher than that in Table 4.6, but at least it appears that the OECD figure includes lottery revenues, since the UK national lottery is operated by a private company. Despite the deficiencies with these data, they are the only cross-national comparison of gambling tax revenues. Table 4.7 presents a comparison based on these data. The table suggests considerable variation in gambling taxes across these OECD countries, with Italy and Finland joining Australia as countries that rely on gambling taxes as a sizeable source of revenue.

Box 4.1. *Specifics of Gambling Taxation: Examples from Four Countries*

The institutional detail of gambling taxation can best be illustrated by describing specific taxes in four countries. Although the following descriptions are simplified, they illustrate the diversity and complexity of actual tax structures.

UK

The UK's biggest source of gambling revenue is its national lottery, which has operated only since 1994. Operated by a private corporation, the lottery transfers about 30 per cent of its sales in mandated allocations to eleven quasi-public bodies that make grants to 'good causes'.[a] As noted above, these allocations are most usefully viewed as an implicit tax, as is the case with the state and provincial lotteries whose net revenues are earmarked for certain government expenditures. In 1999, the allocations to 'good causes' amounted to almost half of Britain's reported revenues from gambling (OECD, 2001a, p. 173). In addition to these allocations, the government also levied a tax on lottery sales – some 12 per cent – which accounted for roughly another fifth of total gambling revenues.[b]

The remaining gambling revenues came from an assortment of five betting and gaming duties. Most significant among these was the general betting duty, levied at a rate of 6.75 per cent on gross wagers on bookmaking, horse racing, and greyhound racing. This tax has recently been replaced, however, by a 15 per cent tax on gross revenue, a change that was taken in part to encourage offshore bookmakers to relocate to the UK.[c] Slot machines, video lottery machines, and other gaming machines were subject to an annual per-machine tax, according to a schedule based on the size of prizes offered. (A machine in the highest class was assessed a tax of £1,815[d] a year (HM Customs and Excise, 2002). In addition, VAT was assessed on the gross revenue from each machine (*International Gaming and Wagering Business*, 2000, p. 14).) Casinos were taxed on gross revenues according to a progressive rate schedule. Bingo was taxed at 10 per cent of gross wagers plus an additional percentage of prizes over a threshold. Football pools were taxed at a rate of 17.5 per cent of gross wager (net of any charitable contributions stated as part of the cost of betting). Although this brief description omits numerous details applying to the actual administration of these taxes, it is sufficient to give a sense of the variety of the taxes applied, each tax designed to fit the peculiar institutional arrangements for each type of gambling.

USA

Most gambling taxation in the USA is done by state governments. The biggest source is the state lotteries, which together yielded revenues of $11.2 billion in FY2000, as shown in Table 4.2. Much more complicated and variegated is the taxation of casinos, which are subject to a variety of taxes and tax rates in the eleven states where they operate. In 1998, those eleven states collected some $3 billion in taxes from casinos, exclusive of corporation income taxes, sales taxes, property taxes, and revenues from casinos operated by Native American tribes. Over three-quarters of this amount was in the form of taxes on gross revenues. Some states also taxed admissions and levied per-machine taxes on slot machines. For example, Nevada levied a graduated tax on the gross revenue of casinos, topping out at 6.25 per cent of gross revenues exceeding $134,000 per month. It also assessed an annual tax of $250 per slot machine and a 10 per cent tax on casino entertainment. By contrast, Indiana levied a flat 10 per cent tax on gross revenues plus a $3 per patron admissions tax for each cruise on its river-boat casinos. Further complicating the casino taxation picture are the arrangements that states have made with Native American tribes (Madhusudhan, 1999).

To illustrate the other forms of gambling taxes in the USA, including arrangements with Native American tribes, consider the case of Connecticut. In 1996, that state taxed pari-mutuel betting, covering greyhound racing and jai alai, on a sliding scale of 2–4 per cent of gross wagers.[e] Off-track betting was subject to a 3.5 per cent tax on gross wagers. According to an agreement with two Native American tribes, the state collected 25 per cent of the gross revenues from gaming machines in the tribes' two casinos.[f] Connecticut also raised some tax revenue through the taxation of charitable gambling. It taxed charitable bingo at a rate of 5 per cent of gross revenue, and pull-tab tickets were taxed at 10 per cent of the purchase price. No tax was levied on raffles, bazaars, and 'Las Vegas nights' run for charitable purposes (WEFA Group, 1997, pp. 1-19–1-20). The USA had one federal gambling excise tax, a minuscule 0.25 per cent tax on betting on sporting events. It also subjected gambling winnings to federal personal income tax, which increased the tax burden on lotteries from 47 to perhaps 53 per cent.[g]

AUSTRALIA

Few countries rely more heavily upon gambling as a source of revenue than Australia, and this reliance has grown in recent years in the wake of the growing popularity of gambling in that country. As a percentage of states' own-source revenue, gambling taxes increased from 7.9 per cent in 1985/86 to 11.2 per cent in 1995/96 (Productivity Commission, 1999, p. 19.7). With legalized lotteries, poker machines, and horse racing all dating from before the Great Depression, Australia features a variety of well-established forms of commercial gambling subject to taxation (Productivity Commission, 1999, pp. 2.1–2.5). In fact, the taxes on gambling in Australia illustrate well a theme of the present chapter, that the structure of gambling taxation is quite complex. Not only do the forms of taxation differ by type of game, but also the tax rates and often the forms differ across states, which are the principal level of government that imposes these taxes. The rates are often differentiated according to the type of operator. And some states return part of the revenues from some taxes to the gambling industry.

A brief listing of the main taxes exemplifies this complexity. Some state governments, including New South Wales, operate their own lotteries, while others tax the profits of a private lottery company, Tattersalls. Such taxes are levied at different rates for lotto, instant scratch-off games, and keno. A second important source of revenue is poker and other gaming machines, which are legal in all states except Queensland. They are taxed on gross wager (turnover) in some states and on gross revenue in others. Most states levy higher rates on machines in hotels than those in clubs. A racing tax, imposed in all the states on gross wager, is a third major source of gambling taxation. Amply illustrating the theme of complexity in structure, the rates levied differ not only by state but also by type of bet.[h] Casinos are a fourth source of taxation, with most states imposing licence fees, levied monthly, annually, or one time only. All states also impose taxes on casino income, usually defined as gross revenue, with the rates ranging from a simple 15 per cent (of gross revenue) in one state to graduated rate schedules elsewhere. Some states assess separate taxes on gaming machines in casinos. The game of keno, available in clubs or casinos, is subjected to separate tax schedules on gross wager in some states, some of which schedules feature graduated rates. Finally, a number of smaller gambling taxes are assessed in some states on various forms of gambling, including football pools, bets on Australian rules football and cricket, sweepstakes, and bingo.[i]

CANADA

As in the USA, the acceptance of commercial gambling in Canada was quite limited prior to the 1960s. Small charity raffles had been legal since 1900, and betting at racetracks had been legal since 1910. It was not until 1969 that provincial governments were allowed to operate lotteries, or to authorize charitable groups to do so. But since that time, provincial lotteries grew alongside US state lotteries. An interesting intergovernmental footnote is an agreement reached in 1985 whereby the Canadian federal government forswore lotteries as a means of raising revenue, in return for an annual payment from the provinces, amounting to $CAN54 million[j] in 1999/2000 (Campbell and Smith, 1998, p. 23; Azmier, 2001, p. 2). Casinos were also legalized along the way, all being owned by provincial governments and some of them also operated by them (Campbell and Smith, 1998, p. 31).

Government net revenue from gambling now comes from three principal, and roughly equal, sources: lotteries, casinos, and electronic gaming machines. In FY2000, these three forms yielded net revenues to government of $CAN5.6 billion,[k] or about 3.4 per cent of the provinces' own-source revenues. By province, the share of own-source revenue ranges from 5.1 per cent in Nova Scotia to 2.2 per cent in Prince Edward Island. By way of comparison, the provinces got slightly more ($CAN5.9 billion[l]) from all alcohol and tobacco taxes (Azmier, 2001, pp. 3–4). These levels suggest that Canada relies relatively heavily on gambling taxes. Gambling has grown rapidly in recent years, boosting its contribution to public revenues. Between 1992 and 2000, gross gambling revenues from the three major forms of gambling increased in real terms at a 13 per cent annual rate.[m]

A useful comparison of gambling taxation in three of these countries – Canada, the UK, and Australia – is given by Vaillancourt (1999), and this compilation is summarized in Table 4.6. It shows not only how the distribution of revenues differs by country but also how those distributions changed over the decade between 1985 and 1995. For Canada, the biggest change was the introduction of gaming machines. This plus the introduction of casinos had the effect of roughly doubling the importance of gambling revenues. For the UK, the biggest change was the introduction of its national lottery, which had the effect of increasing per capita betting and redistributing gambling activity and revenue away from other forms. As a share of total revenue, gambling held steady over this period. In Australia, where all the forms of gambling were established earliest, growth occurred in revenue from poker machines and casinos. As a share of state revenue, gambling is much more important in Australia than in Canada. Measured as revenue per capita in constant US dollars, gambling is shown to be most important in Australia, with per capita revenue of $136 in 1995, compared with $86 in Canada and $42 in the UK.

---

[a] These bodies include four arts councils, four sports councils, the National Heritage Memorial Fund, the National Lottery Charities Board, and the Millennium Commission (UK National Lottery, www.national-lottery.co.uk/news/index.html, visited on 22 January 2002).

[b] OECD (2000) reported gambling taxes of £1,514 million for financial year 2000. The lottery duty was 40 per cent of this total, and the general betting duty was 32 per cent (HM Customs and Excise, www.hmce.gov.uk/business/othertaxes/betting.htm, visited on 21 January 2002).

[c] Inland Revenue, www.inlandrevenue.gov.uk/budget2001/ce1.htm, visited on 22 January 2002.

[d] $US2,728 using £1 = $US1.503.

[e] Except for the Bridgeport Greyhound Track, which was subject to a flat 2 per cent tax rate (WEFA Group, 1997, pp. 1–14).

[f] If the amount collected was less than a specified amount, the agreement provided for rates up to 30 per cent (WEFA Group, 1997, pp. 1–21).

[g] If one-third of all winnings were effectively subject to taxation, by exceeding the threshold withholding amount, and the marginal tax rate for the winners averaged 20 per cent, the income tax on lottery purchases would have been $1.3 billion in 2000, adding an additional tax of 3.8 per cent on lottery sales. Without the income tax, the implicit tax rate was 47 per cent (32/68); with the tax on prizes, the total tax rate, under these assumptions, was 53 per cent (35.868).

[h] Separate rates apply to win/place, quinella, exacta, doubles, trifectas, and superfectas (Smith, 1998, pp. 103–4).

[i] For a detailed summary of Australian gambling taxes, see Smith (1998, pp. 103–9) and Productivity Commission (1998, appendix M).

[j] $US36 million using $US1 = $CAN1.49.

[k] $US3.8 billion using $US1 = $CAN1.49.

[l] $US4.0 billion using $US1 = $CAN1.49.

[m] Azmier (2001, p. 4) reports gross gambling profits of $CAN2,734 million and $CAN9,040 million in 1992 and 2000, respectively. Applying the Canadian consumer price index of 116.4 for 2000 (1992 = 100) puts the 1992 figure at $CAN3,182 million in 2000 dollars (Statistics Canada, web page, http://www.statcan.ca, visited on 6 February 2002).

Table 4.6. *Revenues from Gambling: Canada, UK, and Australia, 1985 and 1995*

	Canada		UK		Australia	
	1985	1995	1985	1995	1985	1995
Percentage of government revenues						
Lotteries	100.0	51.5	0.0	38.9	44.0	29.0
Pool betting	—	—	31.6	12.1	—	—
Casinos	0.0	19.7	—	—	2.0	11.0
Gaming machines[a]	0.0	28.8	11.6	6.8	16.0	38.0
General betting	—	—	42.6	31.1	—	—
Racing and other revenues	—	—	—	—	38.0	22.0
Bingo	—	—	6.8	5.8	—	—
Gambling licences	—	—	7.4	5.3	—	—
Total	100.0	100.0	100.0	100.0	100.0	100.0
Gambling revenue as percentage of GDP	0.20	0.44	0.21	0.22	0.45	0.68
Gambling revenue as percentage of:						
State or provincial revenue	0.93	2.00			9.70	10.90
National revenue			0.63	0.67		
Total gambling revenues (millions of 1995 US$)[b]	1,005	2,511	1,365	2,483	1,177	2,455
Population (million)[c]	25.8	29.4	56.7	58.6	16.0	18.1
Per capita revenue, 1995 (US$)	39	86	24	42	73	136

[a] Canada – video lotteries; UK – gambling machines; Australia – poker machines.

[b] Consumer price index (CPI-U): 1985=107.6; 1995=152.4.

[c] Canada – Statistics Canada, *Canada Year Book*, Ministry of Industry, Ottawa, 2001, table 3.2; UK – *Annual Abstract of Statistics*, 2001 edition, no. 137, The Stationery Office, London, 2001; Australia – Australian Bureau of Statistics, *Year Book Australia*, 1988, no. 71 and 1998, no. 80, ABS, Canberra, 1988 and 1998.

Sources: Vaillancourt, 1999, tables 1, 3, and 4; author's calculations.

4.4 EVALUATION: EFFICIENCY CONSIDERATIONS

Following conventional tax analysis, I apply two sets of considerations to the taxation of gambling – efficiency and equity. The current section first discusses gambling taxation within the standard excess burden model, noting the particular role of legalization in evaluating the efficiency of financing government through gambling and the implications of the theory of optimal commodity taxation in a second-best world. It then considers the importance of negative externalities in any evaluation of the rate of gambling taxation. The related concept of sumptuary taxation is also discussed. Thirdly, it discusses the administrative cost of raising money by way of legalized gambling.

4.4.1 *Excess Burden of Gambling Taxation*

The basic analysis of efficiency aspects of excise taxes on gambling parallels the textbook case for any commodity, with two complications. The first is the ambiguity regarding the proper definition of price and quantity. As noted above, since the major commercial forms of gambling differ significantly in such fundamental respects as prize structure, frequency of payouts, player participation, and payout rates, there is no fully satisfactory way to measure quantity, and therefore price, on any comparative basis. Two candidates for measuring quantity are the gross wager (turnover) and gross revenue (aggregate player losses). Neither concept is obviously right or wrong and, for most purposes, the choice is not at all crucial. For the purpose of analysing excess burden, the concepts may be illustrated well by adopting the first approach, in which gross wager is the measure of quantity demanded. It is then natural to think of quantity as measured by bets in dollar units. Price is simply the cost of this standard bet. This price is the sum of the marginal cost of providing the betting opportunity (the amount per dollar devoted to winnings plus the average cost of operations, including any retail commissions) plus the tax imposed. A demand curve for bets for this generic gambling product is shown in Figure 4.1, where m is the marginal cost per dollar bet. In line with conventional analysis, the rectangle $b(= (1 - m)q_1)$ represents the revenue raised (where $1 - m$ is the per-unit tax), and triangle c is the excess burden, assuming no other distortions exist. As in the usual case, this excess burden is greater the more elastic is demand.[10]

Besides the ambiguity in the definitions of price and quantity, a second complication that arises in assessing the excess burden of gambling taxation is the matter of legalization, an aspect that comes into consideration because taxation and legalization are bound together as a package deal. For most legal forms of commercial gambling, taxation was a condition of legalization. This is perhaps clearest for the case of government-operated lotteries. 'The lottery' is thus more than a tax; it is a state-produced good with a high (implicit) tax rate. Taken as a package, the legalization-cum-taxation creates consumer surplus, evidenced by the fact that people voluntarily play. The tax aspect of a lottery is

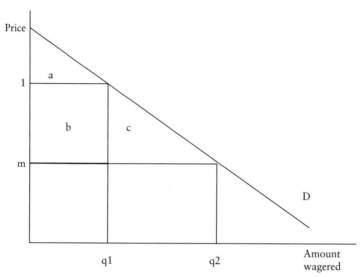

Figure 4.1. *Demand for Generic Gambling Product*

indeed, as its proponents like to say, a 'voluntary' tax, but it is no more voluntary than the tax on alcohol, tobacco, or movies – you don't pay the tax unless you buy the product. The same reasoning applies, of course, to river-boat casinos or poker machines. Thus, while it is proper to discuss the excess burden of the tax or the implicit tax on government-supplied gambling products, it must also be remembered that the *joint* policy of legalization-cum-taxation generally is *efficiency enhancing*, rather than the opposite. The fact that such benefits may be larger or smaller, depending on the government's choice of a tax rate, brings the discussion back into the conventional economic framework of tax analysis. That is, the implicit tax alone may be analysed just as an excise tax is, but only with the proviso that legalization is assumed as a precondition.

But what about the demand curves themselves? Welfare economics relies for much of its force on the information about individual well-being that is contained in demand curves; most individuals are assumed to have sufficient information so that their postulated utility-maximizing behaviour makes them better off. However, some individuals – notably, 'children and madmen' (Stokey and Zeckhauser, 1978, p. 263) – are excluded from this logic; for them, demand curves are not credited with this same welfare significance; these individuals are not assumed to know what is in their own best interest.

The models economists have developed include 'rational addiction' (Becker and Murphy, 1988), 'time-inconsistent preferences' (Gruber and Koszegi, 2002), and a behavioural model based on environmental cues and 'visceral states' (Bernheim and Rangel, 2002). To the extent that demand for gambling is driven by addictive behaviour – and evidence suggests that a small but significant share of gamblers are addicted in some way[11] – the revealed demand for gambling products overstates the social value of that consumption. One suggested approach, no doubt easier said than done, is to 'cleanse' demand curves of this addictive element.[12] Alternatively, legislatures can take on the same paternalistic role they do in dealing with 'merit wants' (Musgrave, 1959), such as education, and, in the tradition of the sumptuary laws of ancient Rome, increase the tax rate to discourage consumption. The justification would be similar to that for raising the tax rate on unhealthy products such as tobacco and alcohol.[13]

Various models of addiction also suggest their own optimal policy remedies. The rational addiction model, for example, implies taxing products subject to addiction only to the extent there are externalities (Gruber and Koszegi, 2002). In contrast, Gruber and Koszegi's time inconsistency model suggests higher tax rates for addictive goods even when there are no externalities. Bernheim and Rangel's (2002) behavioural model suggests that policy should be sensitive to the environmental cues leading addicted individuals to engage in unproductive behaviours; this suggests limitations on advertising.

Putting aside the efficiency-enhancing feature of the joint legalization–taxation policy, what can be said about the desirable rate of taxation? In the absence of externalities and other market failures, the economist naturally turns to the tenets of optimal commodity taxation, and looks to the Ramsey rule to assess commodity taxes in roughly inverse proportion to demand elasticities for the products.[14] To the extent that gambling products are subject to more inelastic demand, their rates ought to be higher. In practice, our empirical knowledge of the elasticity of demand for various gambling products is spotty at best, though what evidence exists suggests that these elasticities do differ (see, for example, Productivity Commission (1999, ch. 19)). Some games, such as daily numbers lottery draws or off-track betting, attract a dedicated, perhaps addicted, clientele, while other games, such as lotto, seem to have an appeal that varies over time and includes a changing set of players.

These considerations are further complicated by features of gambling that move the consideration of optimal taxation decidedly into a second-best world. Because leisure as a good cannot be taxed, the Corlett–Hague rule comes into play, mandating higher excise tax rates on commodities that are complements to leisure (Rosen, 1988, p. 320). Gambling products may well fall into this category, thus implying higher tax rates. However, a second important set of untaxed goods is also quite relevant: illegal gambling. Because they are quite similar to legal games (which is not accidental, since some legal games have been designed expressly to ape the illegal versions) and often easily accessible, high tax rates on legal games had the unhappy consequence of driving players to illegal games, losing tax revenue in the process. That governments are aware of this trade-off is illustrated well by US attempts to tax sports betting after the Second World War. Following a highly publicized scandal in which betters bribed players of the City College basketball team in the national championship, Congress in 1951 enacted a 10 per cent wagering excise tax on the amount bet on sporting events and lotteries (Public Law 183, Sec. 471, 20 October 1951). Worried that this tax was encouraging illegal betting, Congress reduced the rate to 2 per cent in 1974 and to 0.25 per cent in 1983 (Mason and Nelson, 2001, p. 86; Internal Revenue Code, Sec. 4401, 2001). Thus, in the case of gambling excise taxes, these optimal tax rules point in different directions.

4.4.2 *Social Costs and Sin*

Further complicating the assessment of the efficiency of gambling taxes are externalities that arise from gambling. Probably the most serious of these arises from the apparent social fact that there exist some individuals who are especially susceptible to the temptation to gamble excessively. Compulsive gamblers, their gambling stimulated by easy accessibility to opportunities to bet, may spend enormous amounts, driving themselves into bankruptcy, their families into hardship, and their personal relationships into ruin. They are estimated to be of the order of 1–2 per cent of the adult population in countries where surveys have been conducted. Other 'problem gamblers' constitute another 2–4 per cent (Azmier, 2001, p. 10; Volberg, 2001, p. 49). Together, these two groups appear to constitute a small but stubbornly resilient share of the adult population. Research on gambling by these groups suggests that the harmful effects can be mitigated through restrictions on types of games, conditions of play, and marketing,[15] but most experts would agree that legalization will inevitably make life worse for this small subset of the population. Accordingly, most governments that sponsor or allow gambling also provide services to help problem gamblers. This being an inevitable social cost associated with legalized gambling, the logic of Pigouvian taxation implies that gambling taxes reflect, in part, this cost. This justification for a higher rate of tax has parallels to taxes on alcohol and tobacco, although the magnitudes of the social costs arising from consuming those two products may be much larger than those associated with gambling.

A second category of social cost is less visible and probably less severe; it may even be illusory. Some commentators argue that the legalization of gambling, especially when it is endorsed and advertised by the government, may impose a cost to society by undercutting the educational function of government. Government, through its schools, laws, and public pronouncements, advocates certain beliefs, including the value of productive work. To the extent that the sponsorship and, particularly, the promotion of gambling undercut that traditional message, legalized gambling creates a second category of external costs.[16] By the same logic of Pigouvian taxation, these costs would imply higher gambling taxes. This justification is similar to the time-honoured argument for sumptuary laws and 'sin taxes'. Arising out of religious or moral disapproval, sumptuary laws dating from the ancient Greeks have been used to restrict or forbid certain kinds of consumption.[17]

One last form of external cost associated with legalized gambling is crime, specifically organized crime. Although government-operated lotteries do not appear to have attracted or stimulated organized crime activity, some other aspects of the gaming industry have. As with other aspects of social cost, the design and regulation of legalized games will have a major impact on the severity of social costs. But to the extent that these remain external, unbudgeted costs associated with legal gambling, optimal tax theory would imply that these, too, should be reflected in tax rates.

4.4.3 *Administrability*

Critics of state lotteries in the USA have often charged that lotteries are a very inefficient means of raising revenue, since it 'costs' around 68 cents to raise 32 cents in revenue. Clearly, this arithmetic misses the point that lotteries, like any form of gambling operated by the government, involve provision as well as taxation. In order to put the implicit taxes in such government-provided gambling enterprises on a par with taxes and other sources of revenue, it is necessary to isolate the taxation function. On this basis, government-run lotteries, like most of the gambling taxes described above, carry with them no unusual amounts of administrative overhead.

4.5 EQUITY CONSIDERATIONS

Traditionally, two principles have provided the basis for judging the equity of taxes: the benefit principle and the ability-to-pay principle. The benefit principle – that those who benefit from a tax ought to pay the tax – is relevant to gambling taxes in so far as the revenues are earmarked for certain expenditures. This point is discussed below.

4.5.1 *Equity According to the Ability-to-Pay Principle*

Vertical Equity

Of the two norms based on the ability-to-pay principle used in tax analysis, I take vertical equity to be relevant to the excise taxation of gambling. Horizontal equity – the equal treatment of equals – seems to be satisfied a priori, in that those who consume the taxed good are subject to the same taxes and tax rates. Except to the extent that tax regimes differ by jurisdiction, there is nothing in the administration of gambling taxes that would suggest the kind of discrimination implied by horizontal inequity. Gambling taxes may well be what some have called them – a tax on stupidity – and they may disproportionally take from those most susceptible to the urge to wager, but these differences among individuals do not appear to represent classifications on which horizontal equity should be judged, any more than the differences in tastes that cause other excise tax collections to differ among individuals. On the other hand, vertical equity – the differential taxation of individuals with different abilities to pay – is surely an important consideration, as demonstrated by the attention that distributional questions have received in the literature on gambling taxation.

Before considering what is known about the distributional patterns of gambling taxation, it is necessary to highlight once more what policy is being considered. If the analyst's aim is to determine the distributional effect of the joint policy of legalization and taxation for a particular form of gambling, then one will probably be in the business of determining the distribution of consumer surpluses, not excess burdens. Only if one aims to measure the distribution of the loss of consumer surplus occasioned by the imposition of the tax – *given the legalization* of the product – is the conventional tax incidence approach relevant. For most goods subject to excise taxation, the conventional approach is, of course, the correct approach to take; it also happens to be the approach that usually underlies most of the discussions of gambling tax incidence in policy and academic settings. However, since many forms of gambling now taxed have not been legal for long and in fact are not legal in many jurisdictions, and because gambling is typically legalized only on the condition that it will be taxed as well as regulated, it is by no means unreasonable to establish as the primary vertical equity question what the distributional impact is of the joint decisions to legalize and to tax. If the tax is found to be regressive, therefore, this implies that the joint legalize-and-tax decision must be pro-poor, rather than the reverse. In this context, therefore, 'regressivity' as conventionally measured becomes relevant only to the policy question of increasing or decreasing the tax on a form of gambling already legalized.

Incidence of Gambling Taxes

Turning then to empirical studies of the incidence of gambling taxes, one finds virtual unanimity: taxes on gambling are regressive. Tables 4.8 and 4.9 illustrate the patterns that support this conclusion by presenting tabulations of average expenditures on gambling by household income. Table 4.8, based on a nationwide household expenditure survey in Canada in 1996, shows that gambling expenditures as a percentage of income declined as income rose, from 1.5 per cent in the lowest income class to 0.4 per cent in the highest. Table 4.9, based on marketing data produced by the Virginia lottery for 1997, shows the percentage of income devoted to each of three lottery games. All three show declines as income rises, with the daily three- and four-digit numbers games having the sharpest drops. To the extent that taxes on gambling approximate a constant *ad valorem* tax on expenditures – an assumption best satisfied in the case of state lotteries – expenditure patterns such as these imply regressivity of gambling taxes, in that the percentage of income paid in tax falls as income rises.[18]

To show that these patterns are typical, Table 4.10 summarizes a number of empirical studies relevant to the incidence of gambling taxation covering patterns observed since 1982. For each, the measured distribution is summarized by the tax concentration index, an index that may range between −1 and +1, where negative index values indicate regressivity.[19] Most of the studies cover expenditures on lottery products. All of the calculated indices are nega-

Table 4.7. *Government Tax Revenues from Gambling: Twenty-One OECD Countries, 1999*[a]

Country	Total (US$m)[b]	Population (thousands)[c]	Gambling tax revenue per capita (US$)	Gambling tax revenue as percentage of total revenue
Australia[d]	2,166.45	18,730	116	1.7
Austria	303.95	8,078	38	0.3
Belgium	52.83	10,203	5	0.0
Canada[e]	428.67	30,247	14	0.2
Denmark	155.53	5,301	29	0.2
Finland	732.13	5,153	142	1.2
France	2,412.86	58,850	41	0.4
Germany	1,834.97	82,029	22	0.2
Ireland	71.72	3,705	19	0.2
Italy	12,094.98	57,040	212	2.4
Korea	396.19	46,430	9	0.4
Luxembourg	11.49	426	27	0.1
New Zealand[f]	94.08	3,792	25	0.5
Norway	12.57	4,431	3	0.0
Poland	2.02	38,666	0	0.0
Portugal	0.01	9,979	0	0.0
Spain	1,696.87	39,371	43	0.8
Sweden	12.47	8,851	1	0.0
Switzerland	0.67	7,110	0	0.0
UK	4,726.54	59,237	80	0.9
USA[g]	3,674	270,299	14	0.1

[a] All data are for calendar year 1999 ending 31 December unless otherwise stated.

[b] OECD, 2001a, tables 32–71.

[c] OECD, 2001b. Note that data are from reference period 1998.

[d] Fiscal year beginning 1 July.

[e] Fiscal year beginning 1 April.

[f] Fiscal year ending 30 June following year.

[g] Federal government – fiscal year ending 30 September; state government – fiscal year ending 30 June.

Table 4.8. *Household Expenditures on Gambling in Canada, by Income Group, 1996*

Income class ($CAN)	Average expenditure	Average income	Percentage of income
Under 20,000	198	13,200	1.5
20,000–39,999	299	29,900	1.0
40,000–59,999	388	48,500	0.8
60,000–79,999	425	70,800	0.6
80,000 and over	465	116,300	0.4

Note: For conversion to US dollars, the relevant exchange rate is $US1 = $CAN1.37.

Source: Vaillancourt and Roy, 2000, table 2.14, p. 36.

Table 4.9. *Percentage of Average Income Used to Play Lottery, Virginia, 1997*

Income class ($)	Average income ($)	Scratch sales as percentage of average income	Pick 3,4 sales as percentage of average income	Lotto / Cash 5 sales as percentage of average income
Less than 15,000	7,515	0.81	1.22	0.64
15,000–25,000	19,927	0.29	0.39	0.21
25,000–50,000	36,160	0.16	0.15	0.12
Over 50,000	104,266	0.03	0.04	0.04

Notes: Figures for Lotto / Cash 5 also include Big Game multi-state lotto sales. Sales totals are multiplied by 0.88 to account for estimated 12 per cent out-of-state sales.

Sources: Hollenbeck and Kahr, 1999, table 2, p. 140; author's calculations; Virginia Lottery, 1997, p. 3; *International Gaming and Wagering Business*, 1998, p. 49; US Bureau of the Census, 1990 to 1999 annual time series of state population estimates by single year of age and sex, downloaded from www.census.gov/population/www/estimates/st-99-10.html visited on 27 April 2000.

tive, implying that the patterns of expenditures are such that the percentage of income spent on gambling falls with income.

Regarding the regressivity of gambling taxation, the following conclusions may be stated. For lotteries, whose expenditures are subject to a high proportional implicit tax, the incidence is decidedly regressive. Based on available evidence, it is impossible to say for sure which games are the most regressive, but all of them are regressive. There is less information available regarding other forms of gambling. In a study of US gambling patterns, Suits (1977, p. 24) reported a positive index value of 0.26 for casinos in 1974, an index that reflects the comparative inaccessibility of casinos before New Jersey and other states made casino gambling much more widely available in the USA. For Nevada residents alone, however, he found that casino expenditures were regressive, with an index of −0.44.[20] The best evidence on the incidence of other forms is that given in Table 4.10. A household expenditure survey conducted in Canada in 1999 (Marshall, 2001) provides the best evidence on the distribution of spending on gambling products other than lotteries. That survey suggests all were regressive in incidence, with casinos and gaming machines together being the least so. In addition, two separate studies of Australia and Canada (Smith, 1998; Vaillancourt and Roy, 2000) suggest that expenditures on all forms of gambling as a percentage of income in those countries fall as income rises. Again, to the extent that gambling taxes in general can be approximated by a proportional tax on the gross wager, they are regressive as well.

4.5.2 *Equity According to the Benefit Principle*

Seldom applied outside of user fees, some environmental taxes, and property taxes, the benefit principle is relevant to the evaluation of earmarked expenditures associated with gambling taxes. For the common case in which some

Table 4.10. *Calculated Indices of Tax Concentration for Gambling Expenditures*

Product	Jurisdiction, year	Index of tax concentration	Source
Lotto			
	Maryland, 1984	−0.36	Clotfelter and Cook, 1987
	Texas, 1994	−0.06	Price and Novak, 2000
	Virginia, 1997	−0.49	This study[a]
Numbers			
	Maryland, 1984, 3-digit game	−0.42	Clotfelter and Cook, 1987
	Maryland, 1984, 4-digit game	−0.48	Clotfelter and Cook, 1987
	Texas, 1994	−0.04	Price and Novak, 2000
	Virginia, 1997	−0.65	This study[a]
Instant			
	California, 1986	−0.32	Clotfelter and Cook, 1987
	Colorado, 1989–90	−0.10	Hansen, 1995
	Texas, 1994	−0.13	Price and Novak, 2000
	Virginia, 1997	−0.62	This study[a]
Lottery, general			
	Canada, 1982	−0.18	Vaillancourt and Grignon, 1988
	Edmonton, 1983	−0.10	Livernois, 1987[b]
	Canada, 1986	−0.18	Kitchen and Powells, 1991
	Canada, 1992	−0.07	Vaillancourt and Roy, 2000
	Georgia, 1993–98	−0.15	Cornwell and Mustard, 2000[c]
	Canada, 1999	−0.37	Marshall, 2001[d]
Other lotteries, raffles			
	Canada, 1999	−0.29	Marshall, 2001[d]
Casinos, slot machines, VLTs			
	Canada, 1999	−0.21	Marshall, 2001[d]
Bingo			
	Canada, 1999	−0.30	Marshall, 2001[d]
Gambling, general			
	Australia, 1993	−0.31	Smith, 1998
	Canada, 1996	−0.28	Vaillancourt and Roy, 2000

[a] Author's calculations based on tabulations in Virginia Lottery, 1997.

[b] Cited in Vaillancourt and Roy (2000, table 2.15, p. 36).

[c] Author's calculations based on tabulations in Cornwell and Mustard (2000).

[d] Author's calculations based on tabulations in Marshall (2001, p. 50); Statistics Canada, income statistics 2001, 1999 tax year, final basic table 2; Statistics Canada, total income, distribution of economic families, 1997.

portion of gambling revenues is earmarked to deal with problem gambling, the connection between taxpayer and 'beneficiary' is surely very close, although the notion of benefit in that case carries ironic meaning. More generally, the benefit principle leads the analyst to consider the expenditure side of the budget in assessing the equity of gambling finance, which leads naturally to earmarked revenues. If revenues from gambling taxes are earmarked, and if such earmarking is effective, then a full assessment of the equity of such finance must take those earmarked expenditures into account.

In the case of US state lotteries, scholars have devoted some attention to the issue of earmarked expenditures, since about half of the state lotteries earmark their profits for specific state purposes. Such studies that have been done conclude that, for the states devoting funds to the most common beneficiary – public education – such earmarking has no practical effect. The explanation is that legislatures effectively undo the earmarking by diverting general revenues that otherwise would have gone to education, in light of this other source of revenue.[21] The best chance of earmarked funds 'sticking', according to this reasoning, would be for lottery revenues to be devoted to a new programme, thereby taking away the legislature's opportunity to nullify the earmarking. One apparently strong candidate for this condition is the Georgia lottery, whose revenues were earmarked in part for a new scholarship for graduates of Georgia high schools to attend college in Georgia. Analyses of the distributional impact of the Georgia lottery by Cornwell and Mustard (2000) and Rubenstein and Scafidi (1999) reveal that these earmarked expenditures caused the incidence of lottery finance to be even less pro-poor than it was considering only the taxation side. Not only is college attendance more prevalent in middle and upper income classes, but also the amount of the Georgia scholarships did not vary with financial need.[22]

4.6 ADEQUACY, STABILITY

In addition to the concerns over efficiency and equity, practical-minded tax analysts worry about two seemingly mundane aspects of taxes. Do they raise sufficient revenue? Are they stable sources of revenue? 'Sufficiency', of course, is in the eye of the beholder. It surely must be the case that the quantity of revenue raised is relevant to one's consideration of any tax, and this benefit (for those who believe the social value of government revenue is positive) must be traded off against efficiency losses and any unfavourable distributional effects. In the case of gambling taxes, the revenues are rarely large enough to rise to the level of a significant source of government revenue. As shown in Table 4.7, in only two of the OECD countries listed – Italy and Australia – did gambling taxes amount to as much as 1.5 per cent of total tax revenue. To be sure, adding the implicit taxes from government-operated gambling yields higher percentages of own-source revenues of all types, especially in Australia, Canada, and the USA.

Besides adequacy, another pragmatic desideratum in taxation is stability. An unstable source of revenue is one that cannot be relied upon and one whose utilization invites periodic budgetary crises. Concern has been voiced recently, for example, over stagnation in sales of the UK national lottery (Galvin, 2000).

In the USA, one of the common criticisms levelled at state lotteries has been that they are a volatile source of revenue.[23] It is certainly the case that declines in lottery sales have quickly become the subject of public debate in states that have experienced them and that the lottery agencies in these states have typically sought to prevent such occurrences by judicious introduction of new or altered products and through advertising campaigns. To assess the validity of the concern over volatility of lotteries, Szakmary and Szakmary (1995) analysed the performance of state lotteries over the period 1978–92. They concluded that lottery revenues were much more volatile than other state revenues. However, because lottery revenues had a very low correlation with other state revenues, the volatility of state revenue was not aggravated by the lottery. While reassuring to states whose lottery funds go to the general fund, this finding should give pause to states that earmark their lottery funds for specific purposes, particularly for the operating costs of ongoing programmes. Whether it is a lottery or an excise tax on a product whose popularity is subject to variation over time, any narrow source of revenue is likely to be subject to greater instability than a broad-based tax.

4.7 THE POLITICAL ECONOMY OF GAMBLING TAXATION

Some of the peculiarities of how gambling has been institutionalized and taxed in democratic countries arise out of its Jekyll and Hyde nature. On the one hand, it is and has been a popular activity of civilized nations for centuries – and one that has been used to raise funds for public purposes. On the other hand, gambling is also seen as one of society's most notorious vices – certainly one condemned by many religious groups. A result of this dichotomy is a peculiar set of institutional characteristics shaping the political economy of gambling taxation.

The first characteristic, noted from the beginning of this chapter, is that legalization and taxation come as a package. Because of the high level of disapproval of the activity, it can be legalized only if that legalization can be justified on a revenue basis. That it may be subject to very high tax rates is explained by this trade-off, as well as by the desire to 'punish' those who take part and by the willingness of the participants to submit to heavy taxation. In the words of Iowa's Governor Terry Branstad, who had opposed a state lottery in the 1980s until he realized one was inevitable, 'If you're going to have a lottery, you might as well have one that's successful' (Clotfelter and Cook, 1989, p. 160). For those whose first choice was no legalized gambling, the second choice was not legalization with moderate taxation and no marketing. It was to maximize revenue, which in the case of US lotteries meant heavy advertising and high taxes.

A second feature of gambling taxation, which follows this desire to maximize revenues, is that governments themselves have chosen to operate the gambling activity where there was not a pre-existing or ready set of firms able to do it. In the case of lotteries, it has been the practice of governments to run the operation themselves or establish a quasi-public agency to do the same. In this case, any firms already in the 'industry' were quite illegal, so moving in on their turf carried no political cost. In the case of casinos or pari-mutuel betting, government either had no comparative advantage or would have to have moved in on the business of firms already operating. Where no industry existed prior to legalization, such as with lotteries, there were no strong voices to lobby for lower tax rates, which might explain why implicit taxes on lotteries are so high.

An alternative explanation for the comparatively heavy implicit taxation of lotteries looks instead to the mobility of factors of production. By granting themselves local monopolies, states and provinces establishing lotteries put themselves in a position to tax heavily, though these monopolies are by no means absolute. Where states have banded together in multi-state compacts, it has been for the purpose of exploiting the scale economies of lotto without subjecting themselves to competition (see Cook and Clotfelter (1993)). In contrast, governments have been more reluctant to tax mobile resources. For example, the UK has been quite sensitive to the real or threatened prospect that bookmakers would establish themselves offshore. The desire not to drive them to do this was a justification for the recent reforms in the general betting duty (HM Customs and Excise, 2002).

A third feature of gambling taxation that owes its origin to the Jekyll–Hyde quality is earmarking, or hypothecation. One way a new form of gambling can generate sufficient political support is to earmark its revenues for some popular government programme. In US lotteries, the favourite beneficiary for such earmarking is education. Not only are the beneficiaries of public education very widespread, but also this form of earmarking typically enables pro-lottery forces to enlist the support of a large and well-organized special interest group, the public school teachers. Once established, lottery agencies eagerly use earmarking to sell tickets. By saying that a lottery funds schools, cultural monuments, the environment, or programmes for the aged, citizens may be better able to overcome any moral reservations and equate playing the game with helping to support good causes. That earmarking may have little to no effect on actual expenditures is, for this purpose, quite beside the point.

4.8 WHAT ARE THE POLICY QUESTIONS?

When considering policy questions surrounding most types of excise taxation, there are usually more than enough challenging policy issues regarding tax rates, definition of the base, and other administrative details to occupy the serious analyst. In the case of gambling taxation, however, even the most exhaustive consideration of these conventional topics is not always sufficient. In many jurisdictions, gambling in some of its forms is an activity that is illegal, legal in only some areas, or only recently made legal. For these jurisdictions, it is impossible to consider the taxation of gambling without also considering the ramifications of its legalization, including the types and probable success of regulations that will be imposed.

The state of New York serves as a current example. Having lived with a state lottery, pari-mutuel betting, and off-track betting for decades, and having experienced the introduction and growth of casino gaming in its region over the same period, the state legislature passed a law in 2001 that has been called the most significant expansion of legalized gambling in the state's history. This law authorizes the construction of six new casinos, to be operated by Native American tribes, in easy commuting distance to much of the state's metropolitan population. It also provides for the introduction of tens of thousands of new gaming machines in casinos and at race tracks (Perez-Pena, 2001). Besides the economic development benefits anticipated, this new activity will obviously bring new revenue to the state. But, clearly, the policy debate must be about more than the features of the taxes.

Other governments face similar issues, from Korea, which has recently opened casino gambling for its citizens (Peterson, 2001), to North Carolina and Tennessee, which are still debating whether to institute state lotteries. Among the issues to be considered are the effects that legalization and availability will have on problem gambling. One feature of the debate will continue to focus on particular gambling products, since the characteristics of the games themselves contribute, to differing degrees, to social costs. Among the forms of gambling that appear to have particularly great potential for problem gambling, gaming machines are often singled out.[24] But other forms, including betting over the Internet and betting on sporting events, may also have significant, though different kinds of, social costs. Another set of policy questions come to the fore for state-operated gambling such as lotteries. As noted above, some observers worry that government sponsorship has the potential to undermine the teaching of certain values.[25] The implication of these points is that the consideration of gambling taxation must often go beyond the conventional public finance considerations.

Notwithstanding the social costs that inevitably follow the legalization of gambling, it seems reasonable to conclude by stating several propositions that apply to most forms of gambling. Although they go beyond narrow questions of taxation, they are germane to gambling taxes because of the fact that, in the case of gambling, taxes are effectively bundled together with legalization.

1. While some people surely suffer, most of those who participate in legalized gambling are made better off simply by its legalization. Most people who gamble do not win, but that does not make the activity of playing any more 'wasteful' or irrational than, say, playing video games, eating candy bars, or attending a hockey game. They play because they evidently get something out of it.

2. Among those who are worse off are 'problem gamblers', some of whom will have serious financial problems as a result, and those who find the legalization of gambling (and its advertising) to be offensive. This is the

reason some jurisdictions require funds to be set aside for programmes dealing with gambling addiction, or why some governments have placed limits on the amount or nature of advertising.

3. Some gambling products are subject to quite high tax or implicit tax rates. For each dollar bet on a US state lottery, for example, the average lottery pays 56 cents in prizes and spends 12 cents on retailer commissions and other operating costs, leaving 32 cents for the state. If this implicit tax were an excise tax, it would amount to a 47 per cent tax on the cost of operating the lottery (68 cents), making it as high as or higher than the excise taxes levied on alcohol or tobacco products, at least in the USA. Income taxation of winnings makes the tax rate even higher.

4. Since lower-income people spend more on gambling in proportion to their incomes than those with middle and upper incomes, they tend to benefit more from legalized gambling. Although no one can be certain how large the benefits of playing are, economists are inclined to look at people's own behaviour and assume that those who play the most will get the most enjoyment out of it. To be sure, this approach applies to consumers who are not addicted and who have a decent idea of the odds and the prize structure.

5. As a rule, the taxes and implicit taxes levied on gambling are regressive (as distinguished from the combined legalization-plus-taxation package referred to above). Especially when the tax rate or implicit tax rate is high, as in the case of US state lotteries, governments in effect make their revenue structures more regressive than they would be if those taxes were in line with other tax rates. Thus the same lower-income people who benefit from the legalization of gambling could benefit even more if gambling taxes were in line with or lower than taxes on other taxed products, such as alcohol and tobacco.

6. Through heavy marketing of some lottery products, such as state lotteries in the USA, governments can compound this burden on lower-income citizens and increase the social cost to problem gamblers.

7. The taxes and implicit taxes on legalized gambling are therefore bound up with other policy issues, the assessment of which must ultimately depend upon a society's attitude towards gambling. If gambling is seen more or less as harmless entertainment, it can be taxed at rates similar to those on competing forms of entertainment without undue excess burden. If it is viewed, however, as a vice or as an activity with social side effects, government policy must weigh the costs of legalization against the costs of forbidding the activity altogether. A middle ground – one that has been associated with British public policy – is to accommodate the existing, unstimulated demand for gambling, without doing anything to stimulate that demand (Miers, 1996, p. 364). Besides limiting the availability of gambling opportunities, this approach would also be consistent with high, sumptuary tax rates. Tax policy cannot be separated from public policy, especially when it comes to gambling.

Notes

1 See Clotfelter and Cook (1989) for a discussion of the implicit tax in lottery finance.
2 See, for example, Albers and Hubl (1997, p. 128). As an example of large lotto jackpots, the US multi-state Powerball game produced a jackpot in August 2001 advertised to be $295 million, which would have been the sum of twenty-five annual payments. The present value of the jackpot was in fact about $120 million (Behm, 2001; MacQuarrie and Lewis, 2001).
3 See Munting (1996, pp. 69 and 127–43) for discussion of football pools and their relationship to lotteries.
4 For a systematic discussion of dimensions by which gambling forms can be compared, see Abt, Smith, and Christiansen (1985, pp. 39–47).
5 Calculations based on population of 274 million in 2000 (*Statistical Abstract of the United States*, 2000, p. 8).
6 $US0.23 billion to $US1.59 billion using $US1 = FF 5.45 and $US1 = FF 5.90, respectively.
7 Campbell and Smith (1998, p. 30) state: 'VLTs are becoming the game of choice for gambling addicts'. See also Azmier (2001, p. 5), Albers and Hubl (1997, p. 127), and Greenberg (1992, p. 27).
8 For a discussion of 'reinvestment' of gambling winnings, see Productivity Commission (1999, p. U.12).
9 See Clotfelter and Cook (1987). It is worth noting that, in its annual compilation of tax statistics, the OECD does not count profits of government-operated lotteries as tax revenue, but rather as property income in its non-tax revenues (OECD, 2000, annexes 1 and 2). Yet it would appear to be a close call, in that the OECD treats profits from 'fiscal monopolies' as taxes 'because they reflect the exercise of taxing power of the state by the use of monopoly powers' (OECD, 2000, p. 265).
10 Estimates of the price elasticity of gambling have been published. For example, Farrell and Walker (1999) estimate the welfare effects of the implicit tax on lotto. To derive these estimates, however, they redefine the unit of consumption to be monetary units of expected winnings, implying price to be the cost per unit of expected value. They obtain variation in this 'price' by comparing weeks with and without a rollover. In the framework discussed in the present chapter, rollovers actually change the prize distribution, not the price. So these results, despite their originality, cannot contribute to our knowledge of the magnitude of the excess burden without important qualifying assumptions. For a similar approach, see Farrell, Morgenroth, and Walker (1999).
11 The National Gambling Impact Study Commission presented estimates in its 1999 report that about 1.6 per cent of Americans were pathological gamblers and another 4.0 per cent were problem gamblers (National Gambling Impact Study Commission, 1999, p. 4–1).
12 For an extended discussion of this and related points concerning the evaluation of consumer surplus for gambling, see Productivity Commission (1999, appendix C, pp. C.8–C.14).
13 See the discussion of a sumptuary lottery in Clotfelter and Cook (1989, ch. 12). This logic could, in principle, extend to largely harmless products, such as fattening foods, but an assessment of the probable harmfulness would have to be part of the calculus. Where government itself has a role in stimulating demand, such as in the case of lotteries, even stricter scrutiny would be demanded.

14 See, for example, Rosen (1988, p. 319).

15 For a discussion of the effect of availability on problem gambling, see National Gambling Impact Study Commission (1999, p. 4–4).

16 Galston and Wasserman (1996, p. 65) argue that government's promotion of gambling 'belies its commitment to reducing the influence of morally arbitrary factors on the lives of its citizens and to supporting the virtues of thrift, hard work, and responsibility'. See also Clotfelter and Cook (1990).

17 In noting the case of sumptuary taxes, Musgrave (1959, p. 178) sees them as the reverse of public subsidies for what he calls merit goods. He states: 'The economist can only note that both interfere with consumer sovereignty, but it is not for him to say that such an interference must always be inefficient if viewed in the broader framework of social values.'

18 Similar distributions presented in Productivity Commission (1999, p. 19.31) indicate that taxes on lotteries and gaming machines were somewhat more regressive than those on racing and casinos.

19 The index, introduced by Suits (1977), is based on a Lorenz curve plotting the cumulative percentage of taxes or expenditures on the y-axis against the cumulative percentage of household income, when households are ranked according to income. Where L is the area under the Lorenz curve and T is the area under the 45° line, the Suits index is $(T–L)/T$. An item with an income elasticity of 1, which would imply expenditures were a constant proportion of income, results in a Lorenz curve on the 45° line, and thus a Suits index of 0. Items with income elasticities less than 1 imply a declining proportion of income spent on the item as income rises, and thus a Lorenz curve above the 45° line and a negative Suits index.

20 We also have Campbell and Smith's (1998, p. 32) statement that sports gambling is the least regressive form of gambling, but the support for that assertion is uncertain.

21 See, for example, Clotfelter and Cook (1989, pp. 227–8) and Greenberg (1992, p. 25).

22 The example of the Georgia lottery may not be as perfect an example of earmarking immune from the possibility of nullification as one might suppose from the newness of the programme. If the legislature were to reduce other appropriations to colleges and universities at the same time as new scholarships were awarded, part of the new programme's benefit would effectively be nullified.

23 See, for example, Mikesell and Zorn (1986, p. 314).

24 Volberg (2001, p. 58) cites an Australian study that finds a correlation between the density of poker machines and the prevalence of problem gambling.

25 See, for example, Galston and Wasserman (1996).

References

Abt, V., Smith, J. F., and Christiansen, E. M. (1985), *The Business of Risk: Commercial Gambling in Mainstream America*, Lawrence, KS: University Press of Kansas.

Albers, N., and Hubl, L. (1997), 'Gambling market and individual patterns of gambling in Germany', *Journal of Gambling Studies*, 13: 125–44.

Azmier, J. J. (2001), *Gambling in Canada 2001: An Overview*, Gambling in Canada Research Report 13, Calgary: Canada West Foundation.

Barnhart, R. T. (1991), 'Gambling in revolutionary Paris – The Palais Royal: 1789–1838', in W. R. Eadington and J. A. Cornelius (eds), *Gambling and Public Policy:*

International Perspectives, Reno, NV: Institute for the Study of Gambling and Commercial Gaming, University of Nevada.

——(1997), 'Gambling with Giancomo Casanova and Lorenzo Da Ponte in eighteenth century Venice – The Ridotto: 1638–1774', in W. R. Eadington and J. A. Cornelius (eds), *Gambling: Public Policies and the Social Sciences*, Reno, NV: Institute for the Study of Gambling and Commercial Gaming, University of Nevada.

Becker, G. S., and Murphy, K. M. (1988), 'A theory of rational addiction', *Journal of Political Economy*, 96: 675–700.

Behm, D. (2001), 'Now Wisconsin wonders: who won megabucks?', *Milwaukee Journal Sentinel*, 27 August, p. 1B.

Bernheim, D., and Rangel, A. (2002), 'Addiction, cognition, and the visceral brain', Stanford University, mimeo.

Campbell, C. S., and Smith, G. J. (1998), 'Canadian gambling: trends and public policy issues', *Annals, AAPSS*, 556 (March): 22–35.

Christiansen, E. M. (1998), 'Gambling and the American economy', *Annals, ASPSS*, 556 (March): 36–52.

——and——(20 'US growth rate disappoints (gross annual wager)', *International Gaming and Wagering Business*, 22(8): 1 and 32.

Clotfelter, C. T., and Cook, P. J. (1987), 'Implicit taxation in lottery finance', *National Tax Journal*, 40: 533–46.

——and——(1989), *Selling Hope: State Lotteries in America*, Cambridge, MA: Harvard University Press.

——and——(1990), 'Redefining "success" in the state lottery business', *Journal of Policy Analysis and Management*, 9 (Winter): 99–104.

Cook, P. J., and Clotfelter, C. T. (1993), 'The peculiar scale economies of lotto', *American Economic Review*, 83: 634–43.

Cornwell, C., and Mustard, D. B. (2000), 'The distributional impact of lottery-funded aid: evidence from Georgia's Hope Scholarship', University of Georgia, unpublished paper, November.

Ezell, J. S. (1960), *Fortune's Merry Wheel*, Cambridge, MA: Harvard University Press.

Farrell, L., Morgenroth, E., and Walker, I. (1999), 'A time series analysis of U.K. lottery sales: long and short run price elasticities', *Oxford Bulletin of Economics and Statistics*, 61: 513–26.

——and Walker, I. (1999), 'The welfare effects of lotto: evidence from the UK', *Journal of Public Economics*, 72: 99–120.

Forrest, D. (1999), 'The past and future of the British football pools', *Journal of Gambling Studies*, 15: 161–76.

France, C. J. (1901), *The Gambling Impulse*, Worcester, MA: Clark University.

Gabbitas, O., and Eldridge, D. (1998), *Directions for State Tax Reform*, Productivity Commission Staff Research Paper, Canberra: AusInfo.

Galston, W. A., and Wasserman, D. (1996), 'Gambling away our moral capital', *The Public Interest*, 123: 58–71.

Galvin, B. H. (2000), 'U.K. lottery sales slump', *International Gaming and Wagering Business*, 21(7): 22.

Garrett, T. A. (2001), 'An international comparison and analysis of lotteries and the distribution of lottery expenditures', *International Review of Applied Economics*, 15: 213–27.

Greenberg, P. (1992), 'Not quite the pot of gold', *State Legislatures*, (December): 24–7.

Gruber, J., and Koszegi, B. (2002), 'A theory of government regulation of addictive bads: optimal tax levels and tax incidence for cigarette excise taxation', National Bureau of Economic Research, Working Paper 8777.

Hansen, A. (1995), 'The tax incidence of the Colorado state lottery instant game', *Public Finance Quarterly*, 23: 385–98.

HM Customs and Excise (UK), www.hmce.gov.uk/business/othertaxes/betting.htm, visited on 21 January 2002.

Hollenbeck, S., and Kahr, M. K. (1999), 'Individual income tax returns, 1997: early tax estimates', *SOI Bulletin*, 18(3): 126–50.

International Gaming and Wagering Business (1998), 'Worldwide lottery sales', 19(6): 41–9.

—— (2000), 'European Casino Report 2000', 19 (February) Supplement: 1–22.

Johnson, J. (1985), 'Gambling as a source of government revenue in Australia', in G. Caldwell, B. Haig, M. Dickerson, and L. Sylvan (eds), *Gambling in Australia*, Sydney: Croom Helm.

Kitchen, H., and Powells, S. (1991), 'Lottery expenditures in Canada: a regional analysis of determinants and incidence', *Applied Economics*, 23: 1845–52.

Livernois, J. (1987), 'The redistributive effects of lotteries: evidence from Canada', *Public Finance Quarterly*, 15: 339–51.

MacQuarrie, B., and Lewis, R. (2001), 'Maine couple braces for life after Powerball', *Boston Globe*, 28 August.

McQueen, P. A. (1996), 'World gaming at a glance', *International Gaming and Wagering Business*, 17(10): 80–4.

—— (2001a), 'The state of state lotteries', *International Gaming and Wagering Business*, 22(4): 15–22.

—— (2001b), 'Getting a major dose of reality', *International Gaming and Wagering Business*, 22(6): 15–21.

Madhusudhan, R. G. (1999), 'What do we know about casino taxation in the United States?', *Proceedings of the Ninety-First Annual Conference of the National Tax Association, 1998*, Washington, DC: National Tax Association.

Marshall, K. (2001), 'Fact-sheet on gambling', *Perspectives on Labour and Income*, Statistics Canada, (Summer): 47–51.

Mason, J. L., and Nelson, M. (2001), *Governing Gambling*, New York, NY: Century Foundation.

Miers, D. (1996), 'The implementation and effects of Great Britain's national lottery', *Journal of Gambling Studies*, 12: 343–73.

Mikesell, J. L., and Zorn, C. K. (1986), 'State lotteries as fiscal savior or fiscal fraud: a look at the evidence', *Public Administration Review*, 46: 311–20.

Munting, R. (1996), *An Economic and Social History of Gambling in Britain and the USA*, Manchester: Manchester University Press.

Musgrave, R. A. (1959), *The Theory of Public Finance*, New York, NY: McGraw-Hill Book Co.

National Gambling Impact Study Commission, *Final Report* (http://www.govinfo.library.unt.edu/ ngisc/reports/finrpt.html, visited on 22 April 2003).

OECD (2000), *Revenue Statistics, 1965–1999*, Paris: Organisation for Economic Co-operation and Development.

—— (2001a), *Revenue Statistics, 1965–2000*, Paris: Organisation for Economic Co-operation and Development.

—— (2001*b*), 'Basic statistics: international comparisons', in *OECD Economic Surveys, 2000–2001*, Paris: Organisation for Economic Co-operation and Development.

Perez-Pena, R. (2001), 'Gold rush in New York: companies vie for a stake in the untapped gambling market', *New York Times*, 17 December, p. A19.

Peterson, K. E. (2001), 'Winning in South Korea', *International Gaming and Wagering Business*, 22(3): 13 and 42–3.

Price, D. I., and Novak, E. S. (2000), 'The income redistribution effects of Texas state lottery games', *Public Finance Review*, 28: 82–92.

Productivity Commission of Australia (1998), *Directions for State Tax Reform*, Staff Research Paper, Canberra: AusInfo.

—— (1999), *Australia's Gambling Industries*, Report 10, Canberra: AusInfo.

Rosen, H. S. (1988), *Public Finance*, Homewood, IL: Irwin.

Rubenstein, R., and Scafidi, B. P. (1999), 'Who pays and who benefits? Examining the distributional consequences of the Georgia lottery for education', presented at the meetings of the National Tax Association, Atlanta, GA, October.

Smith, J. (1998), 'Gambling taxation in Australia', The Australia Institute, Discussion Paper 16.

Stokey, E., and Zeckhauser, R. (1978), *A Primer for Policy Analysis*, New York, NY: Norton.

Suits, D. B. (1977), 'Gambling taxes: regressivity and revenue potential', *National Tax Journal*, 30 (March): 19–35.

Szakmary, A. C., and Szakmary, C. M. (1995), 'State lotteries as a source of revenue: a re-examination', *Southern Economic Journal*, 64: 1167–81.

The Economist (1999), 'Business: diced', 15 May, p. 68.

United States Code, 1994 edition (vol. 14) (1995), Washington, DC: Government Printing Office.

United States Statutes at Large, 1951 (vol. 65) (1952), Washington, DC: Government Printing Office.

Vaillancourt, F. (1999), 'Government gambling revenues, 1985–1995/1996: evidence from Canada, Great Britain, and Australia', in *Proceedings of the Ninety-First Annual Conference of the National Tax Association, 1998*, Washington, DC: National Tax Association.

—— and Grignon, J. (1988), 'Canadian lotteries as taxes: revenues and incidence', *Canadian Tax Journal*, 36: 369–88.

—— and Roy, A. (2000), *Gambling and Governments in Canada, 1969–1998: How Much? Who Plays? What Payoff?*, Special Studies in Taxation and Public Finance 2, Toronto: Canadian Tax Foundation.

Virginia Lottery (1997), *Who Plays the Lottery*, Richmond, VA: Virginia Lottery.

Volberg, R. A. (2001), *When the Chips Are Down: Problem Gambling in America*, New York, NY: Century Foundation Press.

WEFA Group (1997), 'A study concerning the effects of legalized gambling on the citizens of the State of Connecticut', Hartford, June.

Chapter 5

Environmentally Related Levies

JEAN-PHILIPPE BARDE AND NILS AXEL BRAATHEN[*]
OECD, Environment Directorate

5.1 INTRODUCTION

Thirty years ago, the environmental policies of countries that are members of the Organisation for Economic Co-operation and Development (OECD) relied almost exclusively on direct 'command-and-control' (CAC) types of regulations. Although economists have long promoted the use of 'economic instruments' (mainly taxes, charges, and tradable permits), such instruments have only gradually been implemented (Barde, 1992, 1999; OECD, 1994). Today, the picture remains uneven: economic instruments are used in all countries, but only to a limited, albeit varying, extent. Nevertheless, more consideration is being given to the use of tradable permits, in particular to reduce CO_2 (carbon dioxide) and other greenhouse gas emissions. In addition, greater use is gradually being made of environmentally related taxes, fees, and charges, sometimes in the context of broader 'green tax reforms'.

The theoretical advantages of using taxes – in contrast to regulations – to correct environmental externalities have been clear since the publication of Pigou's book *The Economics of Welfare* in 1920.[1] OECD (2001c) provides an overview of relevant theory on environmental taxation, gives a description of the current use of environmentally related taxes in OECD countries, and provides indications of how obstacles to broader use of such taxes can be overcome. The publication gives due emphasis to the many, sometimes conflicting, objectives the taxes are intended to serve – often forgotten in theoretical discussions of these instruments.

Better and more comprehensive use of market-based instruments, and a reduction or phasing-out of environmentally harmful subsidies, are widely recognized by policy-makers as requirements for sustainable development. This was, for instance, underlined by both finance and environment ministers in the communiqué issued after the OECD's council meeting in 2001. Cur-

[*] The opinions expressed in this chapter are those of the authors and do not necessarily reflect the views of the OECD. The authors thank Muthukumara Mani of the International Monetary Fund, Herman Vollebergh of Erasmus University Rotterdam, and two anonymous referees for useful comments on previous versions of this chapter.

rently, many large polluters *hardly pay any environmentally related taxes at all*. Hence, including these polluters in the coverage of environmentally related taxes should be a step in the right direction – even if the optimal, or Pigouvian, tax level in many cases is not known. A recent OECD survey undertaken among member governments clearly singles out the fear of loss of sectoral competitiveness and the negative impact on the income distribution as the most important political obstacles to the broader use of environmentally related taxes. That survey and OECD (2001*c*) are the starting points of the present chapter, which aims to provide an updated description of the use of environmental levies in OECD member countries and to suggest ways of overcoming the political obstacles to their wider use.

Section 5.2 defines environmentally related taxes, fees, and charges. Subsequently, Section 5.3 provides an overview of the current use of these levies and Section 5.4 lists additional details of recent green tax reforms in OECD countries. Section 5.5 then discusses the distributive and competitiveness impacts of environmentally related taxes in greater detail, while Section 5.6 illustrates the environmental effectiveness of such taxes. Section 5.7 provides some concluding comments.

The focus of this chapter is on OECD member countries, although some information is also given on the use of environmentally related taxes in some non-OECD countries that have relationships with the European Environment Agency. While many of the issues discussed are relevant to the situation in developing countries, the specifics – for instance, concerning institutional capacities – are not discussed.

5.2 DEFINITION AND USE OF ENVIRONMENTALLY RELATED TAXES, FEES, AND CHARGES

There will always be an element of arbitrariness when defining a concept such as 'environmentally related taxes'. This chapter draws to a large extent on information in the OECD/EU (European Union) database on such taxes, fees, and charges, and we use the definitions of that database. The OECD (2001d) defines a *tax* as a *compulsory, unrequited payment to general government*. Accordingly, our definition of environmentally related taxes includes *any tax levied on tax bases deemed to be of particular environmental relevance*. The European Commission, the International Energy Agency (IEA), and the OECD have singled out energy products, motor vehicles and transport services, measured or estimated emissions to air and water, ozone-depleting substances, certain non-point sources of water pollution, waste management, noise, and the management of water, land, soil, forests, biodiversity, wildlife, and fish stocks as the most relevant tax bases in this context.[2]

Obviously, the *name*, or the *expressed purpose*, of a given tax is not an appropriate criterion for deciding whether or not it is 'environmentally related' – *inter alia*, because the names used and the expressed purposes are often arbitrary, and because the purposes of a particular levy can change over time. Therefore, we focus on the potential environmental *effects* of the particular tax, which is determined by its impact on producer and consumer prices, as calculated on the basis of the relevant price elasticities.

A distinction should be made between *taxes* and *fees* or *charges*. Environmental fees or charges are payments for specific services, such as waste collection, treatment of sewerage, and collective water treatment facilities. The term *levy* can be used to cover both taxes and fees and charges.

5.3 CURRENT USE OF ENVIRONMENTALLY RELATED LEVIES

5.3.1 *General Overview*

The use of taxes, fees, and charges in environmental policy clearly goes beyond OECD member countries. The number of levies used in some Central and Eastern European countries (not members of the OECD) is, for example, relatively high compared with the number of levies in OECD countries. Levies on motor vehicles and on motor vehicle fuels constitute a large share of the levies covered by the OECD/EU database, but the number of levies used in, for example, waste management is also important.

A much-focused-on characteristic of environmentally related taxes is the revenues they raise – even if, from an environmental point of view, one would like the tax to be so effective that the revenue diminishes substantially. Figure 5.1 illustrates the revenues from these taxes (i.e. excluding revenues from fees and charges used, for example, in water supply and waste handling) measured as a percentage of GDP in each of the OECD member countries in 1994 and 2000. It can be seen that environmentally related taxes raise revenue of, on average, approximately 2–3 per cent of GDP. For the OECD area as a whole, there is no clear trend in this share between 1994 and 2000. However, in some countries (for example, Austria, Denmark, Finland, Hungary, Korea, and Turkey), the revenues increased considerably as a percentage of GDP. The database demonstrates that this was caused in part by the introduction of new taxes – and the inclusion of more tax bases under existing taxes – and by increases in a number of pre-existing tax rates. At the same time, it should be noted that revenues as a percentage of GDP fell – sometimes noticeably – over this period in a number of other countries, such as Australia, Canada, Greece, Mexico, and the Slovak Republic. The reasons for the fall differ between countries, but to some extent it is linked to the broadening of tax bases not being of particular environmental importance.

Figure 5.2 illustrates estimates of the amount of revenue raised from various environmentally relevant tax bases in OECD member countries. Again, revenues from fees and charges are not included. Motor fuels and motor vehicles dominate the picture: taxes on these products raise more than 90 per cent of all the revenues from environmentally related taxes. Very small revenues are raised from tax bases such as heavy fuel oil, coal, and coke – which are typically used in large quantities by heavy industries.[3]

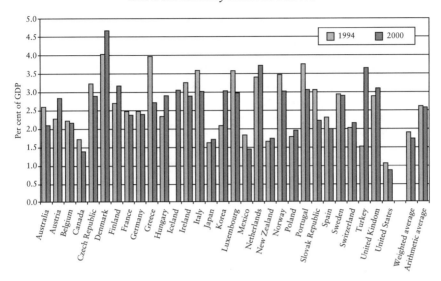

Figure 5.1. *Revenues from Environmentally Related Taxes as a Percentage of GDP*

Note: Revenues from fees and charges are not included.
Source: Based on information from www.oecd.org/env/tax-database.

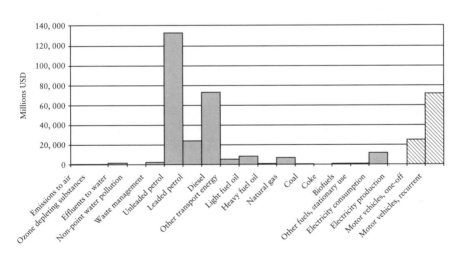

Figure 5.2. *Revenues Raised from Environmentally Relevant Tax Bases: Twenty-One
OECD Countries, 1995*

Note: Revenues from fees and charges are not included.
Source: Based on information from www.oecd.org/env/tax-database.

5.3.2 Some Categories of Environmentally Related Levies

Motor Vehicle Fuels Taxes

All OECD countries levy one or more taxes on motor vehicle fuels, but – as shown in Figure 5.3 – the tax rates applied vary considerably between countries and between fuels. Historically, taxes on motor vehicle fuels were often introduced primarily to raise revenues, but in some countries, significant emphasis is now also placed on using such taxes to limit transport activities – and thereby, *inter alia*, greenhouse gas emissions. With four exceptions (the UK, Switzerland, Australia, and the USA), the tax rates are lower for diesel than for petrol; in many cases, the difference is very substantial – which is undesirable from an

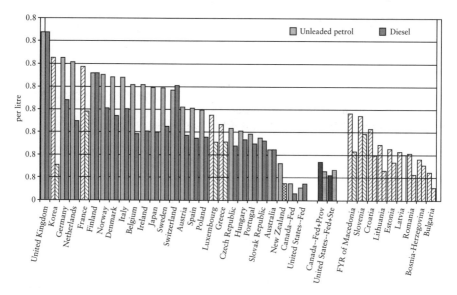

Figure 5.3. *Tax Rates on Unleaded Petrol and Diesel, 1 January 2002*

Notes: For countries with diagonally shaded bars, tax rates on 1 January 2000 are shown. Average exchange rates for 2001 were used to convert tax rates into euros for OECD member countries, while average 2000 rates were used for other countries. When a country applies several tax rates for different environmental qualities of petrol or diesel, the tax rate for the most environmentally friendly quality is included in the graph.

There is no direct taxation of diesel in New Zealand. Instead, there is a tax per 1,000 kilometres driven in diesel vehicles, with tax rates depending on the weight of the vehicle. In this graph, an implicit tax rate per litre of diesel is given for a vehicle weighing less than 2 tonnes assumed to consume 125 litres of diesel per 1,000 kilometres driven.

For Canada and the USA, the graph shows a set of bars that include only federal taxes. In addition, a shaded set of bars include both taxes levied at the federal level and an average of the taxes levied at the provincial or state level. The US average is calculated based on information concerning seventeen states included in the database.

Finally, it should be kept in mind that there are many exemptions in diesel tax rates for the transport sector, which are not reflected in this graph.

Source: Based on information from www.oecd.org/env/tax-database.

environmental point of view.[4] The tax rates for petrol and diesel in the UK are 4.4–6.8 times as high as the combined federal and provincial/state taxes on these fuels in Canada and the USA.

Parry and Small (2002) estimated the optimal petrol tax rates for the UK and the USA under the assumption that the revenues from the petrol tax would substitute for a distorting tax on labour income. Under their central parameter values, the second-best optimal petrol tax is €0.22 per litre ($US1.01 per gallon) for the USA and €0.29 per litre ($1.34 per gallon) for the UK. The congestion externality is the largest component in both countries, and the higher optimal tax for the UK is mainly due to a higher assumed value for marginal congestion cost. Revenue-raising needs also played a significant role in their estimates, as did accident externalities and local air pollution. Climate-related damages only played a minor part in their estimate (€0.02 per litre of petrol or $25 per tonne of carbon).

The current tax rate in the UK is more than twice as high as Parry and Small's estimated optimal level, while the current rate in the USA is only half their estimated optimal level. Parry and Small (2002) found that large gains could be achieved in both countries by switching to a tax on vehicle kilometres with equal revenue yield.[5]

Relatively high crude oil prices triggered substantial political attention in many countries in 2000 and 2001. For example, between 1 January 2000 and 1 January 2002, the tax rate on unleaded petrol was reduced by 15 per cent in nominal terms in Norway and 22 per cent in Portugal, but it was increased by 11 per cent, 12 per cent, and 21 per cent in Ireland, Germany, and Denmark, respectively. A relatively similar pattern can be found for changes in diesel tax rates. Hence, OECD member countries responded rather differently to the increase in crude oil prices. Norway had the second-highest tax rates on both petrol and diesel before the significant reductions were made, while both Germany and Denmark already had relatively high tax rates even before the increases.

Electricity Consumption

The use of fossil fuels in electricity generation causes externalities that, from a theoretical point of view, should be taxed – according to the externalities caused by the fuels used. Taking account only of the climate-change-related damages of Parry and Small (2002) implies that black coal – which contains almost exclusively carbon – should be taxed at about €25 per tonne of coal. Brown coal contains about 70 per cent carbon; hence, a climate-change element in the taxation of such coal used in electricity generation should – based on the numbers used by Parry and Small – be of the order of €17.5 per tonne of coal. The use of (in particular brown) coal can, in addition, cause other serious externalities (for example, sulphur and particles emissions); hence, a Pigouvian tax rate for coal used in electricity generation could be significantly higher than indicated here. Due to a lower carbon (and – often – sulphur) content, the

Pigouvian tax rate on a comparable unit of natural gas used in electricity generation would be lower than that on coal.

However, hardly any country taxes fossil fuels used in electricity generation.[6] This is in part related to the opening-up of electricity markets to cross-border trade. It can be difficult to tax imported electricity on the basis of the fuels used in its generation, and fear of loss of competitiveness of domestic power plants makes countries reluctant to tax fuel usage in such plants unilaterally if some form of border tax adjustment is not possible (see Section 5.5.2).

Instead, a number of countries tax electricity consumption, most often independent of how the electricity has been produced.[7] Figure 5.4 illustrates such tax rates in thirteen OECD member countries.[8] A number of points can be made. First, the tax rates vary significantly between countries, with the highest rates by far being applied to electricity used for (households' and businesses') heating of dwellings and other non-business uses in Denmark, and to the first 10 MWh of annual use of electricity in the Netherlands. Secondly, in almost all countries, the tax rates, if any, that apply to manufacturing and other industries are lower than those that apply to households. The major exception is the UK, where households are completely exempted from the climate change levy. Thirdly, rather different criteria are used to distinguish between groups of taxpayers. For example, in Belgium, only low-voltage electricity consumption is taxable – and hence heavy industries are 'automatically' exempted, as their electricity is supplied at high voltages. In Denmark, the tax rate depends on the purpose the electricity is used for – which requires separate metering in some facilities. In the Netherlands, the tax rate decreases with increasing energy usage, and is zero for any use above 10 GWh per year. In Austria, a tax ceiling is used to protect manufacturing industries, in that the marginal tax rate is zero for goods-producing firms where tax payments under the energy tax constitute more than 0.35 per cent of the firm's value added.

In some countries, the nominal tax rates on electricity consumption increased significantly between 1 January 2000 and 1 January 2002, as follows: Austria (100 per cent, but the tax ceiling concerning goods-producing firms was kept unchanged in nominal terms); Denmark (for example, heating of dwellings: 18 per cent); Norway (non-manufacturing: 20 per cent); and Sweden (non-manufacturing: 22 per cent). In addition, the climate change levy was introduced in the UK on 1 April 2001. No decreases in tax rates for electricity consumption are recorded in the OECD/EU database over this period.

Taxes on the Final Treatment of Waste

A number of countries have introduced taxes related to the final treatment of waste and/or on packaging and certain specific products that can cause special waste-related problems. For instance, some European countries have responded to EU targets on packaging and landfill waste by implementing such taxes. The taxes discussed in this section are in addition to user charges concerning waste collection and treatment, which are levied in most OECD member countries.

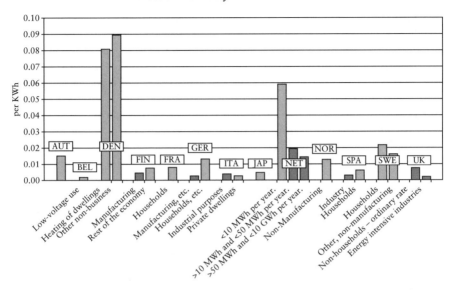

Figure 5.4. *Tax Rates on Electricity Consumption, 1 January 2002*

Notes: The tax rates shown for France and Spain relate to 1998 and 1999, respectively, and are from International Energy Agency (2001). The tax rate in Spain (in 2002) is expressed as 4.864 per cent of the electricity price, which varies between types of users. The dark bars in the graph represent tax rates facing manufacturing industries. In Austria, goods-producing firms face the standard tax rate, but the tax is refunded if electricity use exceeds 0.35 per cent of value added and the tax is more than €363 per annum.

Source: Based on information from www.oecd.org/env/tax-database.

There are many studies of the environmental externalities related to different types of waste treatment. For example, a report prepared for the European Commission (COWI, 2000*a*, 2000*b*) reviews and discusses available studies of environmental externalities related to waste disposal and presents estimates of the externality costs for different categories of both incinerators and landfills.[9]

For an incinerator fulfilling the existing directive on incineration of waste (89/369/EEC), with energy recovery used to generate electricity only, the *net* external costs were estimated by COWI to be €37 per tonne of waste incinerated.[10] If it is assumed that the incinerator generates both electricity and heat, implying a high rate of energy recovery (83 per cent), the net external costs of a tonne of waste incinerated was estimated to be negative: −€43 per tonne. Damage from air pollution (NO_x (nitrogen oxides) and SO_2 (sulphur dioxide) emissions) dominates the gross costs, while replacement of alternative energy generation fully or partially counterbalances the gross costs. For landfills, the COWI studies (COWI, 2000*a*, 2000*b*) distinguish between sites that fulfil the requirements of EC directive EC/31/1999, having a leachate collection and treatment system, and where the landfill gas is collected to generate electricity and heat, and an old site without a liner and with no collection of the landfill gas. In the former case, gross external costs are estimated to be €15 per tonne of waste, while the displacement of pollution from other energy-generation sources reduces net external costs to €11 per tonne of waste. For the old landfill site, both gross and net external costs are estimated to be €20 per tonne. For both cases, the gross external costs are dominated by assumed disamenity costs of €10 per tonne, but the assumed contribution to global warming (€5 and €8, respectively) is also significant.[11]

Figure 5.5 illustrates some of the tax rates on final treatment of waste that apply in OECD member countries. For example, in the UK, an explicit consideration of the externalities involved formed the basis of the rates that were applied when the landfill tax was first introduced. In recent years, the tax rates have, however, been increased beyond the estimated damage levels, in order to achieve EU targets on waste recycling (OECD, 2004). The graph shows that there is considerable variation in tax rates between countries and between different waste categories, with the highest rates being applied for ordinary (municipal) waste in the Netherlands. Rates applying to such waste

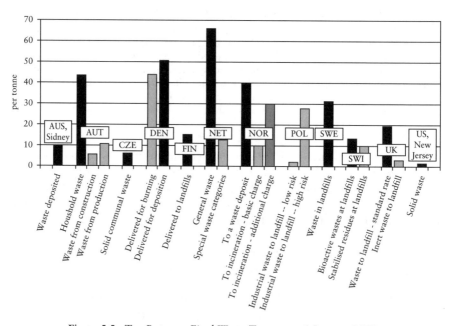

Figure 5.5. *Tax Rates on Final Waste Treatment, 1 January 2002*

Notes: Dark bars represent tax rates that are thought to be best comparable between countries. In Norway, there is a basic charge levied on all waste delivered for incineration. There is also an additional charge that varies proportionally with the degree of energy recovery at the plant, but the bar in the graph represents a case where none of the energy is recovered. The Norwegian parliament has decided to convert this tax into a tax on measured emissions from incinerators of a number of pollutants.

Source: Based on information from www.oecd.org/env/tax-database.

in Austria, Denmark, Norway, and Sweden are more or less of the same magnitude. Rates for ordinary industrial waste – which normally causes less methane emission – tend to be lower than the rates for municipal or household waste. In some cases, tax rates are also lower when waste is delivered for incineration – which can allow for energy recovery, but can also cause other environmental problems (for example, harmful air emissions; see the discussion above).

It should also be noted that in Denmark there is a special tax rate of €1.7 per GJ on heating by incineration of waste, applied under the duty on coal. The aim of this tax rate is to stimulate waste recycling and waste minimization measures.

5.4 GREEN TAX REFORMS

The previous section described some uses of environmentally related levies in OECD countries – in isolation. It showed that whilst there is a wide variety of environmentally related taxes, energy and transport taxes represent by far the largest shares of revenue, an important consideration when deploying and analysing green tax reforms.

Most OECD countries have undertaken significant (general) tax reforms since the end of the 1980s, chiefly in three ways:

1. by reducing tax rates in the higher income tax brackets (which fell on average by more than 10 percentage points between 1986 and 1997) and lowering corporate tax rates (down 10 points over the same period);
2. by broadening the tax bases; and
3. by giving a greater weight to general consumption taxes such as value added tax (VAT).

Such reforms provide an excellent opportunity to introduce an environmental dimension in taxation, i.e. a 'greening' of tax systems. Starting in the early 1990s, a number of countries, in particular in the EU, have implemented so-called 'green tax reforms', which generally consist of three types of approaches:

1. reduction or elimination of environmentally harmful subsidies, including direct public expenditures, 'market price support', and/or exemptions and other provisions in environmentally related taxes;
2. restructuring of existing taxes according to environmental criteria; and/or
3. introduction of new environmentally related taxes.

A 'greening' of fiscal policy could start with a systematic inventory of the environmental impacts of both tax rules and public expenditures. Measures that are harmful for the environment could then be corrected. A green tax reform would normally combine these 'green' components with a reduction of some (other) tax – for instance, social security contributions or taxes on labour income.

5.4.1 *Eliminating Environmentally Harmful Subsidies*

Many fiscal measures can either directly or indirectly produce adverse effects for the environment. One such measure is direct subsidies.[12] For example, subsidies to agriculture in OECD countries (estimated at $US318 billion in 2002, or 1.2 per cent of GDP – see OECD (2003)) are one of the causes of overfarming of land, excessive use of fertilizers and pesticides, soil degradation, and other environmental problems (OECD, 1996, 1998). Similarly, irrigation water is often charged below marginal social cost, which results in wastage. Subsidies for energy production in OECD countries, intended mainly to protect domestic producers and maintain employment in given industries, are estimated at $20–$80 billion per year. Approximately a third of these energy subsidies go to support coal production, the most polluting fossil fuel. Coal subsidies amounted to $5.4 billion in 2000 in five OECD countries, which admittedly was lower than the $11.4 billion for 1990. Industry is also subsidized, although it is difficult to obtain detailed data (industry subsidies were estimated at $44.1 billion in 1992). When subsidies encourage the use of certain raw materials and greater energy consumption, there can be negative fallout in terms of recycling and waste, and a lock-in of inefficient technologies. Subsidies to fisheries are also important: $6.0 billion in 1999, representing 20 per cent of the landed value (OECD, 2000a, 2001b), contributing to overcapacity in fishing fleets and depletion of fish stocks.

More indirect subsidies arise from specific tax provisions (tax rate variations or exemptions) that are environmentally harmful. For instance, coal, the most polluting fuel of all, is only taxed in five OECD countries, and in

Table 5.1. *Trends in Subsidy Levels in OECD Countries*

	Billions of US dollars		Comparison
	1992	Most recent data [Year]	
Agriculture	394	318 [2002]	Equivalent to 1.2% of GDP
Marine capture fisheries	—	5.8 [2000]	Equivalent to 19% of landed value
Coal production	11.9	5.4 [2000]	
Industry	44.1	—	

Notes:

Agriculture: total support estimate for agriculture; data for 1992 represent an average of 1991–3 data.

Fisheries: government financial transfers to marine capture fisheries; does not include market price support.

Coal production: producer support equivalent in selected OECD countries (Germany, Japan, Spain, Turkey, and the UK).

Industry: reported net government expenditures to industry.

Sources: OECD, 2001a, 2001b, 2003a, 2003d.

these countries the most important coal users are subject to many tax exemptions and rebates. The transport sector, a major source of pollution and other harmful effects, is also affected by many indirect subsidies: a case in point is the widespread undertaxing of diesel oil in many countries (see the discussion in Section 5.3.2). This contributes to a constant increase in the number of diesel-driven vehicles, which are more polluting[13] and noisier than petrol-driven vehicles, and to a sharp increase in road freight transport. In OECD countries, the consumption of diesel fuel for road transport grew from 15 per cent of total motor fuel consumption in 1970 to 32 per cent in 1997 (OECD, 1999). Other indirect transport subsidies in many countries include deductibility of commuting expenses from taxable income, the exclusion of the imputed value of company cars from taxable income, and tax exemptions for aviation fuels.

5.4.2 Restructuring Existing Taxes

Many existing taxes could be changed so as to benefit the environment, by increasing the relative prices of the most polluting tax bases. Since energy is one of the main sources both of pollution and of tax revenue, an 'environmental' restructuring of energy taxes is essential. For instance, in most OECD countries, taxes on motor vehicle fuel account for over 50 per cent of the pump price (see, for example, figure 12 in International Energy Agency (2003)). This leaves large scope for restructuring fuel taxes on the basis of environmental parameters, such as sulphur content, as the Nordic countries, Germany, Ireland, and the UK have done. Taxes on other energy products – for example, fuels used for heating purposes and in industrial processes – can also be differentiated according to environmental criteria, such as carbon and/or sulphur content.

It is also possible to restructure taxes on motor vehicles (both one-off sales taxes and annual taxes on vehicle usage) – for example, according to the environmental characteristics of the fuel the vehicle uses, according to the estimated fuel consumption, and/or according to whether or not the vehicle is equipped with a catalytic converter. In Switzerland, such differentiation has now been combined with accurate metering of the number of kilometres driven by various types of heavy vehicles.

5.4.3 Introducing New Environmental Levies

An obvious option is to introduce new levies whose prime purpose is to protect the environment. These may be taxes on emissions (for instance, on atmospheric pollutants or water pollution) or on products that are closely related to environmental problems. The latter are more frequent. Some examples of such taxes were described in Section 5.3.2. Since the early 1990s, other taxes have been introduced on a few types of measured or estimated emissions and on many types of products with harmful environmental impacts, ranging from packaging to fertilizers, pesticides, batteries, chemical substances (solvents), lubricants, tyres, razors, and disposable cameras. The OECD/EU database provides more information on a large variety of such levies.

5.4.4 *Green Tax Reforms in OECD Countries: An Overview*

Since the early 1990s, several countries, mainly in the EU, have introduced comprehensive green tax reforms, in most cases in an equal-yield context in the sense that new environmental taxes are offset by reductions in existing taxes. A constant tax burden is often seen as essential for the political acceptability of a green tax reform, although some countries that need to reduce public deficits, or with relatively low tax revenue, consider revenue-raising reforms.

Finland was the first country to introduce a 'carbon tax', in 1990, followed by a gradual 'greening' of the tax system. While the carbon tax started in 1990 at a fairly modest level of €4.1 per tonne of carbon, the rate was steadily increased until 1998, to reach €62.9 per tonne of carbon. The 'greening' of the tax system included other measures, such as the implementation of a landfill tax in 1996. In addition, Finland has, *inter alia*, taxes on motor vehicles, taxes on beverage containers, and a charge on electricity generation in nuclear power plants which is meant to finance nuclear waste management. The increase in environmentally related taxes was (more than) compensated by a reduction in income tax and social insurance contributions, with the explicit objective of reducing unemployment.

Norway implemented a CO_2 tax on mineral oils in 1991. The scope of the tax has been gradually extended and it covered about 64 per cent of total Norwegian CO_2 emissions in 2002. A tradable permit system in line with the EU's new carbon trading scheme will be introduced from 2005. The intention is to broaden this trading system to other sectors from 2008, as a replacement of the current CO_2 tax. A tax on the sulphur content of fuels is also applied. A reduced rate was levied for a number of years on some industrial uses of coal and coke, but since 2002, this rate has been replaced by a negotiated agreement under which the companies concerned commit to reduce SO_2 emissions. A number of other environmentally related taxes apply to products such as motor vehicles, pesticides, and various types of packaging and waste.

In Sweden, a major revenue-neutral tax reform was introduced in 1991. It included a significant reduction in income taxes, offset by a broadening of the VAT and by a series of new environmental taxes, especially on carbon and sulphur.[14] Energy taxes on industry were halved, nevertheless resulting in higher energy taxation overall. At present, the manufacturing sector pays 50 per cent of the ordinary rates of the CO_2 tax and is totally exempted from the general energy tax. The tax applicable to various categories of diesel and petrol is differentiated according to content of sulphur and benzene, etc. There are consumer and producer taxes on electricity and on domestic air traffic, and Sweden has a charge on NO_x emissions – with the revenue being refunded to the power plants affected, in proportion to the amount of energy they generate.

Denmark introduced a CO_2 tax on fuels in 1992 and continued to broaden its environmentally related taxes until 2002 (Larsen, 1998). The tax reform aimed to: reduce marginal tax rates in all income brackets; eliminate a series of loopholes in the tax law; and gradually transfer tax burden from income and labour to pollution and scarce environmental resources (Danish Ministry of Finance, 1995). The introduction of the 'Energy Package' in 1996 was a milestone, consisting mainly of an increase in the CO_2 tax (with considerably reduced rates for industry) and a new tax on SO_2 emissions. The revenue raised by these taxes is returned to industry through reduced employers' social security contributions and as investment aids for energy saving. Many other taxes – for example, on motor vehicles, waste, waste water, water abstractions, and pesticides – have also been put in place.

The Netherlands introduced a 'general fuel charge' through the 'General Environmental Provision Act' in 1988, which replaced five charges on air pollution, traffic and industrial noise, chemical waste, and lubricants. Between 1992 and 2000, a series of other taxes were introduced (on waste, groundwater, uranium, and small energy users). The 'regulatory tax on energy', introduced in 1996, is levied on small, non-transport, energy consumers, with the revenue recycled in the form of reduced social security contributions (Vermeend and Van der Vaart, 1998). A number of other green taxes – for example, on waste, groundwater, and aviation noise – are in force, and a new kilometre levy to replace existing motor vehicle taxes was discussed but subsequently shelved.

In France, a restructuring of environmental taxes and charges started in 1999. As in the Netherlands, one objective was to streamline and simplify a set of earmarked emission charges. In January 2000, existing charges on air pollution, household waste, special industrial waste, lubricating oils, and noise were merged into a single 'general tax on polluting activities' (TGAP). Taxes on pesticides, granulates, and detergents were also introduced. A progressive reduction of the tax differential between petrol and diesel fuel for cars was initiated in 1999, but discontinued due to political pressures. Also, an extension of the TGAP with a new tax on energy use by industry was rejected by the French Constitutional Council in late 2000 on grounds of an unequal treatment of specific segments of industry.

Germany initiated a green tax reform in April 1999. The main goals were to stimulate energy savings – in the context of the German objective to reduce CO_2 emissions by 25 per cent by 2005, compared with 1990 levels – and to increase employment. The reform comprised two main components: a new tax on electricity and a gradual increase in the taxation of mineral oil over the period 1999–2003. The increased tax burden on energy was compensated by reduced social security contributions for both employers and employees.

In Italy, a carbon tax was introduced in January 1999, to be phased in over five years. The revenue will be used to reduce taxes on labour. However, since 2000, the implementation of the reform has been put on hold.

In the UK, fuel excises were increased by 5–6 per cent per annum in real terms between 1993 and 1999. This 'road fuel duty escalator' was designed to reduce CO_2 emissions and to take into account other environmental factors. A 'climate change levy' on energy use by business and the public sector was introduced in April 2001. Industries entering into negotiated agreements setting targets for emission reductions can obtain an 80 per cent reduction of the tax rate. The revenue is recycled back to industry through lower employers' social security contributions and tax breaks for investments in energy efficiency and renewable energy. As of 2002, firms can opt into a CO_2 emission trading scheme to meet their targets. Firms with negotiated agreements can also fulfil their obligations by buying permits in the domestic UK CO_2 emissions trading scheme (OECD, 2003*b*; Braathen (forthcoming)).

5.5 IMPLEMENTATION ISSUES

Generally speaking, the implementation of environmental taxes is subject to a number of difficulties. There are, of course, technical difficulties, in particular in relation to the design of the taxes. These include ensuring an appropriate 'linkage' between the tax base and the potential environmental damage, without introducing excessive complexity that would undermine the implementation; and fixing an appropriate tax rate that will achieve the environmental objective, while taking into account social and economic constraints. Other issues relate to the use of the tax revenue (for example, earmarking and tax shift), governance and institutions (for example, effectiveness of tax administration, enforcement capacity, tax evasion, pressure groups, and stakeholders), and acceptance building. Dealing with all these aspects would be beyond the scope of this chapter.

A survey undertaken by the OECD clearly indicates, however, that the main political obstacles to broader implementation of environmentally related taxes relate to their impact on the distribution of income between different households and on the competitiveness position of certain industrial sectors. These issues will be briefly analysed below.

5.5.1 *Environmentally Related Taxes and the Distribution of Income between Households*

Environmentally related taxes can have several distributional implications – for instance, increasing regional income disparities. But the issue receiving most political attention in OECD member countries is the distributional impact across household categories – in particular, the possibly regressive impact, measured against income, of such taxes. The income distribution effects of environmentally related taxes, especially those on energy, may be observed in three ways (Smith, 1998):

1. There will be a direct distributional impact related to the structure of household energy expenditure (on heating and transport) for different income brackets. The greater the proportion of low-income households' expenditure devoted to energy, the more regressive will be the impact of the tax.

2. Indirect distributional effects will emanate from the taxation of production inputs. The more energy-intensive the processes, the greater will be the incidence of a tax on the goods produced. Of course, the more the products fall into the basic necessities category, the more regressive the tax will be.
3. The distributional impact will be related to the incidence of the tax. An energy tax may affect end consumers, but it may also affect energy producers or production factors (for example, through a fall in wages or through a lower return on capital). At the same time, part of the tax may be borne by energy-consuming countries, and another part by energy-exporting countries, depending on the elasticities of supply and demand.

In so far as many environmentally related taxes apply to mass consumption products, such as motor vehicles and energy, they can have a negative effect on low-income households.[15] The level of the tax also matters. Other environmental taxes, on products such as detergents, fertilizers, batteries, and pesticides, produce very limited revenue (see Figure 5.2); whether this implies a limited distributive impact, compared with large-scale and fiscally heavier environmental taxes such as those on energy, is an open question. Certain categories may be affected, such as farmers paying taxes on fertilizers and pesticides, and more so if they have to pay water charges according to full social costs.

An evaluation of the distributive implications should also take into account the overall context of the tax reform. For instance, any positive employment effects of a tax reform could reduce the possible regressive effects of the environmental tax. Also, a comprehensive tax reform might comprise reductions in income and/or indirect taxes, which could have positive distributional effects.

The results of an analysis of impacts of a tax reform on income distribution will generally depend on whether the impact on annual or lifetime income is being studied. Most empirical studies address annual income implications.

Finally, one should take into account the distribution of improvements in environmental conditions caused by the reform.[16] For example, low-income households often live in areas in large cities that would benefit the most from measures that would limit road traffic.

Evidence

Evidence on the distributive implications of environmental taxes remains scant. It indicates some, but limited, regressivity, as can be expected from any indirect tax. But little systematic, in-depth, *ex-ante* or *ex-post* analysis has been carried out.

An analysis of possible distributional effects of the carbon–energy tax in the UK, as initially proposed by the European Commission, showed that this tax would clearly hurt poorer households. While a tax of $US10 per barrel (i.e. $88 per tonne of carbon) would reduce total household energy consumption by 6.5 per cent, the reduction would be 10 per cent for the poorest 20 per cent of households (Pearson and Smith, 1991). The figures vary considerably from country to country (Pearson, 1992). To achieve targets concerning climate change, however, a tax on energy might have to be much higher. As mentioned above, the distributive consequences of a reform will depend on the way in which the revenue of the environmentally related tax is recycled.

In its 1997 report, the Swedish Green Tax Commission estimated that doubling the CO_2 tax (from a 1997 rate of SEK0.37 [about €0.04, using exchange rates of April 2003] to SEK0.74 [about €0.08] per kilogram of CO_2) would have a fairly marked regressive impact – see SOU (1997)). In order to maintain the same consumption level, people on the lowest incomes would need to receive compensation of 1.24 per cent of their consumption expenditure, and those on the highest incomes 0.78 per cent. In Norway, environmentally related taxes have not been found to be significantly regressive. However, one issue that has received some political attention is differences in impacts between regions where public transportation is available (and hence it is possible to switch to public transport when fuel taxes increase) and regions where it is not.

A recent study by Bach et al. (2002) estimates the distributive effects of the German green tax reform. The study shows that this reform in itself leads to an increased tax burden for most households, while enterprises in total would benefit. However, as a percentage of household income, the increase in the tax burden is small – below 1.5 per cent of annual disposable income for all the household categories studied. For almost all household categories – grouped according to social status or according to the number of adults and children – the percentage reduction in annual disposable income was estimated to be larger for households with a gross yearly income of under approximately €25,000 than for households with higher incomes.[17]

Policy Options

Basically, two categories of corrective measures to counterbalance any distributive effects of environmentally related taxes can be envisaged: mitigation and compensation.

Mitigation is an *ex-ante* measure consisting of reducing environmental tax rates to alleviate the tax burden on specific segments of the population. This could take at least two forms: establishing a consumption floor below which no tax is levied; or introducing a dual-rate structure with a reduced or zero rate for low-income households.

The main limitation of mitigation measures is that they weaken or even cancel out the desired environmental impact of the tax. Furthermore, the income distribution objective may be poorly achieved; for instance, a consumption floor also benefits the higher-income segment of the population, and hence the deadweight loss is considerable. Using taxable income as a reference also raises difficulties; for instance, taxable income does not necessarily reflect ability to pay when the taxpayer claims significant deductions from gross income, such as mortgage interest. Finally, mitigation measures based on income measures involve substantial administrative complexities and costs.

Nevertheless, a large number of special tax provisions are applied in OECD countries. The OECD/EU database indicates hundreds of provisions such as tax exemptions and reduced rates. Note that these provisions are introduced on both distributive and competitiveness grounds, to the benefit of both households and the business sector, which makes the assessment of the strictly 'social' benefit of these measures quite uncertain.

Compensation measures are basically *ex-post* and outside the realm of the environmentally related taxes as such, i.e. they do not affect their rates or structure, thus maintaining the incentive effect of the tax. They are corrective measures, such as lump-sum compensation, calculated on the basis of average tax payments per household, or subsidies for heat insulation of homes. In this case, compensation will have a progressive incidence on the assumption that, on average, the poorest households pay less tax than the richest. Tax refunds are a typical compensation measure (see Box 5.1); for instance, in several countries, energy taxes are partly repaid to households and/or businesses in the form of subsidies for energy-saving investments or expenditures. Three main forms of compensation can be identified (de Kam, 2002):

1. *Lump-sum compensation*, calculated on the basis of average 'green' tax payments per household, in the form of cash transfers or credits against the income tax liability. Cuts in income taxation may not benefit low-income households because they pay little or no income taxes (Smith, 1998). Tax credits are amounts deductible from tax payable (as distinct from deductions from the tax base). A distinction must be made between so-called 'wastable' and 'non-wastable' tax credits (OECD, 2001c). In the case of wastable tax credits, the environmental tax refund cannot exceed the amount of the income tax liability and will therefore not give rise to a payment by the government to the taxpayer. In the case of non-wastable tax credits, the environmental tax refund can exceed the tax liability, so that the taxpayer can receive a net payment. Therefore, from an income distribution point of view, non-wastable tax credits are the preferred

---

Box 5.1. Examples of Exemptions and Rebates Motivated
by Income Distribution

Germany offers a 50 per cent rebate on the electricity tax for storage heaters installed before April 1999. Such heaters are concentrated in low-income households.

The Netherlands has a tax on domestic energy use (natural gas and electricity), with a fixed tax reduction of €142 (in 2002) for each household connected to the electricity network.

The UK exempts domestic use of energy from its 'climate change levy'.

The Swiss taxes on volatile organic compounds (VOCs) and light heating oil are fully redistributed to the population through the health insurance system. Basic health insurance is compulsory in Switzerland, and the insurance companies will credit each person the amount to be redistributed per person.

Source: Based on OECD (2001c).

option, because there is no ceiling to the tax refund poorer households would be entitled to receive. However, such credits can be relatively complicated to administer.

2. *Income-tested compensation*, with two options (in the case of energy taxes): the compensation paid to *all* households equals the tax due from *average* energy users or polluters; or the compensation is paid only to households below a certain income level, by comparing *actual* 'green' tax payments of households and household income. The rationale for this latter variant might be that poor households sometimes have limited options for reducing their energy use, such as in the case of block heating. However, if it were decided that households need not pay more than, say, 2 per cent of their income in the form of a green tax, the price signal would be ineffective once a household had exceeded this threshold.

3. *Tax shifts*, i.e. the reduction of other taxes, such as labour and income taxes. These are a widespread form of compensation. It is assumed that the regressive impact of the new environmental tax will be compensated by the reduction of other taxes. The net distributional implication of this approach is not clear, however, considering that the poorest households pay the least income tax whereas wealthy households will benefit most from any lowering of income tax. According to Smith (1998), this form of compensation may even prove to be regressive.

Obviously, measures for offsetting the regressive effects of environmental taxes would need to be tailored to specific national and local situations. Scott and Eakins (2001) analyse eleven possible measures in the context of Ireland. Furthermore, Ekins and Dresner (2004) discuss distributive implications of taxes and charges on water, waste, transport and energy in the UK. They show that in most cases a way can be found to redress the regressive effects. In the area of domestic energy, however, the low thermal energy efficiency of many British dwellings makes this difficult to achieve.

Clearly, compensation measures outside the realm of the environmentally related tax are to be preferred to mitigation as they involve a lower risk of defeating the environmental purpose of the tax. For instance, subsidies for more efficient heating systems can be more effective in reducing the burden of increased energy taxation for poorer households living in low-standard apartments.

5.5.2 *Environmentally Related Taxes and International Competitiveness*

A Stumbling Block

It is often claimed in political discussions that environmentally related taxes, particularly on energy, substantially increase the production costs of certain industrial sectors, thus putting them at a competitiveness disadvantage. This is why these industrial sectors (in particular, energy-intensive industries) are strongly opposed to environmental taxes and often formulate an explicit threat of relocation to countries that do not apply such taxes.

In the case of purely local environmental issues, the threat of closing down a heavily polluting firm might not worry political authorities too much. The 'costs' involved in such a closing-down could be (more than) balanced by the environmental benefits reaped. For issues involving cross-border pollution – which is most often the case, for example, in relation to taxes on energy – the situation can be different. Here, the closing-down of a source of pollution in a particular country might not result in any lasting environmental gains if the close-down causes pollution to increase across the border. Hence, there is a fear among policy-makers that the pollution might 'leak out', while they face the political difficulties involved in any plant closures.

If environmentally related taxes are economically efficient (i.e. minimize abatement costs), they should increase the overall competitiveness of the country where they are applied. Reduced damage cost and an improved environment may also enhance competitiveness – for certain sectors and for the country as a whole in the form of, for example, cleaner water for food production and greater attractiveness of the country.

The business community tends to argue in favour of other policy instruments, such as voluntary agreements. Indeed, some countries use 'policy packages', whereby firms can avoid paying taxes (or are granted reduced rates) if they enter into agreements comprising commitments to achieve certain emission reduction targets – see, for example, the CO_2 tax in Denmark, the climate change levy in the UK, and the SO_2 tax in Norway. In practice, such packages often shift a greater part of the total effort to abate a certain type of pollution on to other sectors of the economy – for example, households – or lead to a reduction in the combined abatement effort (OECD, 2003*b*).

The impact of environmentally related taxes on the international competitiveness of a sector is a complex issue depending on various factors:

1. *The market structure.* In relatively competitive markets, increased taxes will result in reduced profits as firms will have no, or limited, opportunity to pass the tax on to consumers through higher prices. Firms with market power will have more opportunity to pass on additional costs in higher prices.

2. *Whether or not taxes replace existing command-and-control regulations.* If taxes replace pre-existing CACs, the impact on competitiveness will depend on whether or not this implies a cost increase, and whether or not the preceding regulatory requirements were devised in a cost-effective way. If efficient taxes are replacing inefficient CACs (thus enabling static efficiency gains), the competitiveness impacts might be positive overall. Note, however, that firms must pay the taxes (for example, on residual emissions and remaining input use) in addition to the abatement cost; this explains the strong opposition from industry. In all cases, with taxes or CACs, there will be winners and losers, depending on the firms' marginal abatement costs. It should also be noted that, in a number of instances, taxes do not replace CACs but come as an additional measure; a negative competitiveness impact is then more likely to occur.

3. *Whether or not the tax reform is revenue neutral.* In a revenue-neutral context, the overall tax burden on the economy remains constant. As environmentally related taxes offset other pre-existing taxes, the tax shift implies primarily a redistribution of the tax burden across the economy. Nevertheless, the tax burden will rise for some firms and sectors of the economy (for example, energy-intensive sectors in the case of a carbon tax).

4. *The nature of the tax shift.* If the revenue of environmentally related taxes is recycled in the form of a reduction in income taxes or social security contributions, thus reducing labour costs, labour-intensive sectors will gain some competitiveness advantages. However, as environmentally related taxes are for the most part paid by members of the labour force, the impact on the tax wedge on labour of such a shift is limited. If the revenue is used to reduce taxes on capital, this could – in isolation – benefit capital-intensive firms or sectors.

5. *The effects of the environmental improvements.* If the tax is environmentally effective, some environmental benefits may improve the competitiveness of certain firms (for example, reduced water-cleaning cost, reduced crop losses, and reduced health cost). This argument is, however, equally valid for any other policy instrument.

Policy Options

Confronted with the competitiveness issue, countries can adopt either of two strategies. One is a wait-and-see attitude: who will go first? This is a 'prisoner's dilemma', where no one wants to start before the others. The other strategy is to introduce environmental taxes, but with special provisions to protect sectors subject to international competition; this is a widespread policy in practice: the OECD/EU database indicates a large number of tax exemptions, many of them for industry (see below).

Five main policy options are open to countries that decide to increase the use of environmentally related taxes but that worry about possible negative impacts on sectoral competitiveness:

1. *Exempt specific sectoral activities or products from the new tax.* This option is widely used: the OECD/EU database includes more than a thousand exemptions in OECD countries. However, the data must be interpreted with caution: exemptions are introduced for a number of social, environmental, and economic reasons, and only part of these exemptions are directly motivated by sectoral competitiveness concerns. One often-applied approach is simply to exclude the main industries completely from the application of a tax, or, for example, by saying that a particular tax does not apply to the use of fuels as input or reduction agents in industrial processes. In other cases, the tax is paid at the outset, but later refunded for polluters that satisfy certain criteria.

2. *Apply reduced tax rates for certain sectors, products, or inputs* – thus providing at least some incentive at the margin to reduce emissions. Many countries apply reduced tax rates – for example, to industrial sectors. For instance, Sweden initially gave a 75 per cent rebate on the carbon tax (and total exemption in the case of the energy tax) to industry and horticulture; this rebate was reduced to 50 per cent in July 1997. In Denmark, a 50 per cent rebate on the CO_2 tax was granted to industry for the period 1993–5. Both countries are interesting 'front-runners' as they were amongst the first to introduce CO_2 taxes. In Germany, electricity taxes are significantly lower for the production sector than for households, and in the UK, tax rates under the climate change levy for energy-intensive companies are 20 per cent of the 'normal' rate.

3. *Apply full tax rates for all polluters, but recycle, fully or partially, the revenue to the affected firms.* One example of such an approach is the Swedish charge on NO_x emissions from power plants. All revenues from this charge are recycled back to the plants in proportion to the amount of energy they have produced. In this way, a strong incentive at the margin is given to the plants to reduce their emissions – but the customers of the power plants do not have an incentive to lower their demand for a polluting product.

4. *Apply border tax adjustments (BTAs).* Environmentally related taxes place domestic producers at a competitive disadvantage if foreign competitors are not subject to similar taxes. Conceptually, BTAs can apply to both products and production processes. Often, it is relatively easy to subject imported products to similar taxes to domestically manufactured products. It is, however, more complicated to tax a product based on the way in which it has been produced. If domestic firms are subject to environmental taxes at the production level (for example, input or emission taxes), applying taxes on foreign competitors implies, *inter alia*, that production processes are deemed to have similar environmental effects. This type of approach can raise formidable legal and practical difficulties. However, such mechanisms do exist under the ozone depletion substances tax in the USA (see US Department of the Treasury, 2002).

5. *International coordination.* The many special provisions and exemptions for industry gravely undermine the environmental effectiveness of environmentally related taxes today. This indicates that, in the absence of international coordination to establish some minimum 'level playing field', green tax reforms are not likely to make significant progress. However, international tax coordination requires consensus among countries, and many countries are reluctant to take part. This is well illustrated in the EU context, with the rejection of the proposed carbon–energy tax in 1992 and the blocking of proposed increases in minimum levels of excises on energy.[18]

Often, competitiveness can be softened through a gradual phasing-in of taxes. For instance, the phasing-in of energy and CO_2 taxes in Denmark was designed to provide industry with clear advance signals, enabling it to plan accordingly. A similar approach is being used with the landfill tax in the UK, where the tax rate per tonne of standard waste will increase by £3 (approximately €4.5) per year until a level of £35 per tonne is reached.

Conclusion

Available studies and data show no significant impact of environmental policies on international trade or on employment in polluting sectors. Jaffe et al. (1995) examined over a hundred studies on the potential effect of environmental regulations (i.e. not only taxes) on the competitiveness of US industry. They concluded: 'Overall, there is relatively little evidence to support the hypothesis that environmental regulations have had a large adverse effect on competitiveness, however that elusive term is defined'. Morgenstern, Pizer, and Shih (2002) found, when examining four heavily polluting sectors in the USA, that 'increased environmental spending generally does *not* cause a significant change in employment'.[19]

These results do, however, provide few indications of the sectoral competitiveness impacts of the broader use of environmentally related taxes. Given the large number of special provisions for industry at present, it is not surprising that no negative competitiveness impacts of environmentally related taxes have been noted to date: when the tax burden is close to zero, the impact of this 'burden' would, in any case, be small.

OECD (2003e) does, however, indicate that the negative impact on the competitiveness of certain heavy industries of the general application of (relatively high) taxes to address climate change would be very significant if a country or a small region applied them unilaterally.[20] This is why international coordination is essential. A useful starting point could be to foster the environmental effectiveness of current taxes by gradually removing the numerous exemptions currently granted to industry. A second step would be to initiate a concerted action between OECD countries for the gradual introduction of environmentally related taxes. Accordingly, OECD (2001c) concludes that 'countries concerned with competitiveness implications of adjusting certain environmentally related taxes on a unilateral basis could consider possible concerted policy options and changes, decided and implemented at the national level, but within a framework which provides for a multilateral dialogue'.

5.6 ENVIRONMENTAL EFFECTIVENESS

5.6.1 *Price Elasticity Estimates*

The environmental effectiveness of a tax can be measured as the extent to which it delivers a reduction in pollution or actual emissions. This is closely connected to the price elasticities of the tax bases to which the tax applies – and to the extent the tax base is comprehensive (see references above to the many important exemptions under existing taxes). The environmental effectiveness will obviously be limited if major relevant tax bases are exempted from the levy.

An important first step, therefore, in evaluating behavioural responses to environmentally related taxes is the collection of up-to-date information on the price elasticities of demand for energy, transport, and other environmentally related goods.

Table 5.2, taken from OECD (2001*c*) – which in turn was based on OECD (2000*b*) – summarizes some of the available price elasticity estimates with regard to petrol or gasoline. While most estimates show relatively low own-price elasticities in the short run (−0.15 to −0.38), some estimates indicate significantly higher values (−0.51 to −1.07). Long-term own-price elasticities are generally estimated to be higher than short-term elasticities (−0.23 to −1.4).

A recent paper by Sipes and Mendelsohn (2001) examines 'whether charging higher taxes [on gasoline] would result in significant emissions reductions'.

Table 5.2. *Selected Estimates of Price Elasticities of Gasoline*

		Short run	Long run	Ambiguous
Pooled time series / cross section	Micro	−0.30 to −0.39 (USA)	−0.77 to −0.83 (USA)	
	Macro	−0.15 to −0.38 (OECD*)	−1.05 to −1.4 (OECD*)	
		−0.15 (Europe)	−1.24 (Europe)	
			−0.55 to −0.9 (OECD 18**)	
		−0.6 (Mexico)	−1.13 to −1.25 (Mexico)	
Cross section	Micro	−0.51 (USA)		
		0 to −0.67 (USA)		
	Macro	Mean −1.07 (−0.77 to −1.34) (OECD*)		
Time series	Macro	−0.12 to −0.17 (USA)	−0.23 to −0.35 (USA)	
Meta-analyses and surveys		Average −0.26 (0 to −1.36) (international)	Average −0.58 (0 to −2.72) (international)	Average −0.53 (−0.02 to −1.59) (USA)
		Mean −0.27 (time series)	Mean −0.71 (time series)	Mean −0.53 (time series)
		Mean −0.28 (cross section)	Mean −0.84 (cross section)	Mean −0.18 (cross section)
				−0.53 (panel data)
				−0.1 to −0.3 (22 estimates)

* OECD except Luxembourg, Iceland, and New Zealand.
** OECD 18 covers Canada, the USA, Japan, Austria, Belgium, Denmark, France, Germany, Greece, Ireland, Italy, the Netherlands, Norway, Spain, Sweden, Switzerland, Turkey, and the UK.

Sources: OECD, 2000*b*, 2001*c*.

Both experimental survey data and actual behaviour in Southern California and Connecticut are evaluated to explore whether people would change their driving behaviour in response to higher gasoline prices. Both sets of results reveal that drivers are price inelastic in the short run (-0.4 to -0.6) as well as the long run (-0.5 to -0.7). Imposing environmental surcharges on gasoline would result in only a small reduction in driving and thus only a small improvement in the environment. Such taxes would therefore place a heavy and clear burden on drivers, and make gasoline taxes extremely unpopular. 'Our results indicate that if an environmental surcharge is added to gasoline taxes, then the additional tax will decrease gasoline consumption only slightly and, therefore, will have little effect on air pollution. For example, the price elasticity estimates suggest that a 33% increase in gasoline prices (a \$0.50 per gallon tax) would decrease gasoline consumption by only 13–23%.'

We find this interpretation of the estimated elasticities too negative. First, if a tax of \$US0.50 per gallon of petrol were added on top of existing federal and state taxes, the combined tax rate in all US states would still be lower than the tax rate applied in all European OECD countries.[21] Secondly, although it is common practice to say that a product with a price elasticity below 1 in absolute value is 'inelastic in demand', we believe that a long-term reduction in petrol use of about 20 per cent would be quite significant. Furthermore, the price elasticity of petrol is likely to be comparatively low anyway in a region such as Southern California, with large distances and little public transport – in other words, few substitution possibilities.

Another illustration of possible impacts of changes in petrol prices is given in Figure 5.6. While more detailed studies would be needed to determine the precise interaction, it is interesting to note that when real petrol prices in the USA increased in the period up to the early 1980s, a significant increase in fuel efficiency of new cars occurred. Later, as real petrol prices decreased significantly (to levels well below those before the first 'oil price shock' in 1973), the increases in fuel efficiency of new cars were brought to a halt. Indeed, the growing popularity of 'sports utility vehicles' has probably led to decreases in fuel efficiency in recent years.

Popp (2002) points to another advantage of environmentally related taxes: 'The most significant result is the strong, positive impact energy prices have on new innovations. ... My results also make clear that simply relying on technological change as a panacea for environmental problems is not enough. There must be some mechanism in place that encourages new innovation'.

Price elasticity estimates of other energy categories are also available. Table 5.3, taken from OECD (2000*b*), presents estimated own-price elasticities of household electricity demand. Furthermore, Nesbakken (1998) quotes a number of estimates, which are reproduced in Table 5.4. Again, the available estimates indicate that a tax on electricity could lead to a relatively significant reduction in electricity consumption. If, for example, a tax increased the price that electricity consumers are facing by 25 per cent, electricity consumption could decrease by some 5–15 per cent in the long term, which would entail clear environmental benefits.

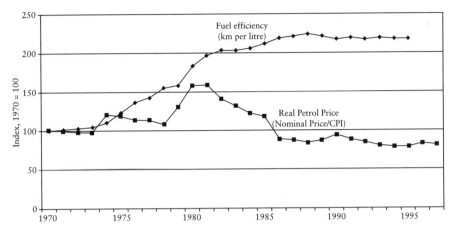

Figure 5.6. *Petrol Prices and Fuel Efficiency of New Cars: USA*
Source: OECD (2001c), based on Birol and Keppler (2000).

Bjørner and Jensen (2002) use a micro-panel database covering the majority of Danish industrial companies over the period of 1983–1997. They find that the average price elasticity of energy in Danish industry is −0.44. Interestingly, the various price elasticities depend on the energy prices firms were facing at the outset. When ranked in increasing order according to energy prices they were facing, the estimated price elasticity of energy for firms in the 10% decile is about −0.4, about −0.6 for firms in the median decile, and about −0.7 for firms in the 90% decile.

Fullerton (this volume) presents a number of estimates of price elasticities related to unit-based garbage collection fees. He concludes: 'The basic message here is that the demand for garbage collection services is inelastic. Substitutes are not readily available. Advocates of unit-based pricing suggest demand may become more elastic in the long run as households learn of available substitutes for garbage disposal, but the empirical literature has yet to address this point.'

5.6.2 Ex-Post Studies of Environmental Effectiveness

Ex-post studies of the environmental effectiveness of environmentally related taxes, implicitly or explicitly, incorporate estimates of relevant price elasticities, but also have to disentangle the effects of the taxes from other developments that have affected demand for the products or services involved. It is obviously always debatable what would have happened if a given tax had not been introduced.

In Belgium, the tax differentiation between heavy fuels with a sulphur content below or above 1 per cent induced a decrease in the use of the fuel with the higher sulphur content from 20 per cent of the market in 1994 to less than 1 per cent in 1998 (also due to a switch to natural gas) (OECD, 2001c). Taxes on non-reused or recycled beverage containers, disposable cameras,

Table 5.3. *Selected Estimates of Own-Price Elasticities of Residential Electricity*

		Short run	Long run	Ambiguous
Pooled time series / cross section	Micro	−0.433 (Norway)	−0.442 (Norway)	
		−0.2 (USA)		
	Macro	−0.158 to −0.184 (USA)	−0.263 to −0.329 (USA)	
Cross section	Micro	−0.4 to −1.1 (Norway)	−0.3 to −1.1 (Norway)	
	Macro			−1.42 (53 countries)
Time series	Macro	−0.25 (USA) −0.62 (USA)	−0.5 (USA) −0.6 (USA)	
Meta-analyses and surveys		−0.05 to −0.9	−0.2 to −4.6	−0.05 to −0.12 (4 studies)

Source: OECD (2001*c*), based on OECD (2000*b*).

Table 5.4. *More Estimates of Own-Price Elasticities of Residential Electricity*

Study	Country	Details	Short run	Long run
Aasness and Holtsmark, 1993	Norway	Household data		−0.2
Halvorsen and Larsen, 1998	Norway	Household data, dynamic model	−0.33	−0.42
Parti and Parti, 1980	USA	Household data	−0.58	
Morss and Small, 1989	USA		−0.23	−0.38
Baker, Blundell and Micklewright, 1989	UK	Paper includes results for subgroups of households		−0.76
Dennerlein, 1987	Germany	Household data, discrete−continuous choice		−0.38
Dubin and McFadden, 1984	USA	Discrete−continuous choice		−0.26
Bernard, Bolduc and Bélanger, 1996	Canada	Discrete−continuous choice	−0.67	
Branch, 1993	USA	Expenditure Survey data	−0.2	
Garbacz, 1983	USA	Partial elasticities	−0.193	

Source: Nesbakken, 1998.

batteries, and various packaging, introduced in 1993, led industry to meet all recycling and reuse targets, thus avoiding payment of the taxes.

In Denmark, the sulphur tax caused a reduction of emissions by 34,000 tonnes between 1996 and 2000. The tax on non-hazardous waste reduced the net delivered waste to municipal sites by 26 per cent over the period 1987–96, and waste to smaller fills and private waste sites by 39 per cent over the period 1990–6. Industrial waste, however, increased by 8 per cent. Recycling also increased considerably: up 77 per cent for paper and cardboard and up 50 per cent for glass (Andersen, 1998).

In Finland, it is estimated that, in the absence of the CO_2 tax, carbon emissions would have been 7 per cent higher in 1998 if taxes had remained at the 1990 level (Finnish Economic Council, 2000).

In Norway, CO_2 taxes introduced in 1991 lowered CO_2 emissions of some stationary combustion plants by some 21 per cent, whereas the drop was much less in other sectors. It is estimated that CO_2 emissions produced by mobile household combustion devices fell by 2–3 per cent as a consequence of the CO_2 tax (Larsen and Nesbakken, 1997). It is also estimated that CO_2 emissions per unit of oil produced by the Norwegian oil sector fell by 1.5 per cent due to measures taken by the industry in response to the CO_2 tax (ECON, 1994).

The Swedish sulphur tax (introduced in 1991) contributed to a fall in the sulphur content of oil-based fuels of more than 50 per cent *beyond the legal standards*.[22] The sulphur content of light oils has now fallen below 0.076 per cent (i.e. less than half the legal limit of 0.2 per cent). The tax is estimated to have reduced emissions of SO_2 by 80 per cent compared with 1980 (Nordic Council of Ministers, 1999). Also in Sweden, a tax differentiation was introduced in 1991 on diesel fuels in order to stimulate the use of less-polluting fuel oils. From 1992 to 1996, the proportion of 'clean' diesel sold in Sweden rose from 1 per cent to 85 per cent, which led to a reduction of more than 75 per cent on average in the sulphur emissions of diesel-driven vehicles (Swedish Environmental Protection Agency, 1997).

In most countries, the tax differentiation between leaded and unleaded petrol, combined with regulations ordering service stations to offer unleaded petrol and the introduction of new emission standards for motor vehicles – based on such requirements as catalytic converters – led to a rapid fall in the market share of leaded petrol (which has now been withdrawn from sale in most OECD countries). The fiscal incentive greatly speeded up the process, despite slow penetration of new vehicles equipped with catalytic converters. Similarly, tax preferences given to ultra-low sulphur petrol and diesel fuels in several countries have lead to a rapid disappearance of fuels with higher sulphur contents.

5.7 CONCLUSIONS

The use of environmentally related levies still remains relatively limited in scope, and their environmental and economic effectiveness is hampered by a number of shortcomings.

- In many instances, the 'linkage' between actual tax rates and calculated externalities is weak or non-existent. For instance, while the tax rate on petrol in a number of countries is relatively high compared with estimated 'optimal' or 'Pigouvian' levels, in many other cases the rates are low compared with such levels.
- This is most evident concerning industry and some other economic sectors, where the existence of a very large number of exemptions, refund mech-

anisms, and other provisions severely undermines the environmental and economic effectiveness of the existing taxes.

- Important tax bases, such as coal, are largely not taxed at all, despite the substantial externalities involved, creating significant distortions and an incoherent picture.

- The levies are often complex, with a confusing variety of tax rates and special provisions. While a complex rate structure might be required to reflect properly the differences in environmental externalities between different products and/or different uses of these products, many of the complexities in existing taxes seem to be due to other political concerns being taken into account. It is often not clear that these concerns are most effectively addressed through special modifications of environmentally related taxes.

- Taxes often combine with other environmental policy instruments in an inconsistent or overlapping way. For example, it is possible that certain regulations on the sulphur content of fuels are redundant if taxes are also levied on it.

- There can also be conflicting incentives between different taxes. For example, while fuel tax rates tend to be lower for diesel than for petrol, one-off or recurrent motor vehicle taxes are sometimes higher for diesel-driven vehicles than for petrol-driven vehicles.

- The fear of loss of international competitiveness of certain industrial sectors remains the main political obstacle to a broader use of environmentally related taxes. The importance of this obstacle could be reduced through increased international coordination. While global cooperation would be required to eradicate the sectoral competitiveness problem, OECD (2003e) indicates that the problem could be very significantly reduced if even a much smaller group of countries decided to cooperate.

In conclusion, environmentally related levies are a potentially effective way of protecting the environment and thus enhancing economic efficiency. It is likely, that countries will give environmental taxes (as well as tradable permits) an increasingly important role in combating greenhouse gas emissions. There is also significant scope for using environmentally related levies to address other environmental externalities. The reduction of environmentally harmful subsidies to agriculture, for example, could be incorporated in a green tax reform. Such reforms should be implemented in the context of broader tax reforms, providing an opportunity to reduce existing tax distortions and modernize taxation systems.

Notes

1 For an excellent, recent presentation of the theory of environmental taxation, see Sandmo (2000).

2 See www.oecd.org/env/tax-database. Figures 5.1 to 5.5 are all based on information from this database.

3 Information for 1995 was used to prepare Figure 5.2, but the main findings are still valid. One exception is that less revenue is now collected from leaded petrol while more is collected from diesel.

4 The lower tax rates on diesel than on petrol – particularly in European countries – probably reflect to a large extent a fear of loss of tax revenues through purchases in neighbouring countries of diesel for heavy vehicles involved in cross-border traffic. The competitiveness position of such vehicles would not be much affected by an increase in diesel tax rates, as they can in practice buy much of their fuel abroad. Vehicles only involved in domestic transport would, however, face increased competition from foreign transport companies if diesel tax rates were increased.

   Another argument sometimes used in the discussion on the relative tax rates for petrol and diesel is that the rates on diesel should be lower than those on petrol since diesel vehicles use less fuel per kilometre, and hence contribute less to the climate-change problem. This argument appears invalid, however, since the Pigouvian tax rate on diesel is higher than that on petrol, due to the higher – non-internalized – externalities related, for example, to NO_x (nitrogen oxides) and particles emissions from diesel-driven vehicles.

5 For an extended discussion of the theory of motor vehicle taxation, see Newbery (this volume). The European Conference of Ministers of Transport (2000) discusses efficient transport taxes and charges in a number of European countries. OECD (1997) presents a number of case studies of the external effects of road transport. Parry (2002) compares the efficiency of alternative policies for reducing traffic congestion.

6 The climate change levy in the UK includes electricity generation, except for high-quality combined heat and power plant. A new tax on coal in Japan also includes coal used for electricity generation.

7 In addition, to serve as a proxy for taxes related to externalities caused by electricity generation (fuel use, landscape damage in the case of hydro-based power, etc.), taxes on electricity consumption can reflect externalities related to electricity distribution, such as damage to the landscape and scenery caused by power lines. There are also claims that power lines can cause harmful radiation.

8 As mentioned, some countries (also) levy taxes on (certain types of) electricity production. For example, in the Czech Republic there is a tax of €0.0015 per kWh of electricity produced in nuclear power plants. In the UK, the tax rate of the 'non-fossil-fuel obligation levy' is 0.7 per cent of the electricity price.

9 Fullerton (this volume) presents an extensive discussion of the marginal social costs of waste generation and the optimal fees on garbage collection. Several chapters of OECD (2004) discuss similar issues.

10 In this estimate, it is assumed that the recovered energy replaces coal-based electricity production. If the incinerator instead replaces electricity generated by an oil-fired power plant, the net external costs increase to €44 per tonne of waste incinerated.

11 The figure for disamenity costs is based on US studies, and COWI (2000*a*) underlines that it might not be applicable to European conditions. For *all* the cost estimates, intervals representing upper and lower bounds are shown in the report.

12 For a detailed assessment of environmentally harmful subsidies, see OECD (1998 I, 2003*c*).

13 This is true particularly for NO_x and particles emissions.

14 According to Statistiska centralbyrån (2002), the tax reform of 1990–91 entailed a SEK18 billion (about 2 billion Euro, using exchange rates as at April 2003) increase

in environmentally related taxes and a SEK71 billion (about 8 billion Euro) decrease in taxes on labour income. Between 1993 and 2000, the share of environmentally related taxes as a percentage of GDP *decreased* 8 per cent, while taxes on labour increased 13 per cent. The 2002 budget included a SEK2 billion (200 million Euro) tax shift from labour to energy.

15 In developing countries and some transition countries, taxes on motor vehicles and motor vehicle fuels can be made progressive in terms of their effect on income distribution, as the poorer parts of the population do not own motor vehicles.

16 For the theoretical underpinning of this point, see, for example, Sandmo (2000, section 5.5).

17 Bach et al. (2002) also include estimates of the impacts on income distribution of the (revenue-neutral) ecological tax reform in combination with a broader tax reform initiated by the German government, involving increases in child allowances and changes in the income taxation of families. The combined reform was found to *increase* the annual disposable income of almost all household categories. However, as the broader reform incorporates a substantial net revenue loss, this finding is not very surprising.

18 For an issue such as climate change, where emissions anywhere in the world cause similar impacts, coordination at a global level would, in principle, be necessary to ensure that no 'leakage' of pollution takes place. Such coordination seems unlikely. The chance is somewhat greater that a limited number of countries – for example, the thirty OECD countries – could agree to some form of coordination. OECD (2003e) indicates that the negative impacts of a relatively high carbon tax on steel production in any of five OECD sub-regions would be significantly reduced if such a hypothetical tax were applied simultaneously in all OECD countries rather than introduced in one of the sub-regions.

19 However, Xing and Kolstad (2002) *do* find a 'significant negative linear relationship between FDI [foreign direct investment] of the US chemical and metal industries and the stringency of environmental regulation in a host country'. However, they point out that 'our empirical study only identifies the impact of environmental regulations on capital outflows and reveals the role of environmental regulations in the decision-making of the FDI of polluting industries. It would not be appropriate to conclude that environmental regulation alone can decide the direction of FDI flow for a polluting industry.'

20 This does not necessarily mean that such taxes should not be applied. For example, it can be cost effective for a country to meet its obligations under the Kyoto protocol by closing down plants.

   OECD (2003e) also indicates that the negative competitiveness impacts can often be significantly reduced through various types of revenue recycling or border tax adjustments.

   Bovenberg and Goulder (2000) and Goulder (2002) show that profits in some of the potentially most affected sectors can be maintained through the grandfathering of a limited share of permits under a tradable permits system, with a modest loss of economic efficiency. As explained in Goulder (2002), 'CO_2 abatement policies have the potential to produce very large rents to the regulated firms. By compelling fossil fuel suppliers to restrict their outputs, the government effectively causes firms to behave like a cartel, leading to higher prices and the potential for excess profit. To the extent that the environmental policy enables the firms to retain these rents – such is the case under a CO_2 policy involving freely offered (or "grandfathered") tradeable permits – the firms can make considerably higher profits under regulation than in its absence. Correspondingly, the government needs to leave with firms only a fraction of these potential rents in order to preserve the profits of the regulated industries.'

Bjertnæs and Fæhn (2004) found similar results in the case of a tax reform in a small, open economy.

21 Incidentally, a \$0.50 per gallon tax increase is – in absolute terms – significantly less than the €0.15 per litre tax increase that was phased in in Germany between 1 April 1999 and 1 January 2003. Comeau and Chapman (2002) have also commented on the article by Sipes and Mendelsohn.

22 According to Statistiska centralbyrån (2002), the tax reform of 1990–91 entailed a SEK18 billion (about 2 billion Euro, using exchange rates as at April 2003) increase in environmentally related taxes and a SEK71 billion (about 8 billion Euro) decrease in taxes on labour income. Between 1993 and 2000, the share of environmentally related taxes as a percentage of GDP *decreased* 8 per cent, while taxes on labour increased 13 per cent. The 2002 budget included a SEK2 billion (200 million Euro) tax shift from labour to energy.

References

Andersen, M. S. (1998), 'Assessing the effectiveness of Denmark's waste tax', *Environment*, May.

Bach, S., Kohlhaas, M., Meyer, B., Praetorius, B., and Welsch, H. (2002), 'The effects of environmental fiscal reform in Germany: a simulation study', *Energy Policy*, 30: 803–11.

Baker, P., Blundell, R., and Micklewright, J. (1989), 'Modelling household energy expenditures using micro-data', *Economic Journal*, 99: 720–38.

Barde, J-P. (1992), *Economie et politique de l'environnement*, Paris: Presses Universitaires de France.

——(1999), 'Environmental taxes in OECD countries: an overview', in OECD, *Environmental Taxes: Recent Developments in China and OECD Countries*, Paris: Organisation for Economic Co-operation and Development.

Bernard, J. T., Bolduc, D., and Bélanger, D. (1996), 'Quebec residential electricity demand: a microeconometric approach', *Canadian Journal of Economics*, 29: 92–113.

Birol, F., and Keppler, J. H. (2000), 'Markets and energy efficiency policy: an economic approach', in *Energy Taxes and Prices*, first quarter 2000, xi–xxiii, Paris: Organisation for Economic Co-operation and Development / International Energy Agency.

Bjertnæs, G. H., and T. Fæhn (2004), 'Energy Taxation in a Small, Open Economy: Efficiency Gains under Political Restraints', Statistics Norway, Discussion Paper 387. Available at www.ssb.no/publikasjoner/DP/pdf/dp387.pdf.

Bjørner, T. B., and H. H. Jensen (2002), 'Energy taxes, voluntary agreements and investment subsidies – a micro panel analysis of the effect on Danish industrial companies' energy demand', *Resource and Energy Economics*, 24(3): 229–49.

Bovenberg, L. A., and Goulder, L. H. (2000), 'Neutralizing the adverse industry impacts of CO_2 abatement policies: what does it cost?', National Bureau of Economic Research, Working Paper 7654. Available at http://www.papers.nber.org/papers.

Braathen, N. A. (forthcoming), 'Environmental agreements used in combination with other policy instruments', in E. Croci (ed.), *The Handbook of Environmental Voluntary Agreements*, Dordrecht, Netherlands: Kluwer Academic Publishers.

Branch, E. R. (1993), 'Short run income elasticity of demand for residential electricity using Consumer Expenditure Survey data', *Energy Journal*, 14(4): 111–21.

Comeau, J., and Chapman, D. (2002), 'Gasoline taxes, CAFÉ and the Kyoto protocol', *Ecological Economics*, 40: 317–20.

COWI (2000a), *A Study on the Economic Valuation of Environmental Externalities from Landfill Disposal and Incineration of Waste*, report prepared for the European Commission, DG Environment. Available at http://europa.eu.int/comm/environment/enveco/waste/cowi_ext_from_landfill.pdf.

—— (2000b), *A Study on the Economic Valuation of Environmental Externalities from Landfill Disposal and Incineration of Waste*, appendices to report prepared for the European Commission, DG Environment. Available at http://europa.eu.int/comm/environment/enveco/waste/cowi_ext_from_landfill_appendix.pdf.

Danish Ministry of Finance (1995), *Energy Taxes on Industry in Denmark*, Copenhagen.

De Kam, F. (2002), Discussion Paper for the Conference on Environmental Fiscal Reform, OECD and German Federal Ministry for the Environment, Nature Conservation and Nuclear Safety, Berlin, 27 June. Available at www.olis.oecd.org/olis/2002doc.nsf/LinkTo/COM-ENV-EPOC-DAFFE-CFA(2002)76-FINAL.

Dennerlein, R. K. H. (1987), 'Residential demand for electrical appliances and electricity in Federal Republic of Germany', *Energy Journal*, 8(1): 60–86.

Dubin, J. A., and McFadden, D. L. (1984), 'An econometric analysis of residential electric appliance holdings and consumption', *Econometrica*, 52: 345–62.

ECON (1994), 'Virkninger av CO$_2$-avgift på olje- og gassutvinning i Norge – Delrapport 4: Sammendrag og hovedkonklusjoner' (Impacts of the CO$_2$ tax on oil and gas extraction in Norway – Partial report 4: Summary and conclusions), Report 326/94, Oslo.

Ekins, P., and S. Dresner (2004), *Green Taxes and Charges: Reducing their impact on low-income households*, York: The Joseph Rowntree Foundation.

European Conference of Ministers of Transport (2000), *Efficient Transport Taxes & Charges*, Paris: Organisation for Economic Co-operation and Development.

Finnish Economic Council (2000), *Environmental and Energy Taxation in Finland: Preparing for the Kyoto Challenge*, Summary of the Working Group Report, Prime Minister's Office Publication Series 2000/4, Helsinki. Available at www.vn.fi/vnk/english/publications/vnk20004e/.

Fullerton, D. (this volume), 'An excise tax on municipal solid waste?'.

Garbacz, C. (1983), 'A model of residential demand for electricity using a national household sample', *Energy Economics*, 5(2): 124–8.

Goulder, L. H. (2002), 'Mitigating the adverse impacts of CO$_2$ abatement policies on energy-intensive industries', Resources for the Future, Discussion Paper 02-22. Available at www.rff.org/disc_papers/2002.htm.

Halvorsen, B., and Larsen, B. M. (1998), 'The dynamics of residential electricity consumption in household production: a microeconometric analysis', in Conference Proceedings, 21st Annual International Conference of the IAEE, Quebec City.

International Energy Agency (2001), *Energy Taxes & Prices*, third quarter 2001, Paris: Organisation for Economic Co-operation and Development / IEA.

—— (2003), *Energy Taxes & Prices*, first quarter 2003, Paris: Organisation for Economic Co-operation and Development / IEA.

Jaffe, A., Peterson, S. R., Portney, P. R., and Stavins, R. N. (1995), 'Environmental regulation and the competitiveness of US manufacturing: what does the evidence tell us?', *Journal of Economic Literature*, 33(March): 132–63.

Larsen, B. M., and Nesbakken, R. (1997), 'Norwegian emissions of CO_2 1987–1994: a study of some effects of the CO_2 tax', *Environmental and Resource Economics*, 9: 275–90.

Larsen, H. (1998), *Energy Taxes: The Danish Model*, Copenhagen: Ministry of Taxation.

Ministerie van Financiën (2001), *'Greening' the Tax System*, summary of the report of the Second Dutch Green Tax Commission, The Hague: Ministry of Finance.

Morgenstern, R. D., Pizer, W. A., and Shih, J-S. (2002), 'Jobs versus the environment: an industry-level perspective', *Journal of Environmental Economics and Management*, 43: 412–36.

Morss, M. F., and Small, J. L. (1989), 'Deriving electricity demand elasticities from a simulation model', *Energy Journal*, 10(3): 51–76.

Nesbakken, R. (1998), 'Price sensitivity of residential energy consumption in Norway', Statistics Norway, Discussion Paper 232. Available at www.ssb.no/publikasjoner/DP/pdf/dp232.pdf.

Newbery, D. M. (this volume), 'Road user and congestion charges'.

Nordic Council of Ministers (1999), *The Scope for Nordic Co-ordination of Economic Instruments in Environmental Policy*, TemaNord, 1999-50, Copenhagen.

OECD (1994), *Managing the Environment: The Role of Economic Instruments*, Paris: Organisation for Economic Co-operation and Development.

——(1996), *Subsidies and Environment: Exploring the Linkages*, Paris: Organisation for Economic Co-operation and Development.

——(1997), *Reforming Energy and Transport Subsidies*, Paris: Organisation for Economic Co-operation and Development.

——(1998), *Improving the Environment through Reducing Subsidies*, Parts I and II, Paris: Organisation for Economic Co-operation and Development.

——(1999), *OECD Environmental Data, Compendium 1999*, Paris: Organisation for Economic Co-operation and Development.

——(2000a), *Transition to Responsible Fisheries: Economic and Policy Implications*, Paris: Organisation for Economic Co-operation and Development.

——(2000b), 'Behavioural responses to environmentally-related taxes'. Available at www.olis.oecd.org/olis/1999doc.nsf/LinkTo/com-env-epoc-daffe-cfa(99)111-final.

——(2001a), *Sustainable Development: Critical Issues*, Paris: Organisation for Economic Co-operation and Development.

——(2001b), *Review of Fisheries in OECD Countries: Policies and Summary Statistics*, Paris: Organisation for Economic Co-operation and Development.

——(2001c), *Environmentally Related Taxation in OECD Countries: Issues and Strategies*, Paris: Organisation for Economic Co-operation and Development.

——(2001d), *Revenue Statistics, 1965–2000*, Paris: Organisation for Economic Co-operation and Development.

——(2003a), *Agricultural Policies in OECD Countries: Monitoring and Evaluation*, Paris: Organisation for Economic Co-operation and Development.

——(2003b), *Voluntary Approaches for Environmental Policy: Effectiveness, efficiency and usage in policy mixes*, Paris: Organisation for Economic Co-operation and Development.

——(2003c), *Environmentally Harmful Subsidies: Policy Issues and Challenges*, Paris: Organisation for Economic Co-operation and Development.

OECD (2003*d*), *Review of Fisheries in OECD Countries*, Paris: Organisation for Economic Co-operation and Development.

——(2003*e*), *Environmental Policy in the Steel Industry: Using economic instruments*, Paris: Organisation for Economic Co-operation and Development. Available at www.oecd.org/dataoecd/58/20/33709359.pdf

——(2004), *Addressing the Economics of Waste*, Paris: Organisation for Economic Co-operation and Development.

Parry, I. W. H. (2002), 'Comparing the efficiency of alternative policies for reducing traffic congestion', *Journal of Public Economics*, 85: 333–62.

——and Small, K. A. (2002), 'Does Britain or the United States have the right gasoline tax?', Resources for the Future, Discussion Paper 02-12. Available at www.rff.org/disc_papers/2002.htm.

Parti, M., and Parti, C. (1980), 'The total and appliance-specific conditional demand for electricity in the household sector', *Bell Journal of Economics*, 11: 309–21.

Pearson, M. (1992), 'Equity issues and carbon taxes', in OECD, *Climate Change: Designing a Practical Tax System*, Paris: Organisation for Economic Co-operation and Development.

——and Smith, S. (1991), *The European Carbon Tax: An Assessment of the European Commission Proposal*, London: Institute for Fiscal Studies.

Pigou, A. C. (1920), *The Economics of Welfare*, London: Macmillan.

Popp, D. (2002), 'Induced innovation and energy prices', *American Economic Review*, 92: 160–80.

Sandmo, A. (2000), *The Public Economics of the Environment*, Oxford: Oxford University Press.

Scott, S., and Eakins, J. (2001), 'Household income effects and compensation options', in *Green and Bear It? Implementing Market-Based Policies for Ireland's Environment*, proceedings of a conference held at the Economic and Social Research Institute, Dublin, 10 May. Available at www.esri.ie.

Sipes, K. N., and Mendelsohn, R. (2001), 'The effectiveness of gasoline taxation to manage air pollution', *Ecological Economics*, 36: 299–309.

Smith, S. (1998), 'Distributional incidence of environmental taxes on energy and carbon: a review of policy issues', presented at the colloquy of the Ministry of the Environment and Regional Planning, 'Green Tax Reform and Economic Instruments for International Cooperation: The Post-Kyoto Context', Toulouse, 13 May.

SOU (1997), 'Skatter, miljö och sysselsättning – Slutbetenkande av Skatteväxlingskommitten', Statens offentliga utredningar 1997:11, Finansdepartementet, Stockholm (Taxes, environment and employment – Final report of the tax-swap committee, Public Studies no. 1997:11, Ministry of Finance, Stockholm).

Statistiska centralbyrån (SCB) (2002), 'Grön skatteväxling?', news bulletin from Statistics Sweden. Available at www.scb.se/press/press2002/press043mi1901.asp.

Swedish Environmental Protection Agency (1997), *Environmental Taxes in Sweden*, Stockholm.

US Department of the Treasury (2002), 'Environmental taxes', Internal Revenue Service, Form 6627. Available at www.irs.gov/pub/irs-pdf/f6627.pdf.

Vermeend, W., and Van der Vaart, J. (1998), *Greening Taxes: The Dutch Model*, Deventer: Kluwer.

Xing, Y., and Kolstad, C. D. (2002), 'Do lax environmental regulations attract foreign investment?', *Environmental and Resource Economics*, 21: 1–22.

Chapter 6

An Excise Tax on Municipal Solid Waste?

*DON FULLERTON**
University of Texas at Austin

Worldwide quantities of household solid waste have been rising. By the year 2000, the USA processed an estimated 544 million tons of solid waste – about 4.4 pounds (2 kilograms) per person per day. Of this total, approximately 370 million tons were put into landfills.[1] Federal legislation has made the siting of new landfills increasingly difficult and costly, while state and local governments continue to pay for landfill costs.

Moreover, most households think garbage collection is free! Traditionally, residents pay for garbage collection services through property taxes or a monthly fee that does not depend on the number of bags or bins placed out at the kerb for collection by the city. This pricing practice provides no incentives for households to reduce quantities of waste generated.

In just the past few years, several cities that face severe waste management problems and revenue problems have begun to adopt some version of a programme that requires households to pay by the bag.[2] Each household must buy special bags at the grocery store, or tags that can be attached to any bag of garbage at the kerb. The city collects only those bags that have paid stickers attached (and provides a small commission to the stores for selling those stickers). While this system can address many cities' waste reduction and revenue needs, the price is not an 'optimal' policy unless it reflects the full social marginal cost at the optimum.[3] That is, the cost per bag of garbage would need to reflect marginal environmental damage (MED) along with the internal or direct costs of collection and disposal.[4]

This chapter sets out to address several related issues. After providing some basic information about household garbage and recycling in the USA, it introduces a simple theory for optimal environmental taxes on disposal options, reviews estimates of demand for garbage collection, and discusses possible effects of these taxes on welfare, illegal dumping, and administrative cost. It

* This chapter has benefited greatly from the research undertaken by Divya Sharma at the University of Texas at Austin, and by comments and suggestions from Carl Bartone, Molly Macauley, and anonymous referees. All remaining errors are the author's.

then uses estimates of the external cost of garbage in landfills to undertake a simple calculation of illustrative prices that might be charged.

Many empirical papers have studied the effectiveness of unit pricing with regard to waste reduction.[5] Many of these studies focus on the relative success or failure of such schemes in a few selected communities, and some use larger cross-section data-sets. Disagreement remains, however, about the effect of unit pricing on garbage collection and its effects on substitutes such as recycling and illicit dumping. In addition, theoretical papers have studied the conceptual problem of how to determine the optimal price per bag. Early writers tend to presume that the optimal price per unit of garbage is the social marginal cost (the direct disposal cost plus marginal environmental damage, MED), but Fullerton and Kinnaman (1995) point out that this price only generates the optimal amount of garbage in a world where the other alternatives, such as recycling, are *also* properly priced. If illicit dumping is an available option and is not properly priced, then charging per bag of garbage could reduce welfare through increased dumping. The authors solve for a pricing system that restores optimality without having to charge directly for dumping: a tax per unit of every output purchased at the store and a subsidy per unit of recycling and garbage collection. With this deposit–refund system (DRS), the consumer indirectly pays for dumping and effectively pays the social marginal cost per unit of garbage as well.

Some of these studies have pointed out that the optimal price per unit of garbage must be higher in densely populated areas of the north-eastern USA and in Europe where landfill space is a scarce commodity, where tipping fees are high, and where households must live close to landfills and thus face higher external costs of litter, noise from the trucks, leachate getting into the water supply, methane gas seeping underground, and the purely aesthetic cost of having a landfill in one's view. Precious few studies have described how costs might vary with characteristics of the locale, and none has tried to calculate that optimal fee for different regions systematically.

This chapter attempts to add to the literature by using the theory of optimal pricing policy to calculate some rough numbers for the optimal price per bag of garbage for states in the USA, at least for landfill disposal. Admittedly, the optimal price is likely to vary considerably within each state because of differences in population density, landfill characteristics including proximity to residential areas, and several other, weather-related conditions. Even the number for any specific state should not be taken very seriously. However, the calculations in this chapter still provide a ballpark figure for the *range* of prices that might optimally be charged across the fifty states, and thus serve as an aid to decision-makers who must weigh up the different waste management alternatives.

Section 6.1 looks at data on the quantities of solid waste disposal in landfills and incinerators and discusses explanations for the increasing fraction of waste that is recycled. Section 6.2 then reviews the basic theory of Pigou (1932), as applied to the problem of household disposal options such as garbage, recycling, and potentially illegal burning or dumping. A tax on garbage might encourage recycling, but it might also increase dumping. To be 'optimal', a tax must apply to *each* form of disposal. A tax on dumping cannot be collected, but this section shows that a DRS can match all of the effects of having both the tax on garbage and the unavailable 'tax on dumping'. This DRS optimally reduces dumping, and it collects the same revenue as the optimal taxes on garbage and dumping. Section 6.3 reviews results of an empirical literature that estimates the elasticity of demand for household garbage collection – the effect of a garbage price on the quantities of garbage and recycling. Those responses are found to be fairly inelastic. Section 6.4 describes some other literature about the potential welfare gains and administrative costs of a garbage tax or DRS. Section 6.5 selects an estimate of each external cost from putting garbage into landfills. Section 6.6 uses those estimates to calculate prices that might be charged across the fifty states, the net revenues that might thus be generated, and the percentage increase in current state revenues from charging this excise tax on garbage. Section 6.7 concludes.

6.1 BACKGROUND ON EACH TYPE OF SOLID WASTE DISPOSAL

Of total household solid waste in the USA, the portion incinerated has remained near 10 per cent over the last decade, but the portion placed in landfills has decreased from roughly 85 per cent in 1989 to just over 60 per cent in 1997.[6] This decrease in use of landfill disposal was associated primarily with the simultaneous increase in recycling. Figure 6.1 shows that the portion recycled in the USA has increased threefold, from just 10 per cent in 1989 to nearly 30 per cent of household waste in 1997.

This dramatic increase in the recycling rate can be attributed to a number of possible interrelated factors. First, the number of kerbside recycling collection programmes increased monotonically from just 1,000 in 1989 to nearly 9,000 in 1997. This trend clearly facilitates household recycling, but then the question is 'what has induced cities to provide this kerbside recycling collection?'

Secondly, some have pointed to increased disposal costs, including the 'tipping fee' charged by landfills per ton of garbage. This cost varies by region, but overall US tipping fees have not increased by much (Glenn, 1998; Kinnaman and Fullerton, 2000b). For example, tipping fees in the more densely populated north-east are greater than those in other regions of the USA where land is cheaper. Over the ten-year period from 1988 to 1997, the average tipping fee in New Jersey has increased from about $50 per ton to about $60 per ton, while the average for the rest of the country has increased only from about $15 per ton to $25 per ton (in nominal dollars). Accounting for increases in the general price level, the real tipping fee has not changed much at all over the past decade. Thus the national rise in kerbside recycling is unlikely to be attributable to increases in the tipping fee. However, kerbside recycling programmes have become most popular in the north-east where the tipping fee is higher. Thus, while the change in recycling cannot be explained by a change in

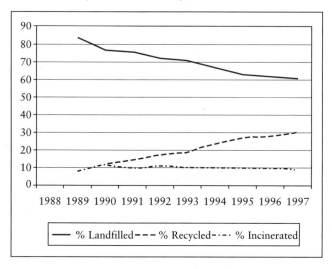

Figure 6.1. *Disposal Trends*

Source: Glenn, 1998.

disposal cost, some other factor may have increased recycling more in the region where disposal costs were already relatively high.

Thirdly, recycling might have increased due to changes in the market price of recycled materials. When accounting for increases in the general price level, however, the prices of recycled materials have remained rather constant over the past decade (Ackerman, 1997). Interestingly, prices of recycled materials are highly variable over time. For old newspaper, six spikes have appeared over the past thirty years, most recently in 1995 when the price for many materials hit all-time highs. This latest spike has been attributed to new recycled-content laws passed by several state governments (Ackerman, 1997). But overall, these trends do not appear to support the argument that economic forces are responsible for the growth in kerbside recycling.

Fourthly, the dramatic increase in the number of kerbside recycling programmes in operation in the USA could be related to changes in voter tastes for the environment and other political concerns. Misinformation may have contributed to the public's perception of a shortage of landfill space. This perception may have emerged in 1987, when the barge 'Mobro', loaded with Long Island garbage, was unable to unload its cargo after repeated attempts (see Bailey (1995) for a discussion of the incident). A wave of state and local legislation encouraging or mandating recycling was passed soon after this incident. In addition, voters read newspaper stories that landfills were closing faster than they were opening. Indeed, the number of landfills in operation in the USA fell by more than half over the period 1988–97, from about 8,000 to only 3,000 (Glenn, 1998).

Yet the USA is *not* running out of landfill *space*. The estimated capacity of remaining landfills has been steadily rising. Based on state-reported estimates, available landfill space has doubled during this period (1988–97), from roughly ten years of remaining capacity to twenty years of remaining capacity. (See Figure 6.2.)

The explanation for the apparent contradiction is the replacement of many small town dumps with fewer large regional sanitary landfills. This trend is due mostly to Subtitle D of the Resource Conservation and Recovery Act (RCRA) of 1976, designed to reduce the negative externalities associated with garbage disposal. This law imposed technology-based standards on the construction, operation, and closure of solid waste landfills. Each new landfill now is required to install thick plastic linings along the base, to collect and treat leachate, to monitor groundwater, and to cover garbage within hours of disposal. Because the fixed costs of constructing and operating a landfill have increased, the cost-minimizing landfill size has increased, and fewer landfills are being built. The trend toward larger landfills is also related to the increased political difficulty in siting them: once decision-makers get past the problem of 'not in my back yard' (or NIMBY), they choose to build a larger one to last longer.

The increase in the percentage of waste that is recycled seems to have come entirely from a reduction in the percentage put in landfills. The portion inciner-ated in the USA has been fairly stable – at 10 per cent of total household solid waste. It reached something of a peak in 1991, when 170 incinerators operated nationally, but then the number of incinerators in operation began to decline gradually. Incineration was once considered a dual solution to the solid waste and energy crises, but that assessment changed with some complicated techno-logical considerations. Fixed costs are high, and so average costs can be reduced by greater garbage throughput. Yet incinerators could not lower their tipping

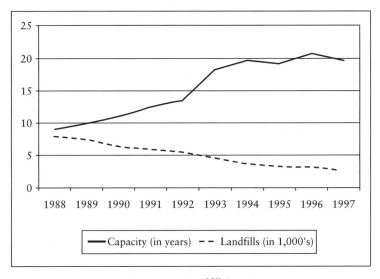

Figure 6.2. *Landfill Crisis?*

Source: Glenn, 1998.

fees to levels necessary to attract more business without incurring financial losses. For this reason, and because incineration was thought to be a good environmental solution to the dual problem of waste and energy, many local governments passed laws *requiring* that all local garbage come to the incinerator, effectively giving the incinerator monopsony power over local garbage.

The US Supreme Court struck down these laws, exposing the incineration industry to competition from cheaper landfills. Then the Supreme Court dealt a second blow to the incineration industry when it ruled that incinerator ash is toxic and therefore disposal of that ash must take place in an expensive toxic waste landfill. A third decision disallowed local control over waste imports. As a consequence of these three decisions, the US private sector built many large regional 'megafills' (Bartone, 2002). These new facilities have state-of-the-art leachate and methane gas management systems, and tipping fees are required to include financial provision for thirty-year environmental aftercare. Thus, external damages are falling.

The increased use of recycling in the early 1990s further reduced the quantity of garbage available to incinerators, adding to their financial problems. Then the public began to oppose the resulting air pollution emitted by incinerators, and policy-makers are no longer eager to rescue the industry.

Because US incineration now accounts for a small share of disposal, calculations below focus on the MED of landfill disposal in the USA. This focus leaves little space for discussion of the external costs of other disposal methods and other countries. Just note, however, that the choice of method depends on land scarcity. Even in the more densely populated north-eastern USA, incineration accounts for 40 per cent of waste disposal. Incineration is also popular in Japan and several European countries where population densities and land values are high.[7] Facing less competition from land-intensive landfills, incinerators in these regions can capture the economies of scale necessary to keep down the average cost of incineration (Halstead and Park, 1996). But even though many countries rely heavily on incineration, Brisson (1997) finds that the private and external costs of incineration exceed those of landfill disposal in most European countries.[8]

Circumstances in developing countries are almost completely different from those in the USA considered here. For example, Medina (1997) suggests that municipal solid waste (MSW) can hardly be reduced from levels that may already be only 0.2 to 0.5 kilograms per person per day. Markets may not work well enough to charge a price or tax on waste. Instead, efforts may need to concentrate just on collection, transportation, and upgrading present open dumping sites into controlled landfills.[9]

6.2 A THEORETICAL FRAMEWORK

A simple skeletal model is developed here to frame the discussion of optimal policy design, but it is a fully general equilibrium model that captures all of the essential elements. We avoid the problems of second-best by assuming that lump-sum taxes are available. Instead, we focus on the technology of waste disposal and include substitution between different methods of disposal. In particular, consumption generates waste that can either go into garbage collection or go into recycling that can be re-used in production.[10]

Assume that n identical consumers each maximize utility subject to a budget constraint and a mass-balance equation given by $c = c(g, r)$, where c is consumption, g is garbage, and r is recycling generated. The general form $c(g,r)$ represents the various combinations of g and r that are consistent with any particular level of consumption, possibly with a varying rate of trade-off (but strict mass balance would require $c = g + r$). All lower-case letters represent per capita amounts, while upper-case letters are aggregate, so $G = ng$ is total garbage. Utility is $u = u[c(g, r), G]$, where each individual can choose g and r (and indirectly c) but cannot affect G. Consumption has a positive effect on utility ($\partial u / \partial c \equiv u_c > 0$), but a negative externality from all others' garbage means that $\partial u / \partial G \equiv u_G < 0$.

The household budget constraint is $y = (p_c + t_c)c(g, r) + (p_g + t_g)g + (p_r + t_r)r$, where y is income, each p is a price, and each t is a tax rate. The price p_r may be negative if consumers are paid by a private firm for recycled material, and any tax rate may be positive or negative. The production function is $c = f(k_c, r)$, where k_c is the amount of labour or other resources used in production of c. General equilibrium conditions require that the amount of recycling generated by households, r, must be the same amount that re-enters production of c. Garbage collection and disposal also use resources through the production function $g = \gamma k_g$, and the overall resource constraint is $k = k_c + k_g$. To get conditions of an optimum, a social planner is assumed to maximize utility subject to this resources constraint, recognizing that choices about individual r and g affect aggregate garbage in utility ($G = ng$). To get private market conditions, consumers view G as fixed but choose g and r to maximize utility subject to their income $y \equiv k p_k$. Private firms maximize profits ($c p_c + r p_r - k_c p_k$) under perfect competition and constant returns to scale, so they set the price of each input equal to its marginal product. Similar conditions for garbage disposal imply that $p_g = p_k / \gamma$. Substitution of these producers' conditions into the consumers' first-order conditions yields a set of conditions for private markets that can be compared to the conditions for social optimality.

Every extra bag of garbage in the landfill might emit more foul odour, pollute more groundwater, worsen the eyesore, and contribute to climate change.[11] If all tax rates are zero, with no government action, then households fail to internalize the full social costs of their disposal decisions. Too much garbage and too little recycling are produced by a decentralized economy. In a similar model, Fullerton and Kinnaman (1995) show that several different tax and subsidy combinations can achieve the efficient allocation of resources in the presence of the external costs from garbage disposal. In the model above, however, the simplest way to make all of the private market conditions match all of the social optimality conditions is to set all tax rates to zero except t_g, which should be set as

(1) $t_g = -nu_G/\lambda,$

where λ is the marginal utility of income at the optimum. Since u_G is negative, this tax rate is positive. It is merely an example of the general principle of Pigou (1932): for an activity that causes a negative externality, the optimal corrective tax is 'marginal external damages' (MED). The expression in (1) reflects the negative effect on utility (u_G) for all n individuals, converted into dollars when divided by the marginal utility of income.

So far, our theory supports not only a price per bag, as would be charged by a private firm (p_g), but also a tax that raises additional revenue (t_g). This excise tax on waste can contribute significantly to local revenue, as discussed below. As intended, the price per bag induces consumers to substitute out of garbage and into recycling.

This optimality disappears, however, if consumers can avoid the tax on proper collection of garbage by instead burning or dumping their garbage. Suppose that the technology of disposal is represented by $c = c(g, r, b)$, where b is 'burning or dumping'. Suppose further that utility is given by $u = u(c, G, B)$, where $B = nb$ and where $\partial u/\partial B \equiv u_B < 0$. A reasonable assumption is that social costs are higher for waste that is dumped than for waste in the landfill ($u_B < u_G$).

In this case, if consumers pay little or nothing to dump their trash, then any positive price ($p_g + t_g$) can induce some households to substitute out of garbage and into the more damaging activity of dumping their waste.[12] The normal Pigouvian solution in this case would require a tax on *each* activity equal to marginal external damages, so that

(2) $t_g = -nu_G/\lambda,$

(3) $t_b = -nu_B/\lambda$

while other tax rates are zero. Yet a simple Pigouvian tax on dumping is generally considered to be infeasible because evasion is easy. Indeed, in this case, just collecting the price per bag ($p_g + t_g$) is a problem, as consumers can avoid that tax by dumping. The revenues from the system in (2) and (3) may be very low indeed.[13]

For one type of alternative, the city could make dumping illegal, impose a stiff fine, and devote police resources to establishing some positive probability of discovery.[14] Using a model where consumers maximize expected utility, the fine can be set such that the *expected* fine per unit of dumping is marginal damages ($-nu_B/\lambda$). The fine revenue bears no particular relationship to the cost of the effort to catch those who are dumping, however, so the net revenue may be small or negative.

Another set of alternatives, though imperfect, is that government could impose an array of command-and-control policies such as mandatory recycling for households and minimum recycled-content standards on producers (Palmer and Walls, 1997). A version of the model above can be used to show the quantity restrictions that achieve efficient outcomes, at least in theory, but the information required to achieve those efficient outcomes is not likely to be available to policy-makers. This point is just a variant of the usual economic efficiency case for incentive instruments rather than mandates.

As a final type of alternative, households could be required to pay an advanced disposal fee at the time of purchase (t_c). This fee by itself cannot achieve the efficient allocation (Palmer, Sigman, and Walls, 1997). In combination with the right subsidies to proper disposal, however, the result is an optimal deposit–refund system. With the strict mass-balance condition $(c = g + r + b)$, Fullerton and Kinnaman (1995) show that the optimum in the above model is achieved by

(4) $$t_c = -nu_B/\lambda,$$

(5) $$t_r = nu_B/\lambda,$$

(6) $$t_g = n(u_B - u_G)/\lambda.$$

Note that the tax on purchase of consumption c is positive, and it reflects the marginal external damages *from dumping*. The tax on recycling is negative, a subsidy that exactly returns the tax collected upon the purchase of the item. Recycling has no 'external' effect, and ends up with no net tax. The proper disposal of garbage also receives back the initial tax upon purchase (since t_g includes nu_B/λ), but garbage gets an additional tax that reflects its own externality, $-nu_G/\lambda$. The basic logic is that any item purchased must eventually become disposal in one of three forms. If the consumer does not get the tax back by recycling the item or by proper garbage disposal, then the item must have been dumped. But the marginal damages from dumping were already collected upon purchase, so even that activity has been properly priced.

A disaggregate version of this model would require many different tax rates and refunds that reflect the toxicity or other social costs of dumping each good. As discussed below, the administrative costs of such a policy might be high indeed, but these costs can be reduced by using few 'categories' of goods, by employing existing sales taxes, and by bulk subsidies to recycling (per ton of glass or aluminium rather than per bottle or can).

Because of the assumption above that dumping must be more socially damaging than proper disposal $(u_B < u_G)$, we know that t_g must be negative. Proper disposal of garbage is subsidized, to avert illicit dumping. If the subsidy is nearly equal to the positive cost of collection (p_g), then the city can save administrative costs just by collecting garbage for free. This logic has already been widely applied, as many cities intentionally collect garbage for free *in order to avert dumping*.

The DRS in (4), (5), and (6) is designed so that all private first-order conditions exactly match the socially optimal conditions, just as would the Pigouvian taxes in (2) and (3). With all the same outcomes, then, the DRS must generate the same *net* revenue as the Pigouvian taxes. But while the tax on dumping is unenforceable, because dumping is unobservable, the DRS applies a tax or provides a subsidy only to observable market transactions: purchase of c, sale of recycled materials r, and collection of garbage at the kerb for disposal at a sanitary landfill. While this chapter will not analyse the relative administrative costs of collecting various excise taxes, it would seem reasonable to believe that the administrative costs of taxing these market transactions are the same as for any other market transactions. The costs of collection of the positive net revenue from the DRS in (4), (5), and (6) must certainly be less than the costs of collection of the Pigouvian taxes in (2) and (3).

Thus, when we discuss the actual revenue that can be collected from the optimal tax rate on waste (equal to MED), we do not even distinguish between the Pigouvian taxes in (2) and (3) and the DRS in (4), (5), and (6). The theory shows they have the same revenue, and discussion here suggests that the DRS has lower collection costs. The point is that the Pigouvian tax on garbage can be collected via the DRS without fear that the tax can be evaded by dumping.[15]

6.3 EMPIRICAL EVIDENCE ON THE EFFECTS OF A PRICE PER BAG

A brief overview of some empirical studies appears in Table 6.1. Wertz (1976) was the first to derive the impact of a user fee on garbage quantities. By simply comparing the average quantity of garbage collected in San Francisco, a town with a user fee, with the average 'urban' town in the USA, Wertz calculates a price elasticity of demand equal to -0.15. In the initial econometric study, Jenkins (1993) uses monthly data gathered from fourteen towns (ten with unit pricing) over several years. Jenkins also finds inelastic demand for garbage collection services: a 1 per cent increase in the user fee is estimated to lead to a 0.12 per cent decrease in the quantity of garbage.

Two studies rely on self-reported garbage quantities from individual households (rather than as reported by municipal governments). Hong, Adams, and Love (1993) utilize data based on a survey of 4,306 homes. Households indicated whether they recycle and how much they pay for garbage collection. Results suggest that a user fee increases the probability that a household recycles, but does not appreciably affect the quantity of garbage produced at the kerb. Reschovsky and Stone (1994) mailed questionnaires to 3,040 households and received 1,422 replies. Each household reported its recycling behaviour, income, and demographic information. The price of garbage is estimated to have no significant impact on the probability that a household recycles. When combined with a kerbside recycling programme, recycling rates increase by 27–58 per cent, depending on type of material.

Miranda et al. (1994) use data gathered from twenty-one towns with unit-pricing programmes and compare the quantities of garbage and recycling over the year before implementation of unit pricing with those the year following it. Results indicate that these towns reduce garbage by between 17 and 74 per cent

Table 6.1. *Empirical Estimates of the Effect of Unit Pricing*

Study	Data	Model	Change in garbage	Change in recycling
Wertz, 1976	Compares subscription programme and flat fee	Comparison of means	$\epsilon = -0.15$	—
Jenkins, 1993	Panel of 14 cities (10 with user fee), 1980–88	GLS	$\epsilon = -0.12$	—
Hong, Adams, and Love, 1993	1990 survey of 4,306 homes in Portland, OR	Ordered probit, 2SLS	No significant impact	Positive relationship
Reschovsky and Stone, 1994	1992 mail survey of 1,422 households in and around Ithaca, NY	Probit	—	No significant impact
Miranda et al., 1994	Panel of 21 cities over 18 months starting in 1990	Comparison of means	17–74% less garbage	Increase of 128%
Callan and Thomas, 1997	1994 cross-section of 324 towns in Massachusetts, 55 with unit-pricing programmes	OLS	—	6.6–12.1 percentage point increase
Fullerton and Kinnaman, 1996	Two-period panel of 75 households in 1992, in Charlottesville, VA	OLS	$\epsilon = -0.076$ (weight) or -0.23 (bins)	Cross-price elasticity is 0.073
Van Houtven and Morris, 1999	Monthly panel for 400 households in Marietta, GA, in 1994	Random effects model	−36% for bags, −14% for bins	No significant effect
Podolsky and Spiegel, 1998	1992 cross-section of 159 municipalities in New Jersey, 12 with unit pricing	OLS	$\epsilon = -0.39$	—
Kinnaman and Fullerton, 2000*a*	1991 cross-section of 959 towns across the USA, 114 with unit pricing	OLS	$\epsilon = -0.19$	$\epsilon = 0.23$
		2SLS	$\epsilon = -0.28$	$\epsilon = 0.22$

Abbreviations:
ϵ = price elasticity of demand
OLS = ordinary least squares
GLS = generalized least squares
2SLS = two-stage least squares

and increase recycling by 128 per cent. These large estimates cannot be attributed directly to pricing garbage: in every case, kerbside recycling programmes were implemented during the same year as the unit-pricing programme. Callan and Thomas (1997) predict that the implementation of a user fee increases the portion of waste recycled by 6.6 percentage points. This impact increases to 12.1 percentage points when the user fee is accompanied by a kerbside recycling programme.

Only Fullerton and Kinnaman (1996) use household data that are not based on self-reported surveys. The weight and volume of the garbage and recycling of seventy-five households were measured by hand over four weeks prior to, and following, the implementation of a price-per-bag programme in Charlottesville, VA. A kerbside recycling programme had already been in operation for over a year. Results indicate a slight drop in the weight of garbage (elasticity of −0.076) but a greater drop in the volume of garbage (elasticity of −0.23). Indeed, the density of garbage increased from 15 pounds per bag to just over 20 pounds per bag.

Since collectors and landfills compact the garbage anyway, the compacting by households does not help reduce the actual costs of disposal. We want to know the change in space used in the landfill, and that is not well measured by the change in the number of bags at the kerb. It is better measured by the change in the weight at the kerb. Unfortunately, with an elasticity of only −0.076, a price per bag is not very effective at reducing that measure of the space in the landfill.

Van Houtven and Morris (1999) look at two policy experiments in Marietta, GA. The traditional bag or tag programme requires households to pay for each additional bag of garbage presented at the kerb for collection. The second programme type requires households to pre-commit or 'subscribe' to the collection of a specific number of containers each week. The household pays for the subscribed number whether these containers are filled with garbage or not. Many towns in California and Oregon have used subscription programmes since early in the twentieth century. One advantage of subscription programmes is that their direct billing systems may reduce administrative costs. Yet most economists believe that the first type of user fee more truly represents marginal cost pricing. The subscription programme does not effectively put a positive price on every unit of garbage, since the bin may be partially empty most weeks. Indeed, Van Houtven and Morris (1999) find that the bag programme reduces garbage by 36 per cent, while the subscription bin programme reduces it by only 14 per cent.[16]

Two studies expand on the work of Jenkins (1993) by increasing the number of towns in the sample. Podolsky and Spiegel (1998) employ a 1992 cross-section of 159 towns clustered in New Jersey, twelve with unit-based pricing programmes. They estimate the largest price elasticity of demand in the literature (−0.39). The authors attribute this estimate to the fact that no towns in their sample had implemented subscription programmes (as was the case for Wertz and Jenkins). Kinnaman and Fullerton (2000a) use a 1991 national cross-section of 959 towns, 114 of which had implemented user fees (none with subscription programmes). They find that accounting for endogeneity of the policy variables raises the demand elasticity to −0.28, but that is still not very high. They also estimate that subscription programmes have less of an impact than bag/tag programmes on garbage and recycling quantities.[17]

The basic message here is that the demand for garbage collection services is inelastic. Substitutes are not readily available. Advocates of unit-based pricing suggest demand may become more elastic in the long run as households learn of available substitutes for garbage disposal, but the empirical literature has yet to address this point. Given the inelastic nature of the demand for garbage collection, however, the potential revenue from an excise tax or DRS can be approximated below by taking the tax rate times the current garbage quantities.

6.4 WELFARE GAINS, ILLEGAL DUMPING, AND ADMINISTRATIVE COSTS

Most cities and towns in the USA still finance garbage collection through property taxes or monthly fees, with no price at the margin. Yet Jenkins (1993) and Repetto et al. (1992) estimate that the full private plus external social marginal cost is $1.43–$1.83 per bag, depending on local conditions.[18] Under the presumption that the price of each activity ought to equal its social marginal cost (SMC), they calculate the welfare cost arising from the current underpricing of garbage. They use estimates of the demand curve discussed above to reflect social marginal benefit (SMB), and they define the optimal quantity where SMB = SMC. In Figure 6.3, the optimal quantity is Q^*, but the current price of zero leads consumers down their demand curve to Q'. The

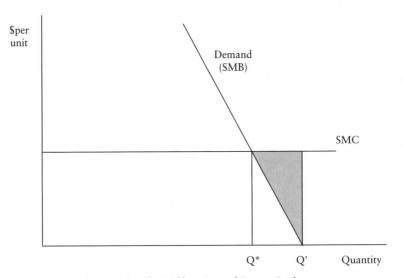

Figure 6.3. *The Welfare Cost of Excess Garbage*

welfare cost of the excess garbage is the extent to which SMC exceeds SMB for each of those extra units of garbage, the shaded area in the figure.

This welfare cost of excess garbage is the welfare gain from charging a price per bag, and Jenkins (1993) estimates this gain to be as much as $650 million per year in the USA, roughly $3 per person per year. Fullerton and Kinnaman (1996) use household data and also estimate the potential benefits of marginal cost pricing to be in the neighbourhood of $3 per person per year. Podolsky and Spiegel (1998) study a cross-section of towns in New Jersey and estimate the economic benefits of charging per unit of garbage to be as great as $12.80 per person per year. Still, inelastic demand in Figure 6.3 makes the triangle relatively small.

Yet even this small welfare gain is not necessarily available merely by charging for garbage, because of three big problems. First, Figure 6.3 is a partial equilibrium model that looks only at garbage, not other disposal methods. It does not convey *why* demand slopes down – that is, what substitutes are available. That welfare gain calculation is correct if recycling is the only alternative, but not if dumping is possible, as that can be *more* costly than garbage.[19] Secondly, the administrative costs of implementing the garbage pricing programme may exceed the social benefits (the shaded area in Figure 6.3). Fullerton and Kinnaman (1996) estimate that the administrative costs of printing, distributing, and accounting for garbage stickers in Charlottesville, Virginia, could exceed the $3 per person per year benefits mentioned earlier. Thirdly, a uniform tax on all types of garbage may be inefficient if materials within the waste stream produce different social costs (Dinan, 1993). If the social cost of disposal of flashlight batteries is greater than that of old newspapers, for example, then the disposal tax on flashlight batteries should exceed that on old newspapers.

These three problems are interrelated. The dumping problem might be fixed by implementation of a DRS, but that system entails its own administrative cost. That administrative cost might be quite low if it is implemented implicitly by the use of a sales tax on all purchased commodities at the same rate, together with a subsidy to all recycling and proper garbage disposal. That practice is currently followed in the USA, at least implicitly, since local governments do impose local sales taxes and they do provide free collection of kerbside recycling and garbage.[20] If the recycling subsidy needs to be larger, administrative costs can be reduced by providing a subsidy per ton, paid to recyclers, rather than providing an amount for each bottle recycled by each household. But then the third problem is that optimality requires a different tax and subsidy amount for each type of material – a plan that might be very costly to administer.

To be a little more specific, consider the general equilibrium model described earlier where c is consumption, g is garbage, and r is recycling. We solved for the optimal DRS in equations (4), (5), and (6) with a tax on c and a subsidy to g and r. That model could be modified to specify that c is a vector of consumption goods, each with its own level of toxicity and its own social cost of dumping (used to determine the optimal initial tax on purchase of that good). Then that individually tailored deposit needs to be returned as a subsidy when that good is recycled or brought to a disposal facility instead of dumped. In other words, the solution to that model looks exactly like (4), (5), and (6) except that the system for optimality needs a vector of tax rates on each good, a vector of subsidy rates to recycling of each good, and a vector of subsidy rates for disposal of each good. Yet tailored tax and subsidy rates are more expensive to administer.

Several economic studies have favoured the use of DRSs to correct for the external costs associated with garbage disposal, including Dinan (1993), Dobbs (1991), Fullerton and Kinnaman (1995), Palmer and Walls (1994), Palmer, Sigman, and Walls (1997), Fullerton and Wu (1998), and Atri and Schellberg (1995). To achieve the efficient allocation, the deposit for each good should be set equal to the social marginal cost of dumping the post-consumer waste, and the refund on return is that deposit minus the marginal external cost of recycling. If the external cost of recycling is zero, then the refund matches the deposit. The deposit could be levied either on the production or on the sale of goods. As long as transaction costs are low, the refund can be given either to the households that recycle the materials or to the producers that use the recycled materials in production. If the refund is given to the households, then the supply increase will drive down the price of recycled materials to firms. If the refund is given to firms, then firms will increase demand for recycled materials and drive up the price received by households (Atri and Schellberg, 1995). In addition, Fullerton and Wu (1998) find that the refund given under a DRS will encourage firms optimally to engineer products that are easier to recycle. Households will demand such products in order to recycle and thereby receive the refund. This result is important, since directly encouraging the recyclability of product design can be administratively difficult.[21]

If the administrative cost of operating the DRS is high, then Dinan (1993) suggests that policy-makers could single out products that comprise a large segment of the waste stream (newspaper) or that involve very high social marginal disposal costs (batteries). Palmer and Walls (1999) argue that a tax on produced intermediate goods combined with a subsidy paid to collectors of recycling would preserve the efficiency effects of a DRS but would be less costly to administer.

Even for a particular commodity with a particular toxicity, the SMC of disposal is not an immutable fact. It depends on where the item is dumped, or on the nature of the landfill or other disposal facility. Anything going into an old landfill might eventually contaminate the land and the groundwater. Indeed, many of these landfills are being added to the Superfund programme's National Priority list of the worst-polluted sites in the USA. On the other hand, new landfills must exclude hazardous materials and must meet other recent regulations.[22] They are constructed with a base of several inches of various grades of plastic lining to keep leachate from seeping. Underground plumbing systems capture and treat leachate, and local groundwater supplies are monitored. These are big improvements, but the landfill may eventually fail to contain all externalities. In terms of operation, garbage must be covered with soil within hours of disposal to reduce foul odour, discourage pests, and reduce the risk of health hazards. All landfills must control explosive methane gas, while many capture it and burn it to produce electricity. Access roads must be watered several times each day to prevent dust from heavy truck traffic. These regulations have decreased substantially the *external* costs associated with garbage disposal but have increased *internal* disposal costs from an estimated average of $9 per ton to $20 per ton (Beede and Bloom, 1995).[23]

Even with the recent advances in the technology of landfill construction and operation, local environmental activist groups still often oppose the creation or expansion of landfills in their region. Landfills are generally found to depress property values. For example, housing values are estimated to rise by 6.2 per cent per mile for the first two miles away from a landfill (Nelson, Genereux, and Genereux (1992), as cited in Beede and Bloom (1995)). Interviewing 150 households in Tennessee, Roberts, Douglas, and Park (1991) estimate that households are willing to pay $227 per year to avoid having a landfill nearby. Reported amounts increase with income, education, and dependency on well water for water consumption. Ten studies reviewed by the Centre for Social and Economic Research of the Global Environment (1993) found significant effects on house prices from being within four miles of a landfill. Prices are 21–30 per cent lower for houses within half a mile of a landfill, and they increase 5–7 per cent for each mile further away. On the other hand, Hite et al. (2001) find that closing the landfill does not necessarily mitigate the impact.

Since these effects pertain to the existence of a landfill, they might not seem to affect the optimal tax per bag at the margin. In the long run, however, any small but permanent increase in garbage per person will eventually necessitate another landfill with negative effects on another neighbourhood. Thus, even though these disamenities are ignored in 'illustrative' calculations below, they do need to be incorporated into any final comprehensive estimate of the optimal price to charge per bag of garbage – at least to the extent that they are not already internalized by the payment of a 'host fee'.

The oldest policy implemented at the state level is DRSs for empty beverage containers. The state of Oregon was the first to pass this form of legislation in 1971, and nine other states followed in the 1970s and early 1980s, but then no state implemented a new DRS until Hawaii in 2002.[24] Instead of administering a detailed set of tax and subsidy rates of a tailored DRS, many states simply regulate household solid waste in particular ways. One item with the lowest SMC of disposal is garden waste, and many states prohibit it from landfills because composting facilities can accommodate it more cheaply. Several other states have passed laws prohibiting from landfills other materials, such as tyres, batteries, motor oil, and old appliances.

It is difficult to determine which items ought to be picked out for a specific DRS. Huhtala (1997) and Brisson (1997) break down the private and external costs of recycling by type of material. Huhtala shows that the social benefits of recycling paper, cardboard, and metal exceed the social costs. Glass and plastic do not pass the benefit–cost criterion. Brisson (1997) finds that the recycling of aluminium produces the greatest social benefits, followed by glass, ferrous metals, paperboard, and rigid plastic. Macauley et al. (2001) note that computer monitors contain lead, which can be damaging to the environment and which can be recycled. They find that 16 million monitors are retired each year at a private disposal cost of $13.5 million and health damages of $2.7 million, but these figures imply a private cost of less than one dollar per monitor and *external* cost of only $0.17 per monitor. If this average external cost is the same as the marginal external cost, as used to calculate the optimal Pigouvian tax or DRS, then the rebate per monitor would be 17 cents. Few monitors would be recycled for that! Indeed, monitors are recycled for other reasons, so a DRS might not be effective. Macauley et al. (2001) investigate alternative policies, but each has costs compared with the low measured benefits.

A DRS can optimally reduce not only the quantity but also the toxicity of waste. An optimal allocation requires an item-specific DRS, however, which can be costly. If a general DRS is employed instead, then various individual quantities may be far from optimal. If no DRS is employed, then a price per unit of garbage can lead to dumping (and we come full circle). Any welfare gain from a garbage tax can be more than offset by the welfare cost of dumping.

Available data rarely allow for direct comparisons between illegal dumping before and after the implementation of unit pricing. Many economists have asked town officials whether they believe illegal dumping has increased, and many have stated that it has, but many more have stated otherwise. Reschovsky and Stone (1994) and Fullerton and Kinnaman (1996) asked individual households whether they observed any change. In the former study, 51 per cent of respondents reported an increase in dumping. The most popular method was household use of commercial skips. For the 20 per cent who admitted to burning trash, the authors were unable to confirm whether these burners did so in response to the programme. Roughly 40 per cent of the respondents to the Fullerton and Kinnaman (1996) survey said that they thought illegal dumping had increased in response to the unit-pricing programme. Many of these lived in the more densely populated urban areas of the city. Those authors also use survey responses with direct household garbage observations to estimate that 28 per cent of the reduction of garbage observed at the kerb was redirected to illicit forms of disposal. Nonetheless, Miranda and Bynum (1999) estimate that more than 4,000 communities in the USA use some form of unit pricing.[25]

6.5 SOCIAL MARGINAL DAMAGE, THE OPTIMAL FEE TO CHARGE

Beginning in the early 1990s, several studies actually try to construct estimates of the full social cost (internal plus external cost) per bag of garbage. Repetto et al. (1992) find that in the states that have high direct disposal costs, the external costs are almost equal to the internal costs (adding up to $1.43–$1.83 per bag). They base these figures on a study conducted in two states with high disposal costs. In particular, the Tellus Institute (1991) studies the full cost of waste disposal for the state of California, employing the 'control cost' method of pollutant evaluation for the external costs. Under that method, the marginal external damage (MED) attributed to a specific pollutant is the cost of preventing a marginal unit of that pollutant from entering the environment.[26]

For the UK, the Centre for Social and Economic Research of the Global Environment (1993) found external costs of £1.30 to £4.00 per ton, depending on whether the landfill has energy recovery from methane gas. These estimates exclude amenity effects, and they helped provide input for setting UK policy: different tax rates were set for inert waste, non-inert waste, and construction debris. These rates are set to increase with time to achieve recycling targets (O'Brien, 2002).

For the Netherlands, Dijkgraaf and Vollebergh (1998) estimate that the external cost of landfill garbage is $US28 per ton (about $US0.28 per 32-gallon bag of garbage).

For the USA, Miranda and Hale (1997, 1999) employ several prior studies to produce a range of estimates for marginal social cost per ton of garbage, including both global and local pollutants. These studies 'use a range of techniques to quantify impacts, including direct estimates of human and environmental health impacts, cost–benefit analysis, abatement costs for specific pollutants, and contingent valuation of changes in human and environmental health' (Miranda and Hale, 1999, p. 24). The numbers provided by Miranda and Hale (1999) form the basis for the external costs used in this chapter.[27]

In the theory above, the optimal price per bag of garbage is $P^* = p_g + t_g^*$, where p_g is the private marginal cost (PMC) of collection and disposal and where is the optimal Pigouvian tax rate, the MED given in equation (1). The city could charge this combined price itself, or allow a private firm to charge $p_g = $ PMC and add a tax rate of $t_g^* = $ MED. Either way, if the city is as efficient as the private hauler, then households pay the same overall price (P^*) and the city gets the same tax revenue (over and above the direct cost of collection and disposal).

The external cost is likely to differ among localities, and waste collection is generally run by local governments in the USA, but a local DRS is likely to find that goods bought in one jurisdiction are carried to another jurisdiction before disposal. Thus sales taxes and refunds are most often administered by states. In any case, sufficient data are not available for different cities in the USA. The next section attempts only to provide some rough indication of the amount by which this overall price might vary from state to state in the USA, given that some states are more rural, with cheaper land, and others are more populated. In addition, the calculations try to account for differences in temperature and precipitation among the fifty states. In other words, the goal is to calculate the two separate costs for each state in order to obtain

$$(7) \qquad\qquad P_i^* = PMC_i + MED_i, \qquad i = 1, \ \ldots, \ 50.$$

Miranda and Hale (1999) show that the average tipping fee in each state is a good measure of the internal cost of disposal (PMC_i). This tipping fee in each state may depend upon the daily quantity intake of garbage in the landfill, the number of years of capacity left before the landfill must be shut down, the initial capital costs incurred during planning and construction of the facility, and the operation and maintenance costs incurred during active use of the facility.

The external costs can include aesthetic costs incurred by individuals, such as the noise pollution from the collection trucks and a less scenic view. So far, no studies have estimated these aesthetic costs per unit of solid waste.[28] The external cost also includes the negative health effects from toxins in the leachate that seeps into the groundwater. It includes the effect of methane gas produced as organic material in the landfill decomposes. Before methane was collected and vented, it could seep through crevices underground, emerge in some neighbouring house or basement, and then possibly ignite and explode. That danger has been virtually eliminated and is not part of calculations here. If the methane *is* vented and released into the atmosphere, then external costs include the greenhouse effect on global warming. Finally, if the methane is 'flared', as required on all new landfills, then the high greenhouse effect of the methane is reduced to the lower greenhouse effect of carbon dioxide (but the flaring creates other air emissions).[29]

Table 6.2 provides estimates of these costs from Miranda and Hale (1999), where each pollutant has an estimated range of external costs. The first entry, under water emissions, is the range for leachate's environmental costs. Leachate is produced from the interaction between degrading landfill material and water from precipitation. It contains toxins that may contaminate groundwater. For present purposes, leachate is a local water pollutant that will be linked with the precipitation level in each state.[30] Because of recent controls, however, the range in the table is small ($0.0–$1.0 per ton of waste).

Under air emissions, methane is the biggest potential problem. In fact, landfills are the source of 35 per cent of methane emissions in the USA, or 4 per cent of *all* greenhouse gas emissions (Environmental Protection Agency, 2001). More is said about the greenhouse effect of carbon dioxide, because so much more carbon dioxide is released into the atmosphere from industries and

Table 6.2. *Environmental Cost Estimates for a Landfill (1997 dollars per ton)*

Cost	No methane flaring	Methane flaring
Water emissions		
Leachate	0.0–1.0	0.0–1.0
Air emissions		
Methane	8.8–59.5	2.1–6.9
Carbon dioxide	0.4–1.4	0.7–2.0
Vinyl chloride	4.3–4.8	4.3–4.8
Benzene	0.1–2.8	0.1–2.8
Others	0.3–4.8	0.3–4.8
Total	*13.8–74.3*	*7.5–22.3*

Source: Miranda and Hale, 1999.

vehicles that burn fossil fuels, but each methane gas molecule has much more greenhouse effect than a carbon dioxide molecule. Thus the row of the table for methane shows a high range of costs from the greenhouse effect ($8.8–$59.5 per ton). If the methane is flared, however, then the combustion converts the methane into carbon dioxide and other air emissions, so the effect of methane from the landfill is much reduced ($2.1–$6.9 per ton). On the other hand, that flaring creates more carbon dioxide, and so the range of estimated costs from carbon dioxide increases (from $0.4–$1.4 per ton to $0.7–$2.0 per ton). These global costs of the two greenhouse gases are *not* specific to any state's temperature or precipitation.

As shown in Table 6.2, Miranda and Hale (1999) also estimate the external cost per ton of waste for vinyl chloride ($4.3–$4.8 per ton), benzene ($0.1–$2.8 per ton), and other gases ($0.3–$4.8 per ton).[31] These ranges are the same whether or not the landfill flares its methane. These gases are local pollutants, and we therefore assume that the different states lie across these ranges depending on their local weather conditions such as temperature.[32]

As Miranda and Hale mention, the range of costs for each pollutant reflects an inherent uncertainty about the quantity and effect of those gases that are produced at any landfill. The range is widely different for the no-flaring and the flaring facilities. On the other hand, the range for the local pollutants largely follows from the differences in local demographic and weather conditions (although, again, some of the uncertainty is about the amount of gas actually emitted and its marginal social damage).

6.6 CALCULATIONS FOR EACH STATE IN THE USA

To prepare for allocating the other costs, the different states are ranked by population in column 1 of Table 6.3. The state with the lowest population gets a rank of 1 and the state with the highest population gets a rank of 50. Similar rankings are given to the states by temperature (column 3) and precipitation (column 5).

For each pollutant, the range from the minimum to the maximum cost in Table 6.2 is divided into fifty equal increments (following Sharma (2002)). High concentrations of benzene can prove fatal, so the cost of benzene from Table 6.2 is assigned using the ranking of states by population.[33] The state with the lowest population – Wyoming – is assigned the lowest cost from the range for benzene. The state with the second-to-lowest population is assigned an amount that is 2 per cent of the way from the minimum to the maximum cost in Table 6.2. The next state is assigned an amount that is 4 per cent of the way from the minimum to the maximum, and so on, until the state with the largest population – California – is assigned the highest cost of that range. The result is shown in column 2 of Table 6.3.

External costs of vinyl chloride and the other gases depend on local weather conditions such as temperature (Environmental Protection Agency, 1999), and so they are assigned in a similar manner using the ranking of states by average temperature. Thus Alaska is assigned the low end and Florida is assigned the high end of the range of external costs from vinyl chloride and the other gases in

Table 6.3. *The Ranking System Used for Local Pollutants*

State (1)	Population rank (2)	Benzene cost (3)	Temperature rank (4)	Emissions cost (5)	Precipitation rank (6)	Leachate cost (7)	Total external cost
Alabama	28	1.59	45	9.09	34	0.67	12.57
Alaska	3	0.21	1	4.60	24	0.47	5.85
Arizona	31	1.75	43	8.89	3	0.04	11.82
Arkansas	18	1.04	41	8.68	38	0.76	11.60
California	50	2.80	39	8.48	11	0.20	12.71
Colorado	27	1.53	13	5.82	7	0.12	8.28
Connecticut	22	1.26	16	6.13	48	0.96	9.24
Delaware	6	0.38	32	7.76	47	0.94	10.05
Florida	47	2.63	50	9.60	31	0.61	14.22
Georgia	41	2.30	44	8.99	28	0.55	13.11
Hawaii	9	0.54	48	9.40	42	0.84	11.93
Idaho	12	0.71	12	5.72	8	0.14	7.28
Illinois	46	2.58	28	7.36	23	0.45	11.50
Indiana	37	2.08	26	7.15	32	0.63	10.93
Iowa	21	1.20	17	6.23	17	0.33	8.59
Kansas	19	1.09	35	8.07	14	0.27	10.44
Kentucky	26	1.48	36	8.17	36	0.71	11.47
Louisiana	29	1.64	49	9.50	46	0.92	13.35
Maine	11	0.65	2	4.70	30	0.59	6.58
Maryland	32	1.81	30	7.56	35	0.69	11.14
Massachusetts	38	2.14	14	5.93	50	1.00	10.04
Michigan	43	2.41	11	5.62	19	0.37	9.30
Minnesota	30	1.70	3	4.80	15	0.29	7.52
Mississippi	20	1.15	46	9.19	37	0.73	12.26
Missouri	34	1.92	33	7.87	21	0.41	11.28
Montana	7	0.43	7	5.21	5	0.08	6.34
Nebraska	13	0.76	21	6.64	10	0.18	8.40
Nevada	16	0.93	25	7.05	1	0.00	8.83
New Hampshire	10	0.60	8	5.31	43	0.86	7.49
New Jersey	42	2.36	29	7.46	39	0.78	11.73
New Mexico	15	0.87	34	7.97	6	0.10	9.90
New York	48	2.69	10	5.52	44	0.88	10.06
North Carolina	40	2.25	38	8.38	41	0.82	12.67
North Dakota	4	0.27	4	4.91	12	0.22	5.97
Ohio	44	2.47	23	6.84	26	0.51	10.88
Oklahoma	24	1.37	40	8.58	22	0.43	11.49
Oregon	23	1.31	20	6.54	13	0.24	8.96
Pennsylvania	45	2.52	19	6.44	27	0.53	10.51
Rhode Island	8	0.49	22	6.74	49	0.98	9.09
South Carolina	25	1.42	42	8.78	29	0.57	11.93
South Dakota	5	0.32	18	6.33	9	0.16	7.55
Tennessee	35	1.97	37	8.27	40	0.80	12.23
Texas	49	2.74	47	9.29	16	0.31	13.67
Utah	17	0.98	24	6.95	4	0.06	8.85
Vermont	2	0.16	5	5.01	45	0.90	6.71
Virginia	39	2.19	31	7.66	25	0.49	11.45
Washington	36	2.03	15	6.03	18	0.35	9.30
West Virginia	14	0.82	27	7.25	33	0.65	9.66
Wisconsin	33	1.86	9	5.42	20	0.39	8.49
Wyoming	1	0.10	6	5.11	2	0.02	5.79

Table 6.2. Other states are arrayed in between. The result is shown in column 4 of Table 6.3.

Leachate costs are assigned using the rankings of states by precipitation level. Thus the state with the lowest precipitation level – Nevada – is assigned the minimum of the range for leachate costs from Table 6.2. The same procedure is used to array the states from the minimum to the maximum cost, up to the state with the highest precipitation level – Massachusetts – which is assigned the highest leachate cost from the range in Table 6.2. The result is shown in column 6 of Table 6.3.

The resulting costs from the different pollutants in Table 6.3 are added up for each state, yielding a number for the total external costs per ton of garbage from local pollutants. Each total local external cost is then converted from 1997 dollars to 2,000 dollars, and shown in column 7 of Table 6.3 (replicated as the total local external cost in column 2 of Table 6.4). This total local cost is the same whether the landfill is a flaring or a non-flaring facility. The local external cost per ton of garbage in each state must be added to internal costs and global external costs to calculate the full social cost per ton of garbage for each state. In Table 6.4, the tipping fee per ton for the year 2000 is shown in column 1.[34] That tipping fee is the only internal cost used here.

Although the global external costs are the same for all the states, Table 6.2 shows a range of costs that are much lower for the new methane-flaring facilities than for the old non-flaring facilities. To begin, for each state in Table 6.4, column 3 shows a low-end total cost for non-flaring facilities – calculated as the sum of the state's tipping fee (column 1), local pollutant cost (column 2), and the low-cost end of the range for global external costs for non-flaring facilities (from Table 6.2 but converted into 2,000 dollars). Analogously, column 4 shows a high-end total cost for non-burning facilities.

Global external costs have a lower range for new methane-flaring facilities (shown in the next two columns of Table 6.4). The low-end total cost for flaring facilities in each state is calculated as the sum of the state's tipping fee (column 1), local pollutant cost (column 2), and the low-cost end of the range for global external costs for flaring facilities (from Table 6.2). Analogously, column 6 shows a high-end total cost for burning facilities.

Finally, the last four columns of Table 6.4 convert all of those numbers to amounts per 32-gallon bag of garbage (using the number of 32-gallon bags per ton of garbage). These columns show four different ways to calculate the total social cost per bag of garbage, including internal costs, local external costs, and global external costs. They differ among states because of different costs at the landfill and different costs of local pollutants (which depend on population, temperature, and precipitation). For each state, this total social cost could reflect the low or high estimate of global external cost, either for flaring or non-flaring facilities.

These calculations cannot be taken very seriously for any particular state. Instead, they are meant to demonstrate how the price per bag of garbage might vary across states. These results only provide a ballpark for the *range* of prices that *might* be charged per bag of garbage.

Until the older non-flaring facilities are phased out, any given state may have both flaring and non-flaring facilities. It would be tempting to calculate a single number for each state using the proportion of facilities in each state that flare methane, but that resulting price per bag would not apply anywhere within the state! Rather, any particular city within a state is likely to be served either by a flaring facility or by a non-flaring facility. If so, then a single charge per bag throughout the city could depend on the kind of landfill facility serving the area.

Interestingly, the low cost for a non-flaring facility in any state is almost equivalent to the high cost for any flaring facility. That is, column 7 is almost identical to column 10 in Table 6.4. In either column, the cost per bag of garbage ranges from a low of $0.31 in Arkansas to a high of $1.03 in Texas. Much of that difference is based on the tipping fee in column 1; less variation among the states is introduced by local external costs in column 2. The states all have higher costs when considering the high end of the range for non-flaring facilities in column 8 (from $0.88 in Arkansas to $1.61 in Texas).

These prices could be used to calculate *gross* revenue from garbage taxes, based on current garbage quantities, but much of that price must be used to pay the direct cost of landfill disposal. The tipping fee must be paid either directly to a private landfill company or instead to cover the costs of a state-owned landfill. However, the portion of the price attributable to the externalities does not need to be redistributed to specific members of society. The Pigouvian tax revenue is an extra source of potential revenue and can be used in the manner best suited to individual community needs. It could be used for solid waste programmes, such as kerbside recycling, or it could be turned over to general funds. The net revenue is calculated here as the external cost in dollars per ton times the quantity of solid waste received in the state, measured in tons per day.

Table 6.5 shows these calculations for the different states. Again, four separate revenue calculations are based on the kind of facility and the range of global external costs for each kind of facility. Column 1 shows the quantity of garbage, in tons, received in each state per day. The next four columns pertain to non-flaring facilities. Column 2 shows the low-end total local and global external costs. Then column 3 shows the corresponding potential revenue per day. Columns 4 and 5 show similar calculations for the high-end cost of the non-flaring facilities. Columns 6–9 provide similar figures for the methane-flaring facilities.

As can be seen from the table, this potential net revenue can be a huge number. California, for example, could receive $1.8 million per day at the low end of the low-external-cost flaring facilities, or $2.6 million per day assuming either the high-cost flaring facilities or the low-cost non-flaring facilities. At the high end of the high-cost non-flaring facilities, this figure grows to $9 million per day.[35]

That sounds like a lot of money, but California has a lot of people. What is that additional revenue as a percentage of the state's current revenue? That is, how much could the state increase its net revenue by charging for garbage? Table 6.6 shows the potential net revenue as a percentage of tax revenue

Table 6.4. *Internal and External Costs per Ton of Solid Waste*

State	Tipping fee per ton (1)	Total local external cost (2)	No flaring		Flaring		Cost per 32-gallon bag			
			Low-end total cost (3)	High-end total cost (4)	Low-end total cost (5)	High-end total cost (6)	No flaring		Flaring	
							Low-end total cost (7)	High-end total cost (8)	Low-end total cost (9)	High-end total cost (10)
Alabama	27.78	12.57	50.5	107.78	43.45	50.20	0.51	1.08	0.43	0.50
Alaska	51.72	5.85	67.8	124.99	60.67	67.42	0.68	1.25	0.61	0.67
Arizona	23.46	11.82	45.5	102.71	38.38	45.14	0.45	1.03	0.38	0.45
Arkansas	9.28	11.60	31.1	88.30	23.98	30.73	0.31	0.88	0.24	0.31
California	32.79	12.71	55.7	112.93	48.60	55.36	0.56	1.13	0.49	0.55
Colorado	29.66	8.28	48.1	105.37	41.04	47.80	0.48	1.05	0.41	0.48
Connecticut	29.72	9.24	49.1	106.39	42.06	48.82	0.49	1.06	0.42	0.49
Delaware	20.01	10.05	40.2	97.49	33.16	39.91	0.40	0.97	0.33	0.40
Florida	32.86	14.22	57.3	114.51	50.18	56.94	0.57	1.15	0.50	0.57
Georgia	28.84	13.11	52.1	109.38	45.05	51.81	0.52	1.09	0.45	0.52
Hawaii	65.97	11.93	88.1	145.33	81.00	87.75	0.88	1.45	0.81	0.88
Idaho	51.84	7.28	69.3	126.54	62.22	68.97	0.69	1.27	0.62	0.69
Illinois	32.37	11.50	54.1	111.30	46.97	53.72	0.54	1.11	0.47	0.54
Indiana	64.42	10.93	85.5	142.77	78.45	85.20	0.86	1.43	0.78	0.85
Iowa	45.15	8.59	63.9	121.17	56.84	63.60	0.64	1.21	0.57	0.64
Kansas	27.33	10.44	48.0	105.20	40.87	47.62	0.48	1.05	0.41	0.48
Kentucky	22.26	11.47	43.9	101.16	36.83	43.59	0.44	1.01	0.37	0.44
Louisiana	51.07	13.35	74.6	131.85	67.52	74.28	0.75	1.32	0.68	0.74
Maine	40.93	6.58	57.7	114.94	50.61	57.37	0.58	1.15	0.51	0.57
Maryland	28.65	11.14	50.0	107.22	42.89	49.64	0.50	1.07	0.43	0.50

Massachusetts	31.04	10.04	51.3	108.51	44.18	50.93	0.51	1.09	0.44	0.51
Michigan	37.77	9.30	57.3	114.50	50.17	56.93	0.57	1.15	0.50	0.57
Minnesota	19.73	7.52	37.4	94.67	30.35	37.10	0.37	0.95	0.30	0.37
Mississippi	25.21	12.26	47.7	104.90	40.57	47.32	0.48	1.05	0.41	0.47
Missouri	44.55	11.28	66.0	123.26	58.93	65.69	0.66	1.23	0.59	0.66
Montana	27.99	6.34	44.5	101.76	37.43	44.18	0.45	1.02	0.37	0.44
Nebraska	25.60	8.40	44.2	101.43	37.10	43.85	0.44	1.01	0.37	0.44
Nevada	26.36	8.83	45.4	102.62	38.29	45.04	0.45	1.03	0.38	0.45
New Hampshire	25.09	7.49	42.8	100.01	35.68	42.44	0.43	1.00	0.36	0.42
New Jersey	58.37	11.73	80.3	137.53	73.20	79.95	0.80	1.38	0.73	0.80
New Mexico	19.76	9.90	39.8	97.09	32.76	39.51	0.40	0.97	0.33	0.40
New York	20.97	10.06	41.2	98.46	34.13	40.88	0.41	0.98	0.34	0.41
North Carolina	39.61	12.67	62.5	119.71	55.38	62.13	0.62	1.20	0.55	0.62
North Dakota	56.70	5.97	72.9	130.10	65.77	72.53	0.73	1.30	0.66	0.73
Ohio	28.75	10.88	49.8	107.06	42.73	49.48	0.50	1.07	0.43	0.49
Oklahoma	32.47	11.49	54.1	111.39	47.06	53.81	0.54	1.11	0.47	0.54
Oregon	22.50	8.96	41.7	98.89	34.56	41.32	0.42	0.99	0.35	0.41
Pennsylvania	53.32	10.51	74.0	131.26	66.93	73.68	0.74	1.31	0.67	0.74
Rhode Island	25.55	9.09	44.8	102.07	37.74	44.49	0.45	1.02	0.38	0.44
South Carolina	30.25	11.93	52.4	109.61	45.28	52.04	0.52	1.10	0.45	0.52
South Dakota	43.40	7.55	61.1	118.38	54.05	60.80	0.61	1.18	0.54	0.61
Tennessee	36.25	12.23	58.7	115.91	51.58	58.33	0.59	1.16	0.52	0.58
Texas	79.59	13.67	103.4	160.69	96.36	103.11	1.03	1.61	0.96	1.03
Utah	14.85	8.85	33.9	91.12	26.80	33.55	0.34	0.91	0.27	0.34
Vermont	49.53	6.71	66.4	123.67	59.34	66.10	0.66	1.24	0.59	0.66
Virginia	36.79	11.45	58.4	115.67	51.34	58.10	0.58	1.16	0.51	0.58
Washington	30.42	9.30	49.9	107.15	42.83	49.58	0.50	1.07	0.43	0.50
West Virginia	21.55	9.66	41.4	98.64	34.31	41.06	0.41	0.99	0.34	0.41
Wisconsin	30.37	8.49	49.0	106.29	41.96	48.71	0.49	1.06	0.42	0.49
Wyoming	50.08	5.79	66.1	123.30	58.97	65.73	0.66	1.23	0.59	0.66

Table 6.5. *Total Potential Revenue*

State	Quantity (tons/day) (1)	No flaring				Flaring			
		Low end		High end		Low end		High end	
		Total external cost/ton (2)	Potential net revenue ($/day) (3)	Total external cost/ton (4)	Potential net revenue ($/day) (5)	Total external cost/ton (6)	Potential net revenue ($/day) (7)	Total external cost/ton (8)	Potential net revenue ($/day) (9)
Alabama	15,300	22.8	348,138	80.00	1,223,944	15.67	239,721	22.42	343,056
Alaska	1,960	16.0	31,422	73.27	143,617	8.95	17,534	15.70	30,771
Arizona	17,040	22.0	375,062	79.25	1,350,470	14.92	254,315	21.68	369,402
Arkansas	19,490	21.8	424,540	79.02	1,540,192	14.70	286,433	21.45	418,066
California	114,480	22.9	2,621,444	80.14	9,174,535	15.81	1,810,229	22.57	2,583,418
Colorado	15,200	18.5	280,708	75.71	1,150,790	11.38	173,000	18.14	275,659
Connecticut	16,850	19.4	327,361	76.67	1,291,893	12.34	207,961	19.10	321,764
Delaware	2,060	20.2	41,688	77.48	159,607	13.15	27,091	19.90	41,004
Florida	52,620	24.4	1,284,474	81.65	4,296,560	17.32	911,604	24.08	1,266,995
Georgia	28,770	23.3	670,302	80.54	2,317,161	16.21	466,436	22.97	660,746
Hawaii	4,930	22.1	109,025	79.36	391,229	15.03	74,091	21.78	107,388
Idaho	670	17.5	11,700	74.70	50,052	10.38	6,952	17.13	11,477
Illinois	42,360	21.7	918,494	78.93	3,343,275	14.60	618,327	21.35	904,423
Indiana	8,160	21.1	172,269	78.35	639,365	14.03	114,446	20.78	169,558
Iowa	840	18.8	15,775	76.02	63,858	11.69	9,822	18.45	15,496
Kansas	14,950	20.6	308,318	77.87	1,164,090	13.54	202,381	20.29	303,352
Kentucky	12,770	21.7	276,604	78.90	1,007,587	14.57	186,115	21.33	272,362
Louisiana	8,950	23.5	210,667	80.78	722,985	16.45	147,246	23.21	207,694
Maine	6,800	16.8	114,025	74.01	503,273	9.68	65,840	16.44	111,767
Maryland	27,190	21.3	579,855	78.57	2,136,271	14.24	387,184	20.99	570,823
Massachusetts	28,610	20.2	578,590	77.47	2,216,290	13.14	375,857	19.89	569,087
Michigan	45,150	19.5	879,927	76.73	3,464,415	12.40	559,991	19.16	864,930
Minnesota	16,450	17.7	291,192	74.94	1,232,827	10.62	174,626	17.37	285,728
Mississippi	12,810	22.4	287,543	79.69	1,020,816	15.36	196,771	22.11	283,288
Missouri	6,940	21.5	149,006	78.71	546,267	14.38	99,829	21.14	146,701
Montana	1,930	16.5	31,892	73.77	142,370	9.44	18,216	16.19	31,251

Nebraska	9,470	18.6	176,001	75.83	718,085	11.50	108,896	18.25	172,856
Nevada	9,290	19.0	176,665	76.26	708,446	11.93	110,836	18.68	173,580
New Hampshire	2,780	17.7	49,148	74.92	208,281	10.59	29,448	17.35	48,224
New Jersey	9,480	21.9	207,740	79.16	750,397	14.83	140,564	21.58	204,591
New Mexico	4,160	20.1	83,556	77.33	321,683	13.00	54,078	19.75	82,174
New York	75,840	20.2	1,535,452	77.49	5,876,704	13.16	998,044	19.91	1,510,261
North Carolina	35,080	22.9	801,701	80.10	2,809,759	15.77	553,122	22.52	790,049
North Dakota	3,760	16.2	60,764	73.40	275,995	9.07	34,120	15.83	59,515
Ohio	45,250	21.1	953,142	78.31	3,543,354	13.98	632,497	20.73	938,112
Oklahoma	10,040	21.7	217,607	78.92	792,319	14.59	146,463	21.34	214,272
Oregon	12,010	19.2	229,992	76.39	917,471	12.06	144,888	18.82	226,003
Pennsylvania	74,890	20.7	1,549,894	77.94	5,836,765	13.61	1,019,217	20.36	1,525,018
Rhode Island	2,780	19.3	53,583	76.52	212,716	12.19	33,883	18.94	52,659
South Carolina	18,560	22.1	410,531	79.36	1,472,947	15.03	279,014	21.79	404,366
South Dakota	1,750	17.7	31,037	74.98	131,211	10.65	18,637	17.40	30,456
Tennessee	26,890	22.4	602,683	79.66	2,461,926	15.33	412,138	22.08	593,751
Texas	30,360	23.9	724,223	81.10	2,462,097	16.77	509,090	23.52	714,139
Utah	16,890	19.0	321,460	76.27	1,288,281	11.95	201,776	18.70	315,849
Vermont	2,720	16.9	45,960	74.14	201,659	9.81	26,686	16.57	45,057
Virginia	16,090	21.6	348,189	78.88	1,269,217	14.55	234,174	21.31	342,845
Washington	27,690	19.5	539,712	76.73	2,124,750	12.41	343,499	19.16	530,515
West Virginia	6,380	19.8	126,603	77.09	491,809	12.76	81,394	19.51	124,484
Wisconsin	12,080	18.7	225,600	75.92	917,087	11.59	140,001	18.34	221,588
Wyoming	250	16.0	3,994	73.22	18,305	8.89	2,223	15.65	3,911

Table 6.6. *Potential Revenue as a Percentage Increase from Current Revenue*

State	Annual tax revenue ($m/year)	No flaring				Flaring			
		Low end		High end		Low end		High end	
		Potential net revenue ($m/year)	% of total tax revenue	Potential net revenue ($m/year)	% of total tax revenue	Potential net revenue ($m/year)	% of total tax revenue	Potential net revenue ($m/year)	% of total tax revenue
	(1)	(2)	(3)	(4)	(5)	(6)	(7)	(8)	(9)
Alabama	15,501.1	127.1	0.82	446.7	2.88	87.5	0.56	125.2	0.81
Alaska	7,312.9	11.5	0.16	52.4	0.72	6.4	0.09	11.2	0.15
Arizona	15,121.9	136.9	0.91	492.9	3.26	92.8	0.61	134.8	0.89
Arkansas	10,361.0	155.0	1.50	562.2	5.43	104.5	1.01	152.6	1.47
California	154,016.7	956.8	0.62	3,348.7	2.17	660.7	0.43	942.9	0.61
Colorado	14,158.1	102.5	0.72	420.0	2.97	63.1	0.45	100.6	0.71
Connecticut	16,437.5	119.5	0.73	471.5	2.87	75.9	0.46	117.4	0.71
Delaware	4,540.4	15.2	0.33	58.3	1.28	9.9	0.22	15.0	0.33
Florida	49,208.7	468.8	0.95	1,568.2	3.19	332.7	0.68	462.5	0.94
Georgia	27,638.5	244.7	0.89	845.8	3.06	170.2	0.62	241.2	0.87
Hawaii	6,646.4	39.8	0.60	142.8	2.15	27.0	0.41	39.2	0.59
Idaho	4,870.4	4.3	0.09	18.3	0.38	2.5	0.05	4.2	0.09
Illinois	43,294.5	335.3	0.77	1,220.3	2.82	225.7	0.52	330.1	0.76
Indiana	19,149.1	62.9	0.33	233.4	1.22	41.8	0.22	61.9	0.32
Iowa	11,629.0	5.8	0.05	23.3	0.20	3.6	0.03	5.7	0.05
Kansas	8,687.1	112.5	1.30	424.9	4.89	73.9	0.85	110.7	1.27
Kentucky	16,853.1	101.0	0.60	367.8	2.18	67.9	0.40	99.4	0.59
Louisiana	17,785.9	76.9	0.43	263.9	1.48	53.7	0.30	75.8	0.43
Maine	5,887.5	41.6	0.71	183.7	3.12	24.0	0.41	40.8	0.69
Maryland	19,612.7	211.6	1.08	779.7	3.98	141.3	0.72	208.4	1.06
Massachusetts	28,119.9	211.2	0.75	808.9	2.88	137.2	0.49	207.7	0.74
Michigan	46,724.4	321.2	0.69	1,264.5	2.71	204.4	0.44	315.7	0.68
Minnesota	25,089.2	106.3	0.42	450.0	1.79	63.7	0.25	104.3	0.42
Mississippi	10,700.9	105.0	0.98	372.6	3.48	71.8	0.67	103.4	0.97
Missouri	19,504.7	54.4	0.28	199.4	1.02	36.4	0.19	53.5	0.27

Montana	3,725.3	11.6	0.31	52.0	1.40	6.6	0.18	11.4	0.31
Nebraska	5,575.5	64.2	1.15	262.1	4.70	39.7	0.71	63.1	1.13
Nevada	7,572.9	64.5	0.85	258.6	3.41	40.5	0.53	63.4	0.84
New Hampshire	4,024.3	17.9	0.44	76.0	1.89	10.7	0.27	17.6	0.44
New Jersey	39,150.0	75.8	0.19	273.9	0.70	51.3	0.13	74.7	0.19
New Mexico	875.7	30.5	3.48	117.4	13.41	19.7	2.25	30.0	3.43
New York	102,241.9	560.4	0.55	2,145.0	2.10	364.3	0.36	551.2	0.54
North Carolina	34,063.9	292.6	0.86	1,025.6	3.01	201.9	0.59	288.4	0.85
North Dakota	2,935.6	22.2	0.76	100.7	3.43	12.5	0.43	21.7	0.74
Ohio	51,273.1	347.9	0.68	1,293.3	2.52	230.9	0.45	342.4	0.67
Oklahoma	11,935.1	79.4	0.67	289.2	2.42	53.5	0.45	78.2	0.66
Oregon	15,666.1	83.9	0.54	334.9	2.14	52.9	0.34	82.5	0.53
Pennsylvania	49,481.7	565.7	1.14	2,130.4	4.31	372.0	0.75	556.6	1.12
Rhode Island	5,478.2	19.6	0.36	77.6	1.42	12.4	0.23	19.2	0.35
South Carolina	14,566.3	149.8	1.03	537.6	3.69	101.8	0.70	147.6	1.01
South Dakota	28,885.9	11.3	0.04	47.9	0.17	6.8	0.02	11.1	0.04
Tennessee	16,903.7	220.0	1.30	781.8	4.63	150.4	0.89	216.7	1.28
Texas	71,648.6	264.3	0.37	898.7	1.25	185.8	0.26	260.7	0.36
Utah	8,742.2	117.3	1.34	470.2	5.38	73.6	0.84	115.3	1.32
Vermont	3,054.8	16.8	0.55	73.6	2.41	9.7	0.32	16.4	0.54
Virginia	26,138.4	127.1	0.49	463.3	1.77	85.5	0.33	125.1	0.48
Washington	28,737.1	197.0	0.69	775.5	2.70	125.4	0.44	193.6	0.67
West Virginia	8,034.3	46.2	0.58	179.5	2.23	29.7	0.37	45.4	0.57
Wisconsin	28,334.1	82.3	0.29	334.7	1.18	51.1	0.18	80.9	0.29
Wyoming	3,092.3	1.5	0.05	6.7	0.22	0.8	0.03	1.4	0.05

generated by the different states. Column 1 shows the annual tax revenue for each state.[36] The next four columns pertain to non-flaring facilities: column 2 shows the potential net revenue from a tax equal to the low-end estimate of local and global MED, and column 3 shows that net revenue as a percentage of total state revenue (ranging from 0.04 per cent for South Dakota to 3.48 per cent for New Mexico). This column 3 is nearly matched by column 9 (for high-end flaring facilities), and both columns are in between the other two calculations. Externalities and thus net revenues are lower assuming the low-end cost for flaring facilities (0.02 per cent for South Dakota to 2.25 per cent for New Mexico) and higher assuming high-end cost for non-flaring facilities (0.17 per cent for South Dakota to 13.41 per cent for New Mexico). These numbers differ among the states both because external costs differ and because baseline revenues differ. For example, New Mexico collects less revenue currently than South Dakota, despite having a larger population.

Finally, note that these revenues are only from external costs, so they implicitly assume that states and cities currently charging no price per bag of garbage are able to use part of the price per bag of garbage to cover the landfill expenses and thus reduce current property taxes or other sources of revenue used to pay for landfill expenses. If those governments choose not to change their other sources of revenue, however, then the entire price per bag of garbage could represent an increase in revenue available to state and local governments. Such percentages would be even higher than those in Table 6.6. The only question in that case is what should be said to represent 'tax revenue', as currently in Table 6.6, and what is 'total government collections'. Obviously, the latter could be a higher figure if governments start to charge for many services that are currently free.

6.7 CONCLUSION

Solid waste quantities have been rising for the past several decades, so waste reduction has become an important item on the agenda of municipalities and other local governments. Under the most common existing pricing arrangement for local garbage collection, the marginal cost to an individual household for disposal of another bag of garbage is essentially zero, even though collection and disposal costs increase with the amount of garbage. Several communities have started a 'pay-by-the-bag' programme, and most of these programmes have been viewed as successful. This chapter shows that the price plus optimal tax rate is the full social cost per bag of garbage. If dumping is not a problem, then this tax can be imposed directly to control waste quantities.

On the other hand, if dumping *is* a potential problem, then this chapter shows that the optimal charge can be collected using a deposit–refund system. This set of taxes and subsidies has the same net revenue as the direct excise tax, but it cannot be evaded by dumping. It therefore has lower enforcement costs.

In order to calculate the full social cost of garbage, the associated external costs are added to the direct resource costs. This chapter finds that revenues from a tax (or DRS) based on external costs can be a substantial amount in many states. Even these substantial estimates of external cost exclude the aesthetic costs associated with garbage, costs that could not be assessed here. These calculations provide only a rough estimate of the true full cost of garbage at the margin.

This chapter undertakes calculations only for two types of landfill facilities. Perhaps similar calculations could be undertaken for other waste management facilities such as waste-to-energy facilities, incinerators, and resource-recovery facilities. Further research could also undertake similar cost-per-bag calculations for different cities based on the kind of disposal facility that serves each particular area.

Another refinement of the current calculations could undertake to use the estimates of demand elasticities reviewed above to predict the change in the quantity of garbage when each state charges its optimal price per bag, and then use the new predicted quantities to calculate the additional revenues. In that case, net tax revenues might be a little lower than estimated here, since those estimated elasticities are quite low, but state budgets might also be helped by the fact that less must be paid for disposal of those lesser quantities of waste.

Overall, this chapter has provided a motivation for looking at waste taxes, background information on trends in the pricing and quantities of waste in the USA, and a theoretical framework for thinking about the optimal price per bag, the welfare gain from charging such a price, and the administrative cost of alternative means by which to collect that price – either as a direct tax or via a DRS. By looking at the range of external costs from garbage across states in the USA, the chapter provides a framework for thinking about actual tax rates that might be employed and the revenue that might be collected.

Notes

1 Both of these figures are taken from the Chartwell website (www.wasteinfo.com). Note that 'municipal solid waste' (MSW) includes not only household garbage and recycling but also some institutional, commercial, and industrial waste, greenwaste (often composted), some construction and demolition debris, and certain special wastes (such as batteries, tyres, solvents, and small quantities of hazardous wastes). This chapter will only discuss policies that might apply to different components of household solid waste.

2 Many adopted unit pricing because it provides revenue without the need to call it a 'tax'. The politics of calling it unit 'pricing' rather than a garbage tax was quite important in many locales.

3 See the theory of Pigou (1932) for optimal environmental policy described in Baumol and Oates (1988).

4 This chapter will use several terms to mean the same as marginal environmental damage, including marginal external damage and marginal external cost (all labelled MED).

5 For a few examples starting with Wertz (1976), see Environmental Protection Agency (1990), Jenkins (1993), Miranda et al. (1994), Strathman, Rufolo, and Mildner (1995), Fullerton and Kinnaman (1996), Nestor and Podolsky (1998), van Houtven and Morris (1999), and Kinnaman and Fullerton (2000*a*).

6 The information in this section is taken primarily from successive issues of *Biocycle*, which in 1989 began annual surveys of the fifty states (Glenn, 1998). Also, see Kinnaman and Fullerton (2000*b*).

7 Landfills are used almost exclusively in the UK, Ireland, and Greece, but incineration accounts for most garbage disposal in Switzerland, Sweden, and Denmark. See Jenkins (1993) and Kinnaman and Fullerton (2000*b*).

8 In Europe, the EU has mandated a waste management policy based on a 'hierarchy' of options that give top priority to waste minimization, followed by recycling, and then incineration, with landfill disposal last. Yet Dijkgraaf and Vollebergh (1998) find that this hierarchy is not justified on economic grounds: incineration has lower external costs than landfills, but sufficiently higher internal private costs – such that incineration has higher total social costs than landfills. The lowest net cost option seems to be landfill disposal with energy recovery through capture and flaring of methane.

9 For more on circumstances in developing countries, see Bartone (2000) and the references therein.

10 The theoretical framework in this section builds on the model of Fullerton and Kinnaman (1995).

11 Decomposition of material in a landfill creates methane gas, which is a greenhouse gas. An estimated 6 per cent of the world's emissions of methane are released from landfills (Beede and Bloom, 1995).

12 Demand for each type of disposal in this model depends explicitly on price and income and implicitly on demographic characteristics and intrinsic motivation. For discussions of these latter variables, see Miranda and Bynum (2002) and Frey (2002). It is difficult for policy to modify the latter variables, however, so we focus here on the effect of changing each price. Some individuals might litter or dump readily, but those who believe it wrong would not do so at any price. This simple model has only one type of individual, but it can be said to represent the average or overall response to a change in any price.

13 The evasion of this excise tax on MSW via illicit dumping is analogous to the evasion of other excise taxes via smuggling. For discussion of other excise taxes, see other chapters in this volume.

14 Again, the model simplifies by aggregation, since different kinds of dumping have costs that would require different prices or enforcement policies. Putting household garbage in a commercial skip may not have the same environmental cost as throwing it along the roadside, and locks on skips might be cheap and effective enforcement, but it does impose social costs by requiring the locks and by transferring the cost of disposal in a way that is economically inefficient. See Miranda and Bynum (2002).

15 If either the Pigouvian tax or the DRS were to encourage recycling of some types of materials more than others, then the change in composition of the remaining

waste stream may change the MED used to calculate the optimal rate of tax (Linderhof et al., 2001). For example, less garden waste would mean less organic material in landfills, which produces methane emissions. For the MED of methane, see later.

16 Miranda and Aldy (1998) find that subscription programmes can be effective if pricing applies to smaller trash containers. Nestor and Podolsky (1998) employ self-reported household data to estimate that subscription programmes are about as effective as bag/tag programmes.

17 Table 6.1 cannot show all relevant studies. Other important studies include Hong and Adams (1999), who look at the effect of unit pricing on aggregate disposal and recycling behaviour, and Jenkins et al. (2003), who use household-level data to look at recycling behaviour by material. They find that unit pricing has no effect on recycling but that kerbside collection has a big effect on recycling of all materials.

18 This estimate includes private and external collection and disposal costs (with a depletion allowance). The external costs are based on the work of Stone and Ashford (1991) and the Tellus Institute (1991).

19 Of the reduction in garbage resulting from pricing garbage at the kerb, Fullerton and Kinnaman (1996) estimate that 28 per cent may have been dumped. Evidence of increased dumping was also found by Blume (1991), Jenkins (1993), Reschovsky and Stone (1994), and Miranda and Aldy (1998). A number of other studies find minimal changes in dumping, including Podolsky and Spiegel (1998), Strathman, Rufolo, and Mildner (1995), Miranda et al. (1994), Miranda and Bauer (1996), and Nestor and Podolsky (1998).

20 Since money is fungible, it does not matter if the subsidized collection of garbage and recycling (the 'refund') is financed from sales taxes (the 'deposit') or from some other source, such as property taxes.

21 On the other hand, this result depends on the assumption that recycling markets are complete. Calcott and Walls (2000*a*, 2000*b*) argue that imperfections in recycling markets prevent attainment of the first-best. It is costly to collect and transport recyclables, and it is difficult for recyclers to sort products according to their recyclability and pay consumers a price based on that degree of recyclability. With these transaction costs, price signals may not be transmitted from consumers and recyclers back upstream to producers.

22 The text describes post-1993 requirements of the Resource Conservation and Recovery Act (RCRA), but some operations require compliance with the Clean Air Act and the Clean Water Act.

23 Thus, as mentioned above, the MED (and thus the optimal tax rate) is lower for garbage sent to new landfills than for garbage sent to old landfills. Also, new regulations that require flaring of methane will make obsolete the calculations below for the optimal tax rate on garbage at older 'no flaring' landfills.

24 According to www.bottlebill.org, the eleven states with current bottle bills are California, Connecticut, Delaware, Hawaii, Iowa, Maine, Massachusetts, Michigan, New York, Oregon, and Vermont.

25 The International Solid Waste Association (2002) reports that a recent study for Denmark recommended against weight-based charges after finding that municipalities with such charges had more illegal disposal and less recycling than other municipalities. Bartone (2002) reports low participation rates and widespread

littering where households contract directly with private firms for collection services in two Latin American cities (Merida, Mexico and Guatemala City, Guatemala). Some municipalities may themselves engage in dumping.

26 Textbooks such as Baumol and Oates (1988) note that the Pigouvian tax rate ought to reflect the marginal damages on others, not the cost of controlling the pollutant. At the optimum, however, the two concepts are the same: reaching the optimal control of pollution means continuing to undertake more control until the marginal cost of control (MCC) equals the marginal benefit of control (the MED from pollution). Moreover, if the MCC is constant, then the current MCC is a good estimate of the MCC at the optimum (which is the MED at the optimum).

27 As their title indicates, Miranda and Hale apply these external cost estimates to data on waste quantities in Puerto Rico. Since no prior study provides estimates of external cost in Puerto Rico, however, they compile prior studies on external costs in the USA. It is this compilation for the USA that is employed here.

28 As mentioned above, hedonic price studies have estimated the effect on house prices from the existence of a landfill nearby, but it is hard to know how to convert these estimates to an amount per bag of garbage.

29 Flaring of methane creates carbon dioxide, a less-potent greenhouse gas, but landfills are also considered to be carbon 'sinks' because they keep the carbon in material such as plastics and other petrochemical products from escaping into the atmosphere.

30 In addition, leachate costs might ideally be linked to the source of drinking water. Places that rely on surface water reservoirs face a different level of risk from leachate from that faced by places relying on groundwater.

31 'Others' includes carbon monoxide, trichloroethylene, carbon tetrachloride, 1,1,1-trichloroethane, chloroform, 1,2-dichloroethane, and methylene chloride.

32 The nature of the damages from each such pollutant is described in Environmental Protection Agency (1999).

33 Population density might be a better way to rank states for the cost of benzene, but the two rankings would be similar and the choice is not unambiguous. Ranking by population may better reflect the total potential cost of release, per unit of benzene. Note, however, that waste may be shipped out of state.

34 Data on the average tipping fee per state were taken from the Chartwell publisher's website at www.wasteinfo.com/products/swd.htm. Calculations follow Sharma (2002).

35 To affect household waste generation, the price can be charged per bag placed at the kerb. To cover the external cost of all material in the landfill, however, another fee must apply to imports of waste. If only one state were to charge such a fee, a change in waste imports may affect this revenue calculation.

36 Data for the 1999–2000 tax revenue are taken from the US Census Bureau website (www.census.gov/govs/state/99rank.html).

References

Ackerman, F. (1997), *Why Do We Recycle?*, Washington, DC: Island Press.

Atri, S., and Schellberg, T. (1995), 'Efficient management of household solid waste: a general equilibrium model', *Public Finance Quarterly*, 23: 3–39.

Bailey, J. (1995), 'Waste of a sort: curbside recycling comforts the soul, but benefits are scant', *Wall Street Journal*, 19 January, p. A1.

Bartone, C. R. (2000), 'Strategic solid waste planning for large cities: a World Bank and CWG approach', keynote address for the Collaborative Working Group Workshop on Planning for Sustainable and Integrated Solid Waste Management, Manila, 18–22 September.

——(2002), 'Comments on the paper "An excise tax on municipal solid waste" by Don Fullerton', World Bank, Washington, DC.

Baumol, W., and Oates, W. (1988), *The Theory of Environmental Policy*, second edition, Cambridge: Cambridge University Press.

Beede, D. N., and Bloom, D. E. (1995), 'The economics of municipal solid waste', *World Bank Research Observer*, 10: 113–50.

Blume, D. R. (1991), 'Under what conditions should cities adopt volume-based pricing for residential solid waste collection?', Natural Resources Branch, Office of Information and Regulatory Affairs, Office of Management and Budget, Washington, DC, unpublished manuscript.

Brisson, I. E. (1997), *Assessing the 'Waste Hierarchy': A Social Cost–Benefit Analysis of MSW Management in the European Union*, Samfund, Økonomi and Miljo (SØM) Publication 19, Copenhagen.

Calcott, P., and Walls, M. (2000*a*), 'Can downstream waste disposal policies encourage upstream "design for environment"?', *American Economic Review: Papers and Proceedings*, 90: 233–7.

——and——(2000*b*), 'Policies to encourage recycling and "design for environment": what to do when markets are missing', Resources for the Future, Discussion Paper 00-30.

Callan, S. J., and Thomas, J. M. (1997), 'The impact of state and local policies on the recycling effort', *Eastern Economic Journal*, 23: 411–23.

Centre for Social and Economic Research of the Global Environment (1993), *Externalities from Landfill and Incineration*, Department of the Environment, London: HMSO.

Dijkgraaf, E., and Vollebergh, H. R. J. (1998), *Incineration or Dumping? A Social Cost Comparison of Waste Disposal Options*, Research Memorandum 9808, Rotterdam: Research Centre for Economic Policy, Erasmus University Rotterdam.

Dinan, T. M. (1993), 'Economic efficiency effects of alternative policies for reducing waste disposal', *Journal of Environmental Economics and Management*, 25: 242–56.

Dobbs, I. M. (1991), 'Litter and waste management: disposal taxes versus user charges', *Canadian Journal of Economics*, 24: 221–7.

Environmental Protection Agency, USA (1990), *Charging Households for Waste Collection and Disposals: The Effects of Weight or Volume-Based Pricing on Solid Waste Management*, EPA-530-SW-90-047, Washington, DC.

——(1999), *The Benefits and Costs of the Clean Air Act 1990 to 2010*, EPA-410-R-99-001, Washington, DC.

——(2001), *Inventory of U.S. Greenhouse Gas Emissions and Sinks: 1990–1999*, EPA-236-R-01-001, Washington, DC.

Frey, B. S. (2002), 'Excise taxes: economics, politics and psychology', University of Zurich, working paper.

Fullerton, D., and Kinnaman, T. C. (1995), 'Garbage, recycling, and illicit burning or dumping', *Journal of Environmental Economics and Management*, 29: 78–91.

Fullerton, D., and Kinnaman, T. C. (1996), 'Household responses to pricing garbage by the bag', *American Economic Review*, 86: 971–84.

—— and Wu, W. (1998), 'Policies for green design', *Journal of Environmental Economics and Management*, 36: 131–48.

Glenn, J. (1998), 'The state of garbage in America', *Biocycle* (April): 32–43.

Halstead, J. M., and Park, W. M. (1996), 'The role of economic analysis in local government decisions: the case of solid waste management', *Agricultural and Resource Economics Review* (April): 76–82.

Hite, D., Chern, W., Hitzhusen, F., and Randall, A. (2001), 'Property-value impacts of an environmental disamenity: the case of landfills', *Journal of Real Estate Finance and Economics*, 22: 185–202.

Hong, S., and Adams, R. M. (1999), 'Household responses to price incentives for recycling: some further evidence', *Land Economics*, 75: 505–14.

——, ——, and Love, H. A. (1993), 'An economic analysis of household recycling of solid wastes: the case of Portland, Oregon', *Journal of Environmental Economics and Management*, 25: 136–46.

Huhtala, A. (1997), 'A post-consumer waste management model for determining optimal levels of recycling and landfilling', *Environmental and Resource Economics*, 10: 301–14.

International Solid Waste Association (2002), 'Fly-tipping increases with weight-based charging', *Waste Management World*, 2(2): 11–12.

Jenkins, R. R. (1993), *The Economics of Solid Waste Reduction*, Aldershot: Edward Elgar.

——, Martinez, S., Palmer, K., and Podolsky, M. (2003), 'The determinants of household recycling: a material-specific analysis of recycling program features and unit pricing', *Journal of Environmental Economics and Management*, 45: 294–318.

Kinnaman, T. C., and Fullerton, D. (2000a), 'Garbage and recycling with endogenous local policy', *Journal of Urban Economics*, 48: 419–42.

—— and —— (2000b), 'The economics of residential solid waste management', in T. Tietenberg and H. Folmer (eds), *The International Yearbook of Environmental and Resource Economics 2000/2001*, Cheltenham: Edward Elgar.

Linderhof, V., Kooreman, P., Allers, M., and Wiersma, D. (2001), 'Weight-based pricing in the collection of household waste: the Oostzaan case', *Resource and Energy Economics*, 23: 359–71.

Macauley, M., Palmer, K., Shih, J-S., Cline, S., and Holsinger, H. (2001), 'Modeling the costs and environmental benefits of disposal options for end-of-life electronic equipment: the case of used computer monitors', Resources for the Future, Discussion Paper 01-27.

Medina, M. (1997), 'The effect of income on municipal solid waste generation rates for countries of varying levels of economic development: a model', *Journal of Solid Waste Technology and Management*, 24(3): 149–55.

Miranda, M. L., and Aldy, J. E. (1998), 'Unit pricing of residential municipal solid waste: lessons from nine case study communities', *Journal of Environmental Management*, 52: 79–93.

—— and Bauer, S. (1996), 'An analysis of variable rates for residential garbage collection in urban areas', Duke University, Nicholas School of the Environment, working paper.

—— and Bynum, D. Z. (1999), *Unit Based Pricing in the United States: A Tally of Communities*, report submitted to the US Environmental Protection Agency, September. Available at www.epa.gov/payt/pdf/jan99sum.pdf.

—— and —— (2002), 'Unit-based pricing and undesirable diversion: market prices and community characteristics', *Society and Natural Resources*, 15: 1–15.

——, Everett, J. W., Blume, D., and Roy, B. A., Jr. (1994), 'Market-based incentives and residential municipal solid waste', *Journal of Policy Analysis and Management*, 13: 681–98.

—— and Hale, B. (1997), 'Waste not, want not: the private and social costs of waste-to-energy production', *Energy Policy*, 25: 587–600.

—— and —— (1999), 'Re-covering all the bases: a comparison of landfills and resource recovery facilities in Puerto Rico', Duke University, Nicholas School of the Environment, working paper.

Nelson, A. C., Genereux, J., and Genereux, M. (1992), 'Price effects of landfills on house values', *Land Economics*, 68: 359–65.

Nestor, D. V., and Podolsky, M. J. (1998), 'Assessing incentive-based environmental policies for reducing household waste disposal', *Contemporary Economic Policy*, 16: 401–11.

O'Brien, C. (2002), 'Policy and potential for reducing landfilled waste in the UK', *Waste Management World*, 2(1): 21–5.

Palmer, K., Sigman, H., and Walls, M. (1997), 'The cost of reducing municipal solid waste', *Journal of Environmental Economics and Management*, 33: 128–50.

—— and Walls, M. (1994), 'Materials use and solid waste: an evaluation of policies', Resources for the Future, Discussion Paper 95-02.

—— and —— (1997), 'Optimal policies for solid waste disposal: taxes, subsidies, and standards', *Journal of Public Economics*, 65: 193–205.

—— and —— (1999), 'Extended product responsibility: an economic assessment of alternative policies', Resources for the Future, Discussion Paper 99-12.

Pigou, A. C. (1932), *The Economics of Welfare*, fourth edition, London: MacMillan and Co.

Podolsky, M. J., and Spiegel, M. (1998), 'Municipal waste disposal: unit-pricing and recycling opportunities', *Public Works Management and Policy*, 3: 27–39.

Repetto, R., Dower, R. C., Jenkins, R., and Geoghegan, J. (1992), *Green Fees: How a Tax Shift Can Work for the Environment and the Economy*, Washington, DC: World Resources Institute.

Reschovsky, J. D., and Stone, S. E. (1994), 'Market incentives to encourage household waste recycling: paying for what you throw away', *Journal of Policy Analysis and Management*, 13: 120–39.

Roberts, R. K., Douglas, P. V., and Park, W. M. (1991), 'Estimating external costs of municipal landfill siting through contingent valuation analysis: a case study', *Southern Journal of Agricultural Economics*, 23: 155–65.

Sharma, D. (2002), 'Optimal pricing policy for municipal solid waste', University of Texas, working paper.

Stone, R., and Ashford, N. A. (1991), 'Package deal: the economic impacts of recycling standards for packaging in Massachusetts', Massachusetts Institute of Technology, working paper.

Strathman, J. G., Rufolo, A. M., and Mildner, G. C. S. (1995), 'The demand for solid waste disposal', *Land Economics*, 71: 57–64.

Tellus Institute (1991), *Disposal Cost Fee Study Final Report*, prepared for California Integrated Solid Waste Management Board.

Van Houtven, G. L., and Morris, G. E. (1999), 'Household behavior under alternative pay-as-you-throw systems for solid waste disposal', *Land Economics*, 75: 515–37.

Wertz, K. L. (1976), 'Economic factors influencing households' production of refuse', *Journal of Environmental Economics and Management*, 2: 263–72.

Chapter 7

Road User and Congestion Charges

*DAVID MICHAEL NEWBERY**
University of Cambridge

7.1 INTRODUCTION

This chapter argues that roads should be treated as a regulated public utility, and road charges set accordingly to yield a stable and defensible revenue stream. An efficient structure of charges would confront road users with the marginal social cost of their decisions, but there are limits to the precision with which this can be done. Congestion externalities make up the larger part of the efficient road user charge, with road damage costs and externalities a relatively small part. Accident externalities are hard to measure, and could be small in comparison with other costs. Other environmental costs affect non-road-users as much as road users, and are therefore best dealt with by corrective taxes (and standards). If governments could set out and defend the total revenue to be collected for road use, and the environmental taxes, then it would be politically easier to move to a more efficient structure of road user charges, such as congestion or road pricing. The levels of road user charges dictated by the regulated public utility model are not inconsistent with an efficient set of road prices, provided that the level of road investment is set efficiently. The public utility model has the additional advantage that it is more likely to deliver efficient investment than current budgetary arrangements.

Road users require access to expensive road infrastructure and impose a variety of external costs on each other (congestion, accident risks) and on non-road-users (accident risks, pollution, noise, environmental degradation). They typically pay special excise duties on fuel and annual licence charges for the right to use highways. They may also pay special taxes on vehicle purchase, though these are less common now in developed countries. Increasingly, countries impose tolls for certain roads and bridges, often as the means to pay the private concession holder, while charges to enter congested urban areas have been introduced in Singapore, Norway, and other countries. Most of these are

* I am indebted to Richard Arnott and Reiner Eichenberger for the detailed written comments, to the participants at the OCFEB conference for their contributions, and to Eurof Walters, Steven Haberman, and Fintan Hurley for help with the mortality calculations in Appendix 7.A.

neither designed for, nor defended as, methods of optimizing traffic flows, as they rarely vary by time of day or in response to traffic conditions. Instead, they are normally justified as a fair means of financing improved transport systems (for motorists and through better public transport). Nevertheless, they remind us that road pricing is likely to be a more efficient way of dealing with traffic congestion than the existing blunt instruments of fuel excises and public transport subsidies.

Figure 7.1 shows the excise taxes (excluding value added tax (VAT)) on road fuels across the European Union (EU), together with the USA and New Zealand, which stand out for their relatively low tax rates. The countries are ranked by the tax on gasoline (petrol), and it is noticeable that diesel is less heavily taxed in all countries except the UK, despite the greater fuel efficiency of diesel vehicles (and hence the lower tax per kilometre even when equally taxed). Heavy vehicles in New Zealand pay weight- and distance-related taxes so that there is no road user charge reason to tax diesel fuel. Road fuels have always been lightly taxed in the USA, in contrast to Europe, raising sharply the question of whether, as Parry and Small (2002) ask, the optimal gasoline tax is closer to the US or European level.

There are conceptually two quite distinct ways of deciding on the appropriate level of road user charges. An ambitious student of optimal public finance might attempt to maximize social welfare subject to a set of tax instruments and a government budget constraint. Social welfare would depend on individual utility, defined over transport services, labour, time spent travelling, accident risk, pollution, leisure, and all other goods. Pollution, accident risk, and travel time would depend on location, demand for travel, and the level of traffic and fuel use. The problem is then to determine the optimal level of such

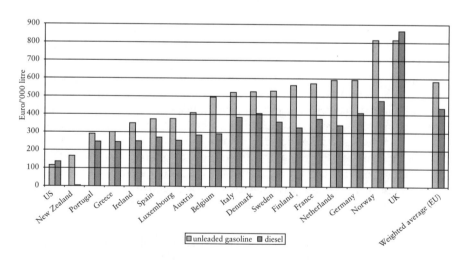

Figure 7.1. *Road Fuel Excise Taxes, 2001*

instruments as the gasoline tax (and all other taxes, possibly subsumed into a labour tax). Parry and Small (2002) provide an excellent example of this approach and show how the gasoline tax should be set to deal with pollution, congestion, and social welfare more generally, balancing the distortionary effects on fuel and vehicle use against the reduction in labour tax distortions. Under certain assumptions, the gasoline tax can be set without regard to these wider policy objectives.

This ambitious top-down or general equilibrium approach can be contrasted with a more partial or bottom-up approach that concentrates on the road sector initially in isolation and only considers wider issues (such as raising additional revenue) at a later stage. Both approaches have their advantages and limitations. As with any exercise in optimal taxation, the model employed has to be greatly simplified to be tractable. It risks overlooking features of congestion and road investment that may be critical for the design of road user charges. The bottom-up approach breaks the problem down into manageable components that can be quantified, and for which tax and charging instruments can be properly tailored. It is relatively silent on the larger question of how much additional revenue should be raised from road users to contribute to general taxation. That answer will depend on the kind of issues addressed by optimal tax theorists and on questions of political economy.[1]

The approach taken here is bottom-up, with a final section discussing some of the wider tax issues. On this approach, an efficient structure of charges and taxes on road users would contain the following components:

- efficient charges for using scarce and costly road space, including congestion charges and road damage costs;
- charges (more properly, corrective taxes) for other externalities, such as pollution, noise, and accidents;
- general taxes that apply to the majority of goods, such as the standard rate of VAT;
- additional taxes or subsidies that are justified by wider policy considerations (or are not justified by any of the preceding).

The last category can be thought of as a balancing item, as most taxing authorities do not distinguish between the separate components that make up the existing system of charging and taxation. For our purposes, it reminds us that there may be additional revenue-raising and redistributive arguments for further taxation that are not covered by any of the previous distinct categories.

The third category can be ignored once we have dealt with one important conceptual issue. The first two categories are corrective taxes or charges to ensure that road users face prices that reflect the social cost of road use. If the prices are right, then so ought to be decisions about vehicle acquisition and use. These prices would then correspond to efficient producer prices elsewhere in the economy, and as such should be subject to the standard rate of VAT. In most developed countries with a system of VAT, excise duties on fuel are also subject to VAT. In some countries, the level of fuel taxes exceeds the amount justified under the first two categories. There will then be additional VAT on the excess of these taxes over the corrective component, and that part of the total VAT should be considered to be part of the residual tax system. At present, commentators typically either exclude all VAT (the convention of the British Office for National Statistics in classifying road taxes) or include all VAT in the total level of road taxes (the practice of the British Automobile Association in arguing that motorists are overtaxed). The proposed approach is conceptually defensible although rather difficult to implement.

The remainder of this chapter shows how to set road user charges following this scheme, illustrating the method with data from Britain. Table 7.1 gives basic data for British traffic and tax revenue from fuel taxes and vehicle excise duty (VED), as well as emissions of various pollutants.

7.2 ROAD USER CHARGES

There are two apparently conflicting approaches to setting road user charges that can be reconciled under not unreasonable conditions. The first approach is to set charges that cover the total costs of operating the network (the way in which privatized network utilities operate). The second is to charge the difference between the marginal social cost (MSC) and the average private cost

Table 7.1. *Traffic Volume, Taxation, and Emissions: Britain, 2000*

	Various units	Tax (£ million)
Traffic (billion vehicle km)	468	27,720
Of which:		
In built-up areas	183	
Cars and light vans	429	21,735
Fuel use (million tonnes)		Fuel tax
Petrol – leaded	1.5	
Petrol – unleaded	19.9	13,665
Diesel	15.6	8,640
Total	37	22,305
Emissions		
Particulates (thousand tonnes)	38	
Nitrogen oxides (thousand tonnes)	730	
Carbon dioxide (million tonnes carbon)	36	
Motor vehicles licensed (thousands)		VED
Motorcycles	790	40
Petrol cars	20,154	3,695
Petrol light goods vehicles	525	96
Diesel cars	3,033	556
Other diesel vehicles	3,911	1,028
Total	28,413	5,415

Source: Department of Transport, Local Government, and the Regions, 2001.

(APC) of road use. If we leave on one side the non-congestive externalities, which will be dealt with below, the main reason why the MSC typically exceeds the APC is that road users impose congestive externalities on other road users. In addition, heavy vehicles cause wear and tear disproportionately to their number (damage increases as the fourth power of the axle weight), and this damage raises vehicle operating costs for other road users. There is therefore both a direct damage cost and an additional road damage externality to be included in the MSC.

Charging efficient prices (to charge for user costs and internalize these two externalities) and charging to recover average costs might appear to be quite different approaches likely to give quite different answers. Newbery (1988*a*, 1989) identifies the conditions under which the two are equal. Road damage externalities averaged over the network are zero provided that the highway authority maintains a condition-responsive maintenance programme – that is, it repairs roads when they fall to a predetermined level of deterioration. Charging efficient congestion prices will exactly recover the total costs of providing road infrastructure (including costs caused by weather damage) provided that the marginal cost of road expansion is constant. The proposition that short-run marginal cost (SRMC) = long-run marginal cost (LRMC) = average cost (AC) for efficiently priced and supplied constant-returns-to-scale industries will be familiar (Mohring and Harwitz, 1962; Mohring, 1970; Strotz, 1965).[2] The result here is more surprising, as AC includes the quite considerable weather damage costs, which may account for half the total operating costs.

This immediately raises two questions: whether there are economies or diseconomies of scale to expanding roads, and whether it is reasonable to suppose that roads are optimally supplied and priced. If we consider the first question, the evidence is mixed. For inter-urban roads in relatively unpopulated areas, there is some evidence of mild increasing returns to scale or decreasing costs. Doubling a two-lane road to a four-lane road almost doubles the capacity per lane and hence almost quadruples total capacity, but the cost of intersections increases considerably. Keeler and Small (1977) analyse US inter-urban data and give their best point estimate as AC/MC = 1.03 (but with a high standard error), suggesting slight increasing returns to scale. Kraus (1981*a*, 1981*b*) combines a number of estimates to get AC/MC = 1.19 explicitly accounting for intersections.

In densely populated and urban areas, the marginal cost of road expansion may be extremely high and exceed the average cost. This suggests that inter-urban and urban roads should probably be treated differently for charging purposes. If we include minor roads that act as feeders to the inter-urban road network, efficient congestion pricing would not be in conflict with average cost pricing, provided the highway authorities expanded roads when justified by social cost–benefit analysis.

The answer to the second question as to whether roads are optimally priced and supplied is almost certainly 'not in all cases'. In Britain, the typical benefit–cost ratio for potential inter-urban road projects is substantially greater than one, suggesting considerable underinvestment and marginal congestion costs that exceed the average costs of expansion. In North America, with suboptimal fuel excises, the opposite may be true. That raises the important issue of advising on the appropriate level of road charges and taxes in sub-optimally managed transport budgets.

The short-run marginal social cost (SRMSC) will be higher, on average, than the long-run marginal social cost (LRMSC) if there is underinvestment in roads. If governments then defend road charges and/or taxes by reference to the SRMSC, they are effectively exercising market power to drive up the scarcity price of the natural monopoly under their control. The standard solution to the abuse of market power for natural monopolies is regulation to prevent exploitative pricing, with the requirement to meet demand at the regulated price. Regulated utilities in the private sector are normally allowed to recover their total costs, while being encouraged to price individual outputs efficiently (subject to the overall revenue constraint). The British model of price caps and private utility regulation has been remarkably successful.[3] It suggests looking at the problem of setting road user charges as one of setting charges for a regulated natural monopoly road network.

7.3 REVENUE CAPS FOR ROAD CHARGES

Where networks are under private ownership, regulation is required to prevent the natural monopoly owner exploiting consumers. Credible regulation is also required to protect the owner against expropriation by politically influential consumers and thus to persuade investors to undertake adequate investment. Over relatively long periods of time in the USA and for more than a decade in the UK, the principles of setting charges for using natural monopolies have been clarified and codified.

The regulated charges should be set to recover the operating and capital costs of an efficiently run network. The capital cost consists of the interest (or return) on the opening value of the regulatory asset base (RAB) and the depreciation (or decrease in value) of this value. A key part of setting the charges therefore consists in determining the RAB, measuring its depreciation, and determining the rate of return allowed on the RAB. In the case of indefinitely lived assets, such as water mains and roads, depreciation may be replaced by the amount of expenditure needed to maintain their modern equivalent asset (MEA) value. Over time, the RAB is increased by new gross investment and reduced by depreciation.

In the USA, the RAB is equal to the written-down book value – that is, the purchase cost (at historic value) less the accumulated value of depreciation. The rate of return is the money rate of interest that lenders would require to invest in that risk class of assets. This approach has the advantage that the assets can be financed by issuing bonds but the drawback that the book value of assets may fall substantially short of the written-down MEA value at current prices, while money rates of interest can be quite unstable. Britain, with a longer and more painful experience of rapid and unpredictable inflation, adopted current cost accounting.[4] Assets are revalued each year by a suitable price index and earn a real rate of return rather than a money rate of return on their opening value.

Where assets are transferred from the public to the private sector, one of the critical issues to resolve is how they will be valued for subsequent resetting of price controls. This issue was essentially sidestepped with the early British privatizations and only returned to haunt the regulators at the first periodic review. Most public assets had been sold at a considerable discount to MEA value, most noticeably for water where the sales price was less than 10 per cent of the MEA. Over time, as investment increases the real value of the assets, the RAB will converge ultimately on the MEA value. In the case of water, this process of convergence was assisted by a K-factor that augmented prices sufficiently rapidly to enable the large required investment programme to be financed.[5] Electricity and gas transmission systems were sold, and remain, at a considerable discount to MEA, and as their rate of investment is relatively slow compared with their asset value, this process of convergence may take decades.

If we consider the road network, and were to adopt the same approach for setting charges to cover operating costs and the return to the owner (the State), there would be a major problem in determining the RAB. It is relatively straightforward to value inter-urban highways. Thus the British Highways Agency estimates that the strategic road network is worth £60 billion at 1998 prices (Drake, 2000). The British strategic road network carries 34 per cent of all road traffic and 67 per cent of freight.

Valuing the rest of the road network, and particularly roads in built-up areas, is intrinsically problematic. The inherited road network reflects a gradual evolution in a largely pre-motorized era and is very unlikely to reflect an efficient road network system designed for motor traffic. It is, of course, possible (in principle) to determine the number of lane kilometres of roads of varying qualities, estimate their current state of repair and the cost of building a new road to that standard, and hence calculate the written-down MEA for the entire system. In 1996, the then Department of Transport in Britain decided to undertake this exercise, but it has not yet produced a result. Newbery (1988b) had already produced estimates from rolling forward the earlier published capital value of the road network by a permanent inventory method of adding new investment to that total. That number would be between £100 billion and £150 billion (1998 prices) for the UK. If the strategic road network value of £60 billion is accepted, the rest of the network is worth between £40 billion and £90 billion, which may appear rather low. If the prime determinant of the cost of roads is the space required for vehicles, then one would expect the cost of the rest of the network to be at least as high as that of the strategic roads. Allowing for the higher costs of road building in urban areas, the amount could be substantially more – perhaps £140 billion, giving the total value as £200 billion.

The practical implications of this are that it may be useful to distinguish between urban and inter-urban roads. Inter-urban roads can probably be expanded in line with traffic demand at moderately constant costs, given sensible planning regulations. Increasing capacity on urban roads, in contrast, is often difficult or very costly. The appropriate capital value of inter-urban roads is therefore relatively simple to compute, but there will be a degree of arbitrariness in determining the RAB for urban roads, where honest opinions may differ by a factor of two or more.

The second controversial element in determining the capital charge for the road network is the rate of return, or its private sector regulatory counterpart, the weighted average cost of capital (WACC). This is typically built up from an assumed debt:equity ratio, the real rate of interest on risk-free debt, plus the (default) risk premium for private sector debt, while the equity return has a further equity risk premium. The correlation between the returns of the regulated asset and the market as a whole, or the value of beta (β), then determines the extent to which the risks cannot be diversified (and hence are socially costly).

If we take Ofgem's recent price control of the gas transport network, Transco, as an example, the risk-free real rate is taken as $i = 2.75$ per cent and the debt risk premium is $\delta = 1.5$–1.9 per cent, giving the cost of debt as $d = i + \delta = 4.25$–4.65 per cent (Ofgem, 2001). The equity risk premium is taken as $\rho = 3.5$ per cent, gearing as $g = 62.5$ per cent, and the equity beta as 1, to give the post-tax cost of equity as $n = \beta(i + \rho) = 6.25$ per cent, or a pre-tax cost of equity as $r = 8.9$ per cent, and a WACC of $gd + (1 - g)r = 6$–6.25 per cent real. This is for a privately owned and regulated network, whereas the road network is publicly owned, raising the standard public economics question of what is the correct rate of interest to use in project appraisal and also for determining the capital charge for the public sector. Under the strong conditions of the Diamond and Mirrlees (1971) theorem that optimal commodity taxation preserves production efficiency, the public sector discount rate should be equal to the private rate of return. If so, and if beta for roads is also unity, then presumably the (pre-2002) UK government test discount rate of 6 per cent real is the correct rate to use.

Atkinson and Stiglitz (1980) discuss the limitations of the result that the public and private sector discount rates should be equal, with the implication that the public sector may discount at a different and probably lower rate. The British Treasury was in 2001 revising its appraisal manual and was arguing for the considerably lower rate of 3.5 per cent real. This was based on the argument that the social discount rate should reflect the rate at which the marginal utility of consumption is decreasing over time as a result of growth in consumption per head (taken as 2 per cent per annum). The elasticity of the marginal utility of consumption was taken as -1, so the rate of fall of marginal utility is 2 per cent, which, corrected by the risk of catastrophe (taken as 1.5 per cent), gives a social discount rate of 3.5 per cent.

This is not the place to resolve the dispute over the correct treatment of the public sector discount rate that it is appropriate to use in determining capital charges, but only to note the considerable discrepancy between the two discount rates advocated for the public sector in Britain. If we take the RAB as £100–200 billion and the required rate of return as 3.5–6 per cent, then the range of annual capital costs is £3.5–12 billion (excluding depreciation, better measured by the required level of maintenance to preserve intact the capital stock). Maintenance is about £3–4 billion p.a. (Newbery, 1998*a*) (though perhaps ought to be somewhat higher), while fuel taxes and vehicle excise duty (the annual licence fee) collected £27.7 billion in 2000–01 (excluding all VAT – see Table 7.1). Investment in the road network is running at about £2–3 billion p.a. (Table 7.2 later), while traffic in 2000 was 468 billion vehicle kilometres (Table 7.1).

Total road costs (made up of maintenance and other operating costs, and the capital charge, but excluding any other external costs) are thus between £7 billion and £17 billion per year, or 1.5–3.6p/VKT (vehicle kilometre travelled), while road taxes were 5.9p/VKT. Section 7.5 and Table 7.2 later estimate the cost of other environmental externalities as £3–9 billion per year. Taking the preferred values of £12 billion for the road costs and £5.45 billion for environmental externalities gives £17.45 billion, on which VAT at 17.5 per cent would be £3.05 billion. Fuel taxes yield £22.3 billion and pay VAT of 17.5 per cent, or £3.90 billion, so there is excess VAT of £0.85 billion. The balancing or pure tax element is therefore £27.7 billion − £17.45 billion + £0.85 billion = £11.1 billion.

One argument for setting road charges like prices for regulated natural monopolies is that it should clarify the role of road pricing, while providing a more secure funding basis for investment. As urban congestion grows, the argument for congestion pricing to improve the efficiency of road use grows steadily stronger. Road pricing has now been made legal in Britain in the Transport Act 2000, as have workplace car park levies. In both cases, the local authority imposing these charges or levies can retain the revenue for ten years provided it is hypothecated to transport improvements. The government has indicated that the revenues so generated will be additional to any transfers made under normal central budgetary arrangements to finance local transport improvements. It has not yet explained how this additionality will be assured, nor what mechanisms will protect road users from possibly rapacious local authorities, other than the power of the local ballot box.

If the total revenue to be collected from road charges were set in the same way as the revenue of private regulated networks, then a change in the form of charging to a more efficient and targeted method, such as congestion pricing, would not increase the total level of road charges. This would reassure road users that road pricing were not an additional charge for using already heavily overcharged and undersupplied roads. Given that a minority of road users create the majority of traffic congestion, a majority of road users would benefit from a rebalancing of road charges. Less-congested and inter-urban roads would attract a lower charge (which would almost certainly be most efficiently collected through fuel and vehicle excise duties), while urban road users would pay a higher charge per kilometre than at present.

The other attraction of treating road charges as regulated utility charges is that it provides the basis for financing investment. In the private sector, the assurance that an efficiently managed utility will be allowed to earn an adequate return on its investment allows the utility to borrow against its future revenues if current profits are insufficient to finance current investment. If the government were to create an independent regulatory agency to set the level of road charges, then that same assurance for proper investment planning could be provided to the agency or agencies responsible for road investment. One can imagine a variety of such agencies – Roadtrack for strategic roads, and various agencies responsible for urban roads (such as Transport for London). A regulator (Ofroad?) would also provide the reassurance that voting motorists need if they are to support any changes in the structure of road charges. Before that happens, though, a number of difficult regulatory and accounting issues would need to be resolved.

The first issue would be the choice of discount rate and of the source of borrowing (and of the required return on the assets to pay to the State as owner). If the revenues really are guaranteed, then Roadtrack and its counterparts would be able to borrow at rather low real rates of interest. Risk would be low, and solvency assured for a public sector entity. If the government attempted to restrict or delay investment, then the solvency of Roadtrack would increase, as revenues would rise in line with traffic (until revised down at the next periodic review), and the ability to invest would increase. That would argue for a rather high valuation of the opening RAB, so that a large fraction of revenue would be payable as a dividend to the State, to prevent surplus funds accumulating and leading to less-responsible investment. A better solution might be for the regulator to monitor investment plans, as for other utilities.

The alternative is for the government to specify a required rate of return comparable to that required by private transport investors (which included Railtrack before it was forced into administration by the government). That would have the Diamond–Mirrlees logic of ensuring comparability between competing transport investments, but would require the Treasury to source the finance and charge an appropriate WACC (perhaps by requiring a specified gearing and dividend yield).

There is no simple solution to creating the right institutional structure for the management of road investment, but the model of the regulated network utility has obvious attractions. It has, with the exception of Railtrack, been a successful method of managing capital-intensive network monopolies and ensuring that they deliver adequate levels of investment. Railtrack suffered from the inherent difficulty that railways are inevitably loss-making. An independent regulator such as the Office of Rail Regulation risks continual confrontation with the Treasury if it requires higher charges to cover necessary investment. As private train operators are only viable with public subsidy, increased track charges feed through to demands for additional subsidies that will be resisted by the Treasury. Roadtrack, if anything, would be in the opposite situation of making embarrassing surpluses, with the regulator acting to restrain charges to avoid paying the Treasury excessive amounts. For our present purpose, though, we are more concerned with setting road charges than with deciding how investment should be managed, and so these difficult institutional design issues can be sidestepped here. Eichenberger (2002) offers another perspective on the institutional and political structure needed to deliver efficient investment.

7.4 EFFICIENT ROAD PRICES

Continuing with the useful benchmark of the regulated network utility, the aim is to ensure an efficient structure of prices for the various services such that their total yield is no greater than the regulated revenue cap. Economists wishing to analyse road congestion and road pricing have usually relied on link speed–flow relationships estimated by traffic engineers to compute marginal congestion costs (see, for example, Newbery (1988*b*, 1990)).

Figure 7.2 illustrates the traditional analysis of congestion externalities. Higher traffic flows lead to lower average speeds and higher travel times and costs per kilometre. Additional traffic imposes an external cost on all other road users. Under congested conditions, particularly in urban areas, and in the absence of efficient road pricing, traffic will be undercharged and hence excessive. In Figure 7.2, the average social cost (ASC) excludes road taxes, while the average private cost (APC) includes road taxes, CB. If the inverse demand is as shown, the equilibrium will occur at point C, where the marginal willingness to pay is equal to the APC. The efficient equilibrium is at point D, where the marginal social cost (MSC) is equal to the marginal willingness to pay. This would be supported by a congestion charge DE (which, as shown, would replace the poorly targeted road tax levied on fuel, CB). The inefficiency of incorrect pricing (the deadweight loss) is then measured by the area DCM.

One obvious objection to this link speed–flow approach is that observations of traffic flows on links may be a very poor guide to traffic conditions in densely meshed urban networks, where most traffic interactions and delays take place at intersections, not on the links between them. This in turn casts doubt on estimates based on these measured simple speed–flow relationships. Fortunately, sophisticated traffic assignment models have been developed to simulate equilibrium traffic flows over a network. SATURN (Simulation and Assignment of Traffic to Urban Road Networks) is an example of such a software package which simulates the results of demands for trips specified by a matrix giving the number of trips between all origin and destination (O–D) pairs (Van Vliet and Hall, 1997). SATURN finds the Wardrop equilibrium, defined as the assignment of traffic in which no trip-maker can reduce total trip cost (the value of the time taken and vehicle operating costs) by choosing a different route from that assigned. Newbery and Santos (2002) use this to compute area-wide counterparts to those shown in Figure 7.2.

There are, however, two major problems with this line of investigation, one conceptual and the other practical. The conceptual problem is that each

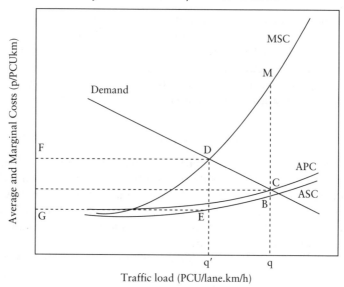

Figure 7.2. *The Standard Analysis of Congestion Externalities on a Link*

segment of each trip will give rise to a different marginal congestion cost, and there is a problem of aggregation if these are to be represented as a single value, as in Figure 7.2. The practical problem is that (supposedly) first-best congestion charging for each link and intersection varying with the prevailing level of traffic is infeasible. It is currently technically impractical, and even if it became technically feasible, it would likely impose excessive information processing costs on drivers. As the aim is to discourage cost-ineffective trips, routes, or times, any pricing signal will have to be sufficiently clear and simple to induce appropriate responses.

Newbery and Santos (2002) show how to address the conceptual problem of aggregation by considering the optimal equiproportional reduction in all O–D trips, for each of which there would then be associated a trip-specific (but not route-specific) charge, the average of which would be as shown. The dead-weight loss (DWL) relative to this (second-best) equilibrium would be accurately measured by the area DCM. While this approach has its advantages and allows a swift screening of towns to select candidates for practical road pricing schemes, the best equiproportional traffic reduction would not be the most effective way to improve traffic efficiency and would itself be hard to implement.

The practical problem of road pricing can be addressed by searching for a feasible set of instruments. The natural choice is a cordon toll, where vehicles are charged for crossing a cordon, typically enclosing the centre of the city. The charge can depend on the time of day and be possibly directional (for example, charging for entering in the morning peak and leaving during the evening peak).

Cordon tolls have been implemented in Hong Kong, Singapore, and three towns in Norway, and were successfully introduced into London on 17 February 2003 (May, Bonsall, and Hills, 1998; Larsen and Ramjerdi, 1991; Menon, 2000; www.cclondon.com). The early cordon tolls were primarily set to raise revenue, in the case of Oslo to pay for the transport improvements that were part of the political deal (Larsen and Østmoe, 2001). As such, they set charges that were frequently constant over the whole day, not charging more in the peak than off-peak, and not optimized to maximize social welfare. It is, at least to an economist, a natural step to require that the cordon tolls be optimally set, where the objective is social welfare, measured as the consumer benefit from travel less the total social cost of that travel.

Designing an efficient cordon toll or tolls turns out to be very complex, and as yet essentially unsolved. The choice variables include the exact location of the cordon and the prices at each crossing point and at each time of day. The net social benefits, after allowing for the quite considerable costs of installing and operating the cordon tolls, are sensitive to all of these (Larsen and Østmoe, 2001; May et al., 2002; Newbery and Santos, 2002). The problem is one of complexity – even in a small town, the number of possible locations rises exponentially with the number of links. A typical cordon may have five to fifteen crossings, and the scheme can yield higher benefits if the charges are varied across these crossings (by up to 40 per cent more compared with finding the optimum uniform toll). Adjusting tolls by time of day makes sense to avoid bunching of traffic just before the start and to encourage efficient time-switching, but it raises the complexity by a further order of magnitude. For example, Larsen and Østmoe (2001) show that dropping the (already time-of-day differentiated) Oslo toll on Saturday increases consumer surplus by 40 per cent. To date (October 2002), all estimates of the correct level of toll and the resulting benefits are based on assumed traffic-flow relationships and behavioural responses, either or both of which could be wrong. It will clearly be important to monitor the performance of and responses to practical schemes to validate the calculations and allow tolls to be adjusted.[6]

Finally, there is no available evidence about the longer-run land-use impacts of cordon tolls, and given that cordon tolls are second- or third-best, there are no useful theorems that ensure that these land-use impacts will be efficient if the tolls are optimally adjusted to achieve short-run efficiency. Eliasson and Mattson (2001) show that in a simulated and symmetric city, the land-use effects of link-based road pricing are small compared with traffic impacts, and they cite a small number of other studies that also suggest small effects. If spatial distortion costs are large and the impacts are long-lasting, small locational changes could still produce significant costs or benefits.

If the problem of optimizing the design of cordon tolls appears daunting, it does not follow that such schemes are not worth implementing. In their study of road pricing for eight British towns, Santos, Newbery, and Rojey (2001) found that the predicted benefits of optimal uniform cordon tolls considerably exceeded the costs of implementation in most cases, provided that the tolls were set correctly. The same appears to be true in Oslo (Larsen and Østmoe, 2001). Detailed investigation of Cambridge (reported in Newbery and Santos (2002)) suggested that the location of the cordon made a considerable difference, and, as a simple rule, maximizing the ratio of traffic terminating within the zone to that passing through (before the toll) increased the benefit–cost ratio. Other studies suggest that additional tolling of particularly congested isolated links can enhance benefits, as can combining cordon tolls with distance charges (though this is likely to require more-sophisticated equipment). One major argument for conducting simple road pricing trials (such as time-of-day cordon tolls) is to test the models that predict driver response and traffic improvement against the reality, as well as to test the political acceptability of road pricing. Refinements and improvements are likely to be simpler once the principle has been adequately tested.

7.4.1 *Integrating Local Road Pricing into a System of Road Charging*

Supposing that initial experiments with local area road pricing, such as cordon tolls, are successful, what would this imply for the overall design of road charges? Suppose also that total road charge revenue is capped and regulated, so any road pricing scheme that generates additional revenue will be associated with reductions in fuel duties and/or VED. This helps to ensure that road pricing commands sufficient voter support. In that case, urban road pricing schemes can be introduced wherever they are sufficiently cost-effective. Each selected town would have a compatible form of electronic charging, and all road vehicles would be equipped with the appropriate transponders to register these charges in whatever town they passed through.[7] As a starting point, road fuel taxes would then be set to cover the average long-run marginal cost of inter-urban roads for typical cars, with VED set to adjust total payments by typical vehicles in each size class to the costs they impose on inter-urban roads. Ideally, urban road prices would recover the remaining revenue.

As most practical forms of road pricing, such as cordon tolls, would only charge for part of the congested area, and as the net social benefits of tolls are sensitive to the level of the toll, there is no guarantee that the revenue collected will be the required amount. If road fuel taxes and VED are set correctly for inter- and non-urban roads, and if the road supply costs are not very much higher in urban areas, then these taxes alone would collect about the right total amount (because fuel efficiency is lower in urban congested areas). Additional road charges would risk exceeding the allowed revenue. If these taxes are set correctly just for inter-urban roads that are currently heavily used, they may not adequately cover the costs of lightly used rural roads, and the surplus from urban areas might balance out the shortfall from the non-strategic rural roads. Again, if the marginal cost of capacity expansion is very high in urban areas, the required revenue per vehicle kilometre may need to be substantially larger from urban roads than from inter-urban roads, and the road charges may help make up the shortfall.

In any case, the difference between the allowed or regulated revenue and that collected from the initial set of fuel taxes, VED, and road prices, either positive or negative, would then be collected from or returned to road users in the least distortionary way. This could be done by adjusting fuel taxes and VED. As a general rule, adjusting the fixed element, or VED, is likely to be more efficient. If there is a shortfall, increases in the VED would be regressive. Increasing the charge on fuel in practice means lowering current rates by less as road pricing is introduced, and is clearly simpler and more in line with willingness to pay for the public good of the road network. If the charges need to be reduced, then some reduction in VED may be attractive, though there is a limit to how much can be returned while retaining the ability to adjust total charges by vehicle class.

There is a significant practical transition problem of introducing urban road prices one town at a time (as is the plan in Britain). In the early years, the road prices would only cover a small fraction of the total vehicle fleet. If all road users continue to pay the old road taxes but some face additional road prices, they will be effectively overcharged and will surely resist the new road prices. Ideally, the revenue from the new road prices would be recycled to the set of road users affected in a non-distortionary way. Practical and politically acceptable schemes might provide transfers to car owners living within the political jurisdiction of the charging authority. The first priority would be to provide any metering equipment for free and provide it with a certain initial level of credit. Road improvements that directly benefit road users are an attractive solution that worked well in Oslo but will not always be available. Providing car-parking vouchers where parking fees are charged, or credits against annual licence fees, may exhaust the remaining credits. As road pricing becomes more prevalent, fuel taxes can be lowered and VED raised, so that the discounts against VED will be targeted on those facing road prices. Surprisingly little attention has been paid to the design of such transitional arrangements, which are likely to be critical for the public acceptability of road pricing.

7.5 CHARGING FOR OTHER EXTERNAL COSTS

Efficiency requires that road users pay the marginal external cost (for noise, pollution, accidents, etc.) that they impose on society. Again, the limited number of instruments available limits the usefulness of this textbook prescription. Logically, the first task is to identify and quantify the external costs, then establish the functional relationship between these costs and road (or fuel) use, and finally set the available taxes or controls at optimal levels. Note that this approach is potentially different from the requirement that road users pay the *total* amount of any social costs, unless, coincidentally, the marginal and average external costs are equal, i.e. damage is a linear function of road use.

Some environmental impacts may be very non-linear, in which case the marginal cost will be very different from the average. Noise pollution is a good example where the marginal cost is below the average cost – doubling noise levels has the same perceived nuisance cost at low and high levels (provided the levels remain below the threshold of physical damage). Increasing the number of cars on a quiet road from nine to ten per hour creates the same nuisance as increasing the number of vehicles from 900 to 1,000 per hour on a busy main road. Thus the marginal noise cost of an extra vehicle in the second case is only 1 per cent of that of the extra vehicle on the quiet road where traffic is only 1 per cent of the level on the main road.

7.5.1 *Accident Costs*

The number of road fatalities in Britain in 2000 was 3,409, of whom 997 were pedestrians, cyclists, or bus passengers. In addition, a further 38,000 people were seriously injured. The Department for Transport estimates the total cost of all road accidents as £17 billion, of which the 'human costs' that reflect willingness to pay to avoid the loss of life or injury amount to about half (Department for Transport, 2002). Some fraction will be an internal cost to the person causing the accident. The average fatal accident caused 1.1 fatalities, 0.41 serious casualties, and 0.5 slight casualties, so if the person causing the fatal accident were killed, the self-inflicted cost would be 87 per cent of the total. Seventeen per cent of fatal accidents involved only one car, and presumably created no external cost (other than grief to friends and relatives). Some costs (for example, to property, which accounted for £5.2 billion) are likely to have been covered by insurance and reflected in insurance premiums. Other costs are borne by the State (health service, police, etc.) and are included in the current estimates of road costs. The remaining costs are external costs visited upon other road users, some very asymmetrically, such as to pedestrians and cyclists. Some external costs are not recorded, and of these the consequential traffic congestion and delays may be appreciable (Arnott, 2002).

The next question is whether road users should be charged for external accident costs, or whether they are better dealt with in some other way (through the criminal justice system or by strict liability and insurance). Where the fault can be proven to lie with the motorist, then penalties or compensation seem appropriate, although there are obvious problems in compensating for death. Logically, the value of a life (£1.44 million in Britain in 2000) should be payable (by the insurance company) to the estate of the victim, though this does not appear to happen. The practical questions are what fraction of external costs are not reflected in insurance costs and how much should be related to distance driven (and weight of vehicle, via fuel taxes).

If, as with other elements of road charging, the aim is to influence behaviour (cause motorists to take proper care), then the question to ask is what is the extra external accident cost per kilometre driven (which is likely to vary with type of vehicle, location, and time of day). As with noise pollution, it is important to distinguish between average and marginal cost. In 1985, 5,165 road users were killed on the roads of Great Britain (Department of Transport, 1996, p. 84), equal to 16.68 per thousand million vehicle kilometres. Ten years later, in 1995, 3,621 road users were killed, or 8.40 per thousand million vehicle kilometres, almost as low as half the 1985 rate despite a nearly 40 per cent increase in traffic.[8] Increases in traffic do not seem to lead to increased numbers of accidents in total, though of course many factors are responsible for the considerable fall in the accident rate. More traffic lights, better vehicle and road design, more use of seat belts and air bags, better campaigns and more stringent enforcement against drinking and driving, and perhaps even slower speeds associated with more congestion have no doubt all contributed to greater road safety.

One less obvious factor is drivers' response to perceived risk – if roads seem more dangerous, drivers take more care, balancing the need to travel quickly against the desire to arrive in one piece. If so, more traffic on the roads makes overtaking and other potentially dangerous manoeuvres less attractive and less frequent, keeping down the total number of accidents even though vehicle kilometres driven increase. If this is indeed the case, then the marginal social cost of the increased risk of accident facing other road users as a result of an extra vehicle will be much lower than the average social cost of accidents.

Of course, the total social cost of accidents is still huge – at £17 billion per year, it amounts to more than half of total road taxes of £28 billion. The *average* accident cost of road fatalities on this estimate would be 3.4p/km or 33p/litre,[9] but the *marginal external distance-related* accident cost might be zero.[10] If all the non-motorist costs (excluding property damage) were attributed to motorists, the figure would be £3 billion per year or 6p/litre. If the likelihood of such accidents increases less than in proportion to traffic, only some fraction of this is attributable, while penalties and insurance costs might reduce this further. Finally, safety standards, such as air bags and survivability, increase the cost of driving and provide additional internalization of risk. There are further complications, discussed by Newbery (1988*b*) and Lindberg (2001), in allowing for the external costs to non-protected (or poorly protected) road users (such as pedestrians and cyclists), and possibly allowing for the suffering to friends and relatives (which, according to Lindberg, might add a further 36 per cent to total costs).

Lindberg (2001) summarizes the present state of theory and evidence. The number of accidents is proportional to traffic on inter-urban roads and urban links, but increases with traffic at intersections (giving rise to a positive externality, as the risk elasticity is between 0.25 and 0.45). Surprisingly, the risk of an accident with a non-protected road user *decreases* with traffic, and the risk elasticity is estimated to be −0.5. Lindberg estimates the marginal external cost in Sweden as 12 per cent of the average cost for non-urban cars, 33 per cent for urban cars, 33 per cent for heavy non-urban vehicles, and 40 per cent for heavy urban vehicles, though some part of these marginal costs will be paid through insurance. For cars, the external cost would justify charges of €0.14 per litre non-urban and €0.35 per litre urban. If these figures are translated and applied to Britain, the total charge would be £6 billion, but the accident rate is somewhat higher in Sweden. The figure seems high compared with the total cost to non-protected victims of £3 billion.

Newbery (1988*b*) estimated accident externalities at perhaps 25p/litre for cars (for 1985, when the accident rate was more than twice the 2000 figure, and using costs of accidents slightly higher in pounds than those used above). This estimate was based on very sketchy information about the risk elasticity, which was taken as 0.25. Halving the cost to reflect the fall in the accident rate would make it similar to Lindberg's estimate.

The conclusion is that accident externalities might be appreciable, but the appropriate level of charges might be considerably reduced if punishment and insurance charges already induce sufficient care. In the absence of convincing calibrated research, accident costs will not be added to the total road user costs, though their value is given in Table 7.2 later.[11]

7.5.2 *Implications of Paying for Environmental Damage*

The idea that road users (and others) should pay for environmental damage has far-reaching implications. To an economist, the obvious way in which road users should pay is through the tax system, as the environment is held in trust for all – there is no obvious owner to whom payments should be made other than the State acting as custodian. Taxes are not the only way, and, indeed, the idea of levying environmental (or 'green') taxes is a fairly novel concept in Britain. The normal way in which polluters have in the past paid is by being forced to undertake otherwise unattractive expenditures to meet mandated standards of quality. The most obvious example in transport is the vehicle emission standards that are set by the government for new vehicles. These require catalytic converters and/or more expensive electronic ignition, and improved fuel, but they have reduced particular emissions per kilometre by between a half and three-quarters since 1993 (Department of Transport, Local Government, and the Regions, 2001, table 2.6). There are also a host of regulations about noise levels and safety standards (alcohol levels, vehicle lights, seat belts, road worthiness, etc.) designed to control the impact vehicles have on the environment and other road users (some literally). However, using green taxes, in addition to various standards, has a number of economic advantages and political attractions.

The political attraction of green taxes is clear – they are likely to command more support than other kinds of taxes. The main economic advantage of taxes that reflect the marginal damage is that they leave the user to decide how best to respond, rather than forcing him or her to make one particular kind of decision. They are also more accurately targeted to the damage caused, and therefore likely to be more effective at lower cost. Perhaps the best-known example is the higher tax on leaded than on unleaded petrol (gasoline). In 1993, 63 per cent of British motorists bought unleaded petrol, compared with only 5 per cent in 1988. Forcing all motorists to switch to unleaded petrol would have required major premature scrapping of older vehicles and would not have been politically acceptable. Just requiring new vehicles to be able to run on unleaded petrol would have discouraged the replacement of older vehicles, as the newer ones would require more expensive engines. Nor would it have provided any incentive actually to buy unleaded petrol. Discouraging replacement would have had a perverse effect on pollution, while not encouraging a fuel switch would have led to a smaller reduction than was possible.

If green taxes are to be both politically attractive and economically effective, they must be clearly distinguished from other taxes or charges, set at levels determined by acceptable methods of computing the cost of the damage done, and applied uniformly to all sources of the same damage. That is, environmental taxes should be *distinct, non-discriminatory,* and *defensibly quantified.* These criteria pose considerable challenges and, if applied, would have radical consequences for fuel taxes more generally.

The principle that environmental taxes should be distinct carries particular force, as it virtually requires that other road taxes be treated as regulated charges for using road space. It forms part of the political compact with road users justifying the total level of taxes, and specifically any changes in those taxes.

7.5.3 Non-Discriminatory Environmental Taxes

Suppose that the government reviews road taxation and reforms the system to distinguish road charges from other forms of taxation, allowing for a separate category of green or environmental taxes, which charge for the environmental damage caused by road users. Unless these taxes were applied in a non-discriminatory way, the full benefits to the environment would not be realized, and the justification for imposing environmental taxes on transport would be undermined. Let us take three simple examples of air pollutants caused by transport: greenhouse gases (GHG), mainly carbon dioxide (CO_2), the main cause of global warming; nitrogen oxides (NO_x), a precursor of acid rain; and particulates (PM_{10}), which cause increased mortality.

Figure 7.3 shows the share of road transport in the total production of these (and other) air pollutants in the UK in 1999. Clearly, road transport is a major contributor to the total emissions of these three pollutants (and also of volatile organic compounds (VOCs), though not of sulphur dioxide (SO_2), the other main cause of acid rain). However, except for carbon monoxide (CO), road transport causes less than half the UK's emissions, and in the case of GHG – singled out as the reason for fuel tax increases – only 22 per cent of the total (though one of the fastest-growing components).

It follows that to tax only transport emissions would involve a very partial and discriminatory environmental tax policy. Carbon taxes have been advocated as one of the simplest forms of green taxation, for they can be imposed very precisely on the source of the problem – the carbon content of the fuel, which is easily measured and completely defines the damaging potential of the CO_2. Such carbon taxes have been proposed by the EU, but were soundly rejected by the Trade and Industry Committee of the House of Commons

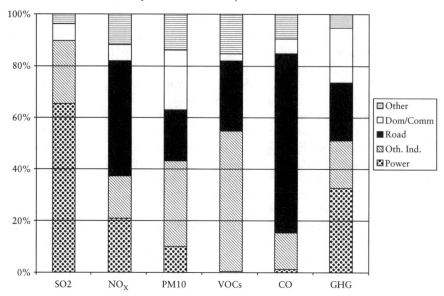

Figure 7.3. *Sources of Air Pollution: UK, 1999*

when it came to examine the market for coal, as being likely to accelerate the decline of the British coal industry. Since then, the Conservative government has been defeated in its attempt to raise VAT on domestic energy from 8 per cent to the standard rate of 17.5 per cent, while the new Labour government has actually reduced the rate to 5 per cent, thus effectively subsidizing domestic gas and electricity use by 12.5 per cent. It then introduced a climate change levy on all forms of electricity generation except renewables, thus taxing non-GHG-emitting nuclear electricity, and taxing electricity generated by low-carbon-containing gas at the same rate per kWh as the considerably higher carbon content of coal- and oil-fired generation. Again, domestic customers were exempted.

British tax policy towards greenhouse gases is thus in a state of disarray. To put the imbalance in the treatment of different fuels in perspective, until recently the British government raised the excise tax on road fuels *each year* by 5 per cent above the rate of inflation. The annual increase of about 3 p/litre amounts to £47/tonne carbon or $US75/tonne carbon, or nearly $10/ barrel, which was the original suggested *total* EU carbon tax (and only half was to be on the carbon content of the fuel, the rest being on the energy content).

Matters are perhaps slightly more even-handed with NO_x, for the power generation and industrial sectors are subject to emission limits which force them to install improved combustion controls or catalytic converters, much as is the case with vehicles (though the cost-effectiveness of reducing NO_x emissions from stationary sources is considerably higher than that for small mobile sources such as vehicles). The same is true for particulates, though for the wrong reason – they are not subject to much control, except when they are from large combustion sources.

If environmental taxes are to be employed as part of a decentralized market-friendly environmental policy, then some of these more obvious imbalances across fuels and sectors will have to be addressed for this element of the total road charge to be defensible.

7.5.4 *Quantifying the Size of the Environmental Costs of Transport*

If environmental taxes are to be justified as correcting externalities, these will have to be quantified. Where the environmental damage can be measured, valued, and attributed to particular causes, then the principle is clear – set the tax equal to the marginal cost of the damage caused and levy it in a way that gives the clearest signals to the polluter responsible. The results of the analysis below are summarized in Table 7.2, and their implications for tax rates in Table 7.3, later.

Global Warming

The only pollutant that is simply related to fuel consumption is CO_2, where there is a direct relationship between fuel used and damage done. The logical tax is a carbon tax on all carbon-containing fuels. Determining the correct level is highly contentious, and the answer depends on the precise question asked, quite apart from any difficulty in quantifying the damage done. Is the tax to be set equal to the global marginal damage on the assumption that all countries impose the same tax, or to the global marginal damage on the best prediction about what other countries may do (but still unselfishly counting all the damage done not just to the UK but to the rest of the world), or to the marginal damage to the UK, based on some view of the response function of other countries to its choice of tax rate? The three answers are likely to be very different.

Even if we agree on the question, there are wide differences between various estimates. Maddison et al. (1996) estimated the shadow prices of controlling the last unit of CO_2 released assuming optimal abatement, where the marginal cost is $US(1993)5.9/tonne carbon (tC). This is only slightly less than the cost assuming 'business as usual', calculated as $6.1/tC. European Conference of Ministers of Transport (1998, p. 70) cites estimates ranging from $2/tC to $10/tC, considerably below the EU's original proposed carbon tax discussed above. Tol et al. (2000) review various estimates and argue for marginal damage costs below $50/tC. The UK Department of the Environment, Transport, and the Regions decided in early 2001 to take as its working assumption a central estimate of $80/tC, with a range from $40 to $160. British road transport emissions were 36 million tC in 2000, implying a cost of £0.9–3.6 billion. It is worth noting that a carbon tax of $80/tC would amount to $53/tonne of coal, or rather more than 100 per cent of the international price. The Danish carbon tax introduced in 1992 was at a rate of 100DKK/tonne of CO_2 or \$38/tC, while Finland levied a carbon tax on all energy at about 500FMK/tC or \$70/tC, roughly twice as high. Parry and Small (2002) review the literature and select a central figure of \$25/tC, with range \$0.7–100/tC.

Even this modest range of citations suggests a range of almost 100:1, with preferred estimates differing perhaps by 10:1. However, even the high figure represents a small fraction of existing road fuel tax rates. There are 0.64tC/t gasoline (0.87tC per thousand litres), so a carbon tax of \$80/tC would be \$0.07/litre, about 0.7 cents/km, or less than 10 per cent of the 2000 UK petrol excise tax. While carbon taxes are potentially of central importance for other fuels, they are relatively small compared with EU road fuel excises.

The Health Costs of Vehicle Emissions

The transport pollutants that are most damaging to health are particulates, NO_x, lead, and SO_2 (though not in most developed countries, where transport fuel has very low levels of sulphur). In most developed countries, tailpipe emission standards on new vehicles have resulted in a dramatic reduction in total levels of road transport emissions, despite the continuing increase in traffic. Newbery (1998*a*) argues for estimating the social costs of the health effects of pollution by estimating the number of quality-adjusted life years (QALYs) lost through premature mortality and morbidity. These costs should then be compared with what it costs the taxpayer to enable the National Health Service (in the UK, or its counterpart in other countries) to achieve an extra year of quality life. The numbers used in the evaluation of transport should be consistent with numbers used elsewhere in health economics. This would enable the money raised in green taxes (which are mainly the costs of health damage) to be allocated to the National Health Service, which should be able to compensate for the quality life years lost through pollution by an equal saving of quality life years gained from improved health services.

Recent work presented at a United Nations Economic Commission for Europe (UN/ECE) symposium, 'The Measurement and Economic Valuation of the Health Effects of Air Pollution', suggests an encouraging convergence in estimates of the mortality effects of the more damaging pollutants.[12] Severe urban pollution reduces life expectancy, and a *permanent* increase in air pollution of $10 \, \mu g/m^3$ of PM_{10} is estimated to raise the daily mortality rate by 1 per cent. That in turn would reduce average life expectancy in Britain by 34 days (weighted by the British age distribution and based on current age-specific mortality rates). In order to relate the loss of QALYs to the annual consumption of fuel, the correct calculation is the total loss of QALYs for a one-year increase in emissions, leaving future mortality rates at the zero emission level. Appendix 7.A shows that road transport may be responsible for $4.4 \, \mu g/m^3$ of PM_{10} in Britain, reducing the loss of life expectancy per person exposed to 0.21 days per year of exposure. If we err on the high side and suppose that QALYs do not decrease with age (as they do), and take the exposed population as all 58 million people, the total number of QALYs lost by one year's traffic particulate emissions is 34,000.

The UK Department for Transport assumes a value of a statistical life saved (VoSLS) in traffic accidents as £1.44 million. The weighted average age of the victim of a fatal traffic accident if all are equally exposed is 38, and life expectancy is then 40 years. We can therefore take a statistical life as 40 QALYs, making the value of a QALY £36,000. The UK National Institute of Clinical Excellence was reported (*The Times*, 10 August 2001) as tentatively accepting a figure of £30,000 per QALY, suggesting a convergence on the valuation side. At £36,000/QALY, the cost of traffic pollution is £1.2 billion per year, negligible compared with road taxation of £27.5 billion in 2000–1 (excluding all VAT). This raises several interesting issues. For example, do we equate the 34,000 QALYs above with 850 statistical lives, and if so, does this mean that traffic pollution is 25 per cent as serious as traffic fatalities, of which there were 3,409 in 2000? One is inclined to think that pollution, which may reduce the life expectancy of a large number of people by a very small amount, is less socially costly than traffic accidents, which reduce the life expectancy of a small number of people by a large amount. If so, then the value of a QALY used above may overstate the pollution cost.

Earlier estimates, in Newbery (1998*a*), suggested a range of values for total air pollution costs of £0.6–3.6 billion, on average rather higher than here, but these pre-dated the UN/ECE evidence and the ability to make the detailed calculations shown in Appendix 7.A. Most (89 per cent in Britain) of this cost is attributable to diesel vehicles, and would amount to 5.6 p/litre of diesel (or 0.9 p/km) and 0.45 p/litre of petrol (or 0.04 p/km). Note that the particulate tax should be 40–50 per cent higher for pre-1993 vehicles than this average value and 50–80 per cent lower for post-1997 vehicles (with diesel cars experiencing the greater improvement). These figures do not include the cost of morbidity (which is not likely to be a large fraction of mortality costs), nor do they include other health costs attributable to other pollutants (which are also likely to be modest compared with particulate mortality costs).

This figure can be contrasted with the estimates from McCubbin and Delucchi (1999) for the USA, where the range for light (i.e. gasoline-powered) vehicles is 0.6–7.7 US (1990) cents/mile. This would be 0.5–6.8 US (2000) cents/km, and higher if all vehicles were included. Parry and Small (2002) select a central figure of 1.3 US cents/km, with a range of 0.3–6.3 cents/km, again for light vehicles. Again, these figures seem on the high side, given the recent downgrading of the health costs of transport pollution based on more careful assessments of effects on mortality rates.

The costs of other emissions are modest and are presented in Table 7.2. They are taken from Newbery (1998*a*) without further analysis, though the allocation across fuels in Table 7.3 is based on data from Department of Transport, Local Government, and the Regions (2001). Maddison et al. (1996) give higher values but they appear to be double-counting particulates, as they distinguish between direct (from mainly carbon in exhausts) and indirect (caused by nitrates and sulphates derived from NO_x and SO_2 emissions). The figures computed here are derived from measured concentrations of particulates, presumably from all sources.

Noise

Noise relationships are extremely non-linear and it is therefore incorrect to compute the total cost of noise and then apportion it to vehicles, as in Tinch (1995).[13] The approach adopted here is to take the traffic noise functions from Department of Transport (1988) and compute the extra noise arising from additional vehicles of different types on different roads. The details are given in Appendix 7.B. The intriguing feature of the noise relationship is the claim that noise costs are linear in decibels (more precisely, dB(A)), which are a logarithmic measure of noise intensity. Consequently, a 1 per cent reduction in traffic on a distant motorway is as valuable to those affected as a 1 per cent fall in traffic on a busy city street or a leafy suburb, for someone sitting outdoors facing the road or inside their double-glazed house. It follows that concentrating traffic on busy roads (such as the M25) reduces total noise damage, for transferring half the traffic on a minor road to a motorway might only increase traffic there by 5 per cent, reducing the cost of noise by 45 per cent. Newbery (1998a) estimates the average marginal cost of noise pollution at 0.2–0.36 p/km. The allocation across fuels in Table 7.3 reflects the higher noise nuisance of heavier (diesel) vehicles.

Water Pollution

Run-off from highways places a considerable load on sewage systems, and a considerable part of that is directly attributable to road traffic. The UK figure for this source of water pollution is 15 per cent of the total cost of sewage treatment, estimated in 1995–6 as £3 billion per year. The marginal cost could be lower, though the capital value of the water infrastructure used to determine costs greatly understates its replacement value, so the long-run marginal costs of total sewage handling would be higher, perhaps as high as £8.9 billion. Some part of highway run-off would take place regardless of traffic, though the extra foul water caused by vehicles puts additional stress on sewage treatment. Newbery (1998a) takes these figures to give a range of £0.5–1 billion per year or 0.1–0.2 p/km, while Delucchi (1997) estimates costs of 0.05–0.13 p/km, which are similar.

7.5.5 Charging for Environmental Damage

Tables 7.2 and 7.3 collect together the various estimates of costs and express them in charges per kilometre or per litre of fuel. In some cases, the costs correlate more closely with fuel than with distance (particularly for emissions).

Table 7.2. *Road User Costs and External Costs: Britain, 2000*

			£ billion
Central and local government road expenditure			
Capital expenditure			2.28
Recurrent expenditure			2.60
Accident costs borne by NHS			0.57
Estimates of various road costs	Low	High	Central
Interest on capital value	3.5	12	7.75
Depreciation	3	4	3.5
Other operating costs	0.5	1	0.75
Total road costs	7	17	12
External costs			
Accident	0	6	1.5
Air pollution:			
Particulates	0.6	1.8	1.2
Nitrogen oxides	0.1	0.3	0.2
Other	0.1	0.3	0.2
Global warming	0.9	3.6	1.8
Water pollution	0.5	1	0.75
Noise	0.9	1.7	1.3
Total environmental costs	3.1	8.7	5.45

Sources: See text and Newbery (1998*a*).

Table 7.3. *Road Charges and Taxes per Kilometre and per Litre: Britain, 2000*

Category	Total (£ million)	Pence per kilometre	Pence per litre of petrol	Pence per litre of diesel
Fuel tax	22,305	4.77	48.8	48.8
VED	5,415	1.16	13.0	8.9
Total	27,720	5.92	61.8	57.7
Road costs	12,000	2.56	25.2	25.2
Accident costs	1,500	0.32	3.2	3.2
Air pollution	1,600	0.34	1.2	6.6
Global warming	1,800	0.38	4.9	4.9
Water pollution	750	0.16	1.6	1.6
Noise	1,300	0.28	3.1	2.1
Total (excluding accident costs)	17,450	3.7	36.0	40.4

Sources: Tables 7.1 and 7.2; Department of Transport, Local Government, and the Regions, 2001.

Pollution damage also varies widely across different vehicles of the same type, raising the question of what form of averaging is appropriate. Fairness (and political support) suggests that the level of charges should not be such that most transport users pay more than the damage done, and that suggests setting any taxes at the rate appropriate for the *median* vehicle user, which may be about half the *average* level.[14] What, then, to do with those who greatly exceed this representative level of damage? There are two possibilities – one is to impose extra charges (or offer rebates to those who meet the standards of lower emissions) and the other is to set standards with penalties for exceeding them.

The main problem with all transport pollution taxes is that the link between cause and effect is not very close. Most of the damage is done as a consequence of emissions, and hence related to distance and fuel use, but the damage per litre of fuel varies widely across vehicle types and ages. The only current instrument in the UK that can be adjusted to the type of vehicle is VED, which is a fixed charge, independent of distance. Vehicle excise duty rebates to lorries have been used to encourage the use of low-emission technology, so the principle has been accepted in the UK at least. The problem is that high fixed charges and low variable charges encourage higher mileage and hence more emissions than the correct vehicle-specific variable charges. Vehicle excise duty rates for cars and light vehicles for vehicles first registered after 2001 are differentiated by CO_2 emissions (g/km) and fuel type, which seems perverse given the greater suitability of fuel as the base of a straight carbon tax.

Parry and Small (2002) argue that emissions damage is proportional to distance driven, rather than fuel consumption, as emissions standards are set in grams per kilometre driven, not grams per litre of fuel. Higher fuel taxes lead to a reduction in distance driven and an increase in fuel efficiency (largely through vehicle choice), with the two effects contributing roughly equally. Taxing fuel is therefore rather an inefficient way of taxing for distance travelled, and hence a doubly indirect instrument for pollution damage (except for carbon taxes). This argument ignores the greater emissions per kilometre of heavier vehicles, and simple calculations show that emissions per litre are more stable across vehicle types than emissions per kilometre. Taxes per litre are simpler than charges per kilometre, although the Swiss government imposes distance (and vehicle-specific) charges for heavy vehicles (Suter and Walter, 2001).

Santos and Newbery (2001), reporting results from Santos, Rojey, and Newbery (2000), examine the effect of cordon charges on pollution and find an extremely close relationship between the congestion and environmental benefits of cordons, at least up to the optimal level of the cordon charge. Their paper examines eight different pollutants – carbon dioxide (CO_2), carbon monoxide (CO), volatile organic compounds (VOCs), nitrogen oxides (NO_x), particulates (PM), methane (CH_4), nitrous oxide (N_2O), and ammonia (NH_3), though only health impacts and global warming effects were valued in the cost analysis. They also find that environmental benefits are a small fraction of the congestion benefits (typically between 1 per cent and 9 per cent across towns and taking a wide range of values for the costs of emissions, with the high value considerably above those defended above).

If road pricing is introduced, then the road charging system can be adapted to levy vehicle-specific charges, but until then any pollution taxes will be relatively crude. It follows that other instruments are likely to be needed as well. Such methods will probably include setting emissions standards not just for new vehicles, but also for existing vehicles, with spot checks for enforcement and fines for exceeding the levels set (perhaps continuing on a daily basis until an emissions test indicates that the underlying problem has been addressed). Other solutions might be to license polluting vehicles only for rural use or to ban vehicles that lack a 'green' licence plate from entering large urban areas on days of high pollution. In windy developed northern cities, such complex solutions are unlikely to be cost-effective.

Accident externalities are even more problematic (Calthrop and Proost, 1998; Jansson, 1994; Johansson, 1997; Newbery, 1988b; Lindberg, 2001). The relationship between distance travelled and accident rate is not well understood, nor do we know how those who are involved in accidents might respond to various disincentives. Taxing fuel is indirect, though it may partially capture the higher external costs of heavier vehicles, which transfer more of the impact to lighter vehicles, but it fails to deal with variations across drivers. The approach consistent with internalizing externalities would be an *ad valorem* tax on the component of car insurance that covers accident costs (as opposed to theft, etc.). Elsewhere, such ideas have been criticized as encouraging drivers to avoid taking out insurance.

7.6 OPTIMAL TAX ARGUMENTS FOR ADDITIONAL ROAD USER TAXES

The theory of optimal taxation sets out conditions under which commodity tax rates should be uniform, in which case there would be no case for differential commodity taxes. These conditions are stringent but in many cases difficult to reject empirically (Deaton, 1987). If there is an optimal non-linear income tax, individuals differ only in the wage rate, and the direct utility function $u(.)$ has goods, x, weakly separable from labour, L, (so $u(x, L) = uN(x), L$), then optimal indirect taxes are uniform (Mirrlees, 1979; Stern, 1987).

Weaker conditions not assuming optimal income taxation apply with linear Engel curves and weak separability between leisure and goods (Deaton and Stern, 1986). The argument that separability removes the case for differential commodity taxation is that, in such cases, the only determinant of the supply of labour is the cost of goods consumed, and this is minimized when relative prices are undisturbed. The case for differential commodity taxes therefore requires that separability breaks down, in which case there is an argument for more heavily taxing goods that are complementary with leisure (Corlett and Hague, 1953).

Parry and Small (2002) use this argument to identify the 'Ramsey' tax element or the additional taxation justified by the impact of road user charges on labour supply. They argue that if leisure is weakly separable in utility, then personal travel is a relatively weak substitute for leisure if the expenditure elasticity for distance travelled is less than one (which, in developed countries, is normally the case). That provides a case for relatively higher taxes on travel, but there is an additional effect to consider. Congestion increases the costs of travel to work, and road prices that reduce congestion therefore increase labour supply and hence reduce the distortionary costs of labour taxation. It follows that there is an additional benefit from reducing congestion over and above the pure efficiency effect, justifying yet more gasoline taxation. If diesel is primarily used for commercial purposes, then there would be no comparable case for additional diesel taxes.

Parry and Small (2002) estimate that the Ramsey component of the optimal gasoline tax would be 6–7 US cents per litre and the congestion feedback would be 0.3–2 cents per litre (the low figure being for the USA, the high figure for the UK). Together, they amount to about one-quarter of the optimal gasoline tax rate. These estimates ignore redistributional effects, which raises serious problems, at least in developed countries, as fuel consumption is relatively income-inelastic. Optimal commodity taxes that may score well on efficiency grounds may do poorly on equity grounds, and in some cases the effects almost entirely cancel out. Mayeres (1999) examines distributional considerations in an applied general equilibrium model of transport in Belgium and finds that if extra fuel tax revenue is used to reduce labour taxes, then, as expected, the rich benefit. On the other hand, recycling fuel tax revenue through lump-sum transfers reduces this effect, and that is the relevant comparison for an optimally designed tax system, where marginal adjustments should be made to the lump-sum element. Much depends on how the government sets taxes, and optimal tax theorists may be placing unjustifiable confidence in the Benthamite credentials of the finance minister.

There is a related literature arguing that corrective taxes (such as environmental taxes) need to take account of distortions elsewhere in the economy (Bovenberg and Goulder, 1996). Newbery (1992) argues that if fuel taxes are used to charge for road use and congestion, then total road taxes should rise by more (perhaps 20 per cent more) than the pure carbon tax, as the carbon tax will induce greater fuel efficiency and hence reduce the tax base on which the road charges are set. Parry and Small (2002) make a similar point, though they estimate rather larger effects. As we have argued that the environmental component of taxes is modest, these corrections are less important.

7.7 ASSESSMENT

Table 7.3 shows that justifiable road user charges for Britain in 2000 are 2.6 p/km. This translates into 2.1p/PCUkm (PCU = passenger car units, the appropriate measure of road space demands and congestive effects). This is equivalent to 25 p/litre of fuel, although it would be more appropriate to relate this more accurately to vehicle type (and hence fuel) and rely on VED to improve cost-targeting. Other externalities (ignoring accidents) were estimated at 0.7–1.9 p/km, with a preferred value of 1.2 p/km. Allocating this by fuel would justify green taxes of 11 p/litre on petrol and 15 p/litre on diesel. These might be somewhat reduced to reflect lower emissions from post-1997 vehicles if higher VED rates on older vehicles were imposed in compensation. Accident externalities might add as much as 13 p/litre, though our (weakly) preferred rate is 3 p/litre. Parry and Small (2002) estimate these as 21 US cents per US gallon or about 4 p/litre, with the accident component about the same size. Green taxes might therefore increase road charges by 45 per cent on average. The pure road charge and green tax elements would amount to 36 p/litre for petrol and 40 p/litre for diesel (€0.6/litre and €0.67/litre respectively) in Britain. If this applied generally across the EU, the Netherlands and Germany would be taxing gasoline at about the right rate and only the UK is overcharging gasoline (see Figure 7.1). All countries except the UK are probably undercharging diesel.

The most controversial element is the 'optimal tax' component, whose value depends sensitively on preferences (specifically, the various elasticities, which are hard to measure), the tax instruments available (road prices versus fuel taxes, optimal income taxes versus proportional labour taxes), and the social welfare function (attitudes to inequality). In practical terms, the British Chancellor of the Exchequer, attempting to justify the current excessive petrol tax rates, might appeal to such arguments (indirectly, by arguing that they are necessary to finance public services such as health and education). It seems doubtful that the US Congress would pay much heed to such arguments, given that the rest of the tax system is hardly a model of the relentless application of Benthamite social welfare optimization.

More to the point, the spirit of building up a defensible cost-based charging structure for road use, combined with general green taxes that apply equally to all pollutants, is contrary to an approach that singles out road use for delicate optimal tax adjustments. Given that the additional tax that might be justified is only a further 30 per cent on top of the road charge and green element, and given the large uncertainties about almost all components of the total, it is difficult to accept that the modest social welfare benefits of such corrective taxes are worth sacrificing the clarity of the approach advocated here.

Arguably the most important aspect of a systematic approach to designing road charges is the philosophy of regulating total revenue, which encourages revenue-neutral adjustments to improve efficiency by shifting over to better-targeted congestion taxes such as cordon tolls and road pricing. Perhaps even more important, once the revenue stream is identified and subject to independent economic regulation, road finance can be put on a sound footing, with even larger potential improvements in transport and economic efficiency (Newbery, 1998*a*, 1998*b*).

APPENDIX 7.A: THE HEALTH COSTS OF VEHICLE PARTICULATE EMISSIONS

The most damaging vehicle emissions are particulates, usually measured by PM_{10} and mainly produced by diesel vehicles. Emissions increase the risk of mortality. The hazard rate, h, (the 'force of mortality') can be estimated from the annual number of deaths, d, of people of a given age, divided by the mid-year population of that cohort, m, so that $h = d/m$ (Miller and Hurley, 2002). The probability of surviving to the end of the year, s, assuming that the hazard rate is constant over the year, is then the ratio of the numbers of that cohort surviving to the end of the year, $m - \frac{1}{2}d$, over the number at the start of the year, $m + \frac{1}{2}d$. This can be rearranged to give $s = (2 - h)/(2 + h)$.

The evidence suggests that the increase in hazard rate is linear in pollutants, so that if in one year pollution increases, the hazard rate will increase to $h' = h(1 + \theta)$. We are interested in relating the mortality impact to the emissions in a single year, which in turn can be related back to the level of traffic in that year, so a single-year change is appropriate. The hazard rate varies with age, a, and can be approximated by an exponential function (which fits extremely well above the age of 30; below that, hazard rates are low in any case). For our purposes, we are interested in the impact of pollution on life expectancy, and particularly on the expected number of QALYs (quality-adjusted life years). The value of QALY per year decreases with age, but we ignore this effect and assume any change in life expectancy is an equal change in QALYs. This will exaggerate the impact of pollution slightly. Let the expected life of a person aged a be L_a and the proportion surviving the year be s_a. Life expectancy of someone dying in the year is taken as half a year, and otherwise survival brings the life expected of a year-older person, giving the recursion relation

$$(1) \qquad L_a = s_a(1 + L_{a+1}) + \frac{1}{2}(1 - s_a).$$

The effect on life expectancy of an increase in s_a to s_a' is then

$$(2) \qquad \Delta L_a = (s_a - s_a')\left(\frac{1}{2} + L_{a+1}\right) = -\theta h_a\left(\frac{1}{2} + L_{a+1}\right).$$

This can be summed over the population, weighting the change in life expectancy by the number of people exposed of that age. The information to make this calculation is available from population statistics, and ONS (2001, section 5) contains the relevant data. As risks are linear in pollution, it is legitimate to take average values, provided the population over which the average is taken has the same pattern of life expectancy.

Many countries monitor concentrations at various sites and identify the contributing sources. Thus for the UK in 1999, 20 per cent of total PM_{10} emissions came from road transport sources, while the annual average concentration of PM_{10} was $20\,\mu g/m^3$ measured at two rural sites, $23\,\mu g/m^3$ in twenty-five urban central and industrial sites, $22\,\mu g/m^3$ in fifteen urban background and four suburban sites, $27\,\mu g/m^3$ at four busy roadside sites, and $37\,\mu g/m^3$ at three city-centre kerbside sites, averaging $22\,\mu g/m^3$.[15] The country-wide average of pollution caused by traffic is then 20 per cent of $22\,\mu g/m^3 = 4.4\,\mu g/m^3$.

It may be that rural traffic contributions to pollution are small, and urban contributions high, as Maddison et al. (1996) argue. Rather than compute the traffic proportion by location and then sum over the affected population, it seems more direct to take the country average share of traffic as 20 per cent, take the country-wide average pollution level, and apply this to the total British population in 1999 of 58 million, relying on the linearity of the damage equation above.

The next step is to relate changes in pollution to changes in hazard rates. The estimated effect of an increase of $10 \, \mu\text{g/m}^3$ in pollution is to raise the daily mortality rate by about 1 per cent (Maddison et al., 1996). Somewhat later estimates from highly polluted developing countries suggest figures as high as 1.3 per cent ($\pm$ 0.5 per cent), the average value found for Bangkok (EF&EE, 2002, p. 5). Thus UK traffic pollution might account for increased mortality rates of $1\% \times 0.44 = 0.44$ per cent, raising mortality rates by a factor of 1.0044 at all ages, and making $\theta = 0.0044$.

This number is in itself hard to interpret, and it is not clear whether it is large or small. In fact, it is very small in terms of reduced life expectancy per person. Using the formula above, the average reduction in life expectancy of a single year's traffic pollution is 0.21 days. The total number of QALYs lost by one year's traffic pollution in Britain is therefore 58 million $\times$ 0.21/365 years = 34,000 QALYs. At £36,000 per QALY, this amounts to £1.2 billion per year.

Figure 7.A1 shows why the reduction in life expectancy is so small.[16] It shows the effect of a 10 per cent increase in mortality rates (corresponding to an increase of pollution of $75 \, \mu\text{g/m}^3$ for ever in a developing country, rather than $4.4 \, \mu\text{g/m}^3$ for one year). Mortality rates are so low for most people that a 10 per cent increase in the *rate* is barely perceptible (note that it is not an

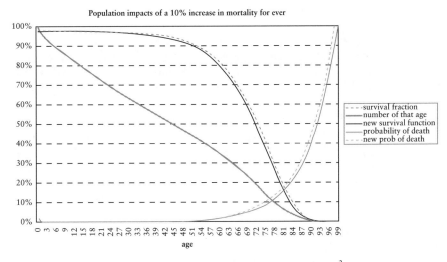

Figure 7.A1. *Effects of a Permanent Increase in Pollution of 75 $\mu g/m^3$: Population Impacts of a 10 Per Cent Increase in Mortality for Ever*

increase to 10 per cent, which would be shockingly high). The shift in the mortality rate to the left is only visible at advanced ages and high background mortality rates, where the fraction of the population at risk is also very small.

APPENDIX 7.B: THE MARGINAL SOCIAL COST OF VEHICLE NOISE

The basic equation for the eighteen-hourly average value of L_{10} (which is the average value of the hourly L_{10}, itself defined as the noise level in dB(A) which is exceeded only 10 per cent of the time) is

(3) $N = 4.343 \ln Q + 14.33 \ln (v + 40 + 500/v) + 3.343 \ln (1 + 5p/v) - 38.9,$

where N is noise in dB(A), ln is the natural logarithm, v is speed in kilometres per hour, $Q = C + F$ is the eighteen-hour traffic flow in vehicles (C is the number of cars or equivalent light vehicles and F is the number of heavy vehicles), and p is the percentage of heavy vehicles in the flow ($100F/Q$). There are additional additive corrections for distance (these values are at the roadside) and barriers or reflections, which are not relevant to the calculations we need to perform.[17]

The effect of increasing the number of vehicles, Q, without changing the proportions of heavy vehicles, p, or their speed[18] can be found by differentiation:

(4)
$$\frac{dN}{dQ} = \frac{4.343}{Q},$$

from which it follows that a 1 per cent increase in traffic (i.e. $\Delta Q/Q = 0.01$) leads to an increase in noise, ΔN, of 0.0434dB(A). Tinch (1995) suggests that the best estimate for the willingness to pay for a 1dB(A) improvement is £7.75/head ($\pm$ £2.25) at 1995 prices, or £9.15 at 2000 prices. Taken literally, this would suggest that a 1 per cent increase in traffic would cost each person 40 pence per year or £23 million for the extra 4.7 billion vehicle kilometres, or 0.5 pence per vehicle kilometre. The intriguing feature of the noise relationship, and the claim that noise costs are linear in dB(A), is that a 1 per cent reduction in traffic on a distant motorway is as valuable to those affected as a 1 per cent fall in traffic on a busy city street or a leafy suburb, for someone sitting outdoors facing the road or inside their double-glazed house. The damage done from a proportional increase in traffic everywhere is also proportional to the affected population, which is here taken as 58 million (i.e. everyone).

These implications encourage a degree of scepticism. The figures might reasonably be halved, as not all the population is likely to be really troubled, since as noise gets worse, so people take evasive action (deciding where to take their weekends or whether to install double glazing, etc.). A more important implication is that transferring traffic from less to more heavily trafficked roads reduces total noise (as the reduction would be a greater percentage of a smaller number than the increase would be of the larger number). Provided that not too many more people are affected by the busier road, there will be a net saving in noise costs. Transport corridors and very-high-capacity motorways are therefore environmentally advantageous.

The next step is to apportion the costs between light and heavy vehicles, as their contributions interact in a rather complex way. Differentiate (3) with respect to the number of cars, C, and heavy vehicles, F, holding other vehicle numbers constant, to give, after some simplification,

$$(5) \qquad \Delta N = 4.343 \left(1 - \frac{p}{100}\right)\left(\frac{1}{1 + 5p/v}\right)\frac{\Delta C}{C}$$

for cars and

$$(6) \qquad \Delta N = 4.343 \left(\frac{p/100 + 5p/v}{1 + 5p/v}\right)\frac{\Delta F}{F}$$

for heavy vehicles. This has the implication that a 1 per cent increase in heavy vehicles creates less increase in noise than a 1 per cent increase in light vehicles in towns if the traffic speed is 50 kph and the percentage of heavy vehicles, p, is less than 9 per cent, or on motorways if $v = 100$ kph and p is less than 15 per cent. Put another way, an extra heavy vehicle at these critical proportions is respectively eleven or seven times as noisy as an extra light vehicle.

As the division between vehicle types depends very much on the level of traffic, the speed, and the percentage share, p, the final estimate was based on a sample of roads of differing characteristics (flow, speed, traffic composition), and the effect of a 1 per cent change in each vehicle type was averaged over these sample roads, resulting in the 9 per cent of vehicle kilometres by heavy goods vehicles (HGV) and buses accounting for 30 per cent of the total marginal cost of noise. At 2000 traffic levels and prices, the marginal cost of a car is 0.4 pence per kilometre (taking the high value of exposed population, or half that for a more cautious assessment) and of an HGV is 2 pence per kilometre (or, more cautiously, 1 penny per kilometre).

Notes

1 Eichenberger (1999, 2002) argues that the form of political institutions will influence the level and type of road taxation that will be acceptable to the electorate. The very large differences in road tax rates in North America and Europe reflect differences in the political process (as well as inertia in tax design).

2 Small (1999) notes the importance of the distinction between economies or diseconomies of scale (which refers to decreasing or increasing unit costs with output) and returns to scale (which refers to the increment of output when all inputs are increased by the same physical proportion). There can be constant returns to scale but if some inputs (such as land) are scarce and only made available at increasing unit price, while others are supplied at constant price, then overall there will be increasing unit costs.

3 For potentially profitable utilities. Railways were less successful as they required the regulator to be able to impose charges that could only be met by public subsidy.

4 Telecoms provide an interesting exception, as the regulated utility – BT – argued successfully for historic cost accounting.

5 Prices are capped by a formula that is indexed to the retail price index, RPI, *less* a productivity term, X, *plus* an amount K to enable the industry to finance the heavy level of anticipated investment, so that the average price is capped by RPI – $X + K$. K thus anticipates the future increase in the RAB that the investment will bring about.

6 Arnott (2002) raises the further question about non-recurrent congestion, which on some estimates may account for half of total congestion. Electricity networks face a similar problem in that available capacity is stochastic, and line or plant failures can precipitate outages. The normal response is to build in a reserve margin and charge very high prices as this reserve falls and the loss-of-load probability increases. In congested urban areas, tolls may have to be set at higher levels than deterministic calculations suggest, or, alternatively, stochastic optimization may be required.

7 The London road charging scheme introduced on 17 February 2003 records and digitally transcribes number plates to match them up with prepayment, so other methods are feasible. See www.cclondon.com.

8 The number of serious injuries dropped even more. From 1995 to 2000, accident rates for cars have declined by a further 10 per cent (Department of Transport, Local Government, and the Regions, 2001, table 1.6).

9 Expressing the cost per litre allocates accidents more in proportion to vehicle weight, which is likely to be more accurately targeted.

10 Of course, the issue is more complex, for there is some cost in having to take more care as a result of the greater perceived risk, and this should be included. The fact that children are not allowed to play in streets and are driven to school rather than walking lowers the child accident rate but has a social cost. Although motorists may be better at avoiding killing each other, they are still killing cyclists and pedestrians at an alarming rate: the ratio of cyclists killed or seriously injured per million kilometres travelled to that of car occupants rose from 14.6 in 1984 to 21.6 in 1994 (Department of Transport, 1996, p. 13), while the ratio for pedestrians rose from 11.2 to 14.6. (That is, in 1994 the risk of being killed or seriously injured per kilometre travelled on a cycle was 21.6 times that in a car.) Improvements in road safety are therefore benefiting car occupants more than cyclists or pedestrians, though the accident rate (killed or seriously injured per kilometre travelled) has fallen for all – by 5.8 per cent per year for car occupants, 1.5 per cent per year for cyclists, and 3.3 per cent per year for pedestrians.

11 Arnott (2002) cites evidence that the partial elasticity of car insurance rates across US states with respect to traffic density is large and highly significant. Without being able to examine the evidence, it is hard to know what other variables might explain this or whether accident *rates* are correlated with traffic levels.

12 The Network of Experts on Benefits and Economic Instruments website of the conference is at www.unece.org/env/nebei. The symposium took place in London on 19–20 February 2001.

13 I am indebted to Paul Nelson of the Transport Research Laboratory and John Knowles of the Department for Transport for discussions on the measurement of traffic noise.

14 The median vehicle owner is the one for whom half the vehicles of that type are less polluting (and half more), and causes much less damage than the average, since a small fraction of vehicles appear to produce most of the pollution.

15 Department for Environment, Food, and Rural Affairs, 2001.
16 Another way to put this into perspective is to note that male mortality rates were uniformly more than 50 per cent higher than female rates in Britain in 1999 and 150 per cent higher for men aged 25–34, though female life expectancy is only 7 per cent higher despite women's considerably lower mortality risk.
17 For example, for a person at a distance d metres, the term $-\ln(d/13.5)$ is added. Presumably the use of average traffic flows implies that this is the relevant average noise for measuring average noise nuisance.
18 The conceptual experiment is thus across roads of similar traffic and speed. Clearly, increasing traffic is likely to reduce speed on any given road.

References

Arnott, R. (2002), 'Comments on "Road user and congestion charges" by D. Newbery', Boston College, mimeo, April.

Atkinson, A. B., and Stiglitz, J. E. (1980), *Lectures on Public Economics*, Maidenhead: McGraw-Hill.

Bovenberg, A. L., and Goulder, L. H. (1996), 'Optimal environmental taxation in the presence of other taxes: general equilibrium analyses', *American Economic Review*, 86: 985–1000.

Calthrop, E., and Proost, S. (1998), 'Road transport externalities: interaction between theory and empirical research', *Environmental and Resource Economics*, 11: 335–48.

Corlett, W. J., and Hague, D. C. (1953), 'Complementarity and the excess burden of taxation', *Review of Economic Studies*, 21: 21–30.

Deaton, A. (1987), 'Econometric issues for tax design in developing countries', in D. M. Newbery and N. Stern (eds), *The Theory of Taxation for Developing Countries*, New York, NY: Oxford University Press.

—— and Stern, N. (1986), 'Optimally uniform commodity taxes, taste differences and lump-sum grants', *Economics Letters*, 20: 263–6.

Delucchi, M. (1997), *The Annualized Social Cost of Motor-Vehicle Use in the U.S., 1990–91: Summary of Theory, Methods, Data and Results*, Davis, CA: Institute for Transportation Studies.

Department for Environment, Food, and Rural Affairs (2001), *Digest of Environmental Statistics*. Available at www.defra.gov.uk/environment/statistics/des/index.htm.

Department for Transport (2002), *Highway Economics Note No. 1: 2000*. Available at www.roads.dft.gov.uk/roadsafety/hen2000/index.htm.

Department of Transport (1988), *Calculation of Road Traffic Noise*, London: DoT.

—— (1996), *Transport Statistics Great Britain 1996 edition*, London: DoT.

Department of Transport, Local Government, and the Regions (2001), *Transport Statistics Great Britain 2001 edition*, London: DTLR.

Diamond, P. A., and Mirrlees, J. A. (1971), 'Optimal taxation and public production, I: production efficiency', *American Economic Review*, 61: 8–27.

Drake, G. (2000), *An Established Privatised Road Maintenance and Operation System: A Government Perspective*, London: Highways Agency.

EF&EE (2002), *Sri Lanka Vehicle Emissions Control Project: Inception Report*, Sacramento, CA: Engine, Fuel, and Emissions Engineering, Inc.

Eichenberger, R. (1999), 'Mit direketer Demokratie zu besserer Wirtschafts- und Finanzpolitik: Theorie und Empriie,' in H. H. von Arnim (Hrsg.), *Adäquate Institu-*

tionen: Voraussetzung für 'gute' und bürgernahe Politik?, Berlin: Duncker & Humbolt.

Eichenberger, R. (2002), 'Road pricing: a political-economic perspective', University of Fribourg, mimeo.

Eliasson, J., and Mattson, L-G. (2001), 'Transport and location effects of road pricing: a simulation approach', *Journal of Transport Economics and Policy*, 35: 417–56.

European Conference of Ministers of Transport (1998), *Efficient Transport for Europe: Policies for Internalization of External Costs*, Paris: Organisation for Economic Co-operation and Development.

Jansson, J. O. (1994), 'Accident externality charges', *Journal of Transport Economics and Policy*, 28: 31–43.

Johansson, O. (1997), 'Optimal road pricing with respect to accidents in a second-best perspective', *International Journal of Transport Economics*, 24: 343–65.

Keeler, T. E., and Small, K. A. (1977), 'Optimal peak-load pricing, investment, and service levels on urban expressways', *Journal of Political Economy*, 85: 1–25.

Kraus, M. (1981a), 'The problem of optimal resource allocation in urban transportation', in B. Maurice and B. Ballabon (eds), *Economic Perspectives: An Annual Survey of Economics*, 2, New York, NY: Harwood Academic Publishers.

—— (1981b), 'Scale economies analysis for urban highway networks', *Journal of Urban Economics*, 9: 1–22.

Larsen, O., and Østmoe, K. (2001), 'The experience of urban toll cordons in Norway', *Journal of Transport Economics and Policy*, 35: 457–71.

—— and Ramjerdi, F. (1991), *Road Pricing as a Means of Financing Investment in Transport Infrastructure: The Case of Oslo*, Oslo: Institute of Transport Economics.

Lindberg, G. (2001), 'Traffic insurance and accident externality charges', *Journal of Transport Economics and Policy*, 35: 399–416.

McCubbin, D. R., and Delucchi, M. A. (1999), 'The health costs of motor-vehicle-related air pollution', *Journal of Transport Economics and Policy*, 33: 253–86.

Maddison, D., Pearce, D., Johansson, O., Calthrop, E., Litman, T., and Verhoef, E. (1996), *Blueprint 5: The True Costs of Road Transport*, London: Earthscan.

May, A. D., Bonsall, P. W., and Hills, P. J. (1998), *The Impacts of Different Road User Charging Systems: Proceedings of Transportation into the Next Millennium*, Singapore: Nanyang Technological University.

——, Milne, D., Shepherd, S., and Sumalee, A. (2002), 'The specification of optimal cordon pricing locations and charges', presented at the 81st Annual Conference of the US Transportation Research Board.

Mayeres, I. (1999), 'The distributional impacts of policies for the control of transport externalities: an applied general equilibrium model', Fondazione Eni Enrico Mattei (Global Network of Environmental Economists), Working Paper 8.99. Available at www.feem.it/web/activ/_wp.html.

Menon, A. P. (2000), 'ERP in Singapore: a perspective one year on', *Traffic Engineering and Control*, 41(2).

Miller, B. G., and Hurley, J. F. (2002), 'Life table methods for quantitative impact assessments in chronic mortality', *Journal of Epidemiology and Community Health*, 57: 200–6.

Mirrlees, J. A. (1979), 'The theory of optimal taxation', in K. J. Arrow and M. D. Intrilligator (eds), *Handbook of Mathematical Economics*, Amsterdam: North-Holland.

Mohring, H. (1970), 'The peak load problem with increasing returns and pricing constraints', *American Economic Review*, 60: 693–705.

—— and Harwitz, M. (1962), *Highway Benefits: An Analytical Framework*, Evanston, IL: Northwestern University Press.

Newbery, D. M. (1988*a*), 'Road damage externalities and road user charges', *Econometrica*, 56: 295–316.

—— (1988*b*), 'Road user charges in Britain', *Economic Journal* (Conference), 161–76.

—— (1989), 'Cost recovery from optimally designed roads', *Economica*, 56: 165–85.

—— (1990), 'Pricing and congestion: economic principles relevant to pricing roads', *Oxford Review of Economic Policy*, 6(2): 22–38.

—— (1992), 'Should carbon taxes be additional to other transport fuel taxes?', *Energy Journal*, 13(2): 49–60.

—— (1998*a*), *Fair Payment from Road-Users: A Review of the Evidence on Social and Environmental Costs*, Basingstoke: Automobile Association.

—— (1998*b*), 'Fair and efficient pricing and the finance of roads', the 53rd Henry Spurrier Memorial Lecture, *The Proceedings of the Chartered Institute of Transport in the UK*, 7(3): 3–19.

—— and Santos, G. (2002), 'Estimating urban road congestion charges', CEPR, Discussion Paper 3176. Available at www.cepr.org/.

Ofgem (2001), *Review of Transco's Price Control from 2002: Final Proposals*. Available at www.ofgem.gov.uk/temp/ofgem/cache/cmsattach/315_26sep01_pub1.pdf.

ONS (2001), *Annual Abstract*, London: HMSO.

Parry, I. W. H., and Small, K. A. (2002), 'Does Britain or the United States have the right gasoline tax?', Resources for the Future, Discussion Paper 02-12. Available at www.rff.org/disc_papers/2002.htm.

Santos, G., and Newbery, D. (2001), 'Urban congestion charging: theory, practice and environmental consequences', CESifo, Working Paper 568. Available at www.cesifo.de.

——, ——, and Rojey, L. (2001), 'Static vs demand sensitive models and the estimation of efficient cordon tolls: an exercise for eight English towns', *Transportation Research Board Record*, Record 1747, TRB, National Research Council, Washington, DC.

——, Rojey, L., and Newbery, D. (2000), 'The environmental benefits from road pricing', University of Cambridge, Department of Applied Economics, Working Paper 0020.

Small, K. A. (1999), 'Economies of scale and self-financing rules with noncompetitive factor markets', *Journal of Public Economics*, 74: 431–50.

Stern, N. (1987), 'The theory of optimal commodity and income taxation: an introduction', in D. M. Newbery and N. Stern (eds), *The Theory of Taxation for Developing Countries*, New York, NY: Oxford University Press.

Strotz, R. H. (1965), 'Urban transportation parables', in J. Margolis (ed.), *The Public Economy of Urban Communities*, Washington, DC: Resources for the Future.

Suter, S., and Walter, F. (2001), 'Environmental pricing – theory and practice: the Swiss policy of heavy vehicle taxation', *Journal of Transport Economics and Policy*, 35: 381–97.

Tinch, R. (1995), *The Valuation of Environmental Externalities*, London: Department of Transport.

Tol, R. S. J., Fankhauser, S., Richels, R., and Smith, J. (2000), 'How much damage will climate change do? Recent estimates', *World Economics*, 1: 179–206.

Van Vliet, D., and Hall, M. (1997), SATURN 9.3 – User Manual, Leeds: Institute for Transport Studies, University of Leeds.

Chapter 8

Excise Taxes: Economics, Politics, and Psychology[*]

BRUNO S. FREY

Institute for Empirical Economic Research, University of Zurich

The imposition of taxes on specific consumption goods and services (i.e. excise taxes) not only is a time-honoured activity but also makes common sense: government financing can be combined with other important social goals, in particular the reduction of externalities (costs imposed on other people) by making the taxed goods more expensive. Thus two goals can be attained at the same time, which makes taxation an attractive option.

Excise taxes[1] enable us to reduce activities considered socially undesirable, such as environmental pollution, tobacco, alcohol, and drug consumption, gambling, and road congestion.[2] The theoretical prediction that the induced relative price effect actually works is supported by considerable empirical evidence.[3] The extensive economic theory of taxation applied to excises produces important insights that are far from being trivial. But this theory concentrates only on a limited number of aspects traditionally considered to be 'economic'; other equally important aspects tend to be ignored. I wish to argue that excise taxation under identifiable conditions leads to undesired and even counterproductive outcomes. This does not mean that excise taxes should not be used, or even that they should be used less. But it does mean that their relative advantages and disadvantages should be evaluated carefully in the light of other methods of taxation and of economic and social policies in general.

This chapter endeavours to focus on the aspects of excise taxation that have been neglected. Section 8.1 deals briefly with some of the largely ignored and unresolved problems arising in the standard theory of excise taxation. Section 8.2 considers excise taxation from the political point of view, based on constitutional economics. Section 8.3 centres on psychological aspects and is based on economic psychology. As these aspects are less well known in economics and in the taxation literature, they are discussed at greater length. Section 8.4 concludes.

[*] The author is grateful for helpful comments from Matthias Benz, Richard Bird, Reto Jegen, John Kay, Simon Lüchinger, Stephan Meier, Silika Tereschtschenko, and an anonymous referee.

8.1 FIVE PROBLEMS IN THE STANDARD THEORY OF EXCISE TAXATION

The following five aspects are well known in the theory of (excise) taxation, but may not always receive sufficient attention, because they are not considered to be fully within the realm of efficiency-focused economic theory. For that reason, they are mentioned but not extensively discussed.

8.1.1 *Externalities*

An attractive reason for using excise taxes is to reduce the externalities generated in the production, and especially consumption, of specific goods and services. The most prominent examples are the taxation of tobacco, alcohol, and gambling.

It is, however, well known that such an approach is only a compelling reason for levying a tax, and only then leads to a socially improved allocation of resources, when two conditions are met:

- The externality must be 'substantial'. The world is full of externalities. If the government decided to tax all externalities, it would be intervening everywhere. Hence, only those externalities that are clearly of greater consequence than others should be addressed. However, it is doubtful whether the excise taxes we observe meet that condition. Is it, for instance, obvious that the social costs of gambling are much larger than the social costs of engaging in dangerous sports (such as, for example, skiing or amateur soccer)? It may well be that dangerous sports produce higher external social costs (for example, in terms of socially insured health costs and working days lost) than gambling. But dangerous sports are not subject to a special excise tax. In fact, many countries heavily subsidize sporting activities. Another instance is overeating, which has become a major problem in developed countries, as the average weight of the population has been increasing rapidly in recent decades. A significant number of people (especially in the English-speaking countries: the USA, the UK, Canada, Australia, and New Zealand) are seriously overweight (see Offer (2001), who gives extensive empirical evidence). This imposes high, partly externalized health costs. Overeating is not tackled anywhere by imposing a specific tax related to increasing body weight.
- Approaches other than taxation may be more effective in reducing external effects. Smoking may be a case in point. The use of tobacco has been penalized for a long time by a substantial special tax, but most countries obviously do not consider that to be sufficient. In recent years, in addition, various types of smoking restrictions have been introduced. According to my subjective impression, the passive smoking imposed on other people in public spaces, especially in restaurants, has thereby been greatly reduced. One reason may be that such direct intervention makes clear that the government disapproves of smoking ('expressive function of the law'). Taxes do not serve this function of moral disapproval.[4]

These considerations suggest that the identification of an external effect is certainly not sufficient reason for imposing an excise tax. This conclusion conforms to economic theory, but its consequences have not always been taken seriously.

8.1.2 *Undesired Side Effects*

Imposing a higher excise tax on a particular good means that the relative price of a substitute good falls at the same time, and that the latter's consumption increases. Empirical research (for example, Farrelly et al. (2001*b*)) indeed suggests that raising the price of alcohol raises the level of consumption of marijuana. But even keeping preferences constant, such an undesired effect does not necessarily occur if the income effect is sufficiently strong. Various goods subject to excise taxation may also be complementary (for the evidence, see Saffer and Chaloupka (1998, 1999)), i.e. taxing alcohol reduces the consumption of both alcohol and drugs.

The econometric estimates are not robust enough to be able to predict whether such undesired side effects occur, but they have to be taken into account when applying a particular excise tax.

8.1.3 *Undesired Effects on Equity*

In order to raise a particular sum of revenue, goods and activities with low price elasticity should be taxed more highly than those with high price elasticity (Ramsey rule). But in many cases, this requirement raises serious distributional concerns. Often, consumers with less ability to find a substitute for more highly taxed goods or services have below-average incomes and are therefore taxed more heavily than higher-income consumers. Moreover, they often belong to minority groups, which need to be protected in the political process. In the USA, women, adults with an income at or below the median income, young adults, African-Americans, and Hispanics are indeed most affected by higher cigarette prices (Farrelly et al., 2001*a*) and therefore by an increase in tobacco taxes. Road pricing also tends to have a regressive income effect (see, for example, Button and Verhoef (1998) and Richardson and Bae (1998)). The conflict between allocational efficiency and equity concerns is well known and should not be overlooked.

8.1.4 *Tax Compliance*

Taxation leads to tax evasion. The crucial question is to what extent this is the case. The standard economic theory of tax evasion (based on Becker (1968) and worked out by Allingham and Sandmo (1972); a recent survey is Andreoni, Erard, and Feinstein (1998)) is based on the deterrent effect of the probability of being caught and the size of the penalty. At least with respect to income taxation, this model has not worked very well: the level of tax compliance is difficult to account for, and in almost all studies, the deterrence variables have no statistically significant effect on evasion (see, for example, Alm, McClelland, and Schulze (1992), Graetz and Wilde (1985), Skinner and Slemrod (1985), and Pommerehne and Frey (1992)).

In addition to the extent of evasion, it is important to consider how the respective underground activities affect societies. In many cases (for example, gambling, drug, and alcohol production and consumption), the external effects are much larger when occurring in the black economy. In so far as this applies to a particular excisable good, the tax should be used restrictively. But it should always be kept in mind that an outright prohibition of such consumption leads to much worse consequences.

8.1.5 *Administrative Costs*

The cost of raising an excise tax varies greatly and often depends to a large extent on technological developments (Cnossen, 2002). Thus, up until recently, road taxes were considered to be costly to administer. This seems to be much less the case today.

8.2 POLITICO-ECONOMIC CONSIDERATIONS

Governments have used certain excise taxes extensively, such as those imposed on alcohol, cigarettes, and gambling. Other excise taxes have been used only reluctantly, such as those placed on drugs, environmental pollution, and especially traffic congestion (road pricing). How can these differences be explained?

Optimal taxation theory, seeking to maximize social welfare, suggests broadly based taxes, which distort the allocation of resources less than narrowly based taxes and secure a steadier stream of revenue. The welfare-maximizing approach therefore finds it difficult to account for the differences observed. In contrast, the politico-economic point of view looks at the incentives faced by politicians seeking re-election. An important means for a government to ensure survival is to finance government expenditures with as little popular resistance as possible. Excise taxes on goods generally known to be harmful (and with respect to which people have a bad conscience when they indulge in their consumption) – in particular, alcohol, tobacco, and gambling – provide a welcome opportunity for politicians. They claim to help consumers overcome their weakness. In addition, the demand for consumption is inelastic and excise taxes are easy to apply. Thus, revenue can effectively be raised by tax hikes.[5] The situation is different in the case of drugs, because the price elasticity of demand is higher and people can quite easily escape taxation. Imposing high taxes on drugs risks driving their consumption underground, which creates problems for the politicians in charge. Both environmental and congestion taxes are unpopular with the population for psychological reasons, which will be discussed in the next section. Politicians are therefore reluctant to use them (see Oberholzer-Gee and Weck-Hannemann (2002)). They prefer direct interventions via commands and controls, which have the added advantage that any successes can more easily be attributed to the government's actions (Frey and Schneider, 1997).

From a constitutional point of view (see, for example, Frey (1983), Buchanan (1991), Mueller (1996), and Cooter (2000)), taxes should be as nearly as possible designed as benefit levies, because this induces governments to provide services valued by the citizens (Brennan and Buchanan, 1980, 1985). Excise taxes are indeed narrowly based and do not ensure a steady source of income. To the extent that consumers react in a price-elastic manner, tax revenue falls when the tax rate is raised. The government therefore has an incentive to restrain substitution possibilities in order to reduce the price elasticity of demand.

Road pricing provides an example. When car drivers are charged on the basis of the traffic congestion that exists, tax revenue can be raised by closing alternative roads to which car drivers could switch. Revenue is also increased when switching to alternative transportation modes – in particular, public transport – is made more difficult, although this policy achieves exactly the opposite of what road pricing should lead to. In an age of environmental awareness, no government will advertise such a policy, but the effect of blocking any possible substitution may still be achieved by turning a blind eye.

If it is to be expected that governments act in a counterproductive way when they switch from income and corporate taxes to excise taxes, the latter become less attractive from the constitutional point of view. Behind a veil of ignorance, citizens must balance the advantage of restricting the growth of the public sector by assigning a narrow tax base with the disadvantage of giving the government the distorting incentives just described. It should be noted that the perverse incentives of the government differ from one excise tax to another. In so far as the supply of alternatives is guided by markets (for instance, in the case of alcohol, by the private supply of non-alcoholic or low-alcoholic beverages), no such counterproductive effect takes place. Economic research must provide the information to the citizens so that they can reach a well-reasoned decision when voting. Direct referendums are well suited for this purpose (see Frey (2001, ch. 9) and Kirchgaessner, Feld, and Savioz (1999) for a collection of the empirical evidence available). As Reiner Eichenberger, in his comment on this contribution, shows, a Swiss commune recently accepted a well-worked-out system of road pricing following a direct referendum. The same result may only indirectly be achieved in a representative democracy by voting for a party supporting a corresponding policy.

8.3 PSYCHOLOGICAL CONSIDERATIONS

Economic psychology[6] suggests three major aspects in which excise taxes depend on psychic influences.

8.3.1 *Fairness*

It has been empirically well established that neoclassical professional econo-mists are fond of the price system (Kearl et al., 1979; Frey et al., 1984), while most other people are reluctant to use it or even abhor it (Kahneman, Knetsch, and Thaler, 1986). In a representative survey of the Zurich popula-tion (Frey, 1999*b*, ch. 10, p. 169), only 27 per cent found the price system 'fair' in a well-defined situation of excess demand, while 73 per cent found it 'unfair'. In contrast, an allocation of the excess demand by the public admin-istration was considered fair by 43 per cent and unfair by 57 per cent. Even more acceptable is an allocation according to the traditional principle of 'first come, first served', where the relationship between fair and unfair is 76 per cent to 24 per cent. Only a random allocation is considered to be less fair than the price system (14 per cent to 86 per cent). While one must always be careful not to overgeneralize such findings, they suggest that governments are rather reluctant to introduce new prices in order to influence people's behav-iour. A pertinent example is road pricing, which often meets with strong resistance in the population (see, extensively, Jones (1995, 1998)). In conse-quence, it has been applied only very rarely.[7] This is only in part due to failure to understand how it is supposed to work, and must also be attributed to a more general lack of trust in the price system. It must therefore be taken into account that an effort to influence consumption behaviour via excise taxes does not meet with much popular support, and in many cases will be strongly opposed.

Quite a different aspect of fairness is also relevant when considering the use of excise taxes. Fairness refers not only to outcomes but also to procedures. As has been shown in psychological research (Tyler, 1990; Tyler and Blader, 2000), people are more willing to accept an outcome unfavourable for themselves if the process leading to this outcome is perceived to be fair. There is a higher degree of consensus with respect to what constitutes a 'fair process' than to what constitutes a 'fair outcome'. Most importantly, the concerns of the people affected must be seriously taken into consideration, and they must have the opportunity to participate in the decision-making process. These are exactly the features of a sound democratic process. It has indeed been argued that, in a well-developed democracy, the citizens are more willing to accept policies in the general interest. They act in a less selfish way and exhibit a higher amount of civic virtue and social trust (see, for example, Mansbridge (1994), Putnam (2000), and Eichenberger and Frey (2002)).

These insights are of direct consequence for the introduction of excise taxes. Even if the citizens are reluctant to accept a new excise tax (as is the case for road pricing and, to some extent, also for environmental taxes), the opposition may be reduced and even won over if the process of introduction is perceived to be fair. The psychological results underscore the importance of using the democratic decision-making process instead of a technocratic ap-proach.

8.3.2 *Weakness of Will*

Excise taxes on tobacco, alcohol, drugs, and gambling not only endeavour to reduce the negative externalities imposed on other people but are also meant to restrict and prevent self-destructive tendencies. Individuals are supposed to be, to some extent, weak willed. They are quite well aware of what would be good for them, but they have insufficient will-power always to act accordingly. Every constrained eater or smoker knows how relevant weakness of will is for daily consumption decisions.

Weakness of will reflects itself in time-inconsistent choices (Strotz, 1956; Hoch and Loewenstein, 1991). There are two very different ways of dealing with this issue (Ainslie, 1992; Loewenstein and Elster, 1992; Elster, 1999).

The standard economic approach, championed by Becker (1976; also Stigler and Becker (1977)), assumes that consumers systematically react to the induced relative price increase of the taxed goods despite a possible weakness of will. Addiction as a manifestation of weakness of will is part of a rational individual consumption plan (see Becker and Murphy (1988)). Therefore, even 'addicts' consume less in the long run when prices rise. This approach is consistent with specific empirical observations (for cigarette consumption, see Becker, Grossman, and Murphy (1994) and Chaloupka (1991); for alcohol, see Cook and Moore (1999); for drugs, see Grossman and Chaloupka (1998)).

Many economists and other social scientists do not find the idea of 'rational addiction' convincing. They prefer not to assume that individuals are rational but to assume that there are areas of life where rationality is less pronounced. For them, weakness of will with respect to the consumption of particular goods, such as drugs, tobacco, or alcohol, is an instance in which rationality is imperfect and its extent has to be explained rather than assumed (Elster, 1979, 1986). An example would be heavy drug addicts who have at least partially lost the ability for rational thinking. Recently, it has become fashionable to suggest that people (and animals) discount future rewards hyperbolically rather than exponentially (Loewenstein and Prelec, 1992; Laibson, 1997). As a result, rewards become more attractive the closer they come in time. At some point, the ranking of preferences is reversed, so that an inferior reward in the here-and-now dominates a superior reward some time in the future. People then act in a myopic way and indulge in consumption activities that they will regret later.

On the basis of empirical evidence, it is not possible to choose between the two approaches, because they focus on different aspects.

Nevertheless, it is possible to derive conclusions about the influence of excise taxes on consumption that are consistent with both approaches:

- An excise tax tends to influence behaviour systematically, but in some cases it is rather ineffective. The marginal effect on consumption of an increase in the excise tax rate often turns out to be small in econometric estimates (for example: Wasserman et al. (1991) for cigarette smoking; Saffer and Chaloupka (1999) and Cook and Moore (1999) for alcohol, cocaine, and heroin consumption; Ramjerdi (1995), Sipes and Mendelsohn (2001), and Newbery (this volume) for road congestion). This could, in principle, be compensated by a correspondingly large increase in the tax rate. However, high rates of taxes have several major drawbacks: they are likely to be perceived as unfair and therefore tend to be opposed. The switch to substitutes may have undesired side effects. Thus, it has been found that smokers in high-tax American states reduce the number of cigarettes consumed per day, but their total daily tar and nicotine intake is unaffected. For young smokers, aged 18–24, the total daily tar and nicotine intake even increases after a tax hike (Evans and Farrelly, 1998). In addition, the incentive to switch to the underground economy increases. As a result, uncertainty about the quality of the substitute product increases. The last effect has had severe health consequences for those individuals buying in the shadow economy, especially in the case of alcohol prohibition in the USA in the 1920s and drug prohibition today (see, for example, Frey (1997)).

It should be noted that these negative effects of excise taxes typically only take place with (very) high, and sometimes even prohibitive, tax rates. In that case, the qualitative effects are similar to outright prohibition. However, the damage produced tends to be smaller because the imposition of taxes allows people to carry the higher cost rather than switch to the shadow economy, which, in the case of prohibition, is the only resort left for consumers.

- A more effective way to influence consumption than raising excise taxes has proved to be curtailing availability in particular locations and for particular groups of people. Pertinent examples are illicit drugs (when Zurich's 'needle park' was closed by the police, a large number of young and casual drug users discontinued their habit; see Frey (1997)) and smoking (which in many countries today has become difficult to practice; see the empirical evidence of the effects in Chaloupka and Grossman (1996)). It is not argued here that reducing availability 'solves' the problem of addiction, but it helps to overcome the weakness of will for many people. As with many other activities, the 'demand' to indulge the weakness of will is, *ceteris paribus*, lower the higher the cost of consumption due to taxes. As easy availability is often the major non-substitutable cost component, reduced availability tends to decrease consumption appreciably for many people in many situations.

The largest effect in terms of negative externalities accompanying the consumption of addictive substances is attained when the availability of such goods for hopeless addicts is at the same time increased. One possibility is that the government provides the opportunity for consumption to that particular class of people. The separation of such markets proves to work much better than often predicted, at least in the case of heavy drugs such as heroin. On both markets, it makes sense not only to steer supply to a certain extent, but also to impose excise taxes.

8.3.3 *Crowding Out Intrinsic Motivation*

The imposition of excise taxes may lead to two undesirable consequences through the negative impact on behaviour undertaken for its own sake (that is, for intrinsic reasons). This effect has been studied by social psychologists as 'hidden costs of rewards' (Lepper and Greene, 1978; Deci and Ryan, 1985; Deci with Flaste, 1995). It has been introduced into economics as 'crowding theory' by Frey (1997). It is supported by a large number of experiments (an important meta-study is Deci, Koestner, and Ryan (1999)) as well as by econometric studies of real-life events (see Frey and Jegen (2001)).

- Government intervention in a market via excise taxes tends to shift perceived responsibility from individuals' own sphere (their intrinsic motivation) to the public realm. This crowding-out effect only takes place if the individuals previously reduced their consumption for intrinsic reasons and if the imposition of the tax is perceived to be controlling. An important case in point is the taxation of pollution according to a market-based environmental policy. The introduction of a tax on the negative external effects runs the risk of undermining environmental morale. Intrinsic motivation not only may be negatively affected in areas where the pollution tax is applied, but may spill over to other areas ('motivation spillover effect'). As not all areas of the environment are suitable for excise taxation, the policy intervention may on the whole worsen, rather than improve, environmental conditions (see, more fully, Frey (1999*a*)).

- The excise is considered a 'licence to do'. The government finds it difficult, and in most cases impossible, simultaneously to condemn an activity and nevertheless benefit from it in the form of revenue. Many individuals lose their bad conscience (a form of intrinsic norm and motivation) and accordingly consider the tax to be just another price. The relative price effect is thereby unaffected, but the intrinsic motivation not to engage in the activity is crowded out. This effect is likely to occur in the case of environmental taxes and also road pricing (see, for example, Goodin (1994), who speaks of 'selling environmental indulgences').

8.4 CONCLUSIONS

Excise taxes in the areas of environmental pollution, tobacco, alcohol, and drug consumption, gambling, and road congestion are faced with five 'classical' problems regarding the identification of negative external effects, undesired side effects, distributional concerns, tax compliance, and administrative costs. These problems are well known and can be analysed successfully within accepted neoclassical economic theory.

The main focus of this chapter has been on aspects that have proved to be difficult or even impossible to approach fruitfully within neoclassical economics. It is argued that important insights can be gained by taking political and psychological elements into account and, if necessary, by going beyond existing theory.

The politico-economic aspects of excise taxation relate to the current policy process as well as to the constitutional level. Reasons are given why some excise taxes are widely applied (especially those on tobacco, alcohol, and gambling) while others are used sparingly (especially road pricing, and also environmental taxes). At the constitutional level, the differing interests of governments and the population at large with respect to the extent and intensity of (excise) taxation are emphasized.

The introduction, as well as the consequences, of excise taxation depends greatly on psychological factors. Such taxation is often considered to be unfair by the consumers affected by it. It is argued that the ensuing resistance can be overcome, at least partially, by a procedure that is considered to be fair. The weakness of will of individuals, or their self-destructive tendencies, is an important reason why government interferes with consumption. This view is disputed by the neoclassical approach built on 'rational addiction'. However, recently, the concept of hyperbolic discounting has gained prominence as an explanation for human myopia. It helps to explain why consumers take short-run decisions that they themselves consider to be suboptimal over the long run. Imposing excise taxes may crowd out people's intrinsic motivation; people may lose their sense of responsibility to act in a socially beneficial way.

Excise taxes are thus faced with many problems. But a reasonable economic policy always compares a policy with feasible alternatives. In the areas where excise taxes are applied, governments often resort to total prohibition. Examples are alcohol prohibition in the USA in the 1920s and 1930s, and today's drug prohibition in, for instance, the USA, France, and Sweden. In some countries, considerable efforts have also been made to prohibit gambling. The chapter repeatedly points out that, in most cases, total prohibition produces much stronger negative external effects than excise taxation does.

There is no such thing as an 'ideal' economic policy, and certainly not an 'ideal' tax policy. Each economic policy has its advantages and disadvantages, which must be studied carefully. When undertaking such comparisons, it is important not to focus on extreme policies, such as total prohibition on the one hand or exclusive application of excise taxes on the other hand – for example, steering all traffic by road taxes. Rather, it is necessary to search actively for ways to apply excise taxes in combination with other policy instruments. Such a policy mix is difficult and cumbersome, but is the only approach promising results in the interest of the population at large.

Notes

1 General discussions on excise taxes are provided, for example, by Shoup (1983), Cnossen (1977), and, in the context of general taxation, Cnossen (2002), as well as by the contributions to this volume.

2 On the environment, see, for example, Cnossen and Vollebergh (1992); on tobacco, see Jha and Chaloupka (2000), Cnossen (2001), and Cnossen and Smart (this volume); on alcohol, see Cnossen (1981) and Smith (this volume); on drugs, see

Frey (1997); and on road congestion, see Johansson and Mattson (1995), Button and Verhoef (1998), and Newbery (this volume).

3 It is possible here to indicate only some results. For the USA, the price elasticities have recently been estimated to be −0.30 for alcohol, −0.28 for cocaine, and −0.94 for heroin (Saffer and Chaloupka, 1999).

For cigarette consumption, a well-known US study is Becker, Grossman, and Murphy (1994), who find that the long-run price elasticity is almost twice as large as the short-run elasticity. Chaloupka and Grossman (1996), also for the USA, estimate the price elasticity for the cigarette demand of youth to be −1.3, but the earlier estimate by Wasserman et al. (1991) finds a lower figure (0.06 for 1970 and −0.23 for 1985). According to Taurus, O'Malley, and Johnston (2001), the consensus estimate for adult demand is −0.3 to −0.5 but the price responsiveness of youth is up to three times as large. In absolute terms, Moore (1996) calculates that a 10 per cent increase in tobacco taxes saves over six thousand lives a year in the USA.

Cook and Moore (1999) and Crawford, Smith, and Tanner (1999) show that alcohol consumption reacts negatively to higher taxes and prices. The negative external effects of drunk driving have been calculated by Mullahy and Sindelar (1994) and Grossman et al. (1993). Levitt and Porter (2001) find that the negative external cost per mile by a drunk driver amounts to at least 30 cents.

Drug prohibition is estimated by Farrelly et al. (2001b) and Saffer and Chaloupka (1999) to have a negative effect on drug consumption. Grossman and Chaloupka (1998) calculate that the price elasticity for cocaine consumption is substantial, at −1.35. Van Ours (1995) estimates that in the Dutch East Indies (1923–38), the short-term price elasticity of opium consumption was −0.7 and the long-run elasticity −1.0.

Farrell, Morgenroth, and Walker (1999) show that the price elasticity of demand for gambling is negative.

The toll price elasticity of road pricing has been estimated to be negative but rather small (for example, for Oslo, −0.04 – Ramjerdi (1995)).

4 After all, governments do not disapprove of work but nevertheless they tax it heavily.

5 According to Cnossen (2001, p. 233), 'governments are addicted to this lucrative and cheap source of revenue'.

6 Surveys are Furnham and Lewis (1986), Lea, Tarpy, and Webley (1987), MacFadyen and MacFadyen (1987), van Raaij, van Velthoven, and Waerneryd (1988), Earl (1990), Rabin (1998), and Frey and Benz (2002). Specific contributions include Scitovsky (1976), Kahneman, Slovic, and Tversky (1982), Frank (1985, 1988), Elster (1998), Frey (1997, 2001), and Frey and Stutzer (2002).

7 'The outstanding fact is that after 30–40 years of analysis, research, and discussion, a pure policy of road pricing has been adopted in only one city, Singapore' (Thompson, 1998, p. 95).

References

Ainslie, G. W. (1992), *Picoeconomics*, Cambridge: Cambridge University Press.

Allingham, M. G., and Sandmo, A. (1972), 'Income tax evasion: a theoretical analysis', *Journal of Public Economics*, 1: 323–38.

Alm, J., McClelland, G. H., and Schulze, W. D. (1992), 'Why do people pay taxes?', *Journal of Public Economics*, 48: 21–38.

Andreoni, J., Erard, B., and Feinstein, J. (1998), 'Tax compliance', *Journal of Economic Literature*, 36: 818–60.

Barde, J-P., and Braathen, N. A. (this volume), 'Environmentally related levies'.

Becker, G. S. (1968), 'Crime and punishment: an economic approach', *Journal of Political Economy*, 76: 169–217.

—— (1976), *The Economic Approach to Human Behavior*, Chicago, IL: Chicago University Press.

——, Grossman, M., and Murphy, K. M. (1994), 'An empirical analysis of cigarette addiction', *American Economic Review*, 84: 396–418.

—— and Murphy, K. M. (1988), 'A theory of rational addiction', *Journal of Political Economy*, 96: 675–700.

Brennan, G., and Buchanan, J. M. (1980), *The Power to Tax: Analytical Foundations of a Fiscal Constitution*, Cambridge and New York, NY: Cambridge University Press.

—— and —— (1985), *The Reason of Rules*, New York, NY: Cambridge University Press.

Buchanan, J. M. (1991), *Constitutional Economics*, Oxford: Basil Blackwell.

Button, K. J., and Verhoef, E. T. (1998), 'Introduction', in K. J. Button and E. T. Verhoef (eds), *Road Pricing, Traffic Congestion and the Environment*, Cheltenham and Northampton, MA: Edward Elgar.

Chaloupka, F. J. (1991), 'Rational addictive behavior and cigarette smoking', *Journal of Political Economy*, 99: 722–42.

—— and Grossman, M. (1996), 'Price, tobacco control policies and youth smoking', National Bureau of Economic Research, Working Paper no. 5740.

Cnossen, S. (1977), *Excise Systems: A Global Study of the Selective Taxation of Goods and Services*, Baltimore, MD: Johns Hopkins University Press.

—— (1981), 'Specific issues in excise taxation', in K. W. Roskamp and F. Forte (eds), *Reforms of Tax Systems*, Detroit, MI: Wayne State University Press.

—— (2001), 'Taxing tobacco in the European Union', *De Economist*, 149: 233–49.

—— (2002), 'Tax policy in the European Union: a review of issues and options', *FinanzArchiv*, 58: 466–558.

—— and Smart, M. (this volume), 'Taxation of tobacco'.

—— and Vollebergh, H. (1992), 'Towards a global excise on carbon', *National Tax Journal*, 45: 23–36.

Cook, P. J., and Moore, M. J. (1999), 'Alcohol', National Bureau of Economic Research, Working Paper no. 6905.

Cooter, R. D. (2000), *The Strategic Constitution*, Princeton, NJ: Princeton University Press.

Crawford, I., Smith, Z., and Tanner, S. (1999), 'Alcohol taxes, tax revenues and the Single European Market', *Fiscal Studies*, 20: 287–304.

Deci, E. L., with Flaste, R. (1995), *Why We Do What We Do: The Dynamics of Personal Autonomy*, New York, NY: Putnam.

——, Koestner, R., and Ryan, R. M. (1999), 'A meta-analytic review of experiments examining the effects of extrinsic rewards on intrinsic motivation', *Psychological Bulletin*, 125: 627–68.

—— and Ryan, R. M. (1985), *Intrinsic Motivation and Self-Determination in Human Behavior*, New York, NY: Plenum Press.

Earl, P. E. (1990), 'Economics and psychology: a survey', *Economic Journal*, 100: 718–55.

Eichenberger, R., and Frey, B. S. (2002), 'Democratic governance for a globalized world', *Kyklos*, 55: 265–88.

Elster, J. (1979), *Ulysses and the Sirens: Studies in Rationality and Irrationality*, Cambridge: Cambridge University Press.

—— (ed.) (1986), *The Multiple Self*, Cambridge: Cambridge University Press.

—— (1998), 'Emotions and economic theory', *Journal of Economic Literature*, 36: 47–74.

—— (1999), *Addictions: Entries and Exits*, New York, NY: Russell Sage Foundation Publications.

Evans, W. N., and Farrelly, M. C. (1998), 'The compensating behavior of smokers: taxes, tar, and nicotine', *RAND Journal of Economics*, 29: 578–95.

Farrell, L., Morgenroth, E., and Walker, I. (1999), 'A time series analysis of U.K. lottery sales: long and short run price elasticities', *Oxford Bulletin of Economics and Statistics*, 61: 513–26.

Farrelly, M. C., Bray, J. W., Pechacek, T., and Wollery, T. (2001a), 'Response of adults to increases in cigarette prices by sociodemographic characteristics', *Southern Economic Journal*, 68: 156–65.

——, ——, Zarkin, G. A., and Wendling, B. W. (2001b), 'The joint demand for cigarettes and marihuana: evidence from the National Household Survey on Drug Abuse', *Journal of Health Economics*, 20: 51–68.

Frank, R. H. (1985), *Choosing the Right Pond*, New York, NY: Oxford University Press.

—— (1988), *Passions within Reason: The Strategic Role of the Emotions*, New York, NY: Norton.

Frey, B. S. (1983), *Democratic Economic Policy*, New York, NY: St Martin's Press.

—— (1997), 'Drugs, economics and policy', *Economic Policy*, 25: 389–94.

—— (1999a), 'Morality and rationality in environmental policy', *Journal of Consumer Policy*, 22: 395–417.

—— (1999b), *Economics as a Science of Human Behavior*, extended second edition, Boston, MA, Dordrecht, and London: Kluwer.

—— (2001), *Inspiring Economics: Human Motivation in Political Economy*, Cheltenham and Brookfield, MO: Edward Elgar.

—— and Benz, M. (2002), 'Oekonomie und Psychologie: eine Uebersicht', in D. Frey and L. von Rosenstiel (eds), *Enzyklopaedie der Wirtschaftspsychologie*, Goettingen: Hogrefe.

—— and Jegen, R. (2001), 'Motivation crowding theory: a survey of empirical evidence', *Journal of Economic Surveys*, 15: 589–611.

——, Pommerehne, W. W., Schneider, F., and Gilbert, G. (1984), 'Consensus and dissension among economists: an empirical inquiry', *American Economic Review*, 74: 986–94.

—— and Schneider, F. (1997), 'Warum wird die Umweltökonomie kaum angewandt?', *Journal of Environmental Law and Policy*, 2: 153–70.

—— and Stutzer, A. (2002), *Happiness and Economics: How the Economy and Institutions Affect Human Well-Being*, Princeton, NJ, and Oxford: Princeton University Press.

Furnham, A., and Lewis, A. (1986), *The Economic Mind: The Social Psychology of Economic Behaviour*, Brighton: Wheatsheaf.

Goodin, R. E. (1994), 'Selling environmental indulgences', *Kyklos*, 47: 573–96.

Graetz, M. J., and Wilde, L. L. (1985), 'The economics of tax compliance: facts and fantasy', *National Tax Journal*, 38: 355–63.

Grossman, M., and Chaloupka, F. J. (1998), 'The demand for cocaine by young adults: a rational addiction approach', *Journal of Health Economics*, 17: 427–74.

——, ——, Saffer, H., and Laixuthai, A. (1993), 'Effects of alcohol price policy on youth', National Bureau of Economic Research, Working Paper no. 4385.

Hoch, S. J., and Loewenstein, G. F. (1991), 'Time-inconsistent preferences and consumer self-control', *Journal of Consumer Research*, 17: 492–507.

Jha, P., and Chaloupka, F. J. (eds) (2000), *Tobacco Control in Developing Countries*, Oxford: Oxford University Press on behalf of the World Bank and the World Health Organization.

Johansson, B., and Mattson, L-G. (eds) (1995), *Road Pricing: Theory, Empirical Assessment and Policy*, Boston, MA, Dordrecht, and London: Kluwer.

Jones, P. (1995), 'Road pricing: the public viewpoint', in B. Johansson and L-G. Mattson (eds), *Road Pricing: Theory, Empirical Assessment and Policy*, Boston, Dordrecht, and London: Kluwer.

—— (1998), 'Urban road pricing: public acceptability and barriers to implementation', in K. J. Button and E. T. Verhoef (eds), *Road Pricing, Traffic Congestion and the Environment*, Cheltenham and Northampton: Edward Elgar.

Kahneman, D., Knetsch, J., and Thaler, R. (1986), 'Fairness as a constraint on profit seeking: entitlements in the market', *American Economic Review*, 76: 728–41.

——, Slovic, P., and Tversky, A. (eds) (1982), *Judgement under Uncertainty: Heuristics and Biases*, Cambridge: Cambridge University Press.

Kearl, J. R., Pope, C. L., Whiting, G. C., and Wimmer, L. T. (1979), 'A confusion of economists?', *American Economic Review*, 69(2): 28–37.

Kirchgaessner, G., Feld, L., and Savioz, M. R. (1999), *Die direkte Demokratie: Modern, erfolgreich, entwicklungs- und exportfähig*, Basle: Helbing und Lichtenhahn; Munich: Vahlen.

Laibson, D. (1997), 'Golden eggs and hyperbolic discounting', *Quarterly Journal of Economics*, 112: 443–77.

Lea, S., Tarpy, R., and Webley, P. (1987), *The Individual and the Economy: A Survey of Economic Psychology*, Cambridge: Cambridge University Press.

Lepper, M. R., and Greene, D. (eds) (1978), *The Hidden Costs of Reward: New Perspectives on Psychology of Human Motivation*, Hillsdale, NJ: Erlbaum.

Levitt, S. D., and Porter, J. (2001), 'How dangerous are drinking drivers?', *Journal of Political Economy*, 109: 1198–237.

Loewenstein, G., and Elster, J. (eds) (1992), *Choice over Time*, New York, NY: Sage.

—— and Prelec, D. (1992), 'Anomalies in intertemporal choice: evidence and interpretation', *Quarterly Journal of Economics*, 107: 573–98.

MacFadyen, A., and MacFadyen, H. (eds) (1987), *Economic Psychology: Intersections in Theory and Application*, Amsterdam: North-Holland.

Mansbridge, J. J. (1994), 'Public spirit in political systems', in H. J. Aaron, T. E. Mann, and T. Taylor (eds), *Values and Public Policy*, Washington, DC: Brookings.

Moore, M. J. (1996), 'Death and tobacco taxes', *RAND Journal of Economics*, 27: 415–28.

Mueller, D. C. (1996), *Constitutional Democracy*, Oxford: Oxford University Press.

Mullahy, J., and Sindelar, J. L. (1994), 'Do drinkers know when to say no? An empirical analysis of drunk driving', *Economic Inquiry*, 32: 383–94.

Newbery, D. M. (this volume), 'Road user and congestion charges'.

Oberholzer-Gee, F., and Weck-Hannemann, H. (2002), 'Pricing road use: politico-economic and fairness considerations', *Transportation Research, Part D: Transport and Environment*, 7: 357–71.

Offer, A. (2001), 'Body weight and self-control in the United States and Britain since the 1950s', *Social History of Medicine*, 14: 79–106.

Pommerehne, W. W., and Frey, B. S. (1992), 'The effects of tax administration on tax morale', University of Zurich, unpublished manuscript.

Putnam, R. D. (2000), *Bowling Alone: The Collapse and Revival of American Community*, New York, NY: Simon & Schuster.

Rabin, M. (1998), 'Psychology and economics', *Journal of Economic Literature*, 36: 11–46.

Ramjerdi, F. (1995), 'An evaluation of the impact of the Oslo toll scheme on travel behaviour', in B. Johansson and L-G. Mattson (eds), *Road Pricing: Theory, Empirical Assessment and Policy*, Boston, MA, Dordrecht, and London: Kluwer.

Richardson, H. W., and Bae, C-H. C. (1998), 'The equity impacts of road congestion pricing', in K. J. Button and E. T. Verhoef (eds), *Road Pricing, Traffic Congestion and the Environment*, Cheltenham and Northampton, MA: Edward Elgar.

Saffer, H., and Chaloupka, F. (1998), 'Demographic differentials in the demand for alcohol and illicit drugs', National Bureau of Economic Research, Working Paper no. 6432.

—— and —— (1999), 'The demand for illicit drugs', *Economic Inquiry*, 37: 401–11.

Scitovsky, T. (1976), *The Joyless Economy: An Inquiry into Human Satisfaction and Dissatisfaction*, Oxford: Oxford University Press.

Shoup, C. S. (1983), 'Current trends in excise taxation', in S. Cnossen (ed.), *Comparative Tax Studies*, Amsterdam: North-Holland.

Sipes, K. N., and Mendelsohn, R. (2001), 'The effectiveness of gasoline taxation to manage air pollution', *Ecological Economics*, 36: 299–309.

Skinner, J., and Slemrod, J. (1985), 'An economic perspective on tax evasion', *National Tax Journal*, 38: 345–53.

Smith, S. (this volume), 'Economic issues in alcohol taxation'.

Stigler, G. J., and Becker, G. S. (1977), 'De gustibus non est disputandum', *American Economic Review*, 67(2): 76–90.

Strotz, R. H. (1956), 'Myopia and inconsistency in dynamic utility maximization', *Review of Economic Studies*, 23: 165–80.

Taurus, J. A., O'Malley, P. M., and Johnston, L. D. (2001), 'Effects of price and access laws on teenage smoking initiation: a national longitudinal analysis', National Bureau of Economic Research, Working Paper no. 8331.

Thompson, M. J. (1998), 'Reflections on the economics of traffic congestion', *Journal of Transport Economics and Policy*, 32: 93–112.

Tyler, T. R. (1990), *Why People Obey the Law*, New Haven, CT: Yale University Press.

—— and Blader, S. (2000), *Cooperation in Groups*, Philadelphia, PA: Psychology Press.

Van Ours, J. C. (1995), 'The price elasticity of hard drugs: the case of opium in the Dutch East Indies, 1923–1938', *Journal of Political Economy*, 103: 261–79.

Van Raaij, W. F., van Velthoven, G., and Waerneryd, K. (eds) (1988), *Handbook of Economic Psychology*, Dordrecht: Kluwer.

Wasserman, J., Manning, W. G., Newhouse, J. P., and Winkler, J. D. (1991), 'The effect of excise taxes and regulations on cigarette smoking', *Journal of Health Economics*, 10: 43–64.

Index